How to Read Architectu

How to Read Architecture is based on the fundamental premise that reading and interpreting architecture is something we already do, and that close observation matters. This book enhances this skill so that given an unfamiliar building, you will have the tools to understand it and to be inspired by it. Author Paulette Singley encourages you to misread, closely read, conventionally read, and unconventionally read architecture to stimulate your creative process.

This book explores three essential ways to help you understand architecture: reading a building from the outside-in, from the inside-out, and from the position of out-and-out, or formal, architecture. This book erodes boundaries between the frequently compartmentalized fields of interior design, landscape design, and building design with chapters exploring concepts of *terroir*, scenography, criticality, atmosphere, tectonics, inhabitation, type, form, and enclosure. Using examples and case studies that span a wide range of historical and global precedents, Singley addresses the complex interaction among the ways a building engages its context, addresses its performative exigencies, and operates as an autonomous aesthetic object.

Including over 300 images, this book is an essential read for both undergraduate and postgraduate students of architecture with a global focus on the interpretation of buildings in their context.

Paulette Singley is a widely read architectural historian and theorist whose work expands the disciplinary limits of architecture across diverse subject matter such as food, film, and fashion. She is a Professor of Architecture at Woodbury University in Los Angeles, California. She received a Ph.D. from Princeton University, an M.A. from Cornell University, and a B.Arch. from the University of Southern California. She co-edited *Eating Architecture*, the first book to explore the intersections of architecture and the culinary arts. She also co-edited *Architecture: In Fashion* and has published chapters in several anthologies as well as essays in architecture journals such as *Log* and *Assemblage*.

How to Read Architecture

Architecture

An Introduction to Interpreting the
Built Environment

PAULETTE SINGLEY

Routledge
Taylor & Francis Group

NEW YORK AND LONDON

First published 2019
by Routledge
52 Vanderbilt Avenue, New York, NY 10017

and by Routledge
2 Park Square, Milton Park, Abingdon, Oxon, OX14 4RN

Routledge is an imprint of the Taylor & Francis Group, an informa business

Library of Congress Cataloging-in-Publication Data
Names: Singley, Paulette, 1960– author.
Title: How to read architecture : an introduction to interpreting the built environment /
    Paulette Singley.
Description: New York, NY : Routledge, 2019.
Identifiers: LCCN 2018061193| ISBN 9780415836180 (hardback) | ISBN 9780415836203
    (paperback) | ISBN 9780429262388 (e-book)
Subjects: LCSH: Architecture–Aesthetics.
Classification: LCC NA2500 .S484 2019 | DDC 720/.47–dc23
LC record available at https://lccn.loc.gov/2018061193

ISBN: 978-0-415-83618-0 (hbk)
ISBN: 978-0-415-83620-3 (pbk)
ISBN: 978-0-429-26238-8 (ebk)

Typeset in Univers LT Std
by Servis Filmsetting Ltd, Stockport, Cheshire

Cover image: Photograph by Gerard Smulevich "Barceloneta" 2006 of an installation by
the artist Marieke Polocsay (Marika) "#Rehabilitacion"

If not for you…
David Hall and Connor Stankard

Contents

Acknowledgments   viii

Introduction: Ground Rules   1

Part 1
Reading Between the Lines   **13**

  1. Engraving   15
  2. Inscription   32

Part 2
Outside-In Architecture   **49**

  3. *Terroir*   57
  4. Scenography   89
  5. Criticality   130

Part 3
Inside-Out Architecture   **149**

  6. Atmosphere   153
  7. Tectonics   185
  8. Inhabitation   223

Part 4
Out-and-Out Architecture   **251**

  9. Type   257
 10. Form   296
 11. Enclosure   337

  Index   379

Acknowledgments

Given the scope and breadth of this work the number of individuals, particularly my colleagues, students and former professors, to whom I owe a debt of gratitude is innumerable. This book would not have been initiated were it not for the vision and support of Routledge and Taylor and Francis editors, particularly Krystal LaDuc, Julia Pollacco, Wendy Fuller, Kalliope Dalto, Nick Craggs, and Fran Ford. Copy-editor Jon Lloyd was intrepid. Cover designer Jo Griffin and indexer Angus Barclay also did a tremendous job. Woodbury University in general and Ingallil Wahlroos-Ritter in particular were highly supportive of this project at every juncture. I am grateful to the American University of Sharjah for an academic year in the middle east. I am particularly grateful to colleagues who spared time to read chapters: Jeffrey Balmer, Matthew Bell, Amy Converse, Deborah Fausch, Alicia Imperiale, Mark Jarzombek, Romolo Martemucci, John Montague, Pat Morton, Mikesch Muecke, Eric Olsen, Vikram Prakash, and Mark Stankard. Gavin Friehauf and Hitisha Kalolia completed careful diagrams and drawings. Thanks to Sean Dockray having initiated the knowledge-sharing platform of Aaaaarg, I was able to complete much of this work in remote locations. I should also mention the strategic interventions of Ron Evitts, Alessandra Ponte, David Rifkind, Georges Teyssot, Nick Roberts, Kazys Varnelis, and Astrid Virding. To David Hall, whose relentless image-finding breathed life into the visual arguments being made here, I am eternally indebted. There would be no book without his support and encouragement.

Paulette Singley
Altadena, California; Guildford, Connecticut; Rome,
Italy; Sharjah, United Arab Emirates;
Rocca di Caprileone, Sicily

Introduction

Ground Rules

Greek legend insists that Daedalus was the first architect, but this is hardly the case: although he built the Cretan labyrinth, he never understood its structure. He could only escape, in fact, by flying out of its vortex. Instead, it may be argued that Ariadne achieved the first work of architecture, since it was she who gave Theseus the ball of thread by means of which he found his way out of the labyrinth after having killed the Minotaur.[1]

—Beatriz Colomina

Imagine you are standing in front of a building you previously have not seen. Without the aid of a guide book or other supplemental information, but equipped with your native ability to reason and a basic knowledge of the culture with which you are engaging, how would you begin to interpret, that is to say "read," this work of architecture? Perhaps you would examine the way the building engages its site, study the configuration of interior spaces as they evidence themselves on exterior surfaces, or compare it to similar precedents you remember having seen. If the building you are reading is an ancient ruin or prehistoric monument, then you might adopt the perspective of an archaeologist and seek to identify primary site alignments or mentally reconstruct the edifice from remaining wall fragments. The seemingly dumb stone blocks from which a building was constructed may carry information that communicates architectural knowledge—the proximity of the quarry to the building site, chisel marks remaining from the extraction process, and more. To study an extant structure instead of a ruin, one might survey the ways in which the building responds to the nature of the site or consider its familial parallels to adjacent buildings. These techniques of observation, combined with an understanding of larger cultural forces such as socio-religious practices, contribute to an *explication de texte* of architecture.

The title of Paul MacKendrick's seminal work *The Mute Stones Speak: The Story of Archaeology in Italy* suggests that the key to unlocking architecture's communicative value, no matter what language the builders spoke, remains embedded in the work itself, waiting for an interpreter to reveal its intrinsic mysteries.[2] While it certainly helps, as the Rosetta Stone demonstrates, to be able to read inscriptions as an epigrapher does, the process of deciphering an archaeological site also relies on close observation that leads to extracting useful information from mute material. After years of excavating in the Valley of the Kings with little result, during his final season of digging in 1922, Howard Carter discovered a half-buried rock step. Excavation revealed a stairway leading down to a sealed door that opened onto a passage leading to King Tutankhamun's tomb. A small piece of evidence and sharp eyes revealed one of the world's greatest archaeological discoveries.

Simple site surveying may indicate complex subterranean architectures waiting to be liberated by the archaeologist's trowel. The density of plant growth on a contemporary farmer's field may index subcutaneous patterns of inhabitation: either though lush vegetation growing over hidden canals or sparse growth over building foundations. Adding the technological advantage of aerial photography to the practice of visual observation, the reconnaissance John Bradford and Peter Williams Hunt completed while flying above the *Tavoliere delle Puglie* at the close of the Second World War exposed the presence of over 2000 subterranean settlements lying just under the surface of fields scarred by a light braille of vegetation growing out from otherwise hidden trenches. Their work brought to light the inhabitations of Neolithic farmers who dwelled on this plain over 7000 years ago. MacKendrick observed that the typical wattle and daub huts found here featured a sunken floor, central hearth, and smoke hole. This simple hut formed "the remote and primitive predecessor of the atrium-and-impluvium house of historic Roman times, whose central apartment has a hole in the roof with a pool below to catch rainwater."[3] MacKendrick drew an historical link from these prehistoric dwellings to the typical Roman house found in archaeological sites such as Pompeii and in so doing even implicated contemporary Mediterranean houses displaying courtyard fountains as part of this genetic lineage.

Georges Perec reminds us that: "The earth is a form of writing, a geography of which we had forgotten that we ourselves are authors."[4] While hiking in foothills overlooking the Nazca Desert in southern Peru in 1927, Toribio Mejia Xesspe discovered a precise geography of secret writing, becoming the first archaeologist to observe a series of geoglyphs dating from approximately 500 BCE to 500 CE. Formed by shallow marks carved into the ground, the Nazca lines depict hundreds of abstract geometries and cyclopean drawings of natural figures such as hummingbirds, monkeys, jaguars, sharks, flowers, and trees. This site remains one of archaeology's great enigmas, with theories about its meaning ranging from an astronomical observatory to a system of canals. The lines themselves, however, demonstrate the power of a humble incision in the ground to endure for thousands of years and to describe numinous spatial fields. The simple but important practice of close visual observation that Bradford and Hunt, Carter, and Xesspe illustrate remains our most effective tool for interpreting architecture. While more recent archaeological practices may deploy drones and photogrammetry to modernize the techniques of aerial site surveying—yielding significant knowledge about the

Figure 0.1 Photo by John Bradford with his caption reading: "APULIA. A low oblique photo of a Neolithic settlement found from the air near Foggia. It is outlined by the circular crop-mark of its buried enclosure ditch, and by those of the circular 'compounds' inside it. (F) The inturned entrance to the site." From John Bradford and John Spencer Purvis Bradford, *Ancient Landscapes: Studies in Field Archaeology* (London: G. Bell, 1957)

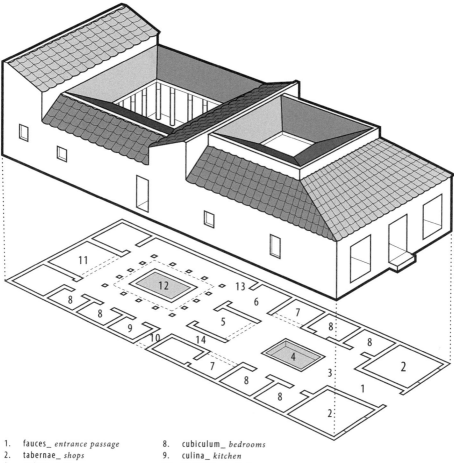

1. fauces_ *entrance passage*
2. tabernae_ *shops*
3. atrium_ *hall*
4. impulvium_ *rainwater basin*
5. tablinum_ *passage room*
6. triclinium_ *dining room*
7. alae_ *side-rooms*
8. cubiculum_ *bedrooms*
9. culina_ *kitchen*
10. posticum_ *back-door*
11. exedra_ *garden-room*
12. piscina_ *fishpond*
13. peristylium_ *garden-court*
14. andron_ *passage*

Figure 0.2
Diagram
of a typical
Pompeiian
house, drawn
by Gavin
Friehauf

past without ever having to scratch a surface—the rule of close observation nonetheless holds.

Stepping across the threshold of that imaginary edifice, you might consider studying the distribution of artifacts, clarity of circulation, sequential hierarchy of rooms, public-private interface, or exterior-interior adjacencies in order to interpret the spatial story lingering therein. Having momentarily adopted the archaeologist's point of view for reading an historical ruin, other professional personas also provide useful interpretive tools for disencrypting architecture— the detective who seeks clues hiding in plain sight, the anthropologist who traces patterns of inhabitation across material culture, the psychologist who interprets the symbolic value of mythological objects, the engineer who is

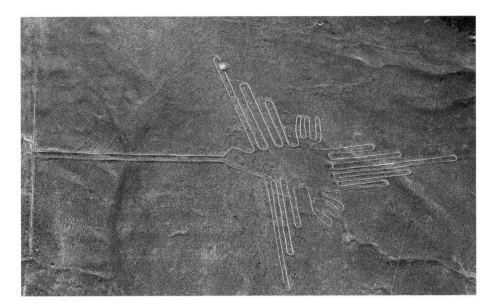

fascinated by structural forces and failures, or the writer interested in attics, basements, and buried narratives. Each provides methodologies for the canny interpreter to shuttle between poetic and prosaic ways of reading architecture. A window, for example, may be subjected to diverse analytic perspectives; an artist might focus on natural light, a mechanical engineer on air movement, a general contractor on costs, a carpenter on framing, and an architect on proportions. These combined perspectives offer a toolkit for reading a building that may be triangulated between its response to context, performance, and abstract composition—three of the four parts in this book.

The ability to read architecture—to interpret a building's conceptual resonance—is something we do intuitively as part of our everyday lives as we negotiate the labyrinth of our built environments with the thread of legibility that personal experience provides. Throughout our day-to-day lives, we negotiate highly explicit yet often unspoken behavioral codes and navigational clues within architecture that rely on tacit reading skills. Taking the remote example of 12th–13th century Italian city-states, where supporters of the Pope or the Holy Roman Emperor fought fierce battles against each other, the fortresses defending these warring territories announced their respective political alignment as Guelph or Ghibelline through the architecture of rectangular or swallowtail-shaped battlements. More recent spatial territorialization may be determined by the defensive walls surrounding a gated community, graffiti tagging a neighborhood, or the threshold of a cultural institution across which it may be daunting to pass. Not only have we learned to read the role of architecture and how to comport ourselves accordingly therein, but also we generally know when we don't belong. We generally know the difference, moreover, between what constitutes an ordinary building and a

Figure 0.3
Aerial view of "The Hummingbird," geoglyph from Nazca Desert in southern Peru (between 500 BCE and 500 CE), photograph by Diego Delso, courtesy of delso.photo.

building whose set of representational systems designates it as carrying extraordinary formal significance—of a building that an architect is likely to have designed.

That we have intuited such readings but have not necessarily articulated them is where this book enters the conversation concerning architecture's ability to engage epistemological systems broader than simple use. Our understanding of the built environment may be enriched beyond these afore-mentioned soft readings into a self-conscious study that begins to provide a systematic approach to developing spatial literacy by reading architecture through its external, internal, and intrinsic pressures.

Returning to the imaginary *threshold* you just crossed, this term reso-nates with the traditional practice of separating the threshing area adjacent to the exterior of a house from the interior living space. A divider between the inside and outside, the threshold often featured some kind of sill or lintel at the building's entrance that also designated it as a liminal space of being neither inside nor out, but both. Liminal zones describe sites and rites of passage from one developmental stage to another and, as with thresholds and states of mind, a transitional space of neither here nor there, but both. The Latin root of *lintel* resides in *limitaris*, a term describing the borders and boundaries ancient Romans defined with *limes*, defensive lines and boundary limits etched into territories that may still be seen from the air. *Liminal* similarly describes the limits of a threshold condition. While architecture operates as defining boundaries between inside and outside and performs in response to these pressures, it also operates autonomously by sublimating (with its root of *sublime* stemming from *sub* "up to" + *limen* "lintel, threshold, sill") context and use into the dynamics of form and space. In this respect, the analysis of form examines a building's composition as a self-referential organization of mass, space, line, and color. Formal analysis, then, emerges as a way to read architecture as an autonomous spatial practice that adheres to the same aes-thetic and compositional principles as do works of art isolated from the world behind the walls of a museum. This book provides a repertoire of approaches to interpreting architecture organized across a topological axis leading from external contexts to internal performances, an axis that isolates these very exigencies as independent from the processes of formal analysis in order to underscore formalism's role.

The limits between what constitutes *architecture*, the production of an enclosure that carries surplus meaning, and simple *building*, an enclosure whose purpose remains purely utilitarian, conventionally relies on the added and often ineffable aesthetic value an architect may bring to the design process. For Umberto Eco, an early theorist of architecture's potential to communicate as a language, "architecture is the art of the articulation of form and spaces."[5] One difference between *building* and *architecture* resides in the necessity for architecture to deliver a message regarding its own compositional logic. Eco distinguished between *building*, "the construction of manufactured objects that circumscribe spaces set aside to foster practical functions (a hen-house, a hangar, an 'unsightly' block of flats)," and *architecture*, spaces that permit practical functions but "are valued above all for their aesthetic auto-reflectiveness."[6] As Sir John Summerson similarly insisted: "A bicycle shed is a building; Lincoln Cathedral is a piece of architecture. Nearly everything that encloses space on a scale sufficient for a human being to move in is a building; the term architecture applies only to buildings designed with a view to aesthetic appeal."[7] Roland Barthes synthesized these various distinctions when observing that "architecture is always dream and function, expression of a utopia and instrument of a convenience."[8]

Despite the distinction between architecture and building, numerous built works merit inclusion in art and architectural history survey books that possess neither architectural pedigree nor a uniquely self-reflective design process, produced as they were through enduring cultural patterns of construction and inhabitation. James Ackerman describes the parallel process in Renaissance Italy as a "self-unconscious revival " of classical architecture that was accompanied by the "unconscious survival" of building traditions "in which forms of art are handed down from generation to generation like myths, without evidence of their original sources."[9] In order to locate unconscious traditions on an equal footing with more canonical architecture, this book blurs any strong distinction between architecture and building at the level of the subjects selected to be discussed. Moreover, this distinction also underscores a subtle dynamic between high design and popular culture, where architecture conceived in the incubator of elite clientele or academic theory stands in stark contrast to buildings produced by commercial developers or amateur hands. This is not to undervalue the important work architects have completed in positively transforming our built environment, but to recognize that the architecture we inhabit on a daily basis is what we read, and reads us, most frequently. The process of interpretation necessarily relies on being able to read our built environment from numerous perspectives and at multiple scales. Given that buildings result from numerous influences and participants, reading architecture resides in an interpretive milieu that extends beyond a designer's specific intentions.

While social media expands awareness about architecture's role in shaping our world, as well as fostering a cult of personality, it further demonstrates that the general public already possesses considerable tools for reading buildings. Perhaps the best example of this is documented in the animated sitcom *The Simpsons*. Episodes have depicted Frank Gehry as deriving his architectural inspiration from a crumpled piece of paper, showed Bart Simpson on the High Line in Manhattan, and inserted Rem Koolhaas into a world of Lego architecture—all instances of popular culture assimilating and parodizing capital "A" architecture for mass consumption.

Operating from a more conceptual point of departure in his 1966 photo essay "Homes for America," Dan Graham studied large-scale tract housing developments in New Jersey to arrive at the following dry observation: "When the box has a sharply oblique roof, it is called a 'Cape Cod.' When it is longer than wide, it is a 'Ranch.' A two-story house is usually called 'Colonial.' If it consists of contiguous boxes with one slightly higher in elevation, it is a 'Split-level.'"[10] Cape Cod, Ranch, Colonial, and Split-Level. As with real estate advertisements, these terms identify an architectural language shared in the "poetry of banality" Graham sees in these homes.[11] He dwells, as Kirsten Swenson explains, "on the era's depersonalized home, which no longer reflected individual tastes and needs but was built 'to be thrown away.'"[12] As Graham argues, the predetermined, synthetic order of these housing developments lacks "organic unity connecting the land site and the home."[13] For Graham, these suburban enclaves transition into indeterminate transitional zones of bowling alleys, shopping plazas, big box stores, and a labyrinth of parking lots. Although Graham's alienated New Jersey appears as a featureless land of in-betweeness, he also demonstrates the potential for navigating the anonymity and confusion of the commercial strip through the *limes* of highways. Perhaps most importantly, Graham reads his home state through ancient Roman terminology, common parlance, and simple observation.

If, as Walter Benjamin wrote, "To live means to leave traces," then to read a building requires paying attention to the way in which use-patterns imprint themselves upon spaces and surfaces.[14] Quotidian inhabitation leaves legible traces on the surfaces of architecture—the wear and tear that everyday life inflicts on a building such as scuffmarks, mends, scratches, and stains. This patina of use that life imposes on buildings describes the ways in which architecture inflects to the demands of habitual use. When a chair rail or dado, stemming from Latin *datum*, projects from a wall, it protects the surface from the daily scraping of furniture at the height of a sitting body. The molding, in fact, indexes the memory of scratched surfaces and anticipates the bumping of chairs against the wall as people sit themselves to table. The dado molding simultaneously aids in the material transition between the lower level of a wall's protective wainscoting and the upper level of more fragile wallpaper. The ever-purposeful Shakers placed a higher rail on the wall that they fitted with knobs for hanging furniture off of the floor when not being used. As the story of a simple chair rail attests, a building's details and ornaments offer the potential to reveal big ideas condensed within small moments of design intensity—the proverbial world in a grain of sand. We inhabit many different architectures on a daily basis—from home, to work, to school, to places of worship—that augment the rote activities of life. We therefore have become expert at reading the traces of wear and the patterns of use which indicate an architecture's ability both to absorb memories and to delineate a spatial plane across which we navigate.

Reading architecture, deciphering a building's conceptual apparatus, is an act we complete intuitively as part of everyday life, negotiated across connotative and denotative codes that structure the built environment. As we routinely inhabit buildings and the spaces in-between them, we negotiate an arbitrated system of signification that allows us to navigate the built environment. Our lived experiences have already taught us how to intuitively read architecture, while cultural institutions such as heritage sites and museums round out the difference between instinct and insight. In general, finding a building's bathroom is clearly indicated by architectural codes such as scale (smaller spaces), siting (hidden behind the scenes), symmetry (pairing of men's and women's rooms), and signage (graphics to assist with way finding). Likewise, proportion, materiality, and massing can suggest different uses, exemplified by schools scaled to the size of children, churches with bell towers, or prisons with small windows. When radical experimentation overthrows these established conventions, normative forces such as gravity, materiality, and public circulation remain ways in which to begin navigating these uncharted territories until they too become absorbed into our architectural unconscious.

Fredric Jameson develops the concept of cognitive maps, the mental compasses and cartographies of a built environment we produce internally to navigate our worlds. Basing himself on Kevin Lynch's important book *The Image of the City* (1960), Jameson argues that cities have become alienated spaces where people are able neither to navigate cognitively nor to locate the invisible power structures. Jameson echoes Graham when observing that places like Jersey City, where it is challenging to find the traditional navigational markers such as monuments, nodes, and natural boundaries, intensify this alienation.[15]

Even the most abject of cities and suburbs maintain a semblance of cartographic legibility enough for inhabitants to negotiate socio-political systems of power inscribed in the monuments and public spaces that compose these worlds. Were it not for the experience of everyday life providing the basic tools with which to navigate public space and interpret built form, it would be impossible to perform an act as simple as going to work or purchasing groceries. To progress from intuitively navigating architecture and urban space as a system of invisible ideological maps that define one's subjectivity to intentionally unraveling architecture's theoretical underpinnings by learning how to read with greater precision makes room for taking ownership of the spaces we inhabit and for drawing our own maps.

Interpreting a space's light, detail, color, texture, sound, and views involves experiential observation that only an actual site visit may elicit. In the absence of this opportunity, we rely on published descriptions, drawings, photography, and film to embroider the lack of physical experience with memories of similar spaces. These various strategies for reading architecture both align with and disregard the architect's own design intentions which often are shaped unconsciously by larger forces flowing through a stream of technological innovation or blowing in the wind of a stylistic zeitgeist. The architect's agency and authorship of her design persists in reciprocity with the unintended influence of cultural contaminants and a global *force majeure*. Likewise, architecture emerges from a highly collaborative process wherein multiple individuals contribute to the completion of a collective work that ultimately results in a built form much larger than the work of a single person. Buildings therefore reside in an interpretive milieu in which the architect's singular, heroic voice may be displaced by sequential interpretations, translations, and observations that emerge independently from and even transform the valence of any original design intentions.

If not solely derived from the architect's intentions, which may or may not explicate a building's conceptual trajectory, then examining a building in response to its external contexts and internal performances liberates interpretation from rote intentionality. Moreover, evaluating a building's abstract compositional relationships independent of both external and internal forces describes the epistemological system for interpreting the built environment that outlines *Reading Architecture's* organizational strategy. Divided into four parts of (1) Reading Between the Lines, (2) Outside-In Architecture, (3) Inside-Out Architecture, and (4) Out-and-Out Architecture, the complex interaction among the ways in which a building engages its context, addresses its performative exigencies, and operates as an autonomous aesthetic object offers a comprehensive approach to interpreting the built domain, one that unites the increasingly distinct practices of landscape, interior, and building design into a holistic appreciation of what constitutes architecture. This book focuses on built works whose siting, response to nature, cultural context, environmental systems, tectonic exigencies, and overall form constitute narrative devices leading to the expository process of architectural story telling.

According to the architect Aldo van Eyck: "What you should try to accomplish is built meaning. So get close to the meaning and build."[16] Adopting a broad approach to considering a wide range of historical and geographical subjects, this book considers the study of architecture through the ways in which it produces cultural meaning, through a combination of historical, theoretical, and material investigations that contribute to making our built environment legible. *How to Read Architecture*, as this title signals, adopts the position that architecture's primary role is as a cultural communicator, one which evidences systems of legibility that may be interpreted through myriad modes of expression we negotiate on a daily basis in states of distraction or in moments of concentrated attention. It also provides tools for turning buildings outside in and inside out as a way of bracketing the space in-between as a formal zone autonomous from exigency.

This book privileges the idea that architecture draws from a complex and oscillating field of inquiry that engages a plurality of voices in a multicultural context. Above all, it asserts that architecture's legibility engages a formal system of representation that encompasses and absorbs its functional performance. It aims to offer its readers a conceptual apparatus for interpreting the built environment that, in turn, augments their confidence in assessing a building's merit, even in opposition to conventional architectural criticism. The building you entered at the beginning of this chapter and the twists and turns you have crossed to arrive at the end introduces a labyrinth of thresholds for which the following chapters operate as Ariadne's ball of thread, as a navigational tool for reading architecture.

Notes

1 *Architectureproduction*, eds. Beatriz Colomina and Joan Ockman (New York, NY: Princeton Architectural Press, 1988), p. 7.

2 Paul Lachlan MacKendrick, *The Mute Stones Speak: The Story of Archaeology in Italy* 2nd ed. (New York: Norton, 1983), p. 5.

3 Ibid, p. 8.

4 Georges Perec, "The World," in *Species of Spaces and Other Pieces*, ed. John Sturrock (New York: Penguin, 2008), p. 79.

5 Umberto Eco, "Function and Sign: The Semiotics of Architecture," in *Rethinking Architecture: A Reader in Cultural Theory*, ed. Neil Leach (New York: Routledge, 1997), p. 183.

6 Umberto Eco, "A Componential Analysis of the Architectural Sign/Column/" *Semiotica 5*, no. 2 (1972), p. 100.

7 Sir John Summerson, *An Outline of European Architecture* (Harmondsworth: Penguin, [1942] 1957), p. 23.

8 Roland Barthes "The Eiffel Tower," in *A Barthes Reader*, ed. Susan Sontag (New York: Hill and Wang, 1982), p. 239.

9 James Ackerman, "Sources of the Renaissance Villa," in *Distance Points* (Cambridge, MA: MIT Press, 1991), p. 316. Originally published as James Ackerman, "Sources of the Renaissance Villa," in *Studies in Western Art: Acts of the Twentieth International Congress of the History of Art*, vol. II, ed. Millard Meiss (Princeton: Princeton University Press, 1963), pp. 6–18.

10 Dan Graham, "Homes for America," in *Rock My Religion, 1965–1990*, ed. Brian Wallis (Cambridge, MA: MIT Press, 1993), pp. 14–23.

11 Interview with Dan Graham, November 1, 2011, interviewed by Sabine Breitwieser, MoMA Chief Curator of Media and Performance Art, the Museum of Modern Art Oral History Program, http://www.moma.org/momaorg/shared/pdfs/docs/learn/archives/transcript_graham.pdf.

12 Kirsten Swenson, "Be My Mirror," *Art in America*, May 1, 2009, https://www.artinamericamagazine.com/news-features/magazines/dan-graham-be-my-mirror-kirsten-swenson.

13 Barry Schwabsky, "Beyond Exhaustion: Dan Graham's Period Pieces," *The Nation*, August 26, 2009, https://www.thenation.com/article/beyond-exhaustion-dan-grahams-period-pieces.

14 Walter Benjamin, "Paris, Capital of the Nineteenth Century," in *Reflections: Essays, Aphorisms, Autobiographical Writings*, trans. Edmund Jephcott, ed. Peter Demetz (New York: Harcourt Brace Jovanovich, 1978), p. 156.

15 Fredric Jameson, *Postmodernism, Or, the Cultural Logic of Late Capitalism* (New York: Verso, 1991), p. 51.

16 Aldo van Eyck, *Team Ten Primer*, ed. Alison Smithson (London: Standard Catalogue, 1966), p. 7, as cited by Colin Rowe in his introduction to *Five Architects: Eisenman, Graves, Gwathmey, Hejduk, Meier* (New York: Wittenborn, 1972), p. 2.

Introduction to Part 1
Reading Between the Lines

Our buildings, above all the public buildings, ought in some fashion to be poems. And the images they offer to our senses must excite in us sentiments analogous to the functions to which the buildings are devoted.[1]
—*Étienne-Louis Boullée*

Architect and architectural theorist Marco Frascari unequivocally asserted that "buildings are texts which are generated by assembling three-dimensional mosaics of fragments, excerpts, citations, passages, and quotations."[2] While the conceptual parallel between buildings and writing dates back at least to the late eighteenth century, when Étienne-Louis Boullée articulated his analogy between architecture and poetry, the linguistic turn rekindled toward the end of the 1960s inaugurated a system for interpreting architecture according to the rules of language and semiotics. "Linguistics, semiotics, rhetoric, and various models of 'textuality'" as W. J. T. Mitchell observed in 1994 "had become the lingua franca for critical reflections on the arts, the media, and cultural forms."[3]

Lebbeus Woods perfectly summarized the search for meaning at this time when explaining that the grammar and syntax of written language were believed to organize a coherent and meaningful system that clearly related to architecture. As Woods put it, by the 1970s and 1980s, linguistic and literary theorists concluded "that written texts do not have a fixed meaning established by what its author intended to say, but rather multiple meanings that readers have to interpret for themselves by using various cultural codes and references."[4] In other words, while architecture could be read as a cultural text, the actual meaning of that text was fluid. Meaning therefore paradoxically was evacuated from both architecture and the architect's intentions, with the end result for Woods being that "form does not follow any *a priori* function but has autonomous existence that must, in the end, be 'read' on its own terms."[5] As Woods concluded, "the meaning of architecture is to be found only in architecture itself."[6] The comparison between books and buildings that promised to vitalize architecture as a potentially legible enterprise rebounded into an alibi for evacuating meaning from form and thereby further rarefying its interpretive capacity for an elite audience indoctrinated in its abstruse jargon. The linguistic cure had become literary poison.

In this section the linguistic turn operates as both an historical moment suspended in amber and a contemporary approach to the reading of architecture that begins on the surfaces of buildings featuring supplementary textual content. Chapter 1 approaches engraving as a process of carving into a building's surface that carries gravitas, as in a grave or serious meaning, where architecture operates as communicator of cultural meaning through its originary status in burial. From signage as contemporary inscription to signs as linguistic tools to scripting as autonomous design, Chapter 2 considers architecture as a process of inscription. It considers the ways in which daily life and roadside attractions inscribe themselves on architecture, often in contradistinction to a designer's will. Both chapters explore the enduring quarrel between buildings and books.

Notes

1   Etienne-Louis Boullée *Boullée's Treatise on Architecture & Complete Presentation of the "Architecture Essas sur l'art" which forms part of the Boullée papers (Ms. 9153) in the Bibliothèque Nationale Paris* (London: Tiranti, 1953), p. 26.

2   Marco Frascari, "Carlo Scarpa in Magna Graecia: The Abatellis Palace in Palermo," in *AA Files 9* (London: Architectural Association School of Architecture, 1985), p. 3.

3   W. J. T. Mitchell, *Picture Theory: Essays on Verbal and Visual Representation* (Chicago: University of Chicago Press, 1994), p. 11. Mitchell is referencing Richard Rorty, *Philosophy and the Mirror of Nature* (Princeton: Princeton University Press, 1979), p. 263.

4   Lebbeus Woods, "Libeskind's Machines," November 24, 2009, https://lebbeus woods.wordpress.com/2009/11/24/libeskinds-machines.

5   Ibid.

6   Ibid.

Chapter 1

Engraving

The circle, the square, are the letters of the alphabet used by the architects for the structures of their best works.[1]

—*Claude Nicolas Ledoux*

Long before books were printed and the Internet established worldwide connectivity, architecture was the most accessible and durable form of public media. Architecture emerged as a conduit of cultural expression whose greater function had been to frame rituals, consecrate sites, suspend thresholds between sacred and profane zones, and articulate these spatial performances in conjunction with meaning written on and by its material surfaces. If past civilizations combined inscriptions, symbolic images, and sculptural groups on building surfaces as allegorical programs to expand legibility to less literate audiences, then the complementary presence of words and symbols on today's architecture remains the most direct means of ascertaining a building's purpose. In short, focusing on the words, signs, symbols, and emblems appended to a building offers a good place to start to read architecture. While neon lights and digital screens may substitute for words carved in stone, studying the signs and symbols of these more recent contributions to writing on buildings merits the same close attention epigraphists apply to deciphering ancient inscriptions. Inscriptions and their contemporary counterpart of signage may directly or indirectly identify a building or monument's purpose, construction period, patron, architect, historical context, or poetic aspirations. When it comes to reading architecture, then the first place to start is by seeking out any words, epigraphs, icons, numbers, or symbols that may be appended to it.

Emblematic of the space that writing occupies in ancient architecture, the great hypostyle hall of Amun-Re at Karnak in Egypt features inscriptions, cartouches, and bas-relief sculpture on every surface. Built during the time of Sety I (reigned 1294–1279 BCE) and his son Ramesses II (reigned 1279–1213 BCE), the hall's dense intercolumniation represents a primordial papyrus thicket, while its relief carvings illustrate historical and religious stories. This petrified forest contains 12 giant columns in the central space, or nave, standing at about 70 feet tall and 10 feet wide, and 122 columns at the lower side

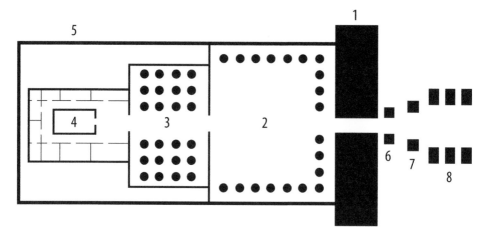

1. pylon
2. court
3. hypostyle hall
4. sanctuary
5. enclosure wall
6. colossal statues of Pharaoh
7. obelisks
8. avenue of sphinxes

Figure 1.1
**Diagram
of a typical
Egyptian
temple, drawn
by Gavin
Friehauf**

aisles standing at about 33 feet tall. The hall's surfaces depict the daily rituals priests conducted in the temple sanctuary. The sanctuary was the house of the deity, the final and lowest room in the temple's processional route that led from an entrance pylon to a peristyle court to a hypostyle hall to the final naos or central shrine. Papyrus column capitals, with open blossoms in the nave and closed buds on the flanking aisles, represent the mythological marsh of creation and the fertile Nile flood plain from out of which they grew. The entire hall operates at multiple levels and scales of legibility: as a shelter for religious practices, an edifice that depicts the rituals it instantiates, a primordial grove, and the deity's domicile.

Painted in bright colors, bas-relief sculpture depicts temple rituals and augments the hieroglyphic inscriptions of sacred rites so that even an illiterate public would have been able to glean the message of scenes such as the pharaoh being crowned with a diadem, sacrifices to Amun-Re, or the procession of annual festivals. These engraved surfaces also depict the foundation rites of the temple itself, including such tasks as surveying, designating a sacred boundary, and molding a brick. In temples such as those at Karnak, extensive textual references and ornamental programs transform the building into a guidebook of itself, where deep ritual mysteries are carved on stone pages.

Hieroglyphs mythologize the origins of writing, a gift that liberated people from the burden of having to preserve stories through memorization. This gift, however, was paradoxical. Writing in *Phaedrus*, Plato described the discovery

Figure 1.2 Transverse section of the Great Hypostyle Hall from the Precinct of Amun-Re in the Karnak Temple Complex at Thebes. From *Description de l'Égypte: ou, Recueil des observations et des recherches qui ont été faites en Égypte pendant l'expédition de l'armée française publié par les ordres de Sa Majesté l'empereur Napoléon le Grand* (Paris: Imprimerie impériale, 1809–1828)

Figure 1.3
Ramesses II molding a mud brick before Amun-Re using a wooden mold, a ritual similar to laying the cornerstone of a building ceremonies, from the Great Hypostyle Hall at Karnak. Photo by Dr Peter Brand and image courtesy of P. Brand/Karnak Hypostyle Hall Project

of writing as a *pharmakon*: a cure that also acts as a poison. According to Egyptian legend, the god Theuth (Thoth) developed the art of letters among his other inventions of arithmetic, geometry, and astronomy. The Egyptian King Thamus replied to this offering with circumspection, arguing that "this discovery of yours will create forgetfulness in the learners' souls, because they will not use their memories; they will trust to the external written characters and not remember of themselves."[2] A prescription to save memory, inscription transforms the surfaces of architecture—an art form whose endurance uniquely ties to the *ars memoriae* or memory arts—into permanent historical records, and indeed into books. But, in this poison–cure dynamic the pharmacological tensions between inscription, prescription, architecture, writing, forgetting, and remembering also identify a fundamental rivalry between words and buildings. Does writing render buildings into mere surfaces awaiting inscriptions or does architecture's monumentality dwarf the words inscribed on its walls? For John Ruskin, a 19th-century architectural critic: "It is as the centralization and protectress of this sacred influence, that Architecture is to be regarded by us with the most serious thought. We may live without her, and worship without her, but we cannot remember without her."[3]

Trajan's Column, a commemorative *columna cochlis* in Rome dating from 113 CE, offers a case in point to demonstrate this rivalry. It is a marker that depicts sequential sculptural groups of the emperor's two victories over the Dacians on a narrative frieze spiraling from the base to the capital of its cylindrical shaft. While the direct content of this spiral book is that of Trajan's defeat of barbarians at the borders and the expansion of empire, the collateral text is a highly illustrated story of the Roman war machine, from the building of bridges or fortifications to styles of armor and weaponry. At its upper-most edge, the continuous narrative stops to reveal 24 flutes of the Doric order, as if peeping out from under a story-board, positioning the entire work as an ancient scroll or book covering an existing stone column. Further delineating the column as an ancient Roman book standing within Trajan's monumental complex, its siting between Greek and Latin libraries would have allowed curious readers to begin at ground level and then continue reading at the level of second-floor balconies projecting from these buildings. Indicating the column's narrative function as superseding that of enclosure, its interior volume occupies the narrow shaft of space for a spiral staircase that wends its way from the bottom entrance to the top of a viewing platform like a corkscrew.

The column also serves as an urban marker establishing an elevated position from which it is possible to survey the city, telling a story of power as monumental as the narrative of battle campaigns. Standing at 125 feet tall, the column indexes the prodigious engineering feat of having removed a saddle-shaped piece of land that attached the Capitoline and the Quirinal hills, a geophysical transformation that permanently transformed Rome's topography, in order to make room for Trajan's forum and market. The pedestal, which contains a chamber to house the golden funerary urns of Trajan and his wife Plotina, features inscriptions that explain the column as having been built "to demonstrate how lofty a hill and (what area of) ground was carried away for these mighty works."[4] By providing important textual evidence about the way in which it marks a dramatic change to Rome's topography, the inscription becomes the primary alibi for constructing the column as a marker that documents Trajan's engineering prowess.

Commemorative columns and triumphal arches, imagined in their original state of extreme polychrome and sparkling bronze letters, served as giant billboards with narrative sculptural groups enacting historical events to a semi-literate public. Where Trajan's Column describes a condition of minimal spatial enclosure, the triumphal arch or fornix slightly expands the potential for inhabitation by creating a shelter from the elements under its arches and hiding a secret room in its attic story.

Dating from 203 CE, the arch of Septimius Severus commemorates the emperor's victories over the Parthians and the Osroeni. It served as a threshold along the *Via Sacra* (Sacred Way), a celebratory pathway leading through the Roman Forum that delineated a general's triumphal procession through the city. This arch and others like it established a formal strategy for Renaissance architects to apply a classically inspired façade to a Christian basilica section. It also developed a model for the separation of vehicular and pedestrian pathways by providing a large central opening for chariots or wagons and two smaller flanking arches scaled to people. After Severus died, his son Caracalla organized the assassination of his brother Geta, thereafter

Figure 1.4
Giovanni Battista Piranesi, section through Trajan's Column, from *Trofeo o sia magnifica colonna coclide di marmo composta di grossi macigni ove si veggono scopite le due guerre daciche fatte da Traiano* **(1775–1776)**

Figure 1.5
**Giovanni
Battista
Piranesi, View
of the Arch
of Septimius
Severus from**
*Vedute di
Roma* **(1740)**

issuing an order of *damnatio memoriae* commanding that all mention of Geta be removed from public view. It is possible to identify this act of erasing Geta from memory on the arch because archaeologists connected the dots of the holes drilled into the marble to attach the bronze letters Caracalla had had removed, which originally read *P. Septimio L. fil Getae nobilissi(mo)*, the most noble son of Lucius Septimius, Publius Septimius Geta.

The Arch of Septimius Severus describes the military history of the empire as well as a story that turns on Rome's foundational mythology of Romulus killing his brother Remus to become the sole ruler of the newly formed city. As the story of this arch demonstrates, inscriptions, sculptural groups, bas reliefs, wall paintings, petroglyphs, graffiti, signage, and more operate as an architectural metalanguage that floats above a building's structural and spatial imperatives, allowing the reader to move laterally from denotative words to connotative ideas such as power, fratricide, and ritual that the arch frames.

Carved surfaces maintain the power to evoke architecture's conceptual underpinnings as they problematize the status of its primary role to provide shelter with larger representational concepts such as burial and remembrance. When contemplating architecture's essential role in marking the place of death, architect Adolf Loos wrote in 1910: "If we were to come across a mound in the woods, six foot long by three foot wide, with the soil piled up in a pyramid, a somber mood would come over us and a voice inside us would say, 'There is someone buried here.' That is architecture."[5] Writing in his *Essays Upon Epitaphs* (1810), William Wordsworth further problematizes the relationship between monument and text, arguing that: "It needs scarcely be said, that an Epitaph presupposes a Monument, upon which it is to be engraven."[6] As the epitaph conjures the monument, so too writing anticipates architecture.

But this argument could be reversed. A headstone without an inscription lacks an identity but not necessarily its meaning as a marker of burial, while an inscription without a surface destination may float in ether.

Although *How to Read Architecture* focuses on the built domain, no publication on this subject would be complete without at least some mention of Giuseppe Terragni's *Danteum*, designed in 1938 for a site on Benito Mussolini's newly constructed Via dell'Impero in the heart of Rome. The *Danteum* was to be a memorial and study center for Dante Alighieri, author of the *Divine Comedy* (1320) and of the modern Italian language. Terragni translated the three sections of Dante's hell, heaven, and purgatory into a series of sequential rooms that explicitly reference the spatial quality of these spaces as Dante described them. Terragni also used inscriptions and mathematical proportioning systems to reference both the words and the organization of Dante's masterpiece. He marshaled words, space, form, and building material to arrive at a design that translated Dante's poem into a work of architecture. As Terragni wrote of this project: "The spiritual reference and direct dependence upon the first canto of the Poem must be expressed in unmistakable signs by an atmosphere that influences the visitor and appears physically to weigh upon his mortal person, so that he is moved to experience the 'trip' as Dante did."[7]

To return to the world of built work, if providing shelter is one of architecture's essential roles, then marking and memorializing space is another. Inscriptions remain as relevant to the construction of contemporary buildings as they were to ancient ones, articulating tensions between architecture's role as an abstract form-giver and as a conveyor of symbolic content. Maya Lin's Vietnam Veteran's Memorial exceeds the role of serving as a mere destination for carving the names of deceased veterans to emerge as sacred architecture in and of its own right. Here architecture and engraving remain inseparable from the stone upon which they cleave. As a silent space that speaks volumes, little more than a submerged wall, visitors descend into the ground of interment, contemplate their own image reflected in the polished black granite, and tactilely probe a carved letter that summons an absent body through their fingers. The V-shaped incision the memorial cuts into the earth, with one angle pointing toward the Lincoln Memorial and the other toward the Washington Monument, cuts a wound in the landscape rather than building a conventional work of architecture. As one walks down into the subterranean valley, the linguistic homology between *grave* and *engraving* fuses into the space of an incision—both on the ground and in the stone.

The carvings, sculptural groups, and ornamental programs that supplement edifices with larger informational systems, commonly referred to as iconography, draw upon the applied and decorative arts to produce architectural meaning. In his *Iconologia overo Descrittione Dell'imagini Universali cavate dall'Antichità et da altri luoghi* (*Iconography; or, A Description of Universal Images Derived from Antiquity and Other Sources*, 1593), Cesare Ripa codified a number of emblems, personifications of concepts such as *wisdom*, whom he depicts as holding an open book and carrying and illuminating torch.

Figure 1.6
Perspective views from Maya Lin's original design submission for the Vietnam War Memorial (1981) from the Library of Congress, American Treasures exhibit

The numerous paintings and sculptural installations covering the surfaces of Baroque architecture with emblems and iconographical programs, such as those Ripa outlined, tell stories through a symbolic language of socially contracted allegories. Indeed, the use of iconographic programs to communicate sacred stories or dynastic authority has been a dominant mode through which architecture has been read for centuries around the world.

S. A. P. 1. E. N. Z. A.

Figure 1.7
**Cesare Ripa,
"Wisdom" or
"Sapienza,"
from Cesare
Ripa,
"Sapienza,"
*Iconologia
overo
Descrittione
Dell'imagini
Universali
cavate
dall'Antichità et
da altri luoghi*
(1611 edition)**

Although illicit, graffiti is an important form of architectural media. Stemming from the ancient Greek *graphein*—meaning to scratch, draw, or write—graffiti is as old as architecture itself. Speaking through his alter-ego of Claude Frollo, the reverend archdeacon of Notre Dame de Paris (Our Lady of Paris). Victor Hugo fictionalized a piece of graffiti scratched into the wall of one of the towers. "Black with age, and quite deeply graven in the stone," as Hugo described it, Frollo discovered the word ἈΝΆΓΚΗ, meaning *fatality*.[8] Narrating this event in his 19th-century novel *The Hunchback of Notre Dame*, Hugo demoted architecture from its role as public media when causing Frollo to utter what perhaps has become the most poignant words ever spoken about architecture: "ceci tuera cela" or "this will kill that."[9] The book will kill the edifice.

In part, Hugo wrote The *Hunchback of Notre Dame*, to draw attention to the church's condition of neglect and to argue for the value of Gothic architecture that had fallen out of style at that time. And yes, this written phrase transferred the dominant vehicle for the dissemination of cultural knowledge from buildings to books. Johannes Gutenberg's introduction of moveable type printing to Europe in the 15th century saw to it that biblical accounts no longer required translation into the stone carvings and stained glass windows of gothic cathedrals such as Notre Dame. Those rare and inaccessible illuminated manuscripts that had been passed down one tome at a time to be painstakingly copied by hand onto precious papers and stored in remote libraries eventually became mass-produced volumes placed directly in the hands of the laity. Until the invention of the printing press, architecture was the most accessible communicative medium through which a culture expressed itself, not only by translating biblical lessons into the legible pictographs of stained glass windows and carved stone, but also as a record of the society that produced these structures.

For a medieval village dwelling in the shadow of its great cathedral, the structure represented generations of builders, radical new building technologies, effigies of people who modeled for portraits, and, perhaps most importantly, the public spaces within and without the church where the town would gather in communion to celebrate sacraments such as matrimony, baptism, and burial. Gothic cathedrals such as Notre Dame, built from 1163 to 1345, exemplify a building's ability to communicate through several forms of architectural writing. Ranging from more abstract concepts of god demonstrated through the components of light, symmetry, and proportion, to the daily rituals of monastic life, to precise semblances of writing such as didactic art programs, sarcophagi, inscriptions, or consecration dates, the cathedral absorbed, reflected, and transformed the world through its constructed words. During the gothic period, according to Hugo, architecture conveyed a deep cultural significance that it would never again possess. So great was the loss of this role that architecture's ontological foundation as a conveyer of meaning would cease to exist and die.

The story less often told regarding Hugo's proclamation of architecture's death is that Gutenberg breathed new life into architecture through the book's ability to disseminate, theorize, and ultimately develop an entire profession that heretofore possessed little formal training or epistemological rigor. In this respect, the book "built" the building by codifying a disciplinary lexicon for spatial literacy and a systematic theoretical approach to design. Throughout the Middle Ages and prior to Gutenberg, architectural knowledge primarily passed from generation to generation through the transcription of important texts, apprenticeships with master craftsmen, trial and error, and the vast amounts of knowledge buildings themselves held in reserve. Gutenberg's press led to the definition of *architecture* as a specific term and profession. On the contrary, as Lewis Mumford countered, "the real misdemeanor of the printing-press was not that it took literary values away from architecture, but that it caused architecture to derive its value from literature."[10]

The centuries separating the building of Notre Dame from Leon Battista Alberti's publication of *De re aedificatoria* (*On the Art of Building*, 1443–1452) witnessed the emergence of architectural theory and pedagogy, the printing of books, and the discovery of Marcus Vitruvius Pollio's 1st-century treatise *De architectura* (*The Ten Books on Architecture*). The printing press that Hugo blamed for the destruction of architectural meaning helped to disseminate Alberti's Renaissance publication, the essential text for having elevated architecture to the systematic theorization of a fine art. Embedded in the very title of *De re aedificatoria* is an understanding that architecture's cultural role is to transcend shelter with meaning. Taken from its Latin root of *ædificare*, which translates as "to build or construct" and to "improve spiritually or instruct," this double meaning conveys the idea that the edifice may edify us. Architecture's primary role as a conveyor of meaning, in this sense, assigns buildings with the responsibility of representation, of teaching society how to read the alphabet, words, and stories it may express.

The printing press disseminated the words and images of architects such as Leon Battista Alberti, Andrea Palladio, Sebastiano Serlio, Claude Perrault, Antoine-Chrysostome Quatremère de Quincy, Claude Nicolas Ledoux, Étienne-Louis Boullée, Gottfried Semper, and Eugène Emmanuel Viollet-le-Duc, and more recently of Le Corbusier, Robert Venturi, and Rem Koolhaas—authors whose writings translate building traditions into published theoretical treatises. In particular reference to the affinity between books and buildings, the printing press allowed for the publication of Ledoux's *Architecture considérée sous le rapport de l'art, des moeurs et de la legislation* (*Architecture Considered in Relation to Art, Morals, and Legislation*, 1804). In this treatise Ledoux published designs for the buildings he intended to populate Chaux, an ideal city he conceived as the second half of the semi-circular plan he designed for the Royal Saltworks constructed at Arc-et-Senans, France. He proposed a series of suburban pavilions for Chaux that explore architecture's symbolic alphabet of primary shapes. For the house and workshop of the barrel makers, he shaped the façades with interpenetrating concentric circles pierced by cylinders. The key to unlocking this architectural rebus resided in the reader's ability to connect the dots between the metal hoops binding a barrel's staves and the house's circular geometry. *Architecture parlante*, translated literally as "speaking architecture," is a French academic term that emerged in response to Ledoux's work. *Architecture parlante* identifies the potential for architecture to communicate its purpose through external symbolism.

Figure 1.8
Claude Nicolas Ledoux, House and Workshop of the Coopers, from *L'architecture considérée sous le rapport de l'art, des moeurs et de la législation,* **vol. 1 (1804)**

Figure 1.9
**Claude Nicolas
Ledoux,
House of the
Agricultural
Guard, from**
*L'architecture
considérée
sous le rapport
de l'art, des
mœurs et de
la legislation,*
vol. 1 (1804)

Recourse to designing architecture as an expression of its conceptual purpose gave architects license to do away with the imitation of ancient classical canons. Ledoux's House of the Agricultural Guard, shaped as a perfect sphere, illustrates the magnitude of this shift in perception that divided those architects who followed the ancients and those who elected to become modern. A metaphorical seed or pure platonic solid, this pavilion appears to have landed from another planet, so extremely radical is its form in comparison to anything preceding it. Modern architecture was born with the explosion of classical architecture this very seed disseminated when planted in the 18th-century garden of political revolution. Even if the shape of this sphere contradicted any reasonable use, the ruptured authority of the classical orders that *architecture parlante* inaugurated contributed to a quarrel among the ancients and the moderns that resulted in protracted research into architecture's uniquely performative and/or representational, rather than imitative, role.

In terms of built work that exemplifies *architecture parlante*, Ledoux's plan for the Royal Saltworks at Arc-et-Senans demonstrates salt's vital role in food preservation that elevated its status to a precious commodity. As the French government sought to regulate the salt economy through the imposition of taxes and the construction of salt works, it required systems of control and surveillance that the placement of the Director's house in the center of Ledoux's semi-circle and the gated threshold guarding the entrance make clear. Ledoux rendered the entrance as a giant salt grotto and located stone portals at the base of the building from out of which salt brine has been petrified into a permanent state of leakage. In this example, architecture's expressive potential relies as much on the building's overall form as it does the kind of salient details the Royal Salt Works at Chaux exhibits.

Figure 1.10
Detail of salt
brine exuding
from out of
the entrance
to the Royal
Saltworks at
Arc-et-Senans
(Chaux,
1774–1779) by
Claude-Nicolas
Ledoux

Figure 1.11
Automotive
details on
William Van
Alen's Chrysler
Building (New
York City,
1928–1930),
photograph by
Norbert Nagel

27

Figure 1.12
**Capitol Records
Headquarters
by Louis
Naidorf of
Welton Becket
Associates,
courtesy of
the Marc
Wanamaker-
Bison Archives
of Hollywood
Historic Photos.
com**

Figure 1.13
**Eliot Noyes's
Aerospace
Research
Center for
IBM (now Otis
College of Art
and Design,
Los Angeles,
1964). Courtesy
of International
Business
Machines
Corporation, ©
International
Business
Machines
Corporation**

Figure 1.14
Foreground:
PTW Architects'
"Water Cube"
(Beijing 2008
Olympic
Games Aquatic
Center);
background:
Herzog &
de Meuron's
"Bird's Nest"
(Beijing 2008
Olympic
Games
National
Stadium)

Figure 1.15
Milton J.
Black's Tail o'
the Pup hotdog
stand in Los
Angeles (1946),
courtesy of
the Marc
Wanamaker-
Bison Archives
of Hollywood
Historic Photos.
com

Several select examples of *architecture parlante* demonstrate its trajectory into the iconography of modern and contemporary architecture. Not only was William van Alen's Chrysler Building in New York (1929) the world's tallest building in the world at the time it was completed, but also the "gargoyles" on the corners of the 61st floor were over-scaled replicas of the 1929 Chrysler Deluxe Roadster hood ornament. Welton Beckett's Capitol Records Headquarters in Hollywood, California (1956) is a 13-story cylindrical tower whose asymmetrical spire evokes the image of a turntable needle playing on a stack of records. Now the main building on Otis College of Art and Design's campus, Eliot Noyes's Aerospace Research Center for IBM (1963) in Los Angeles, California reflects the company's products with façades that look like computer punch cards. The four L-shaped buildings forming Dominique Perrault's National Library of France (Paris, 1995), bracket the corners of an open plaza as a vertical tower that easily read as open books. PTW Architects' Water Cube, the aquatic center for the 2008 Summer Olympics in Beijing, features an exterior envelop based on a three-dimensional geometry that represents foam bubbles. While they indicate a building's purpose but not necessarily its function, these projects do begin to suggest the way in which form follows figure. While these projects make clear that the production of contemporary architecture finds antecedents in eighteenth-century architectural theory, the challenge remains for architects to elevate them from the more prosaic roadside architecture of the 1920s and 1930s, where hot dogs were sold from buildings shaped like buns and ducklings were sold from buildings shaped like ducks, a paradigm that the following chapter explores.

Notes

1   Ledoux writes "Le cercle, le carré, voilà les lettres alphabetiques que les auteurs emploient dans la texture des meilleurs ouvrage." C. N. Ledoux, *L' Architecture Considérée sous le Rapport de l'Art, des Moeurs et de la Législation* (Paris, 1804), p. 135.

2   Benjamin Jowett, "Thamus and Theuth (Phaedrus 274b-278d)," in *The Dialogues of Plato in Five Volumes*, 3rd ed. (Oxford: Oxford University, 1892) unpaginated, at http://www.john-uebersax.com/plato/myths/phaedrus.htm.

3   John Ruskin, *The Seven Lamps of Architecture* (London: Waverly, 1920), p. 186.

4   The full dedicatory inscription reads: "The Senate and the People of Rome to the Emperor, Caesar Nerva, son of the deified Nerva, Traianus Augustus, Germanicus, Dacicus, Pontifex Maximus, invested with the power of the tribune seventeen times, hailed imperator six times, elected consul six times, father of the fatherland, to demonstrate how lofty a hill and (what area of) ground was carried away for these mighty works." From D. R. Dudley, *Urbs Roma* (1967: Aberdeen), http://www.trajans-column.org/?page_id=208.

5   Adolf Loos, "Architecture," in *The Architecture of Adolf Loos* trans. Wilfried Wang (London: Art Council of Great Britain, 1985), pp. 104–109.

6   William Henry Wordsworth, "Essay upon Epitaphs," in *The Complete Poetical Works of William Wordsworth*, ed. Henry Reed (Philadelphia: Troutmon and Hayes,

1854), p. 700. This interpretation is indebted to Eugenio Donato's interpretation of sepulchral inscriptions, in the grave or engraven. According to Donato, "through graphic inscriptions, that is to say, that which is most inimical to presence, funerary monuments are the twice removed representation of an empty center" in "The Mnemonics of History: Notes for a Contextual Reading of Foscolo's Dei Sepolchri" *Yale Italian Studies 1*, no. 2 (Winter 1977), pp. 1–23.

7   Thomas L. Schumacher, *The Danteum: A Study in the Architecture of Literature* (Princeton: Princeton Architectural Press, 1985), p. 133.

8   Victor Hugo, "Preface," in *Notre-Dame De Paris Also Known as: The Hunchback of Notre Dame*, trans. Isabel F. Hapgood, http://www.gutenberg.org/files/2610/2610-h/2610-h.htm.

9   Ibid.

10   Lewis Mumford, *Sticks and Stones: A Study of American Architecture and Civilization* (New York: Dover, 1955), p. 134.

Chapter 2

Inscription

Las Vegas, Los Angeles, Levittown, the swinging singles on the West-heimer Strip, golf resorts, boating communities, Co-op City, the residential backgrounds to soap operas, TV commercials and mass mag ads, bill-boards, and Route 66 are sources for a changing architectural sensibility.[1]
—*Denise Scott Brown*

When it comes to reading the way in which inhabitants adapt to the abstract and minimal spaces of modern architecture's machine aesthetic to meet their individual needs, Le Corbusier's *Cité Frugès* worker housing complex in Pessac, France (1924) stands out as an emblematic project. By 1981, when Ada Louise Huxtable visited Pessac, a number of tenants had modified the original structures according to their own designs with additions and remode-lings substantial enough to have supposedly spoiled the original architecture.[2] And yet, these presumed violations of Corbusier's original work evidence the pliability of his designs to adapt to the particular needs of individual people. In developing her argument in favor of the project's ability to accommodate change, Huxtable referenced Philippe Boudon's study *Lived-in Architecture, Le Corbusier's Pessac Revisited* (1972) showing "photographs of garage doors where there once were open entrances, small, shuttered windows replacing large expanses of glass, tile roofs and endearing touches of kitsch."[3] Upon entering one of the row houses, Huxtable encountered "flowered wallpaper, overstuffed furniture, and the accessories of a comfortable bourgeois life style." Instead of "the architect's will imposed," as Huxtable narrated, "the then-radical open plan could be reorganized and subdivided in many ways; a terrace could be roofed over for an extra room; windows of one's choice could be fitted into the large openings without knocking out a wall."[4] Architectural sensibilities seem to have changed enough since Huxtable found the need to defend the inhabitants' transformation of their property at the expense of the architect's control, to the extent that Alejandro Aravena built into his design of the Incremental Houses Complex in Iquique, Chile (2004) the ability for the tenants to transform and expand their homes.

In an earlier essay about the necessity of architects to consider the every-day needs of their inhabitants entitled "Learning from Pop" (1971), Denise

Scott Brown asked: "If high-style architects are not producing what people want or need, who is, and what can we learn from them?"[5] Through their built work and theoretical treatises, Robert Venturi and Denise Scott Brown taught generations of architects to read ordinary houses and roadside attractions as offering valuable insight to the design of the built environment. In so doing they updated the ancient art of inscribing words upon stone with modes of communication delivered by the electric light of commercial signage. They offered a significant contribution to the transformation of architecture from modernism's functionalist doctrine to a stylistic trend that came to be termed post-modernism, a return to expressing architecture's representational or communicative potential, often implemented through eclectic stylistic references to various historical time periods.

Figure 2.1 Alejandro Aravena, Incremental Houses Complex in Iquique, Chile (2004), courtesy of Alejandro Arevena: Ludovic Dusuzeau

In *Signs of Life: Symbols in the American City*, a 1976 exhibition at the Renwick Gallery of the Smithsonian Institution, Venturi and Scott Brown depicted the three topological sites of home, commercial strip, and street with full-scale installations of these environments accompanied by large panels depicting photographs highlighted with explanatory thought balloons. They analyzed important iconography of American architecture at that time and studied the ordinary homes and the extraordinary features of the commercial strip. The exhibition highlighted middle-class aspirations for colonial shutters, Cape Cod shingles, and Currier and Ives motifs as well as objects from popular culture, furniture from everyday life, and the exterior symbolism of the suburban landscape. Citing Dan Graham's 1966 photo essay *Homes for America* as an important influence on their research into the architecture of everyday life, they identified the pervasive tropes or metaphorical themes that allow the lay public to read architecture. Among Venturi and Scott Brown's many influences, other artists including Andy Warhol and Richard Hamilton introduced the genre of Pop Art to the discussion. Hamilton created a collage for the Independent Group's 1956 exhibition catalogue *This is Tomorrow* entitled "Just what is it that makes today's homes so different, so appealing?", which depicts a scantily dressed couple inside a domestic interior filled with the paraphernalia of consumer goods and a giant Tootsie Pop stick candy that purportedly gave rise to the nomenclature of "POP" architecture.

Figure 2.2
Signs of Life:
Symbols in
the American
City, Renwick
Gallery (1976),
courtesy of
Venturi, Scott
Brown and
Associates, Inc.

From triumphal to golden arches, in 1968 Venturi and Scott Brown took their research on the road and traveled with a group of architecture students from Yale University to study the Las Vegas Strip, a trip that ultimately resulted in the provocative publication *Learning from Las Vegas: The Forgotten Symbolism of Architectural Form* (1972). They iconoclastically compared Rome's ancient monuments with the Las Vegas strip, Nevada's version of the *Forum Romanum.* They argued that the advertising billboard of capitalist production parallels the triumphal arch of imperial rule and the "Las Vegas is to the Strip what Rome is to the Piazza."[6] Along with their comparative analysis of

Figure 2.3
Richard Hamilton, "Just what is it that makes today's homes so different, so appealing?" from *This is Tomorrow* (1956)

Las Vegas architecture, Venturi and Scott Brown produced a genealogy of buildings whose broad façades operate as informational signage, including Amiens Cathedral, the pylon of an Egyptian temple, a highway billboard, an electric sign in front of the Stardust Hotel, and an ancient Roman triumphal arch.

Possibly the most useful provocation in this publication is Venturi and Scott Brown's distinction between a building that is a "duck" and one that is a "decorated shed." The duck and decorated shed emerge as an influential set of paradigms for identifying the different ways in which a building may communicate to the general public while simultaneously challenging modern architecture with ironic examples of its own tenets. In a straightforward interpretation of this dichotomy, the duck transmits meaning as an inhabitable sculpture that reflects its contents—as with the building in Suffolk County, New York that sells ducks and is shaped like a duck—while the shed relies on signage to communicate the purpose of what would otherwise remain a generic and utilitarian structure. A more nuanced interpretation of the decorated shed, as Deborah Fausch offers, is to understand it as a case in which a building's expression of function may be detached from its form, a comment on modern architecture's organic approach to laminating interior and exterior functions upon each other.

Figure 2.4
**The "duck" and
the "decorated
shed" from
*Learning
from Las
Vegas: These
Forgotten
Symbolism of
Architectural
Form* (1972),
courtesy of
Venturi Scott
Brown and
Associates, Inc.**

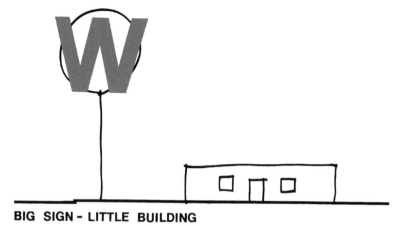

BIG SIGN – LITTLE BUILDING

OR

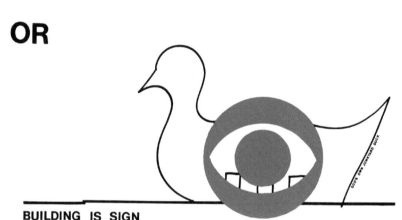

BUILDING IS SIGN

As Fausch continues, for Venturi and Scott Brown, "the decorated shed *was* an expression of structure and function: the structure was separated from the function of communication." The duck, as she continues, operates as a combination of "sculptural symbol and architectural shelter," in contrast to the false front of old west, Cowboy-type main streets that the shed implies.[7] Equally, the duck is as much of a decoy of *architecture parlante* within a context of wit and humor as it is an assessment of architecture's sculptural expression.

Both in their design practice and published theories, Venturi and Scott Brown remained committed to engaging architecture through media to the extent that they risked reducing buildings to signs. Take their BASCO showroom in northeast Philadelphia from 1976 as a radical example of this trajectory. When asked to increase the visibility of a 16-foot high by 1,100-foot long showroom for a catalog department store, the architects responded with five 34-foot-tall aluminum sheathed capital letters spelling out BASCO that they placed in front of the building. Their polemic of placing building and signage on an equal footing undermines architecture's formal capacity in favor of its

Figure 2.5
**Showroom and
Warehouse,
BASCO Inc.,
Philadelphia,
1977–1978,
Photograph by
Tom Bernard,
courtesy of
Venturi, Scott
Brown and
Associates, Inc.**

communicative role, what has come to be referred to as *representation*, and in so doing positioned Venturi and Scott Brown as outliers among the discipline's more entrenched formalists.

The word *sign* in the title of Venturi and Scott Brown's Smithsonian exhibition identifies a privileged mode of reading buildings that emerged in the late 1960s through s*emiotics*, the systematic study of signs. For semioticians, a *sign* is a communicative term constructed by two indivisible components: a *signified* (the thought concept) and a *signifier* (the entity that stands in for a thought concept). In his 1916 *Cours de linguistique générale* Ferdinand de Saussure articulated the definitive diagram for outlining his system, in which a sound-image or *signifier* (*un significant*) such as a *tree* (*arbor*) and the concept-image or *signified* (*un signifie*) such as the image of a tree combine to produce a sign.

Since semiotics concerns "all aspects of culture as communicative processes," as Umberto Eco posited in his 1972 essay "A Componential Analysis of the Architectural Sign */Column/*," it should be possible to analyze architecture from the perspective of a sign's language. For Eco, the communicative aspect of architecture predominates over and precedes its functional role. A stair, in this respect, communicates the ability to ascend or descend in advance of our using it to transition from one level to another. Indeed, as John Hejduk notes: "The stairs of a house are mysterious because they go up and down at the same time."[8]

In assessing the double imperative of communication and function, Eco distinguishes between primary functions, what "the functionalist tradition

Figure 2.6
**Diagram of
Ferdinand de
Saussure's
concept of
a sign from
his *Cours de
linguistique
générale*,
drawn by Gavin
Friehauf**

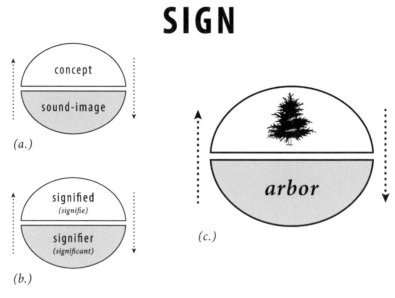

SIGN

recognizes as functions in the true sense of the word (going upstairs, standing
at the window, taking the air, enjoying the sunlight, living together, etc.)," and
secondary functions, what "art-historians and iconologists have preferred to
classify as the 'symbolical values' of Architecture."[9] Comparing Peter Cook
and Colin Fournier's Kunsthaus (2003) in Graz, Austria to a "slug," referring
to Norman Foster's Swiss Re Tower in London (2004) as a "gherkin," calling
Herzog and de Meuron's Beijing National Stadium a "bird's nest," or nicknaming

Figure 2.7
**Peter Cook and
Colin Fournier,
Kunsthaus in
Graz, Austria
(2003)**

Figure 2.8
**Foster +
Partners,
Swiss Re
Tower, London
England (2004),
courtesy of
Nigel Young /
Foster +
Partners**

the Office for Metropolitan Architecture's (OMA) Central Chinese Television Headquarters (2008) in Beijing "pants" similarly exemplify the ways in which figural form invites analogical readings that transform architecture into a built symbol, one that also risks reducing important work to one-liners.

As a primary building component, the column carries myriad potential for multiple readings that go far beyond even what Eco considered. The three classical Greek orders, known as Doric, Ionic, and Corinthian, describe a series of column profiles that extend upwards from a temple's base to its entablature. Columns, then, may serve as the architectural equivalent of linguistic signs. Their denotative value, a column's literal meaning, is to support a beam. Their connotative value, symbolic references that columns evoke, begins with forming a screen of cylindrical vertical elements that subtly veil

Figure 2.9
**Office of
Metropolitan
Architecture
(OMA), Central
Chinese
Television
Headquarters,
Beijing, China
(2008), Rem
Koolhaas and
Ole Scheeren,
courtesy of
OMA**

views from the public exterior into the private *cella*, the sacred interior where an effigy of the god or goddess would dwell. Their connotative value extends to an interpretive sequence concerning their analogy with the human body and even the gender of these bodies. Columns approximate the human body semantically, functionally, and proportionally. The term for the top of a column is *capital*, meaning head. Statues of women supporting beams on their heads, as seen at the "Temple of the Maidens," or Erechtheion, on the Acropolis in Athens, are called Caryatids, while their male counterparts are called Persians.

As Vitruvius recounted in the first century CE, the Doric order evidences the thick and muscular proportions of a masculine nature; the Ionic order displays volutes on its capital that represent the curls of a matronly woman's

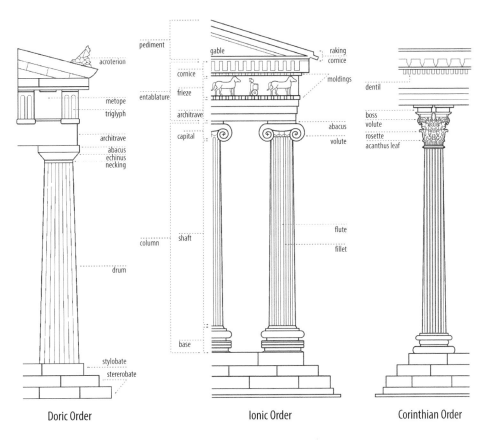

Doric Order

Ionic Order

Corinthian Order

(Doric Order labels) pediment, acroterion, cornice, entablature, metope, triglyph, frieze, architrave, capital, abacus, echinus, necking, column, shaft, drum, stylobate, stererobate

(Ionic Order labels) gable, raking cornice, moldings, abacus, volute, flute, fillet, base

(Corinthian Order labels) dentil, boss, volute, rosette, acanthus leaf

Figure 2.10
Doric, Ionic, and Corinthian orders drawn by Gavin Friehauf

Figure 2.11
Caryatids on the Erechtheion of the Acropolis in Athens, Greece

41

hair; and the Corinthian order maintains "the graceful elegant appearance of a virgin."[10] By way of a distinction, Trajan's Column seems to lack denotative value, with no other structural capacity than to support itself. In comparison, in Adolf Loos's 1922 competition entry to design a skyscraper for the *Chicago Tribune* newspaper—where he proposed an inhabitable Doric column over 30 stories tall—the column's denotative value is that of a typical skyscraper delineated by a base, shaft, and, cornice. As with Trajan's Column, its connotative value references monumentality, duration, and power. Importantly, the legibility of both columns oscillates between semantic references to the human body inhabiting the classical language of architecture and to the syntactic references of the column as an ornamental structure, insofar as these colossal vertical elements support nothing but themselves.

Of particular interest to reading architecture as simultaneously abstract script and figural form are the decorative motifs found in Islamic architecture where ornament, building, and text become co-spatial through the process of calligraphy. The art of transforming calligraphy into figures offers a visual embodiment of the sacred word in Islamic architecture, a way of imprinting the holy book of *Qur'an* onto the sacred edifice of the mosque.[11] Conventional wisdom understands that the ornamental program of Islamic architecture was a response to the prohibition against using graven imagery, which in fact references the same prohibition in the Old Testament. And to a certain extent this holds true. But the rules banning iconographic art were applied inconsistently to the extent that the so-called practice displays numerous exceptions and complexities that rendered Islamic architecture as textual. Rather than overtly break with the prohibition, Islamic architects deployed the figurative ability of Arabic calligraphy to deform into identifiable shapes when covering the surfaces of their buildings with decorative yet instructive ornamentation. Great latitude between words and images inhabits Islamic calligrams, writing that conforms and deforms to accommodate the shape of an external image or concept—a poem about trees typeset in the shape of a tree. To achieve this effect, 17th-century calligraphers in Turkey, Persia, and India initiated the contrivance of words such as "Allah" or "Muhammad" into anthropomorphic or zoomorphic figures like the depiction of Imam Ali as "The Lion of God" or a bismallah in the form of a hawk. Calligraphic architectural ornaments may be found throughout the Islamic world, from the upper part of the Dome of the Rock in Jerusalem, to the mihrab of the Great Mosque in Cordoba, to the interior domes of the Blue and Suleymaniye Mosques in Istanbul, to the *Masjed-e Jāmé* ("Friday mosque") in Isfahan, Iran.

The figuring of inscriptions, or the inscribing of form, is central to more recent discussions regarding architecture's legibility that privileges syntax over semantics. In other words, the set of rules determining the arrangement of words in sentences, versus the actual meaning of that sentence, becomes prioritized. The Iraqi architect Zaha Hadid acknowledged the combined influence of figuration and Arabic calligraphy on her work. She contended that both Kazimir Malevich and Wassily Kandinsky must have looked to Chinese

Figure 2.12
Adolf Loos,
*Chicago
Tribune* Tower
competition
entry (1922)

Figure 2.13
**Ornate Arabic
Calligraphy
on the Oljeitu
Mihrab at
the Jameh
Masjid ("Friday
mosque") in
Esfahan, Iran,
courtesy of
Alamy**

Figure 2.14
**Pictorial
Calligraphy of
a Lion, India,
17th century,
opaque
watercolor, ink,
and gold on
paper, 12 x 19
cm © The Aga
Khan Museum**

and Islamic scripts for inspiration. As she described her time as a student at
the Architectural Association School of Architecture in London, Rem Koolhaas
"noticed that only the Arab and Persian students like myself were able to
make certain curved gestures. He thought it had to do with calligraphy."[12]
Zaha Hadid Architects's design for the Bergisel Ski Jump in Austria (1999)
evokes the fluidity of a single brush stroke, while their design of the Heydar
Aliyev Center in Baku, Azerbaijan (2012) suggests a poem locked within a
calligram, making the potential for a cursive architecture explicit. As Saffet
Kaya Bekiroglu, the project architect, explains, the office considered the

Figure 2.15
Heydar Aliyev Center in Baku, Azerbaijan (2012), photograph by David Hall

region's cultural heritage when developing the design of this highly curvilinear building. In particular, the office explored the "cursive flow of the Islamic world's calligraphy, which was etched into mosques scattered around Baku in centuries past."[13] As Bekiroglu continues, "Fluidity has always been part of the Islamic world's architecture," in structures such as the 400-year-old Blue Mosque in Istanbul, where "Calligraphy and geometric patterns flow through the interior surfaces of domes and walls, and onto the carpets within, establishing this continuity."[14]

Zaha Hadid Architects captioned an illustration of the process they deployed for the design of the Kartal-Pendik Masterplan in Istanbul (2006) as "Scripting Calligraphy Block Patterns" to describe various computer scripts they developed to configure random variations within the opening of the perimeter blocks of this project according to parcel size, proportion, and orientation. This process generated forms that imply some new architectural alphabet in their shapes.[15] If the office's work may appear to be letters without meaning, syntax without semantics, or form without specific legibility, it nonetheless evokes architectural writing, while the process to arrive at this place is referred to as *scripting*.

What may initially appear to be a long comparative reach, in fact, delivers a uniquely motivated bridge between architecture and writing that contains essential tools for reading architecture conjured in an era of electronic media and design intelligence. This bridge centers on the term *script* and the emergence of concepts such as "shape grammar" that serve as more than digital metaphor. A script is a computational language allowing human operators to write programs that automate sequences of commands that otherwise would have to be executed one at a time. According to Malcolm McCullough, the first architectural product manager for Autodesk, in the early stages of software, scripting, and coding "computers operated on relatively simple geometrical data, following sets of alphabetic or algorithmic instructions" so that when image manipulation did occur, it derived from rule-based scripts.[16] This rule-based design process allowed for the straightforward sequencing of architecture into a set of mathematical commands that resulted in a digital program for intelligent design to emerge with minimal human agency.

In an inspiring marriage between Renaissance architectural theory and embryonic research into the potential for computers to perform autonomous design processes, Rudolf Wittkower's publication *Architectural Principles in the Age of Humanism* (1962) initiated a debate in the 1960s on the numeric value of proportional systems that, as Kari Jormakka recounts, "inspired Bill Mitchell, George Stiny and a host of other CAD experts to proclaim the era of automatically generated architecture, based on similar geometrical principles as Palladio's villas."[17] In 1972 George Stiny and James Gips published "Shape Grammars and the Generative Specification of Painting and Sculpture," where they presented their method for form generation "using shape grammars which take shape as primitive and have shape specific rules."[18] As with grammatical structures in language that can generate an infinite range of sentences, shape grammars allowed for the identifying and quantifying of a set of rules that can generate an infinite range of architectures, fueling an entire field of parametric design research in which forms are generated by a complex set of rules or algorithms, a discussion that will re-emerge in Chapter 9.

William J. Mitchell entitled a chapter of his book, *The Logic of Architecture: Design Computation and Cognition Languages of Architecture Form* (1990), "Languages of Architectural Form." In this essay he walks the reader through a step-by-step process of transforming the internal logics of Andrea Palladio's architecture into a digital language and, ultimately, a program for automatically designing neo-Palladian villas. He initiated this discussion by explicating a precise analogy between language and architecture. Insofar as nouns in English are governed by specific rules of grammar, they only communicate in specific combinations or strings with other words and only those strings that follow the proper rules of grammar form actual sentences.[19] Mitchell turned Wittkower's analysis of Leon Battista Alberti's system for combining columns, piers, entablatures, and arches into an architectural syntax that performs according to an internal set of grammatical rules. Following models he researched in classical Roman architecture, Alberti avoided placing arches on freestanding columns, preferring instead to have a straight entablature to span between these vertical elements and also preferring for arches to spring from rectangular pillars that appeared as residual segments of leftover wall. Specific rules such as this describe a linear sequence of combinatory elements that allowed programmers to embed grammar in algebra. When programming more complex grammatical sequences, the strategy was to assign parameters to specify geometric transformations of their spatial relationships from a chosen lexicon.

Palladio's villas constructed in the Veneto region of Italy and his idealization of them in his publication *I quattro libri dell'architettura* (*The Four Books of Architecture*, 1570) provided sufficient internal design logics to test these operations through a complex set of rules that could generate villa floor plans in the style of Palladio. An architect who conveniently distinguished himself by developing numerous iterations of a single planimetric geometry, Palladio's designs could be broken down into a set of iterative building blocks. Much like a parametric "shape grammar," a term Stiny and Gips coined in 1972, Palladio's buildings acted as original forms embedded with a set of rules that function as a generative engine for other forms. Taking the Villa Foscari (Villa Malcontenta) as a case study, the generative stages of grid definition, exterior-wall definition, room layout, interior-wall realignment, principal entrances-porticos and exterior wall inflections, exterior ornamentation-columns, windows and doors, and termination offered a catalogue of original architectural plans for Mitchell to program the computer to design in the manner of Palladio.

In this trajectory from the dissection of existing buildings and their rule sets to the generation of a series of parametric shape grammars, the status of the author remains in an indeterminate zone between the programmer, the program, and the architect who eventually will use this software. To this extent a designer's agency, his or her unique fingerprint, may become a wrinkle in a system whose terminus is the purity of entirely autonomous processes. If the architectural text at this point is to script a program, then the author may disappear into the algorithm that invariably takes over the work. Conversely, once it became possible to generate architecture from a set of rules derived from an existing building, it would be possible to do so from alternative sources and to begin to adjust the software into aberrant behaviors. If one end of this spectrum idealizes the abstract purity of rule-based, self-generating geometries, then the other romanticizes the computational potential to create hybrid monsters from the radical perversion of normative software systems. In either case, scripts have moved from words to algorithms while authorship dwells in the software. Icons have become buttons on screens as we keyboard our way into built form through electronic writing.

Notes

1   Denis Scott Brown, "Learning from Pop" originally published in *Casabella* (1971) in *Architecture Theory Since 1968*, ed. K. Michael Hays (Cambridge, MA: MIT Press, 1998), p. 62.
2   Ada Louise Huxtable, "Le Corbusier's Housing Project-Flexible Enough to Endure" *New York Times*, March 15, 1981, http://www.nytimes.com/1981/03/15/arts/architecture-view-le-corbusier-s-housing-project-flexible-enough-endure-ada.html?pagewanted=all&mcubz=0.
3   Ibid.
4   Ibid.
5   Ibid.

6   Robert Venturi, Denise Scott Brown, and Steven Izenour, *Learning from Las Vegas* (Cambridge, MA: MIT Press, 1972), p. 18.

7   Deborah Fausch, "The Context of Meaning is Everyday Life: Venturi and Scott Brown's Theories of Architecture and Urbanism (dissertation, Princeton University, 1999), p. 17. See also "Ugly and Ordinary: The Representation of the Everyday," in *Architecture of the Everyday*, eds. Steven Harris and Deborah Berke (New York: Princeton Architectural Press, 1997), pp. 75–106.

8   John Hejduk, "Sentences on the House and Other Sentences," in *Such Places as Memory: Poems, 1953–1996* (Cambridge, MA: MIT Press, 1998), p. 119.

9   Umberto Eco, "A Componential Analysis of the Architectural Sign /*Column*/" *Semiotica 5*, no. 2 (1972), p. 98. See also Umberto Eco, "Function and Sign: The Semiotics of Architecture," in *The City and the Sign*, eds. M. Gottdiener and K. Lagapoulous (New York: Columbia University Press, 1986).

10   Marcus Vitruvius Pollio, *De Architectura* (*The Ten Books on Architecture*), Book IV, Chapter 1, http://penelope.uchicago.edu/Thayer/E/Roman/Texts/Vitruvius/4*.html.

11   Cf. Doris Bittar, "Inside Arabic Calligraphy From Alef to Zaha: An Artist's View," presented on April 1, 2006 for the DIWAN Conference, Arab American National Museum, Dearborn, Michigan.

12   Massimo de Conti, *Design Talks: Contemporary Creatives on Architecture and Design* (Victoria, Australia: Images Publishing, 2012), p. 56. See also: http://www.vogue.com/873780/form-in-motion-architect-zaha-hadid-on-her-exhibit-at-the-philadelphia-museum-of-art.

13   Kevin Holden Platt, "Heydar Aliyev Center," *Arcspace*, February 12, 2014, https://arcspace.com/feature/heydar-aliyev-center.

14   Ibid.

15   Patrik Schumacher "Parameticism: A New Global Style for Architecture and Urbanism," in *AD Reader: The Digital Turn in Architecture 1992–2012*, ed. Mario Carpo (Chichester: Wiley, 2013), p. 250.

16   Malcolm McCullough, "Scripting," in *AD Reader: The Digital Turn in Architecture 1992–2012*, p. 182.

17   Kari Jormakka, "Paper, Rock, Scissors: Analog and Digital Pictures in Architectural Design" *Schriften der Bauhaus-Universität Weimar 120–122* (2008), p. 162.

18   George Stiny and James Gips, "Shape Grammars and the Generative Specification of Painting and Sculpture," presented at the IFIP Congress 71 in Ljubljana, Yugoslavia. Published in the Proceedings: *Information Processing 71*, ed. C. V. Freiman (Amsterdam: North-Holland, 1972), pp. 1460–1465; republished in *The Best Computer Papers of 1971*, ed. O. R. Petrocelli (Auerbach, Philadelphia, 1972), pp. 125–135. This is the version reproduced below.

19   Malcolm McCullough, "20 Years of Scripted Space," in *Programming Cultures: Art and Architecture in the Age of Software, AD Profile 182*, ed. Mike Silver (Chichester: Wiley, 2006), pp. 12–15.

Introduction to Part 2
Outside-In Architecture

The map is not the territory.[1]

—Alfred Korzybski

Standing outside architecture, in the most basic sense of where rain falls or wind blows, is the position from which we observe a building before entering it. From this exterior vantage point, the practice of reading begins with surveying the ways in which context—weather, views, site lines, landscape, solar orientation, built adjacencies, or cultural milieu—influences architecture. When approached from this orientation, as an object in space whose primary role is to provide shelter against the elements, architecture necessarily stands outside of nature as an inherently artificial artifact.

Being outside—whether in a forest, city, desert, or suburb—places us in the realm where the forces of nature may exert themselves. As part of the outside world, the built environment becomes naturalized. Skyscrapers may evoke vertiginous cliffs and buildings recall the form of trees or mountains. Conversely, nature becomes architecturalized. Parks may seem like green carpets rolled over asphalt while the arrangement of trees and plants suggests roofless rooms. Ilmari Lahdelma and Rainer Mahlamäki's design for the Museum of the History of Polish Jews (2013) in Warsaw, Poland features an entrance hall that cuts through the building with a curvilinear space almost indistinguishable from the stone canyon leading up to the ancient Nabataean rock-cut architecture in Petra, Jordan. When berms conceal buildings underneath or plants are made to grow on walls and roofs, architecture enters a fluid continuum between nature and artifice. At the Musée du quai Branly-Jacques Chirac in Paris (2006), Jean Nouvel and Patrick Blanc transformed the north façade into a living green wall off of which plants from around the world grow. And at the *Bosco Verticale*, or Vertical Forest, in Milan, Italy, Boeri Studio designed a pair of skyscrapers with surfaces supporting over 700 trees, developing a model of biological architecture that produces a micro-climate of vegetation to absorb air pollution and filter sunlight.

Any neat distinction between nature and artifice no longer holds in our anthropocene era. In a moment of time when human activity has permanently transformed the environment—from glaciers in Antarctica to surfaces on Mars—what we build impacts where and when rain falls and wind blows. The binary separation of inside and out or of nature and artifice erodes as architects turn toward living organisms in developing biomimetic and biodynamic buildings. Achim Menges designed the Elytra Filament Pavilion, a canopy system that evolved across the timespan of its construction at the Victoria and Albert Museum in London during 2016. The fibrous structure found in flying beetles called Elytra provided this pavilion with its name and structural logic of biomimicry. The structure was composed of lightweight hexagonal building elements prefabricated at the University of Stuttgart, where robots wove glass and carbon fibers around metal frames. Vertical columns spread upward like tree branches to support hexagonal cells off of which other cells cantilevered. Fiber-optical thermal imaging sensors monitored "changes to the structural systems caused by the further growth and adaptation of the canopy."[2] Elytra's onsite fabrication evolved in response to real-time data, rendering the building process into performance architecture that would

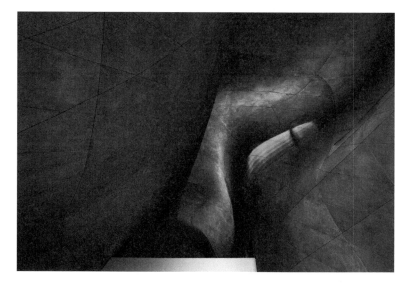

Figure P2.1
Lahdelma and Mahlamäki, Museum of the History of Polish Jews in Warsaw, Poland (2013)

Figure P2.2
Façade of Al Khazneh (The Treasury) in Petra, Jordan, capital of the Nabataean Kingdom (ca. 4th century BCE), photograph by Paulette Singley

"grow and reconfigure over the time of the exhibition, based on the behaviour of the garden's visitors, and their preferred places to walk, stroll, rest or meet."[3]

From biomimicry to biodynamic forms, while architects and engineers such as Menges and his team revolutionize architecture based on models derived from systems found in natural organisms, others propose building with nature itself. Mitchell Joachim's group at Terreform One has developed the Fab Tree Hab as a "Living Graft Prefab Structure" grown from trees. The concept is that Prefabricated Computer Numeric Controlled (CNC) scaffolds bend the growth of tree branches into the shape of inhabitable structures.

Figure P2.3
Jean Nouvel, Musée du quai Branly-Jacques Chirac, Paris, France (2006) with "green wall" by green wall, or wall of vegetation, created by Patrick Blanc

Figure P2.4
Stefano Boeri, Gianandrea Barreca, and Giovanni La Varra, *Bosco Verticale* (Vertical Forest), Milan Italy (2014), courtesy of Stefano Boeri Architetti

Writing and reading outside of architecture also implies more than exploring the impact of a given site on a building's design and vice versa. Studying *Architecture from the Outside*, the title of Elizabeth Grosz's book and the subject of this section, is also to consider the disciplinary apparatus of exclusivity and inclusivity that architecture defines. As Grosz writes, the outside implies "what resists assimilation, what remains foreign even within a presumed identity, whether this is the intrusion of a minor language into a majoritarian one or the pack submerged within an individual."[4] While the outside engages the dynamics of deterritorialization and reterritorialization, As Grosz argues, it potentially inserts minor irritants into dominant epistemological

systems such as architecture, where distinctions between inside and outside serve to protect against invasions of what is alien to its disciplinary apparatus. Outsider Art, work produced by creators excluded from officially sanctioned institutions, suggests that there is an Outsider Architecture comprised of buildings, conceptual design practices, or theoretical positions that emerge despite dominant normative practices. Simon Rodia's Watts Towers (1921–1954) in Los Angeles, California and Ferdinand Cheval's Palais idéal (1890–1934) in Hauterives, France exemplify architecture produced by untrained hands, but have been recognized as a significant contribution to the field.

Finally, this part posits that architecture's situatedness requires examining it as a product of its cultural, socio-political, and temporal contexts, the response to which produces a critical response to a site.

Figure P2.5
Achim Menges, Elytra Filament Pavilion (2016), Victoria & Albert Museum, London, ©ICD University of Stuttgart.

Figure P2.6
Terreform One, Fab Tree Hab, courtesy of Terreform One

Figure P2.7
**Simon Rodia,
Watts Towers,
Los Angeles,
California,
(1921–1954)**

Figure P2.8
**Ferdinand
Cheval,
Palais ideal,
Hauterives,
France
(1890–1934)**

Notes

1 Alfred Korzybski, *Collected Writings, 1920–1950*, ed. Marjorie Mercer Kendig Gates (Englewood, NJ: Institute of General Semantics, 1990), p. 299.

2 http://icd.uni-stuttgart.de/?p=16443.

3 http://www.achimmenges.net/?p=5922.

4 Elizabeth Grosz, *Architecture from the Outside: Essays on Virtual and Real* Space (Cambridge, MA: MIT Press, 2001), p. 64.

Chapter 3

Terroir

Cuisine is a function of the genius loci, the spirit of the place. And one who says "place" also says "season," one who says "earth" also says "heaven." The goût de terroir (the taste of the earth, meant in the literal and not pejorative sense) that typifies so many wines and foodstuffs is only the most immediate manifestation of this gastronomic specificity.[1]

—Allen S. Weiss

Terroir, a term generally used in the culinary arts with particular respect to vintner culture, summarizes the environmental factors nuancing the flavor, taste, and aroma of what we eat and drink. It references the ways in which flora and fauna absorb site-specific flavors from the terrain on which they were grown. Factors such as seasons, solar orientation, soil content, water sources, prevailing winds, and adjacent crops combine to affect the taste of a region's foodscape. Architecture too possesses a *terroir*, the way in which buildings respond to a region's aforementioned environmental factors. But architectural *terroir* is more than the sum total of these pieces; it is the ability of a building to engage or reflect its site so that it transforms as much as it communicates the nuanced flavors and bouquet of its context.

In this respect, Antoni Gaudí's work in Catalonia exemplifies architectural *terroir*. Gaudí emphasized regional craft traditions such as ceramics and mosaics when designing works like Park Güell (1926) in Barcelona, Spain. He drew inspiration from Moorish architecture and ornament when contributing to the development of a Catalonian national style. His often-monstrous ornamental details on buildings such as the Casa Batlló or the "sand castle" towers of the *Basílica i Temple Expiatori de la Sagrada Família* (Basilica and Expiatory Church of the Holy Family, 1882–present) inserted a fantastical mythology into his work. His constructions of regional legends were potent enough to provoke Salvador Dalí to describe his work as "the bony structures and the living flesh of his delirious ornamentation."[2]

Figure 3.1
**Detail of
Casa Batlló
by Antoni
Gaudí (1904,
Barcelona,
Spain)**

Compass Points

To take bearings or dead reckon is to navigate the environment by aligning our bodies with natural elements, a process architects similarly deploy when aligning their buildings with existing paths, landmarks, monuments, or topographies. In its role of defining boundaries, thresholds, and sacred spaces, architecture also performs as a navigational instrument. Apropos of architecture registering our location between heaven and earth, King Sawai Jai Singh II built the *Jantar Mantar* in Jaipur, India (1734 CE) as a conceptual garden for astronomical observation. It contains 19 separate instruments for measuring the heavens, forming a scientific park of inhabitable devices replete with stairs and sloped curvatures upon which visitors may climb, walk, and observe the universe. These instruments were developed according to design principles written in ancient Hindu Sanskrit texts and from the tables of *Zij* (Persian: زيج), an Islamic book used for astronomical calculations. The architecture describes Ptolemaic positional astronomy, which places the earth at the center of the solar system and, by extension, the entire universe.

Among the various celestial machines located at this site, the *vrihat samrat yantra*, meaning "great king of instruments," operates as the world's largest sundial. Standing at 88 feet tall, it centers on a stairway that leads upward through a wedge that terminates in an observation tower that intersects with a crescent-shaped wall. The tower's shadow tells the time of day while the small cupola or Hindu *chhatri* at its summit provides an elevated vantage point used to announce impending eclipses and monsoons. Other instruments register information such as the declination of the sun at four specified times of the day, the location of a pole star, or distances

Figure 3.2
**Jantar Mantar
(1734, Jaipur,
India) by the
Rajput King
Sawai Jai
Singh II**

of other celestial bodies. Taken as a larger composition, these freestanding architectural instruments orient to various axes rotated off of true north. They project upward to the sky or carve space into the ground and form a collection of pavilions engaged with the universe across a spatial, material, and metaphysical dialogue.

Excavation

From architecture that maps the sky to one that digs into the earth, the city of Lalibela in the Lasta region of northern Ethiopia is a major historical center of Orthodox Christian worship known for its 11 monolithic churches carved entirely from out of the solid rock ridge upon which they have been built. Exemplifying the reciprocity between a building's site and its architectural materialization, the churches at Lalibela seamlessly emerge from the foundational ground that seems to fold upward vertically into an inhabitable enclosure whose walls and roof are made of the same continuous material. The city was named after the Zagwe King, Gebre Mesqel Lalibela (1181–1221) who moved the capital here and initiated a major building campaign to construct a landscape in imitation of the biblical Holy Land. When Muslim expansion and Salah-ad-Din's conquest of Jerusalem in 1187 made pilgrimage to this part of the world increasingly hazardous, King Lalibela envisioned his city as an alternative pilgrimage destination and derived place names such as the Churches of Golgotha, the Holy Sepulchre, and Mount Sinai from locations in the Holy Land.

It is likely that wood-burning foundries used for extensive metal production in this area caused deforestation to the extent that the most proximate alternative building material was sourced by excavating inhabitable space

Figure 3.3
**Bete Giyorgis
(Church of St
George) (12th
or early 13th
century CE
in Lalibela,
Ethiopia).**
Photograph
by Bernard
Gagnon

directly from the solid geological floor. That the churches were submerged in the ground also made them less conspicuous to hostile eyes. Not only are the churches at Lalibela constructed as the negative space of what was left over from the process of excavation, but they are also constructed from the very site itself.

Architecture attaches to the ground through its literal and metaphorical establishment of foundations, the stone or solid substructure supporting a building or an idea. The subject of the underground introduces mythological associations that digging into the earth evokes. Stemming from ancient Greek *khthōn*, meaning *earth*, chthonic summons a *subterranean* realm, in the sense of the underworld, the domain of Hades entered by crossing the River Styx. Digging into the ground places us closer to mysterious apparitions that dwell in the earth. "Excavation sought a rational past," as Rosalind

Williams summarizes, but "uncovered a quasi-mythological one."[3] By 1800, according to Williams, "the concept of a universal stratigraphic column had been firmly established," providing the world with the concept of near-infinite chronologies locked in vertical sections in the earth.[4] Insofar as archaeology demonstrated that ancient myths dwelled among scientific facts, the sequential discoveries by Heinrich Schliemann in Troy (1878–1879), Arthur Evans at the Palace of Minos (1900), and Howard Carter at King Tutankhamun's tomb (1922) dematerialized the underground into a porous stratigraphy layered with ancient architectures, artifacts, sepulchers, and spirits. These discoveries also provided Sigmund Freud with ample evidence for his analogy between the work of the analyst and the process of archaeology. When referencing the ruins of Pompeii, hidden by the eruption of Mount Vesuvius in 79 CE, Freud observed: "There is, in fact, no better analogy for repression, by which something in the mind is at once made inaccessible but preserved, than the burial of the sort to which Pompeii fell as a victim and through which it could emerge once more through the work of spades."[5] Architecture digs into the earth to locate its foundations: mythological, archaeological, and psychological.

Hydrology

Lalibela's rock-cut churches demonstrate a close affinity to water, with the depth of their excavation marking the level where the ground begins to become saturated, a somewhat remarkable condition given that that the city is located on a 2000-meter high hill. As Mark Jarzombek surmises, Lalibela selected this site due to water stored in an artesian aquifer, whose source is miles away in the high Lasta Mountain Range to the north.[6] Either in its natural state or as part of permanent infrastructure such as at Lalibela—flowing naturally or diverted through aqueducts to public distribution centers—water maintains the potential to animate architecture with fecundity, beauty, hygiene, delight, and community.

The city of Rome, Italy is animated by baroque fountains located at the terminus of aqueducts designed as architectural celebrations displaying the largesse of those who repaired ancient conduits or built new ones in order to quench the city's thirst for water. The popes who commissioned these liquid displays of munificence from the fifteenth to the eighteenth centuries—such as Sixtus V at the Aqua Felice, Paul V at the Acqua Paola, or Clement XII at the Trevi—made water available for public consumption through these highly visible displays of hydro-engineering called a *mostra*, an exhibition fountain. Although architecture's usual role in response to water is to direct it away from the potential to damage building surfaces—through systems such as sloped roofs, gutters, scuppers, downspouts, flashing, positive grading, and drains—developing ways to celebrate and preserve this resource through cisterns, pools, baths, fountains, channels, and porous landscapes finds important antecedents in Rome's liquid infrastructure. The house or *domus* in ancient Pompeii displayed a system for harvesting rainwater through a *compluvium*, the opening in the atrium framed to slope inward toward the *impluvium*, a shallow basin in the floor located to catch this run-off. Fountains in peristyle courtyards of these houses would have helped cool the interior while animating spaces with the cheerful sparkle and splash of flowing water. See Figure 0.2 in the Introduction.

It also appears in India's remarkable step-wells that harvest rainwater in deep subterranean cisterns, often with scant surface indication of the serene environments they shelter below. They demonstrate how climate and culture interact in submerged public spaces whose silhouettes have been excavated as negative volumes. Annual monsoon rains fill these wells and the aquifer below, providing sources of water that lasts into the dry season. As the demarcation of a sacred place or *tirtha*, water performs a special role in Hinduism with particular reference to the River Ganges as the embodiment of all sacred waters and a significant site for ritual ablution and burial. Writing in 1864, Louis Rousselet described the lush ecosystem of a step-well as a "vast sheet of water, covered with lotuses in flower, amid which thousands of aquatic birds are sporting … encompassed with a screen of Banyans and other giants of the tropics, of somber foliage."[7] While these public wells provided a reliable water source for the surrounding community, their terraced stairways isolated a micro-climate, some six degrees cooler at the bottom, which fostered social interaction and provided space for gathering, meditating, and praying. They provided spaces of profundity to probe telluric forces while simultaneously measuring the abundance of water one step at a time.

The village of Abhaneri, in the province of Rajasthan, contains the Chand Baori ("moon" or "silver" well) stepped pond, India's deepest and steepest well. The addition of a Mughal arcade at ground level in the 18th century surrounded and privatized what had been a public well built by King Chanda between 800 and 900 CE. Three sides of this square room terrace down into an interlocking network of 3500 steps descending steeply into a pool of water 100 feet below ground. Hindu shrines dedicated to Mahisamardini and Ganesh are located at the lowest level, supporting a Mughal palace balanced above. Not only a measure of water depth, the well also acts as a stratigraphic column indexing India's religious chronology. Thick post and beam trabeated columns describe the lower Hindu zone while cusped arches on columns identify the Muslim zone above. As an abode of the mother goddess Nāga, a pool of water defines an axis mundus between the universe and the earth that provides an alternative orientation to the horizontal line prevalent in Western perspective. Similar to Indian temples, where the darkest and most sacred space is called a womb chamber (*Garbhagriha* or *Garbha gruha* in Sanskrit), as Morna Livingston observes, "the stepwell embodies a cosmic reference to the contrast between light and dark."[8]

Whether rock-hewn church or submerged well, the work of architecture stands to bring nature, earth, and sky closer to human understanding. Peter Zumthor expresses the poetry of throwing stone into water as an analogy to

Figure 3.4
**Chand Baori
(stepwell),
India by
King Chanda
(between 800
CE and 900
CE, Abhaneri,
Rajasthan).
Photograph by
Doron**

a building transforming its site: "Sand swirls up and settles again. The stir was necessary. The stone has found its place. But the pond is no longer the same."[9] At the thermal baths in Vals, Switzerland (1996), Zumthor inverts this poetry when throwing water into stone. A hydrotherapy center sited over thermal springs that supply Valser mineral water, in this restorative bathing complex walls appear as a rock-hewn monolith carved directly out of the stone beneath the surface of the site. The entire effect relies on the natural appearance of Vals Gneiss, a metamorphic rock locally quarried about one kilometer from the site that frequently displays alternating light and dark layers referred to as gneissic banding. Carved from out of a grass terrace, a swimming pool appears like the basin of a partially submerged archaeological ruin, while a sequence of interior pools seem to have been excavated from millennial-old geology. Further emphasizing the sense of swimming in an ancient quarry, inside the baths, water flows unimpeded over sloping stone floors and between large stone piers, while light penetrates through thin glass fissures in the roof terrace and sparkles off of the wet stone surfaces.

As the examples of Lalibela, the Chand Baori step-well, and the thermal baths at Vals suggest, no building site is ever a complete tabula rasa. The ground from which architecture draws its gravitational strength may feature traces of previous inhabitation, contain significant adjacencies, serve as the dwelling place of a deity, or articulate a pattern of ritualized uses. However barren, a building site always maintains a relationship with the cardinal compass points, prevailing winds, solar alignments, climactic activity, geophysical forces, and existing use patterns. The architect may elect to ignore these profundities in pursuit of more distant inspiration, but the existing conditions of a given context will inevitably reform the built work in a combined process of entropy and overgrowth.

Public water sources such as the step-wells in India, which had been reserved for common use, introduce the concept of banality to this discussion on architecture inflected from the outside in. This term typically references ideas that are commonplace, predictable, mundane, or even dull. But it also indicates an essential part of architecture's response to external social needs. *Banal* stems from the 13th-century French *banel*, meaning communal, and from *ban*, meaning decree, legal control, or payment for the use of a communal space. A ban delimits spaces set aside for public use—such as

Figure 3.6
Old arcaded washhouse in Mollans-sur-Ouvèze, Drôme, Rhône-alpes, France (18th century) from Mireille Roddier's *Lavoirs, Washhouses of Rural France* (2003). Photograph by and courtesy of Roddier

mills, shared ovens, grazing land, or water sources—made available to a community as a collective space, as the public commons. A ban also determines the borders between the inside and outside of a community from which members who break with established prohibitions may be banned, banished, or abandoned.

A perfect example of water establishing a common place within an architectural setting are the rural French *lavoirs*. These communal washhouses, as Mireille Roddier observes, embodied ineffable qualities of rural France and performed as a "uniquely feminine space of relative emancipation."[10] "The space of the lavoir has been compared to a woman's version of the café," as she writes, where "women vociferously argued over the latest elections, the loss of tradition to modern conveniences, or local issues."[11] She continues: "Implicitly, the comparison ignores men's lack of physical effort while sipping pastis. But no such social gathering space was available to women without an associated domestic function."[12] While banal means *commonplace*, as in ordinary, a common place or a public commons held in reserve for shared uses such as baking bread and washing clothes expands this definition into the realm of architecture.

Light

After independence and the Partition of 1947, when Jawaharlal Nehru became India's first Prime Minister, the Punjab's capital at Lahore was ceded to Pakistan, necessitating the building of a new city to accommodate refugees and a new administrative seat. The site for the future capital city of Chandigarh, named after "Chandi," the Hindu goddess of power, was located between two river valleys and in view of the mighty Himalayas. The project of determining the overall plan eventually fell to Charles-Édouard Jeanneret, otherwise known as Le Corbusier, who designed residential districts and a government complex for Chandigarh. As the titular head of the city's body politic, the capital complex terminated the axis of a street leading northeast from the gridded residential quarters. For the main government buildings—including the Palace of Assembly, the Secretariat, and the High Court—Le Corbusier developed innovative design responses to the Punjab's symbolic landscape and extreme climate.

One of the challenges facing architects working with passive solar energy is to control the negative effects of the sun such as glare, heat gain, and destructive ultraviolet rays while maintaining access to natural light, air, and views. Le Corbusier developed a system of external screens called *brise-soleil* (sun-breaker) that surrounded windows with top, bottom, and side panels to prevent the sun from directly entering a building at almost all hours of the day, while simultaneously allowing reflected light to illuminate the interior. The government buildings at Chandigarh feature deep *brise-soleils* façades with a variety of geometric patterns derived from the *modular*, Le Corbusier's proportioning system based on the human body and the mathematical sequence of the Fibonacci series. Likewise the highly textured concrete façades of these buildings capitalized on local building traditions to provide a timeless patina of craft and context.

William Curtis identifies the parasol as an architectural leitmotif Le Corbusier developed into a protective overhang to shelter buildings from the harsh sun and fierce rain, as well as to collect cool breezes and frame views.[13] This conceptual apparatus appears on verandas, scoops, porticoes, and curved roofs. Le Corbusier's sketchbooks from India contain studies of vernacular

Figure 3.7
Le Corbusier's Palace of Assembly in Chandigarh, India (1950s). Photograph by Duncid

structures, colonial verandas, loggias of Mogul pavilions, and shaded walks of Hindu temple precincts he adapted into a passive response to solar heat gain. He applied these lessons to the form of the parasol, "an ancient symbol of state authority, found on top of Buddhist *stupas* and in a much later domical or arched form in Islamic monuments."[14]

The Palace of Assembly features an oversized scoop to sluice monsoon rain. The portico of concrete piers supporting this scoop delimits a deeply shaded exterior room. While Le Corbusier sketched a comparison between the light quality of the dome of Hagia Sophia in Istanbul with the Assembly's conical dome, Curtis sees a parallel with the cooling towers Le Corbusier observed in Ahmedabad, interpreting them as "an appropriate image for Nehru's policies of modernization and industrialization … blended with ancient sacral images."[15] The crescent on top of the conical dome also references the horns of bulls, an animal sacred to Hinduism that he sketched during his time in India, and the Jantar Mantar observatory described at the beginning of this chapter.[16] Writing of the curved and angled structures composing this astronomical theater, Le Corbusier stated: "They point the way: relink men to the cosmos … Exact adaptation of forms and organisms to the sun, to the rains, to the air…"[17]

Resilience

Staking a claim for the importance of vernacular architecture, in 1964 Bernard Rudofsky published *Architecture Without Architects: A Short Introduction to Non-pedigreed Architecture*, celebrating a broad range of nonconfirmist global building techniques. Rudofsky developed a strong visual polemic in favor of anonymous architecture produced in response to communal patterns of inhabitation and available materials. As highly inventive and resilient design models, indigenous buildings provide regional responses to challenging environments or idiosyncratic sites. They inspired Rudofsky, himself an architect, to question the homogenizing forces of modernization that he understood to have resulted in sterile and formulaic design processes. Rudofsky pioneered vernacular or "non-pedigreed" architecture as sources of experimentation and renewal that stood outside of the Eurocentric canon.

A small sampling of the vast compendium of illustrations Rudofsky published includes an image of a floating village in China reproduced from Erasmus Francisci's *Lustgarten* of 1668, house boats in Shanghai's Soochow Creek, and the framework for a men's clubhouse at Maipua, in the Gulf of New Guinea. He published pictures as diverse as underground settlements near Tungkwan (Honnan), granaries from the Spanish province of Galicia, miniature silos from the Ivory Coast, shorings supporting the salt mine of Wielicza, Poland, and the wind scoops of Hyderbad Sind in Pakistan, used to cool spaces by natural means.[18] His collection of images offers diverse, delightful, and highly inspiring alternatives for the production of architecture that explores indigenous and opportunistic building strategies. Carefully taking advantage of existing site

Figure 3.8
**Framework
for a men's
clubhouse at
Maipua, in the
Gulf of New
Guinea made
of bamboo
poles that will
be covered
with thatch;
Underground
settlements
in the Chinese
loess belt near
Tungkwan;
Miniature
silo from
Korhogo on the
Ivory Coast;
Windscoops
of Hyderbad
Sind in West
Pakistan,
from Bernard
Rudofsky's**
*Architecture
Without
Architects:
A Short
Introduction to
Non-pedigreed
Architecture*
(1964)

opportunities, minimizing a building's carbon footprint, developing nature as a living environmental system, sharing common places, extending a building's lifespan, and capturing wind for power and human comfort are all examples of proven methods for producing an architecture of resilience. Readers of architecture may look to the way in which a building evidences material reactions to these conditions when seeking to understand how we might amplify climatic responsiveness. Autochthonous buildings provide excellent examples of collaborative design processes and elegantly simple responses to environmental challenges.

After the Second World War unleashed what heretofore had been unimaginable destruction from and of humankind, the world witnessed a planet careening into climatic disaster and increasing social unrest. Preindustrial and vernacular architectures offered immediate models for sustainable and simple responses to living in harmony with nature, creating community, and locally sourcing building materials. A series of publications emerged in the 1960s engaging a general zeitgeist that questioned humankind's destructive potential and responded with a call for resilient design practices that offered a holistic response to combined social, economic, and environmental pressures.

In 1961 Jane Jacobs published *The Death and Life of Great American Cities*, in which she addressed the reckless demolition of historic city centers under the pretext of urban renewal. Jacob's model urban enclave was Greenwich Village—a vibrant neighborhood in Manhattan with storefronts animating pedestrian life, buildings that rose to the maximum height an individual could climb stairs, dwellings that provided protective eyes on the street, and public parks that fostered community gatherings. One year later Rachel Carson published *Silent Spring,* an exposé on the pernicious effects environmental pesticides such as Dichlorodiphenyltrichloroethane (DDT) had on natural ecosystems. In 1969 Ian L. McHarg published *Design with Nature*, a series of design instructions for determining a site's intrinsic suitability for development. So that "man becomes the steward of the biosphere," McHarg developed a meticulous approach to landscape analysis and the planning of human settlements.[19] His formidable analytic compendium considered topography in terms of slope, surface drainage, soil drainage, bedrock foundation, soil foundation, susceptibility to erosion, land values, historic values, scenic values, recreation values, residential values, forest values, wildlife values, and institutional values.

These values itemize the diverse factors architects consider before and during the design process in response to the external forces that impact architectural form. Slopes may suggest a process of cut and fill to balance the displacement of earth a building's footprint occupies so that it remains at a natural angle of repose. In contrast, columns may rise up from the ground so that the building floats above irregular topography. Land values may accelerate buildable densities as a way to capitalize on square-foot profits. Heritage-based zoning ordinances may require responsiveness to certain historical styles. Existing animal migration patterns or designated sacred lands may prohibit any building whatsoever. Existing trees may determine the location of open spaces, drainage patterns may prescribe a building's footprint, solar orientation and prevailing breezes may influence the envelope, and so on. When substantial financial and technological resources make it so that today almost any building strategy is possible, if not always reasonable, working with or against existing site conditions becomes a decision of conscience rather than a physical necessity.

Nodes and Lines

Kevin Lynch's important work *The Image of the City* (1960) is essential reading for understanding the fundamental ways in which space may be defined through his five operative terms of paths, edges, districts, nodes, and landmarks. Lynch provided an invaluable taxonomy both for mapping an existing site and designing a new one. Although Lynch focused on elements found primarily in cities, his terms translate well to the study of landscapes wherein

Figure 3.9
Erik Gunnar
Asplund and
Sigurd Lew-
erentz, *Skog-
skyrkogården*
or Woodland
Cemetery in
Stockholm,
Sweden,
(1915–1935).
View from the
main entrance
with the
crematorium
to the left and
the meditation
hill to the right.
Photograph by
Holger Ellgaard

natural elements such as groves, precipices, valleys, arroyos, cliffs, rivers, orchards, and glens perform as architectural elements.

In this respect, Erik Gunnar Asplund and Sigurd Lewerentz's design for *Skogskyrkogården* (Woodland Cemetery) in Stockholm, Sweden (1915–1935) poetically illustrates Lynch's five elements as it integrates architecture and landscape into a synthetic whole. An existing pine forest and gravel pit helped to organize the cemetery design across a processional sequence of spaces that ritualize the landscape into a site for mourning and reconciliation. The entrance leads southward past a stone wall washed by a continuous trickle of water. This path defines the edge of a bright meadow, a former gravel pit, which slopes upward toward the silhouette of a dark forest appearing at the crest of the hill. The first of two districts, the meadow is defined on the north by the forest, on the west by a large mound surmounted by Weeping Elms, and on the east by a complex of buildings containing a crematorium, columbarium, and chapels. The entire site plan alternates between paths organized on a somewhat rectilinear grid and those that follow the curvilinear topography. The Willows on the hill, planted in the shape of a perfect square, enclose a meditation area that operates as an exterior room or node. This meditation grove, as Caroline Constant points out, "draws upon Swedish burial mounds, such as those of the Swedish kings at Old Uppsala, dating from the 5th to 7th century."[20]

The path continues through the forest to terminate at the entrance to Lewerentz's *Uppståndelsekapellet* (Chapel of the Resurrection), described as a freestanding temple front that forms a threshold to the rectangular chapel beyond. Rotated ever-so-slightly off-axis from the building it almost touches, the temple pavilion serves as both a landmark and a portal into a realm suspended between life and death. The Chapel of the Resurrection acts as a filial counterpart to Asplund's *Skogskapellet* (Woodland Chapel), sited in the forest as a primordial work of architecture built as if its columns had been grown from living trees hewn in situ. The chapel adopts the language of an unassuming cabin with a steeply pitched roof covered in black wood shakes. The roof covers a single room fronted by a deep columnar porch, both of which have been covered in whitewash. The simple rustic exterior by no means communicates that it has swallowed the negative volume of a semi-circular dome supported by eight columns that register a circle on the floor of a rectangular space.

Figure 3.10
**Sigurd
Lewerentz,
*Uppståndelse-
kapellet* (the
Resurrection
Chapel),
at *Skog-
skyrkogården*
(Stockholm,
Sweden).
Photograph
by Bengt A.
Lundberg /
Riksan-
tikvarieämbetet
for the Swedish
National
Heritage Board**

According to Constant, Woodland Cemetery "infused the profane and generalized infinite space of modernism with the spirit of the concentrated and particular *locus sacer* of antiquity, amplifying the cemetery's symbolic resonance through a direct appeal to essential experiences."[21] In synthesizing an abstract unity between architecture and nature, the Woodland Cemetery gathers into itself a symbolic landscape between the sky and the earth in which buildings extend beyond their own identity to engage in a dialogue

Figure 3.11
**Erik Gunnar
Asplund,**
Skogskapellet
**(Woodland
Chapel),**
at *Skog-
skyrkogården,*
**photograph by
Holger Ellgaard**

with the places they share in making. Buildings inflect to the slight presence of nearly invisible site lines by forming a horizontal axis linking sunrise with rebirth and a vertical axis tying the earth and sky to death and heaven. The architecture, then, engages ceremonial ritual as well as phenomenological, or experiential, responses to light and shadow, delineated through the design tools of paths, edges, districts, nodes, and landmarks. It works in a similar manner to the way Martin Heidegger describes how a stream and its banks unfold under a bridge's span. He wrote that "the banks emerge as banks only as the bridge crosses the stream" as the bridge "brings stream and bank and land into each other's neighborhood" and "gathers the earth as landscape around the stream."[22]

Paths and edges generally rely on lines or linear formations. Architectural drawing is a form of site delineation wherein the act of engraving lines on two-dimensional planes anticipates its three-dimensional expression on a site. When architects draw a vector on a computer screen, they project a line in space that inhabits two temporal locations: the present moment of the drawing itself and its future as built form. Jean Luc Nancy writes that: "The line that divides and draws a form is similar to the arrow fired by a bow."[23] Insofar as it anticipates this future presence in time and space, architectural design is projective. As the noun for a job carefully planned and the verb for the action of extending outward, the double duty of the word *project* indicates that architects launch their ideas into the future as they anticipate changing the world with their designs.

From 1585 until his death in 1590, Pope Sixtus V, born Felice Peretti di Montalto, radically transformed Rome into a Baroque city with the construction of new, straight streets cutting diagonal axes through the dense medieval fabric. These lines projected themselves into an evolving transformation of

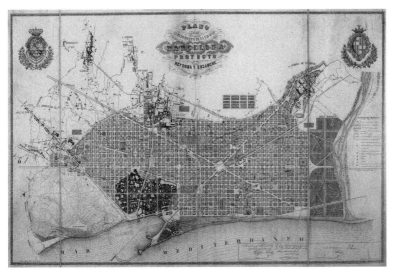

Figure 3.12
Ildefons Cerdà i Sunyer's *Eixample,* **officially entitled "Enlargement map of Barcelona. Map of the neighborhoods of the city of Barcelona and project for its improvements and enlargement, 1859." From** *Museu d'Historia de la Ciutat,* **Barcelona**

Rome he could not have entirely anticipated. He made sense of the city's existing labyrinth of streets and alleys by connecting visual axes with vertical markers, such as Egyptian obelisks and triumphal columns, which linked squares and streets like so many pins and strings marking the main thoroughfares of a one-to-one map of the city superimposed upon itself. In providing important infrastructure—such as streets accessing yet uninhabited areas of the city or a 15-mile-long aqueduct known as the Aqua Felice—Sixtus V projected his design into future building campaigns that eventually would fill in the spaces between the lines he drew. Edmund Bacon describes the impact of Sixtus's plan as "the establishment of lines of force which defined the tension between various landmarks in the old city" whose interrelationships set into play a series of cohesive urban forms these lines projected.[24]

A similarly projective urban design occurred in 1854 in Spain, when Madrid demolished Barcelona's medieval walls and awarded Ildefons Cerdà i Sunyer the portentous opportunity to expand the city beyond the historical center. Cerdà's *Eixample* (Catalan for "expansion") proposed a grid of streets defined by perimeter block buildings, filled with shared garden courts, whose corners were chamfered to introduce miniature plazas, light, and air in the city. This simple but entirely human response to urban expansion determines, as most city plans do, the basic configuration of the architecture built therein as it continues to influence Barcelona's urban fabric.

A final and perhaps subtler example of architectural projection may be found in a Japanese process called *sengu*, meaning *rebuilding*. The Ise Grand Shrine or Jingū is a Shinto complex consisting of two major sanctuaries: Naikū, the Inner Shrine dedicated to Amaterasu Omikami (the ancestral deity of the Imperial Family), and Gekū, the Outer Shrine dedicated to the deity of food, clothing, shelter and industry. Each shrine houses a sanctuary built in Japan's oldest

73

Figure 3.13
**Ise Grand
Shrine or
Jingū (Ise,
Mie, Japan),
photograph by
Rekishi-JAPAN**

architectural style of "shinmei-zukuri," featuring gables, a raised floor, plank walls, and a thatch roof typifying a *honden*, a small structure built of cypress wood and joined without the use of nails. Under the guiding principle that rebuilding renders sanctuaries eternal, the Shikinen Sengu ceremony requires these buildings to be demolished and reconstructed on an adjacent site every 20 years, a tradition that dates back to 692 CE. The adjacent forest of sacred Japanese cypress trees provides the wood for a cyclical rebuilding process that establishes a constructional continuum of carpentry techniques that date back hundreds of years to the first shrine whose generative DNA dwells within its progeny. This reconstruction process projects a building into its future twin in a process of doubling that occurs when both structures co-exist next to each other. This process of doubling also demonstrates the power of multiple identical structures to establish their own self-referential contexts, to mirror existing buildings with reflective enclosures or proportional relationships, or even exact copies that produce an uncanny doppelgänger.

Fields

When a site exhibits a certain aura, an auspicious characteristic that demarcates a special place—perhaps a panoramic view, dramatic geology, or a distinctive grouping of trees—then it also may possess a *genius loci*, an ancient Roman term meaning the spirit of a place. In *Genius Loci: Towards a Phenomenology of Architecture* (1979) Christian Norberg-Schulz distinguished between "landscapes" as varied and continuous extensions of space, and "settlements" as enclosed entities. The potential interplay between a landscape's extended ground and a settlement's enclosed figure determines the interface of open and closed spaces. When superimposed, these open and closed spatial properties oscillate into a figure-ground, or figure-field, pattern of solid building and spatial void that suggests a cartographic process of depicting existing enclosures as solid black forms on a white page and the reverse representational strategy of rendering the spaces in-between as white. The solid void relationship between a building and its site is denser in urban than in extra-urban contexts, while all too often it is also denser in historical urban centers than in their modern expansions.

From projected lines to oscillating fields, site responsiveness relies on an ability to analyze the physical evidence of both static and dynamic systems. Giambattista Nolli's ichnographic plan of Rome, his *Pianta Grande di Roma* of 1748, describes Rome's historical center as a dynamic oscillation between figural voids and equally figural solids. In this 12-plate engraving, Nolli delineated Rome's public spaces of courtyards, colonnades, and church interiors as figural voids within a field of buildings cross-hatched in solid black, a technique of filling in spaces in drawings otherwise known as *poché*. The almost symmetrical balance between black and white in this cartography depicting Rome's intricate and complex spatial patterns minimizes the significance of individual buildings while it foregrounds the importance of the public spaces they frame. Concomitantly, Nolli's model applies just as well to the design and analysis of individual buildings whose technique of delineation relies on the convention of *poché*, but where the hatching designates background features which may be inhabitable or uninhabitable behind-the-scenes zones. Focusing on a detail of Nolli's plan at the baroque Chiesa di Sant'Ignazio di Loyola in Campo Marzio (Church of St Ignatius of Loyola in the Campus Martius) by Orazio Grassi from 1650, it is possible to clearly see the way in which Filippo Raguzzini's systemization of the piazza (1727–1735) in front of the church extends the interior chapels into the public sphere. This roofless room in the city of Rome roughly mirrors the church's interior plan of altar and four side chapels across the edge of the façade, producing a figure field reversal between inside and out that extends the sacred space into the secular realm.

Just as a black and white drawing of a wine glass may oscillate into the spatial void produced between the profiles of two human heads, architecture too has the potential to construct the negative space around itself as a powerfully figural object. According to the lessons of figure-field analyses, simply designing a sculptural object that floats in an abstract field no longer fully describes a building's spatial impact. Rather, the space surrounding architecture serves as an equally important component of a dynamic continuum that exists in a suspended state of permanent fluctuation. For the purposes of reading architectural contexts in situ, studying the negative space between buildings as if they were solid figures extends this interpretive approach.

In what amounts to a response to Nolli's authority among architects, Stan Allen explores the limitations of the figure-field dynamic in a world characterized by a shift from analog to digital technologies and the introduction

Figure 3.14
**Giambattista
Nolli,** *La Nuova
Topografia di
Roma* (*The
New Plan of
Rome*, 1748)

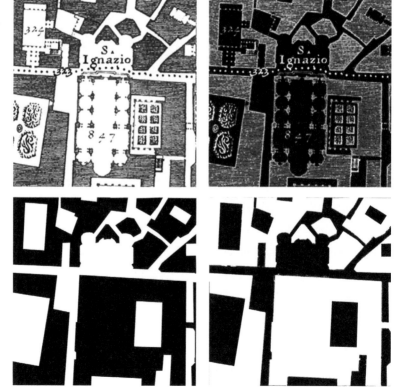

Figure 3.15
**Figure-field
diagrams
derived from a
detail of Nolli's
map located at
the church of
Sant'Ignazio,
drawn by
Paulette
Singley**

Figure 3.16
Danish psychologist Edgar Rubin developed the cognitive optical illusion of two human heads facing each other to produce the silhouette of a vase in the void between them around 1915. Painted by Emil 2005

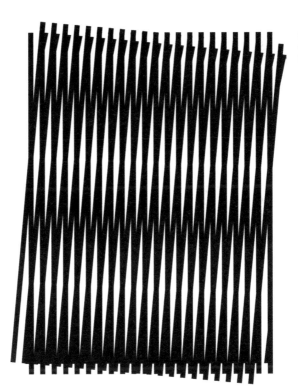

Figure 3.17
Moiré pattern, drawn by Gavin Friehauf

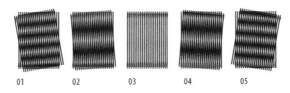

01   02   03   04   05

of new telecommunication infrastructure to the modern city, the likes of which are linked in open-ended networks. According to Allen, field conditions relate to "mathematical field theory, nonlinear dynamics, and computer simulations of evolutionary change," while it also resonates with "a more tactical sense, as it would for an anthropologist or a botanist engaged in 'fieldwork,' for a general facing the field of battle, or the architect who cautions a builder to 'verify in field.'"[25] Field conditions work as open-ended, self-referential systems with a highly dynamic solid and void relationship similar to the operation of swarming or the optical distortions present in a moiré pattern. Among the examples Allen proposes, moiré patterns appear as visual interferences appearing from the asymmetrical superimposition of two or more fields upon each other. Think of the oscillating bands that appear when two window screens are laid one on top of another at a slightly skewed angle. Just like the murmuring of starlings that momentarily converge into figural shapes, quickly blur into a disparate cloud, and then just as quickly reappear in new torsional geometries, field conditions approximate the dynamics of crowd behavior, the scatter pattern of reindeer disturbed by an overhead helicopter, or the action of swarming.

Allen develops the Mezquita-Catedral de Córdoba (Mosque-Cathedral of Córdoba) in Spain, 784–987 as a model architectural field condition. "Constructed over a span of nearly eight centuries," as he writes, "the form of the mosque had been clearly established: an enclosed forecourt, flanked by a minaret tower, opening onto a covered space for worship (perhaps derived from market structures. Or adapted from the Roman basilica)" with an enclosure oriented "toward the qibla, a continuous prayer wall marked by a small niche (the mihrab)."[26] Allen constructs the argument that this mosque differs from the closed unity typical of Western classical architecture insofar as it is possible to add onto the structure infinitely without substantial modifications to either the original or the addition.

For Allen, the Great Mosque evidences a field condition through a series of independent elements that combine additively into a limitless whole and describe a self-referential system where the relations of part to part remain consistent with the first and last versions built. Inherently expandable, field conditions retain the structural seeds of their own incremental growth. For the purposes of reading architecture, figures and fields determine the internal dynamics of an architectural system as either open to expansion or designed to limit growth. The way in which this system then engages its contexts may perform as centrifugal or centripetal spatial forces: one spinning outwardly to an infinite appropriation of space and the other inwardly to oscillating solids and voids.

Context

Even when a building entirely ignores its context as a radically different addition to a given setting, it nonetheless exists in dialogue, even if a querulous one, with the surroundings it will ultimately shape into a new set of physical

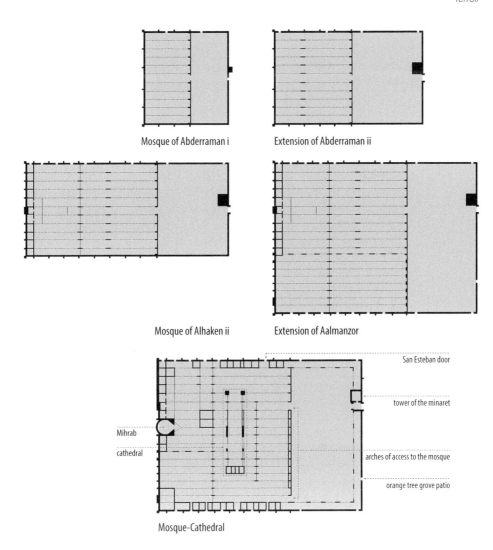

Mosque of Abderraman i

Extension of Abderraman ii

Mosque of Alhaken ii

Extension of Aalmanzor

San Esteban door

tower of the minaret

Mihrab

cathedral

arches of access to the mosque

orange tree grove patio

Mosque-Cathedral

and cultural contingencies. "The act of joining, with *con* meaning together, and *text*, from the Latin *texere*, meaning to join, or weave," as Sandy Eisenstadt clarifies, determines the root meaning of the term *context* in relation to the Greek *tekton*, the person who makes wattle, and to the master of all tectonics, the *arch-tekton*, or *architecte*. For Eisenstadt, "context takes its place in a spectrum of terms concerned with perception of place and the creation of placefulness."[27] Given that *text*, in the sense of a piece of writing, also refers to the Latin *texere*—meaning to weave, join, construct, fabricate, or build—Eisenstadt's research actuates meaningful intersections among *weaving* a story, *writing* a building, and *fabricating* a site.

In response to modern architecture's drive to treat the historical city as a tabula rasa, Alison and Peter Smithson designed a complex of three buildings

Figure 3.18 **Growth of the Mosque-Cathedral of Córdoba, drawn by Gavin Friehauf**

79

for *The Economist* newspaper (1964) as irregular polygons that defer to the 18th-century context of St James's Street in London. With expressed vertical ribs clad in shell-filled Portland stone, the project reflects the window proportions of nearby historical buildings and establishes a context of hi-tech historicism. The Smithsons also anticipated a different kind of context for this project, the stains produced from the pollution of London fireplaces. Peter Salter reports that the Smithsons detailed the façades "to channel rainwater from window sills to the column gutters, at which point the stone was scoured by the effects of rain and up-draught winds and its whiteness renewed."[28] As he summarizes, "the facade, which originally had little modulation of its structure, acquired great visual depth, understood through the control of the shadows of soot and the scouring of the stone." The Smithsons collaborated with Gordon Cullen to sketch *The Economist* cluster as referencing a village townscape and to publish these drawings in the *Architectural Review*, further cementing the position of this project as contextually responsive.

Yet another strategy for addressing a building's context through technology involves the ubiquitous mirrored façade found in cities around the world. As an apparently neutral enclosure, the mirrored glass building was supposed to disappear into its reflected surroundings. But as the cladding on I. M. Pei's 200 Clarendon Tower (formerly John Hancock Tower, 1976) in Boston demonstrates, while it successfully mirrors Henry Hobson Richardson's Trinity Church (1877) across the street, the reflective skin simply cannot make a 60-story tall building disappear from view. Similarly, depending on the time of day and the orientation of the sun, Doug Aitken's site-specific installation "Mirage" (2017) set in the Southern California desert is a seemingly generic suburban house completed clad in mirrors that reflect the desert landscape, the sky, and distant views while simultaneously dematerializing its stereometric stability but not its silhouette.

The responsive metallic *brise soleil* that Jean Nouvel designed for the Institut du Monde Arabe (Institute of the Arab World, 1987) in Paris derives inspiration from Arabic *mashrabiyas*, traditional latticework screens typically found in Middle-Eastern architecture that provide sunshade and, like an ornate mask, a privacy screen for inhabitants. For this project he designed a polygonal screen of moveable diaphragms, mechanized lenses that dilate in response to solar movement. His description of the project's enclosure explains his response to context: "If the south side of the building, with its motorized diaphragms, is a contemporary expression of eastern culture," then the north side literally mirrors Western culture in its reflective glass skin where images of the Parisian cityscape across the Seine are metaphorically "enameled on the exterior glass like chemicals over a photographic plate."[29] Introverted on one side and extroverted on the other, the *Institut du Monde Arabe* offers a Janus-faced building to the public realm.

Responding to a building's context in the most prosaic sense of a site's physical adjacencies is often dictated by building codes and planning ordinances that determine form. Decisions such as allowable building heights

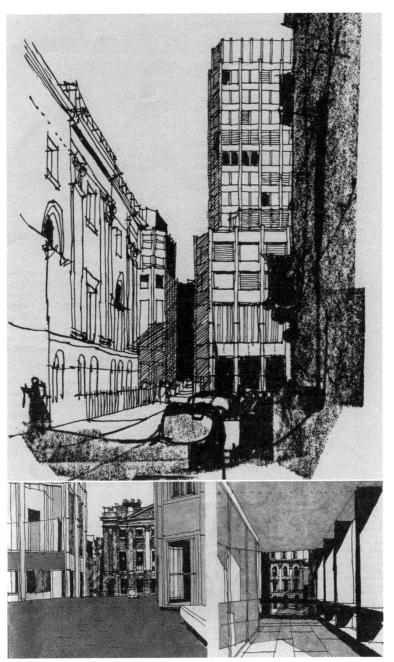

Figure 3.19
The Economist
Newspaper
buildings by
Alison and
Peter Smithson
(London)
as drawn
by Gordon
Cullen for the
Architecture
Review in 1965

Figure 3.20
**I. M. Pei, 200
Clarendon
Tower (formerly
Hancock Tower)
with H. H.
Richardson's
Trinity Church
in Reflection,
photographed
by Boris
Hasselblatt**

Figure 3.21
Doug Aitken,
Mirage 2017,
acrylic mirrors,
steel, plywood.
Courtesy of
the Artist,
303 Gallery,
New York;
Galerie Eva
Presenhuber,
Zürich; Victoria
Miro Gallery,
London; Regen
Projects, Los
Angeles, and
Desert X

Figure 3.22
Jean Nouvel,
Institut du
Monde Arabe
(Institute of
the Arab World,
1987) in Paris,
photographed
by Gerard
Smulevich

and square footages, setbacks, materials, and even stylistic choices may be determined by review boards and local governments trying to ensure neighborhood continuity and quality. In Pacific Palisades, California, the firm of Johnston Marklee transformed the supposed limitations of a zoning ordinance into a design opportunity at the Hill House (2004), where they maximized legal set back regulations to their geometric limits as a way of determining the

Figure 3.23
**Institut du
Monde Arabe,
photographed
by Gerard
Smulevich,
and a typical
mashrabiya**

Mashrabiya from Isfahan

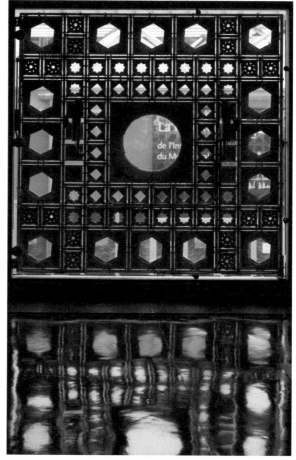

Smulevich Arab Monde

building envelope. In another example of transforming a site constraint into a design strategy, the firm of Escher and GuneWardena based the House on Two Towers in Pasadena, California on the dimensions of the largest structural member a truck could import to the site on a narrow hillside road, affirming the context of California car culture. While two concrete towers support long steel beams that span 84 feet above the hillside lot, Frank Escher explains that "the width of the building was determined by the size of the biggest floor joist that could be transported up to the hill."[30] Acting as an unfinished bridge across the site, the House on Two Towers also references the nearby hillside campus of the Art Center College of Design. Craig Ellwood's 1974 building spans 192 feet over an arroyo and acts as a dramatic gateway for the road below.

Most famously, Frank Gehry's iconoclastic design for his own house in Santa Monica, California (1978) reflects the larger context of Los Angeles's experimental building materials and the influence of the local art scene more so than its staid and manicured neighbors. As Gehry's house makes clear, even

Figure 3.24
Johnston Marklee, Hill House Pacific Palisades, California (2004). Courtesy of Johnston Marklee; photography by Eric Staudenmaier

Figure 3.25
Escher and
GuneWardena,
House on
Two Towers
in Pasadena,
California
(1997–2007).
Courtesy of
Escher and
GuneWardena;
photography
by Gene Ogami

Figure 3.26
Craig Ellwood,
The Art Center
College of
Design in
Pasadena,
California
(1974)

when a building rejects a site's physical adjacencies, it still may respond to a different kind of context. Gehry's friendship with artists such as Ron Davis, for whom he designed a studio, also demonstrates that if a work of architecture seems to have emerged from the blank page of an architect's sketchbook or the anti-gravitational field of a computer screen, cultural continuums may influence creative processes and techniques to the extent that context appears to be inescapable.

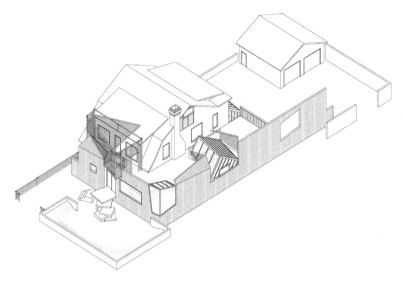

Figure 3.27
Diagram of Frank Gehry's Santa Monica House by Connor Gravelle and Ramiro Diaz-Granados of the Southern California Institute of Architecture (SCI-Arc)

Notes

1   Allen S. Weiss, "Culinary Manifestations of the Genius Loci," in *Eating Architecture,*eds. Jamie Horwitz and Paulette Singley (Cambridge, MA: MIT Press, 2004), p. 26.

2   Salvador Dalí, "The Vision of Gaudí" *Surrealism and Architecture, Architectural Design, Profiles 11* (1978), p. 141.

3   Rosalind Williams, *Notes on the Underground: An Essay on Technology, Society, and the Imagination* (Cambridge, MA: MIT Press, 1990), p. 27.

4   Ibid, p. 29.

5   Sigmund Freud, "Delusion and Dream in Jensen's Gradiva," in *Writings on Art and Literature* (Stanford: Stanford University Press, 1997), p. 35

6   Mark Jarzombek, "Lalibela and Libanos, the King and the Hydro-engineer of 13th Century Ethiopia" *Construction Ahead: Bi-monthly Interface with the Construction Industry in Ethiopia 10* (2007), p. 19.

7   Morna Livingston, *Steps to Water: The Ancient Stepwells of India* (New York: Princeton Architectural Press, 2002), p. 14.

8   Ibid, p. 42.

9   Peter Zumthor, *Thinking Architecture* (Basel: Birkhäuser, 2006), p. 30.

10 Mireille Roddier, *Lavoirs: Washhouses of Rural France.* (New York: Princeton Architectural Press, 2003), p. 23.

11 Ibid.

12 Ibid.

13 William Curtis, *Le Corbusier: Ideas and Forms* (New York: Rizzoli, 1986), p. 192.

14 Ibid, p. 193.

15 Ibid, p. 196.

16 Ibid.

17 Ibid.

18 Bernard Rudofsky, *Architecture Without Architects: A Short Introduction to Non-pedigreed Architecture* (New York: Museum of Modern Art, 1964).

19 Ian L. McHarg, *Design with Nature* (New York: John Wiley, 1992), p. iv.

20 Caroline Constant, *The Modern Architectural Landscape* (Minneapolis: University of Minnesota Press, 2012), p. 79.

21 Ibid, p. 78.

22 Martin Heidegger, "Building, Dwelling, Thinking," in *Rethinking Architecture: A Reader in Cultural Theory*, ed. Neil Leach (New York: Routledge, 1997), p. 99.

23 Jean-Luc Nancy, *The Pleasure in Drawing*, trans. Philip Armstrong (New York: Fordham University Press, 2013), p. 98.

24 Edmund Bacon, *Design of Cities* (New York: Viking Press, 1974), p. 1.

25 Stan Allen, "Field Conditions," in *Stan Allen Architect: Points + Lines* (New York: Princeton Architectural Press, 1999), p. 92.

26 Ibid, p. 93.

27 Sandy Eisenstadt, "Contested Contexts," in *Site Matters: Design Concepts, Histories, and Strategies*, eds. Carol Burns and Andrea Kahn (New York: Routledge, 2005), p. 160.

28 As cited by Jonathan Hill, *Weather Architecture* (New York: Routledge, 2012), p. 248 from *Climate Register: Four Works by Alison & Peter Smithson*, Volume 6 by Lorenzo Wong, Alison Margaret Smithson, Peter Smithson, and Peter Salter (London: Architectural Association, 1994), p. 40.

29 From the architect's website: http://www.jeannouvel.com/en/desktop/projet/paris-france-arab-world-institut1.

30 From the architect's website: https://openformarchitecture.wordpress.com/2007/09/04/jamie-residence.

Chapter 4

Scenography

[T]he Picturesque emerged primarily as an aesthetic of decay. For an edu-cated elite, it justified the visual enjoyment of objects previously excluded by the classical theory of representation; if the bright, the new, the whole, the symmetrical, the strong, and the smooth pertained to the Beautiful, the decayed, the worn, the aged, the dirty, the ragged, and the unevenly lit characterized the Picturesque. It may be said that the eighteenth-century notion of the Picturesque prefigured the Kantian perspective of "disinterested pleasure," detaching the visual appearance of things from their existence in a social, political context.[1]

—Alessandra Ponte

As part of the celebrations for the 950th anniversary of its founding, in 1990 the provincial Dutch capital of Groningen invited Daniel Libeskind to curate a series of temporary public art pavilions to mark the city's boundaries. Publishing this work as *The Books of Groningen*, a folio of 12 aluminum plates bound together with nuts and bolts, Libeskind proposed erecting entrance markers at the city's nine major access routes, the number of which he deter-mined by the letters in the city's ancient name of *Cruoninga*.[2] He assigned nine eminent artists and scholars to design each marker, charging them to respond to one of the assigned letters in *Cruoninga* along with a specific time, color, and the name of one of the nine muses of Greek mythology. The sculptor Thom Puckey proposed nine bronze branches growing from out of a factory chimney. The choreographer William Forsythe planted a quarter mile-long row of Willow trees, referencing local shipbuilding techniques by warping their growth into the shape of arcs with the aid of metal tension wires. And the architect John Hejduk marked his site with three towers, one composed of giant playing cards, one supporting the name of Groningen, and one with a joker sitting on top. The scenographic devices published in *The Books of Groningen* distill picturesque landscape theory into a contemporary demonstration of these principles. The formatting of architectural plans as the pages of a book, Libeskind's reliance on writing as a design prompt, and the pavilions' diverse characteristics locate the project within the sequence of a narrative journey.

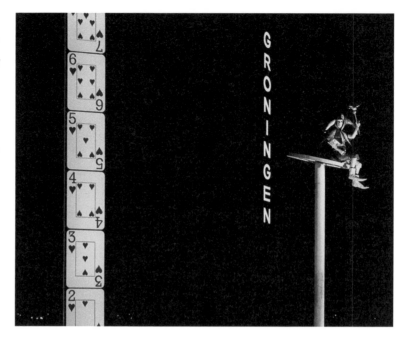

Figure 4.1
"Tower of
Cards and One
Joker," 1990.
Groningen City
Marker, part
of The Books
of Groningen,
in celebration
of the 950th
anniversary
of the city,
photograph by
Hélène Binet

Groningen's conceptual underpinning traces back to 18th-century concepts of picturesque landscape design, which established complicity between architecture, narration, and scenography that continue to perform in architecture's contemporary design theater. Picturesque landscape theory involves intertextuality, sharing of references and concepts among subjects such as architecture, literature, art, and science. It leverages human memory and experience into nascent theories of subjectivity regarding the transformative psychological impact a work of art may have upon its viewer. While the term usually evokes ideas of sentimentality, nostalgia, emotionality, quaintness, ungoverned compositional techniques, and the subordination of built form to mere story telling—these so-called deficiencies define architecture through its anxiety of being reduced to mere *mise-en-scène* or set design. This chapter, on the contrary, posits the persuasive power of this very scenography.

Translated most directly as "placing on stage," *mise-en-scène* encompasses the visual themes that tell a story, generally expressed as an art form in theatrical and cinematic production design. While scenography is an inherently architectural term, insofar as it applies to constructing stages and their sets, it also tends to describe structures that are temporary, quickly built, hiding something, relying on trickery, and tied to external narrative content for meaning. Nonetheless, an important aspect of architecture is the theatricality accomplished by manipulating the interplay of light, sound, texture, and spatial drama. Architecture's optical role, the ability to frame and be framed by views, suggests that its exterior countenance matters as much, if not more than, its planimetric organization. Reading architecture as scenography requires rotating one's focus away from fixating on the arrangement of floor plans and to examining the invisible line projecting from our eyes to the horizon line in order to survey the views that lie in-between. Exploring some of the precepts surrounding architectural optics likewise initiates a journey into the panorama of gardens, landscapes, scenic devices, and optical illusions that fasten architecture to the narrative content of spatial itineraries.

Having emerged from the Italian *pittoresco*, meaning "in the manner of a painter," the term *picturesque* borrows its spatial identity from the compositional strategies found in landscape painting. When describing the idea of *movement* in the *Works in Architecture of Robert and James Adam* (1773–1779), the Adam brothers define the essence of their architectural theory as deriving from a term "meant to express the rise and fall, the advance and recess, with other diversity of form, in the different parts of a building, so as to add greatly to the *picturesque* of the composition."[3] They contend that the "rising and falling, advancing and receding, with the convexity and concavity, and other forms of the great parts, have the same effect in architecture, that hill and dale, fore-ground and distance, swelling and sinking have in landscape."[4] The goal of architectural composition for the Adam brothers was "to produce an agreeable and diversified contour, that groups and contrasts like a picture, and creates a variety of light and shade, which gives great spirit, beauty, and effect to the composition."[5] Just as painters deployed specific rules such as these as ways to govern their compositions, picturesque architects would design buildings and landscapes with similar scenographic objectives. Such exuberance for designing architecture according to the principles of painterly composition brought with it the collateral narrative dimension these paintings illustrated. The allegorical imaginary journeys to mythical destinations that paintings illustrated found their way into the design of gardens, where classical architectural ruins and wild scenery formed a scenographic backdrop to semi-natural contrivances such as artificial grottoes and lakes.

The moral lessons appending to these scriptural or mythological tableaux entered gardens in the guise of architectural pavilions that would perform as guideposts for triggering a range of emotions intended to transform a viewer's comportment and judgment. Such episodic stratagems to align architecture with moral enlightenment established a bond between buildings and human behavior that would underpin modernism's messianic impulse to transform society through the space it occupied. Architecture's ability to reference literary descriptions of journeys described in classical literature established its role as a conveyor of cultural content, a mnemonic device for storing memories, and a vehicle for personal transformation.

Sharawadgi
When it comes to examining the pedigree of the English picturesque garden, as Jurgis Baltrušaitis recounts, the Duc d'Harcourt summarized three kinds of tendencies prevalent in 18th-century landscape design, writing: "A Frenchman

puts geometrical figures in his garden, an Englishman sets his house in the midst of a field, a Chinaman sets frightening shapes in front of his windows."[6] As Baltrušaitis notes, an important source for the scenographic impulse expressed in picturesque design is found in classical Chinese landscape gardens.

In particular, Chinese scholars' rocks or *gōngshí* are irregularly shaped limestone formations of various sizes that were valued for their natural deformations and whose decorative use dates back to the Tang dynasty (618–907 CE). A common source for these stones was Lake Taihu in the Jiangsu province of China. Known as Taihu stones, these twisted rock formations were highly sought-after landscape features that were transported as far as 600 miles north via the Grand Canal to Beijing. Valued for their porosity and cavernous depths, produced by hundreds of years of water surging against rock, they often configured the shape of animals, humans, or mythical creatures. Their natural cracks and crevasses also suggested mountains, grottos, and caves. Their forms echoed Chinese ink brush paintings of natural landscapes known as *shan shui*, a term which translates as "mountains-water." "The two major axes of landscape painting, vertical and horizontal," according to Yi-Fu Tuan, "are abstracted from the juxtaposition of steep hills and alluvial plains that is characteristic of Chinese topography."[7]

Linking the writing of poetry with garden design, according to Robert M. Craig, they inspired "Chinese literati, painters, poets, and garden architects, whose themes and designs universalize the role of nature in Chinese thought."[8] Around 1631, Ji Cheng authored *Yuanye* (園冶) or *Craft of Gardens*, purportedly the earliest manual of landscape gardening in the Chinese tradition. In the last chapter, entitled "Borrowed Scenery" (*Jiejing*, 借景), he posited what would become standard theory in picturesque garden design: "Skill is shown in the

Figure 4.2
Taihu stone in the Lingering Garden at the Classical Gardens of Suzhou

ability to 'follow' and 'borrow from' the existing scenery and lay of the land, and artistry is shown in the feeling of suitability created."[9]

With their jagged contours and figural allusions, scholar's rocks enjoyed a conceptual place in the concept of *sharawadgi*, a term visitors to China imported to England as a way to express the idea of composed irregularity. While the precise source of *sharawadgi* remains uncertain, it has been traced to garden design vocabulary in Chinese expressions such as *sale guaizhi*, which means the "quality of being impressive or surprising through careless or unorderly grace," and *sanlan waizhi* or "space tastefully enlivened by disorder," as well as to Japanese terms like *sorowaji* or *sorowazu* which refer to irregularity.[10] *Sharawadgi* condenses the reciprocity between Chinese garden design and what later would become the English picturesque garden into a game of mutual influence played out through mistranslation. From this cultural exchange, English architects and gardeners began to explore unleashing, rather than disciplining, nature's irregularity, while sublimating architecture to the background of a larger program of idyllic reverie.

Formal Gardens

Baltrušaitis cites the Marquis de Girardin's assessment that French gardens express "nature subjected to the dwelling" while their English counterparts demonstrate "the dwelling subjected to Nature."[11] Working in collaboration with the painter Charles Le Brun, André Le Nôtre designed an exemplar *jardin à la française* in the gardens at the Palace of Versailles. King Louis XIV had been inspired to transform his hunting lodge into a proper palace by a visit to the elaborate gardens Le Nôtre implemented around the magnificent building Louis Le Vau designed for Nicolas Fouquet, the Château de Vaux-le-Vicomte (1661). In what would become an exact science for tyrannizing nature, the gardens at Vaux-le-Vicomte demonstrate the precise geometric intricacy that characterizes French Baroque landscape design. After Louis XIV imprisoned Fouquet, who apparently compromised his position as Superintendent of Finances in France with the elaborate campaign to build Vaux-le-Vicomte, he elevated Le Nôtre to work at a significantly more elaborate scale and transform the garden and parks of the Château de Versailles.

The high degree of spatial contrivance French designers such as Le Nôtre exercised over their gardens may be found in a lexicon of terms such as *broderie* (embroidery), a complex curvilinear pattern formed with plants; *parterre*, the division of plantings into orthogonal frames; *allée*, a straight tree-lined path; *art topiaire*, bushes cut and wired into ornamental shapes; *rond d'eau*, a circular pool of water; *grotte*, grotto; or *miroir d'eau*, reflecting pool. Other French garden design terms—such as *salle*, *chambre*, *fabrique*, and *théâtre*—describe an exterior architecture of roofless rooms delineated by hedges and other planting material, a synthetic space combining architecture and landscape design. As structured and geometric arrangements of spaces, French gardens could appear as whole suites of salons, rooms, and small retreats.

Figure 4.3
André le Nôtre, garden of Vaux-le-Vicomte (1658–1661), photograph by Esther Westerveld

According to Baltrušaitis, landscape designers created domed or vaulted pavilions out of foliage "with decorated architectural doors and windows all created by tying and clipping."[12]

Framed by a wet moat and aligned to a seemingly infinite axis three kilometers long, Vaux-le-Vicomte occupied the center of grounds so immense they required Fouquet to purchase and demolish three villages in order to complete his monumental vision for the château. Allen Weiss considers these gardens from the viewpoint of scenography and *anamorphosis abscondita* (hidden distortion), a design process that transforms the geometry of a perfect square into a trapezoid as a way to accelerate or decelerate the perspectival distortion of space toward a distant vanishing point observed from a fixed position. Perspective diminution, the recession of objects toward the horizon, means that ordinarily what would exist in plan as a perfect square resembles a trapezoid when viewed from afar. In order to manipulate, that is, accelerate or decelerate perspective distortion, substituting a trapezoid for a square in plan begins to force optical distortions in the space of vision.

The manipulation of perspective is a particularly notable design tool at Vaux-le-Vicomte. From the position of the terrace at the back of the house, visitors are able to look across to the *rond d'eau*, to the *miroir d'eau*, to the *vertugadin*, to the Statue of Hercules (after the Farnese Hercules) that marks the vanishing point. A series of manipulated geometries and submerged terraces create a forced perspective that makes the garden appear closer to the viewer than it actually is. The garden contracts visually as the perspective shortens, slows down, or decelerates what otherwise would appear to be a dauntingly long axis to circumnavigate on foot. The vertugadin, a sloping lawn near the end of the vista, further decelerates the perspective distortion with an angular plane that tips upward toward the château. When standing from the position of the exterior stairs at the rear of the château, a panorama of the estate unfolds, as Weiss observes, into a "seemingly perfect, extremely painterly perspectival view, giving the impression that the gardens are entirely revealed in a single glance."[13]

Distortion

Perspective abhors nature. This is to say that one-point linear perspective works best when depicting edges, grids, and straight architectural elements instead of curvilinear forms such as hills, valleys, wild vegetation, and people, which tend to resist being illustrated by strict rectilinear geometries. In contrast to the geometrical gardens at Vaux-le-Vicomte or Versailles, the elements typically found in English gardens, such as the curvilinear volumes of hills and dales or the irregular patterns of trees and lakes, do not easily lend themselves to depiction in the rigid system of a perspective grid. In *Tutte l'opere d'architettura, et prospetiva* (ca. 1545; "Complete Works on Architecture and Perspective"), a volume concerned with perspective painting, Sebastiano Serlio published three designs for theatrical performances concerning comic, tragic, and satiric plays that demonstrate this principle.

The comic scene, which includes a brothel, an inn, and a church, depicts a medieval village with an irregular array of buildings projecting and receding from the street and with façades featuring pointed arches—an additive composition as if having grown over time. The tragic scene depicts a Renaissance town composed of loggias, or arcades, and a triumphal gate all designed as a complete entity with classically inspired semi-circular arches and buildings aligned to the street grid as if having been built at once. And finally, the satiric or pastoral scene depicts trees aligned along a path with rustic huts hidden in the forest. While *Serlio* describes how to depict space in three dimensions, in contrast to the other two scenes framed as small cities, the satiric scene scarcely depicts depth, except for the trees and architectural fragments vaguely aligned to a vanishing point.

Conceived in the experimental hothouse that the design of ephemeral architecture, theaters, and public festivals would stimulate, the comic and tragic scenes represent public spaces in urban centers. So too were the images depicted on stages such as Andrea Palladio's Teatro Olimpico (Olympic Theater) in Vicenza and Vicenzo Scamozzi's Teatro all'antica (theater in the style of the ancients) in Sabbioneta. Both of these theaters house permanent scenographic apparatuses in which space is visually accelerated three-dimensionally through the mechanism of perspectival distortion. By applying perspective theory to urban design, Serlio began to codify an approach to the city already

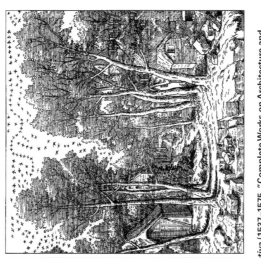

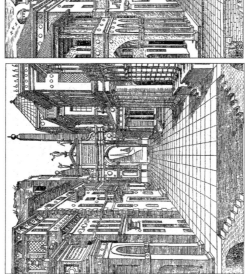

Figure 4.4 **Tragic, Comic, and Satiric stage sets** from Sebastiano Serlio's *Tutte l'opere d'architettura, et prospetiva* (1537–1575, "Complete Works on Architecture and Perspective")

appearing in public plazas, such as Michelangelo Buonarotti's Campidoglio in Rome (1536), whose exterior civic spaces displayed geometries distorted according to the rules of foreshortening.

Locating the human body at eye level in front of a pictorial frame contrasts with the viewing position of Chinese scrolls, which describe space from above. Their continuous roll of paper eschews Western framing methods for seamlessly interconnected sequences that seem to go on infinitely. In the film *A Day on the Grand Canal With the Emperor of China (or Surface Is Illusion But So Is Depth)* (1988) David Hockney analyzes the differences between Western and Eastern spatial constructs, comparing one-point linear perspective from Antonio Canaletto's painting *Capriccio: Plaza San Marco Looking South and West* (1763) and Wang Hui's 72-foot-long painted scroll entitled *The Kangxi Emperor's Southern Inspection Tour (1691–1698), Scroll Seven*. In contrast to

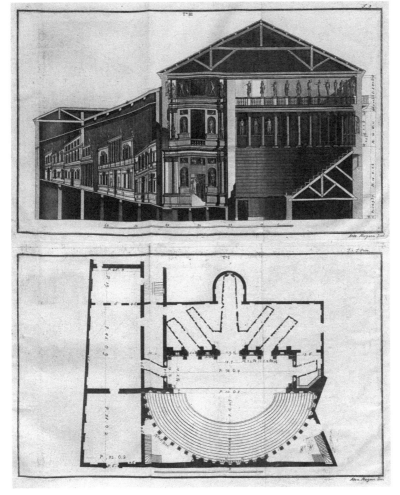

Figure 4.5
Section and plan of Andrea Palladio's Olympic Theater from Ottavio Bertotti Scamozzi's *Le fabbriche e i disegni di Andrea Palladio* (1776)

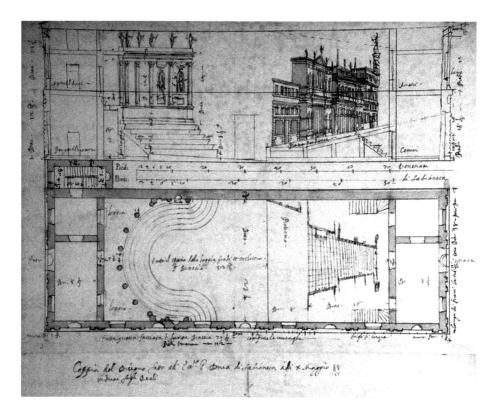

Figure 4.6
Vincenzo
Scamozzi,
design for the
Teatro all'antica
(theater in the
style of the
ancients, 1590)
in Sabbionetta,
Italy (Firenze,
Uffizi 191 A)

the Canaletto view, which focuses the viewer's eye on the single vanishing point of a work whose edges are defined by an enclosing frame, Hui depicts space without vanishing points or separating frames. Hockney points out that in the scroll, the viewer takes charge of what to look at by rolling the paper backwards or forwards and allowing his or her eye to trace the directions of shifting viewpoints that lead from one scene into another. For Hockney, this makes the scroll "far more spatial than Canaletto's one point perspective."[14] With linear perspective, the landscape is apprehended in a powerful, singular gaze, while with Chinese gardens, spatial sequences are absorbed through a series of glances, "designed to be walked through, to be experienced over time from many viewpoints, without any single place, object, or viewpoint being privileged over the others."[15]

Looking more closely at the geometry of Hui's architecture, planes remain parallel to each other rather than transforming into perspectival trapezoids and the buildings closely resemble having been delineated by an oblique drawing technique called axonometric projection. Oblique drawing allows architects to project lines vertically from a plan to construct measurable and precise volumes that display exterior walls, roof, and ground plane simultaneously. As a type of drawing useful for depicting the exploded views of engineered machines, parallel projection allows architects to project the plan directly onto

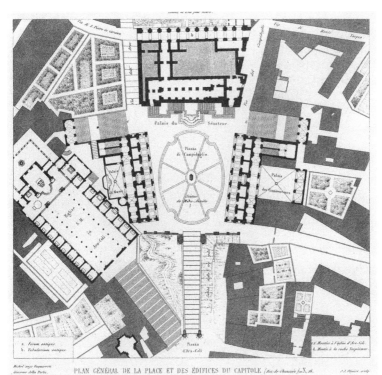

PLAN GÉNÉRAL DE LA PLACE ET DES ÉDIFICES DU CAPITOLE (Rez-de-Chaussée) Pl. X. ch.

VUE GÉNÉRALE DE LA PLACE ET DES ÉDIFICES DU CAPITOLE Pl. X. ch.

Figure 4.7
Michelanagelo Buonarotti, Campidoglio in Rome, Italy (1536), engraved by **Paul-Marie Letarouilly,** *Édifices de Rome moderne: ou recueil des palais, maisons, églises, couvents, et autres monuments publics et particuliers les plus remarquables de la ville de Rome* **(1840–1855)**

Figure 4.8 **Detail from Wang Hui's** *Kangxi Emperor's Southern Inspection Tour, Scroll 7, Wuxi to Suzhou* **(1698)**

Figure 4.9 **Antonio Canale, called Canaletto,** *Piazza San Marco Looking South and West* **(1763), courtesy of Los Angeles County Museum of Art**

its adjacent elevation as reciprocally informative surfaces for linking interiors with exteriors. Massimo Scolari finds early examples of axonometric drawing on ancient Greek vases, Pompeiian frescoes, and Byzantine mosaics, while he attributes its codification to military engineering from the mid-16th century, when precise delineation was required to estimate ballistic trajectories. In explaining the significance of *prospettiva soldatesca* (soldierly perspective) he concludes: "A bullet's lethal trajectory had to be measured with the same precision as the bulwarks that were built to deflect it. The *ars mechanica* of war, like the practice of applied geometry (*geometria pratica*), used techniques other than perspective."[16] According to Scolari, modern architects saw perspective drawing as deceptive, subjective, and geometrically distorted, while orthographic projection delivered an honestly represented object, measurable

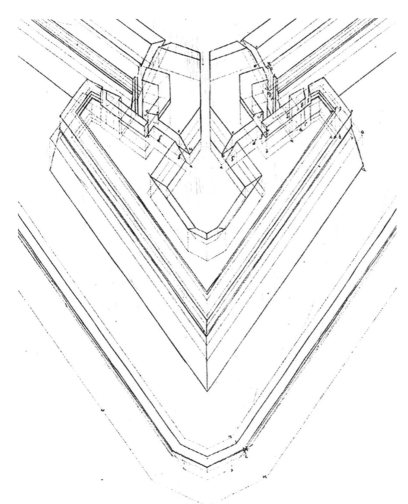

Figure 4.10
Three-dimensional construction of a bulwark based on perpendicular lines drawn over the plan lines from Ambroise Bachot's *Le timon du capitain Ambroise Bachot...* **(Paris, 1587)**

101

and pure. In contrast, Jan Krikke offers that "axonometry originated in China. Its function in Chinese art was similar to linear perspective in European art."[17] Regardless of its precise origins, axonometric drawing was important to Chinese art and conceptions of space, describing a world seen from an aerial position of mathematical distance.

Cult of Ruins

Introducing travelers to the pleasure of ancient ruins scattered across the *campagna* (countryside), a requisite trip to Rome, Italy was an essential part of an architect's education during the 18th century that also contributed to the development of picturesque gardens. A pioneer of the Grand Tour, as this trip came to be known, Inigo Jones introduced Renaissance architecture to England after traveling to Italy around 1603. He carried with him a 1601 edition of Andrea Palladio's *I Quattro libri dell'architettura* (*The Four Books on Architecture*, 1570) and compared the idealized versions of drawings published in this book with differences found in the actual built work. Palladio published woodcuts of ancient Roman buildings, new Renaissance architecture, and his own work, including his designs for numerous villas. Jones annotated the pages of this book with copious marginalia and even drew on top of them as if in a sketchbook. Jones's built work delivered an experimental interpretation of Palladio's principles to England, with projects such as the Queen's House in Greenwich directly referencing the Palazzo Chiericati in Vicenza. Meanwhile, numerous editions of the *Quattri Libri* were translated into English and initiated the spread of neoclassicism across England and beyond.

A parallel contribution to picturesque design therefore emerged from Palladio's work in the area of the Veneto in northern Italy and with his drawings of small houses and temples finding their way into English gardens. Palladio's influence was far-reaching enough for an entire architectural movement, called Palladianism, to adopt his name. It reaches to the design of those iconic white pedimented porticos prevalent on southern mansions and fraternities across the United States and beyond.

By the second half of the 18th century, traveling to Italy and returning home with published surveys of ancient sites became *de rigueur* for architects seeking to elevate their professional stature. Sponsored by the Society of Dilettanti, James "Athenian" Stuart and Nicholas Revett published *The Antiquities of Athens and Other Monuments of Greece* in 1762, being followed by Robert Adam's *Ruins of the Palace of the Emperor Diocletian at Spalatro in Dalmatia* from 1764. As both of these publications attest, another way to read architecture is with a tape measure, wherein the hands-on investigation of a building extracts numerical secrets from its proportional dimensions. A lingering influence of publications such as these concerns two distinct theoretical agendas—one sought architectural models from antiquity as perfectly reconstructed orthographic projections and the other derived inspiration from picturesque ruins depicted in situ. While it was standard to publish both types

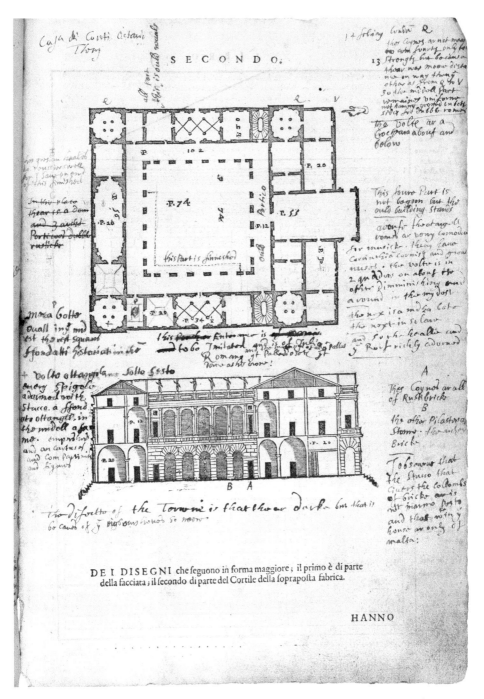

SECONDO.

DE I DISEGNI che seguono in forma maggiore; il primo è di parte della facciata; il secondo di parte del Cortile della soprapposta fabrica.

HANNO

Figures 4.11 and 4.12 **Inigo Jones's annotations on Andrea Palladio's *I Quattro libri dell'architettura* (Venice, 1601), courtesy of the Provost and Fellows of Worcester College, Oxford**

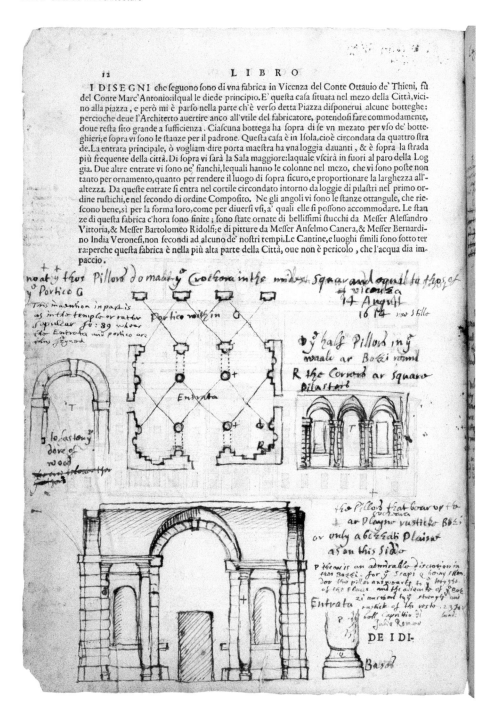

12   L I B R O

I DISEGNI che seguono sono di vna fabrica in Vicenza del Conte Ottauio de' Thieni, fù del Conte Marc'Antonio:il qule le diede principio. E' questa casa situata nel mezo della Città, vicino alla piazza , e però mi è parso nella parte ch'è verso detta Piazza disponerui alcune botteghe: percioche deue l'Architetto auertire anco all'vtile del fabricatore, potendosi fare commodamente, doue resta sito grande a sufficienza . Ciascuna bottega ha sopra di se vn mezato per vso de' botteghieri;e sopra vi sono le stanze per il padrone. Questa casa è in Isola,cioè circondata da quattro strade.La entrata principale, ò vogliam dire porta maestra ha vna loggia dauanti , & è sopra la strada più frequente della città. Di sopra vi sarà la Sala maggiore:laquale vscirà in fuori al paro della Loggia. Due altre entrate vi sono ne' fianchi,lequali hanno le colonne nel mezo, che vi sono poste non tanto per ornamento,quanto per rendere il luogo di sopra sicuro,e proportionare la larghezza all'altezza. Da queste entrate si entra nel cortile circondato intorno da loggie di pilastri nel primo ordine rustichi,e nel secondo di ordine Composito. Ne gli angoli vi sono le stanze ottangule, che riescono bene,sì per la forma loro,come per diuersi vsi,a' quali elle si possono accommodare. Le stanze di questa fabrica c'hora sono finite ; sono state ornate di bellissimi stucchi da Messer Alessandro Vittoria,& Messer Bartolomeo Ridolfi;e di pitture da Messer Anselmo Canera,& Messer Bernardino India Veronesi,non secondi ad alcuno de' nostri tempi.Le Cantine,e luoghi simili sono sotto terra:perche questa fabrica è nella più alta parte della Città, oue non è pericolo , che l'acqua dia impaccio .

Figures 4.11 and 4.12 **(Continued)**

104

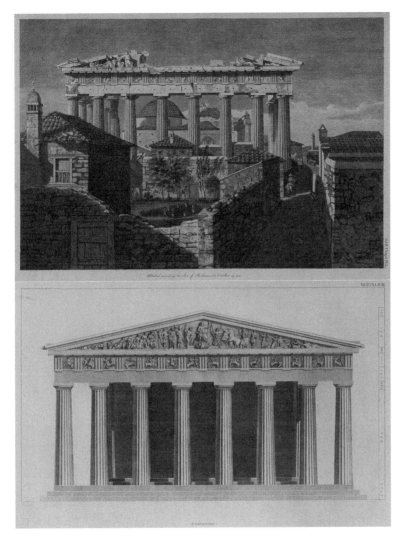

Figure 4.13
**The Parthenon
in situ (before
mosque
and other
additional
structures were
removed) and
restored, from
James Stuart
and Nicholas
Revett's *The
Antiquities
of Athens
and Other
Monuments
of Greece*
(London, 1762)**

of drawing in these archaeological compendia, the first approach (rational, measured, and abstract) countered the second (interpretive, perspectival, and rendered in context): the first being attached to Neoclassicism and the second to Romanticism.

Let us briefly consider how picturesque design works in the quintessential English garden of Stourhead. Henry Hoare, heir to a banking dynasty, acquired the ancestral estate of the Stourtons and employed Colen Campbell, author of *Vitruvius Britannicus* (1715–1725), to build a new Manor House based on Palladio's Villa Emo. In 1735 his son Henry Hoare II "the Magnificent," working with his architect Henry Flitcroft, initiated the garden design by damming the River Stour to create a lake around which he distributed architectural pavilions

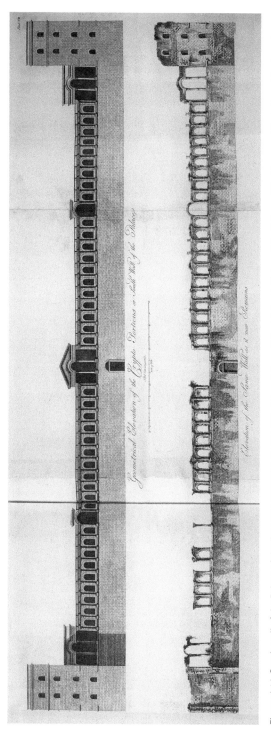

Figure 4.14 **South wall of the Palace of the Emperor Diocletian in situ and restored, from Robert Adam's** *Ruins of the Palace of the Emperor Diocletian at Spalatro in Dalmatia* **(London, 1764)**

Figure 4.15
View of the garden at Stourhead

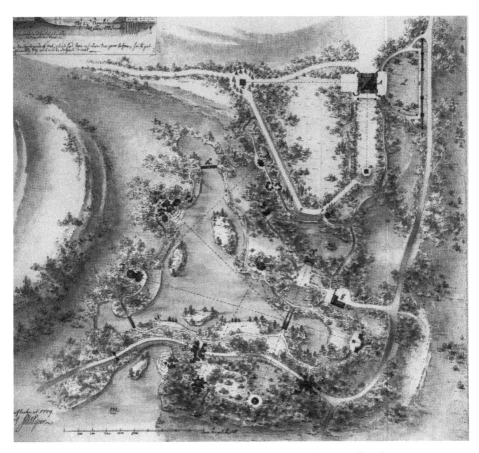

Figure 4.16 **Detail of Fredrik Magnus Piper's plan of the** *Valley Garden at Stourhead* **(1779)**

such as the Temple of Ceres/Temple of Flora (1744), the Temple of Hercules/Pantheon (1754), and the Temple of Apollo (1765). Hoare theorized the proper compositional techniques for garden design, writing: "The greens should be ranged together in large masses as the shades are in painting: to contrast the dark masses with light ones, and to relieve each dark mass itself with little sprinkling of lighter greens here and there."[18] On his drawing, "Plan of the Valley Garden at Stourhead" (1779), the Swedish landscape architect Fredrik Magnus Piper used dashed lines to depict the views visitors would see as they strolled from one building to another, looking from the five-arched "Palladian" bridge to the underworld grotto, from the Temple of Flora to the Pantheon, from the Pantheon to the Palladian bridge, and so on. Unlike the gardens at Vaux-le-Vicomte, the Manor House at Stourhead is removed from the garden sequence and multiple views are discovered by staged, almost filmic, accidents rather than a single view presented on axis.

The disposition of gardens such as Stowe and Rousham adopted models of pastoral or Virgilian landscapes, with temples distributed in wooded groves next to fields of peacefully grazing animals. Artists such as Claude Lorrain, Nicolas Poussin, and Gaspard Dughet established important compositional sources for picturesque gardens. In fact, Hoare possessed a large collection of paintings, including Andrea Locatelli's copy of Claude's *View of Delphi with a Procession* and Claude's *Landscape with Aeneas at Delos* (1672) illustrating a scene from Book III, I.69–83 of Virgil's *Aenied*. A pemented portico fronting

Figure 4.17
***Landscape with Aeneas at Delos* by Claude Lorrain (1672, National Gallery, London)**

a domed temple reminiscent of the Pantheon at Stourhead enunciates the visual parallel with Claude's landscape at Delos.

Claude's painting offers an important key to unlocking the garden as an allegory of Aeneas's journey from Troy, descent into the underworld, and founding of Rome, while it establishes a nexus among literature, garden design, ancient mythology, and architecture. Walking counterclockwise around the lake, a body of water thought to represent Lake Avernus where Aeneas entered the underworld, the first major stop on the recommended circuit is the Temple of Flora. An inscription from the Aeneid found on the pediment of this small pavilion—"the Sybil warns Aeneas 'begone, you who are uniniti-ated, begone!'"—offers a second important clue to deciphering this encrypted narrative. The itinerary continues with a visit to a grotto featuring a river god and the Temple of Hercules, each evoking the River Tiber and the Pantheon in Rome respectively. It culminates at the Temple of Apollo, a round pavilion with a scalloped entablature resembling the circular temple at Baalbek that evokes the golden age of Augustus and his descent from Aeneas. Stourhead's literary itinerary, natural features, pavilions, and statuary demonstrate how to read a garden through its topography, iconography, and painterly composition.

The picturesque garden married painterly composition, ancient archi-tecture, and living nature in a ceremony conducted among quasi-mythical temples, simulated ruins, false grottoes, and faux bridges dispersed across a landscape that was anything but natural. It created an actual journey through an imagined classical past that allowed visitors to develop sequential pavilions into an *ars mnenonica*, or "memory arts," that often relied on architecture to help memorize long passages of literature. A *locus* is a place for those tasked with memorizing long pieces of writing, such as stories by Homer or Virgil, to cognitively store words in an imaginary or real location, to which they might return in their minds when required to retrieve the text. While other mnemonic systems existed, the method of *loci* is specifically tied to architecture, demon-strating the power of buildings to trigger memories. English gardens render this relationship among *ars mnemonica*, architecture, landscape, and narrative explicit.

They also provided evidence for the emerging theory of *associationism*, a theory that George Hersey summarizes through the lenses of 18th-century French architectural theory and Sebastiano Serlio's three scenic styles. As Hersey summarizes, in *Livre d'architecture* (1745) Germain Boffrand suggested that edifices, as if appearing on stage, should indicate "that the scene is pastoral or tragic, that it is a temple or a palace, a public building destined to a specific use, or a private house."[19] Introducing an embryonic functionalist discourse, Boffrand claimed that "these different edifices, through their disposition, their structure, and the manner in which they are decorated, should announce their purpose to the spectator" while they also should arouse emotions such as "joy, sadness, love, hate, even terror."[20]

To adopt Boffrand's approach to reading architecture is to identify the way in which an edifice may convey emotions and moods to the observer.

A building's ability to convey a mood, express a purpose, or even elicit a pre-scribed feeling becomes evidenced across the diversity of garden pavilions that could suggest a range of accompanying emotions and trigger a series of mental associations. Emerging from the Scottish Enlightenment, the circle in which the Adam brothers moved, David Hume and Henry Home, Lord Kames outlined the ways in which a building could initiate a chain of associations in observers that would lead them to contemplate elevated and psychologically transformative thoughts. Developed across the diverse designs of pavilions that had no real purpose other than to ornament gardens, Associationism resulted in the idea that buildings could express an affect uniquely tied to their exterior form and powerful enough to trigger a stream of thoughts, which, in turn, could transform the observer's disposition. The repertoire of styles expanded to include Gothic and Asian structures amplified the range of asso-ciations provided by the usual temples, classical ruins, grottos, and rustic huts. Writing in *Elements of Criticism* (1762), Kames considered the way in which a building elicits a chain of associations, asking: "Should a ruin be in the Gothic or Grecian Form? In the former, I think; because it exhibits the triumph of time over strength; a melancholy, but not unpleasant thought: a Grecian ruin suggests rather the triumph of barbarity over taste; a gloomy and discouraging thought."[21]

Sublime Beauty

When unleashed from the propriety of English gardens, nature may display the awesome incomprehensibility of abyssal cliffs, wild rivers, and precipitous mountains. She is prone to extreme upheavals such as landslides, volcanoes, ice storms, and more that produce vistas and spectacles that incite sublime emotions in the solitary observer watching from a relatively secure distance of contemplative terror. Caspar David Friedrich's painting *Wanderer Above the Sea of Fog* (1818) epitomizes this state of sublime pleasure. In 1757 Edmund Burke published *A Philosophical Enquiry into the Origin of Our Ideas of the Sublime and Beautiful*, discharging the awesome powers of nature as an aesthetic complement to beauty. Terms such as *obscurity*, *vastness*, *infinity*, and *magnificence* thematize Burke's sublime as delightful terror. In contrast to beauty, which draws aesthetic principles from neoclassical order, proportion, and reason—what Johann Joachim Winckelmann referred to as "noble sim-plicity and quiet grandeur"—the sublime celebrated the effects of passion, difficulty, and power, which helped to construct romanticism's terrible and dark persona.[22]

Architecture enters the conversation with Burke's assessment of the sublime through the properties of succession, uniformity, infinity, chiaroscuro, magnitude, and difficulty. Succession suggests that the repetition of a build-ing's parts impresses "the imagination with an idea of their progress beyond their actual limits."[23] Uniformity requires that a building remains free of many parts to prevent "the termination of one idea, and the beginning of another."[24]

Figure 4.18
Caspar David Friedrich's painting ***Wanderer Above the Sea of Fog*** **(1818, Kunsthalle, Hamburg)**

Uninterrupted progression suggests infinity. *Chiaroscuro* refers to the brightness that makes darkness even more terrible. *Magnitude* describes great size that makes everything else seem insignificant. And *difficulty* stems from a building that requires an immense force of labor to construct it. For Burke, Stonehenge's "huge rude masses of stone, set on end, and piled each on other, turn the mind on the immense force necessary for such a work."[25] Ruins played an invaluable role in translating the sublime from a literary theory into built form, as demonstrations of nature reclaiming wilderness from architecture. Reading sublime architecture seeks to identify gargantuan scales, deep shadows, and repetitive elements suggesting an infinite expanse.

The ability of architecture to express awe and power eventually will find expression in the *Sturm und Drang* of Nazi rallies such as the *Lichtdom* (Cathedral of Light, 1933) in Nuremberg that Albert Speer orchestrated by aiming 152 anti-aircraft searchlights skyward at the *Zeppelinfeld*. It also references his concept of *Ruinenwert* (Ruin Value), the desire for buildings to collapse into beautiful ruins. His designs for the Third Reich, such as the *Zeppelinfeld*, relied upon gargantuan neoclassical forms that reference the unbuilt work Étienne-Louis Boullée published in his late 18th-century treatise *Architecture, essai sur l'art* (*Essay on the Art of Architecture*). So too, Boullée's

Figure 4.19
**Cathedral
of Light or**
Lichtdom
above the *Zep-
pelintribune*
**(Nuremberg,
1936) from
Allgemeiner
Deutscher
Nachrichtendi-
enst – Zentral-
bild (Bild 183)**

Source gallica.bnf.fr / Bibliothèque nationale de France

Figure 4.20
**Étienne-Louis
Boullée,
"Circus,"**
from his
*Architecture,
essai sur
l'art,* (*Essay
on the Art of
Architecture,*
1778–1788)

accompanying text seems to anticipate the rhetoric of Speer's pyrotechnics: "surrender yourselves completely to all the pleasure that this sublime passion can procure! No other pleasure is so pure. It is this passion that makes us love to study, that transforms our pain into pleasure and, with its divine flame, forces genius to yield up its oracles. In short, it is this passion that summons us to immortality."[26]

The progression of neoclassicism into romanticism moved from a rational and malleable model of architectural classicism to the creation of hybrid monsters that willfully broke rules and mixed styles. Francisco Goya's etching *El sueño de la razón produce monstruos* (*The Sleep of Reason Produces Monsters*, 1798), where creatures of the night haunt a writer's sleep, perfectly summarizes the release of rationalism's repressed emotions into 19th-century romanticism. As with the Chinese fascination with scholars' rocks, rough and mutilated objects displaying the ravages of time were substituted for the noble simplicity of smooth marble surfaces. Romantic artists and writers feared not

Figure 4.21
Francisco Goya,
El sueño de la
razón produce
monstruos
(*The Sleep*
of Reason
Produces
***Monsters*) from**
Los Caprichos
(1799)

gazing into the depths of nature's grotesque amalgam of eclectic form to produce an architecture of magnificent and terrible invention. Ruins, by virtue of their white marble fragments, could be naturalized as a bunch of old bones lying about the architectural graveyard storing the terribleness of the events they had witnessed.

Whether classical or industrial, ancient or modern, ruins maintain the distinct ability to invoke sublime sensations in those who gaze upon them. In his *Vedute di Roma* (*Views of Rome*, starting in 1747), Giovanni Battista Piranesi depicted ancient architecture as charged with eruptive forces and cyclopean scale. The interior views he published in *Le Carceri d'Invenzione* (*The Imaginary Prisons*, starting in 1745) offer menacing images of subterranean vaults filled with stairs disappearing to infinity. The prisons demonstrate an emphasis on two-point and multiple-point perspective in scenic design derived from Ferdinando Galli-Bibiena's development of the *scena per angolo*, a device for designing stage sets where a corner faces the audience and flanking sides diminish to two vanishing points. If two vanishing points emerge simply by rotating a square in plan, then an infinite number of vanishing points enter the scene with each new line that rotates off of this initial rectilinear system, exploding space into a centrifugal phantasmagoria.

"Study the sublime dreams of Piranesi," Horace Walpole implored, because he "seems to have conceived visions of Rome beyond what it boasted even in the meridian of its splendor ... He piles palaces on bridges, and temples on palaces, and scales heaven with mountains of edifices."[27] Among the numerous writers and artists who were transformed by Piranesi's prodigious work of documenting and distorting antiquity, Sir John Soane points to a synthesis of the sublime and the picturesque. In taking over the design of the Bank of England in London starting in 1788 he developed a series of discreet rooms—each with its own thematic identity—including the Four Percent

Figure 4.22
Giovanni Battista Piranesi, "The Drawbridge," from *Carceri d'Invenzioni* (*Imaginary Prisons*, 1750), plate 7

Figure 4.23
Demonstration of a two-point perspective scene from Ferdinando Galli Bibiena's *L'architettura civile: preparata sú la geometria, e ridotta alle prospettive: considerazioni pratiche* **(***Civil Architecture...,***1711)**

Office surmounted by a pendentive dome supporting a ring of caryatids, the Rotunda, a circular dome on arches, and the Three Percent Console Transfer Office, another pendentive dome now supporting a ring of ionic columns. With rooms buried deeply inside a building that occupied an entire city block, the only way to bring natural light into these spaces was through courtyards and a complex system of skylights. These apertures transformed the entire complex

115

Figure 4.24
Joseph
Gandy's
painting of
Sir John
Soane's Bank
of England
rendered in
ruins (1830, Sir
John Soane's
Museum)

into a subterranean world illuminated from above. Joseph Gandy's rendering of the Bank of England in ruins (1830) intensifies reading the architecture as sustaining both sublime and picturesque personae.

Sequences

Just as picturesque landscape strategies may describe a series of episodic and interlinked spaces connected on a path, so too do the interconnected sequence of spaces in cities, as Serlio's set designs reveal. Town plans that adopted the lessons of Renaissance and Baroque cities favored the tragic scene, projecting broad axes into newly expanded urban enclaves. Towns that display the irregular pattern of historic cities that grew over time reference the comic scene, producing sequential spaces offering the potential for picturesque urban design.

The 19th-century transformation of Vienna followed the model of the tragic scene. At least it was a tragedy for Camillo Sitte, who proposed its redesign according to the communal scale of historic city plazas. After Emperor Franz Josef began removing the medieval fortifications separating Vienna's historical center from its suburban expansion, in 1857 construction of the *Ringstraße* began according to his specifications. This was a broad ring road circumambulating the city with new monumental buildings. Otto Wagner won a competition to expand this plan, advocating, as Henry Francis Mallgrave observes, for "the straight, clean, practical street leading us to our destination in the shortest possible time."[28] In contrast, he writes, Camillo Sitte proposed a painterly strategy of "composed urban panoramas based on scientific laws of perspective."[29] Although Sitte warned against copying the additive and irregular morphology of medieval towns, the images illustrating his book *Der Städtebau nach seinen künstlerischen Grundsätzen (City*

Figure 4.25
**Camillo Sitte,
*Brügge, Rue
des Pierres*
from *Der
Städtebau
nach seinen
künstlerischen
Grundsätzen*
(*City Planning
According
to Artistic
Principles,*
1889)**

Planning According to Artistic Principles, 1889) tell something of a different story. They depict curving and irregular street alignments providing ever-changing vistas reminiscent of picturesque towns across Europe, offering a useful alternative to the purely rational planning philosophy modernist city planning would implement.

Picking up Sitte's mantel of picturesque planning, Gordon Cullen developed a sequential drawing technique that keyed town plans to the location where perspective drawings had been completed. From Oxford, England to New Delhi, India, he studied the historic cores of cities, documenting the intricate and often labyrinthine circuit of navigating by sight and intuition. He published these drawings in his 1961 book, *The Concise Townscape*, where he pioneered the process of analyzing and designing cities from the point of view of a pedestrian. He analyzed space through serial vision, positing the design of towns as a sequence of pressures and vacuums, exposures and enclosures, and constraint and relief. He advocated for concepts such as deferred views, place making, enclaves, and focal points. He invited readers to join him on an imaginary walk through a town while being guided by captivating views at the end of a street, only to be led astray by lateral glances down side alleys or glimpses into colorful courtyards. His book celebrates bottom-up planning processes, organic growth over time, and the human scale of historic town centers. It also develops the irregular circulation patterns and clustered silhouettes of additive design processes associated with concepts of

Figure 4.26 Thomas Gordon Cullen, *Serial Vision*, from *The Concise Townscape* (1961)

CASEBOOK: SERIAL VISION

To walk from one end of the plan to another, at a uniform pace, will provide a sequence of revelations which are suggested in the serial drawings opposite, reading from left to right. Each arrow on the plan represents a drawing. The even progress of travel is illuminated by a series of sudden contrasts and so an impact is made on the eye, bringing the plan to life (like nudging a man who is going to sleep in church). My drawings bear no relation to the place itself; I chose it because it seemed an evocative plan. Note that the slightest deviation in alignment and quite small variations in projections or setbacks on plan have a disproportionally powerful effect in the third dimension.

the picturesque—aesthetically driven planning principles that place eye-level experience above numeric calculations and planimetric patterns.

Projects such as Frank Gehry's Loyola Law School campus (1978) in Los Angeles and Peter Eisenman's Wexner Center for the Arts (1989) on the Ohio State University's campus evidence a return to considering the massing and intricate growth patterns of villages as a viable approach to university planning initiatives that follow in the tradition of the picturesque—sentimentality and all. Given that, in the late 1970s, postmodern architecture initiated a critique of the stark geometries characteristic of modernist planning principles, it inflected urban design with compositions such as these. Eisenman, in fact, develops a narrative component and explores the cult of ruins when referencing an armory that once had inhabited the site with the insertion of brick tower-shaped forms into his rotated grid frames. The rotated grids begin to approximate the palimpsest organization of a building site insofar as it appears to have been constructed over buried layers, above the invisible strata of an imaginary archaeological dig where the geometry of hidden foundations projects upward to influence the orientation of new construction.

Andrés Duany and Elizabeth Plater-Zyberk codified the application of picturesque scenography to urban design, outlining systematic principles for neighborhood-based planning derived from historic town centers. After establishing their firm in 1980, Duany and Plater-Zyberk wrote the design codes for Seaside, Florida, a small beach resort that models traditional town

Figure 4.27 **Peter Eisenman, Wexner Center for the Arts at the Ohio State University (1989)**

Figure 4.28 **Seaside, Florida, courtesy of M. Timothy O'Keefe and Alamy Stock Photo**

planning ideals on a systematic set of written guidelines. They applied these principles to the Congress for the New Urbanism (CNU), a non-profit organization they co-founded in 1993 with Peter Calthorpe, Elizabeth Moule, Stefanos Polyzoides, and Daniel Solomon. "Established with the goal of transforming the built environment from ad-hoc suburban sprawl towards human-scale neighborhood development," as Duany and Plater-Zyberk state, New Urbanism focuses on transit-oriented neighborhoods, mixed-use development, and walkable communities.[30] New Urbanism's mining of traditional town plans also suggests an attachment to architectural styles that look backward nostalgically to historic revival with implicit codes and covenants that restrict experimenting with unconventional forms. For its nostalgic and revivalist aesthetics, it remains a controversial approach among avant-garde designer circles, while it garners popular appeal for its traditional architectural references, human scale, and pedestrian-oriented design.

Promenade Architectural

Bernard Tschumi developed an approach to the design of sequential movement in relation to cinematic space that he and Michael Photiadis applied to the design of the new Acropolis Museum in Athens (2001–2009). As Tschumi writes, spatial sequences emphasize "a planned path with fixed halting points, a family of spatial points linked by continuous movement."[31] While the museum's circulation expresses Tschumi's concept of spatial sequences, it also interiorizes the Panathenaic Way by introducing a path of continuous movement that merges cinematic and architectural space.

In use from around the 6th century BCE until the 6th century CE, it formed a processional route for a summer festival called the Panathenaea, celebrated annually on the goddess Athena's birthday. Also known at the *Dromos*, the path wound its way from the *Dipylon*, or main city gate, through the *Agora*, around the base of the *Acropolis* (the high city or "polis" and sanctuary of ancient Athens), across the *Propylaea* (gateway), and into the Acropolis proper. The procession concluded at the altar of the city's patron goddess Athena, standing about halfway between the Erechtheion and the Parthenon, where sacrifices of the processional animals would be made in honor of Athena Polias (Athena protector of the city-state or *polis*). The festival lasted several days and featured a variety of events including chariot races, musical competitions, gymnastic events, footraces, wrestling, boxing, and javelin throwing. The procession featured maidens carrying a *peplos*, priestesses carrying gifts, sacrificial cows and sheep, musicians, men carrying olive branches, chariots, *ergastinai* or the weavers of the *peplos*, infantry, cavalry, winners of the games, and the remaining Athenian population. The high point of the festival was the ceremony of the *peplos*, a garment Athenian women wove and which high priestesses used to dress the *xoanon*, a life-sized cult statue of Athena Polias constructed of olivewood and located in the Erechtheion. Every four years Athenians would weave a colossal *peplos*, delivered on a wheeled ship and hanging on the mast like a sail, to dress the gigantic, chryselephantine statue of Athena Parthenos ("virgin") sculpted by Phidias and occupying the *cella* (inner chamber) of the Parthenon.

The Propylaea, Temple of Athena Nikê, Erechtheion, and Parthenon constitute the most significant monuments surviving at the summit of the acropolis and designate a building complex that emerged during Athens's Golden Age under the leadership of Pericles (ca. 495–429 BCE). These buildings represent the pinnacle of Greek architecture and set the standards against which classical architecture is measured. They also encapsulate the origins of democracy and philosophy in Greek civilization. The Temple of Athena Nikê (ca. 420 BCE) is built out of white marble from Mount Pentelicus according to a design by Kallikrates. It displays Ionic tetrastyle (four-column) porches on an amphiprostyle (featuring a portico both at the front and the rear) structure. As one approaches the Propylaia, this small temple sparkles from the southwest corner of the Acropolis, appearing as a near-seamless continuation of the monumental retaining wall holding up the entire sacred precinct.

Constructed according to designs by Mnesicles and Phidias (ca. 406 BCE), the Erechtheion encapsulates an etiology of archaic myths that form the center of Athenian worship and houses altars dedicated to both Athena and Poseidon. The "Porch of the Maidens" forms the most distinctive component of this temple, where female figures called caryatids stand in for columns (see Figure 2.11).

The most monumental structure on the citadel is the Parthenon (438 BCE), designed by Ictinus with a sculptural program by Phidias. A peripteral temple (surrounded on all sides by columns), with an octastyle façade (eight columns on the front), proportioned in the Doric order and constructed with a trabeated system (post and beam), the exterior of the cella displays a continuous frieze depicting the Panathenaic procession described above. Here the games, sacrifices, and citizens carved in white marble mirror the Athenians back to themselves on the very site where this event occurs.

Figure 4.29
Auguste Choisy,
Acropolis: Propylaea, Parthenon, Erechtheion,
from
Histoire de l'Architecture
(1899)

The approach to the Acropolis and the general organization of its temples on the summit describe an architecture designed to be viewed in motion. Nineteenth-century art historian Auguste Choisy published a series of illustrations in *Histoire de l'Architecture* (*The History of Architecture*, 1899), where he sequentially diagrammed the Acropolis with perspective drawings keyed to plans indicating the point of view from which they were drawn and rotated to the correct angle of vision. The prevailing pattern in ancient Greek spatial

Propylaea

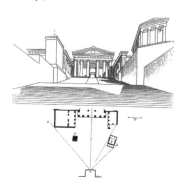

View of Acropolis from Propylaea

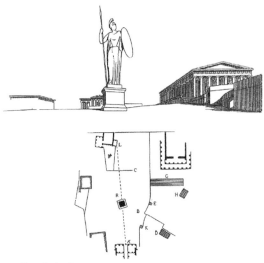

Parthenon

Erechtheion

organization that he documented was to rotate buildings off of an orthogonal plan in order to show two sides rather than one, thereby eroding the more rigid organization of public space around a fixed grid into a panorama of multiple privileged views.

Along with Piranesi's *Carceri*, Choisy's analysis of the Acropolis in Athens inspired Sergei Mikhailovich Eisenstein, a Soviet Russian filmmaker who also had been trained in architecture, to develop the concept of cinematic montage as a technique for editing films that forced space into a collision of dynamic cuts. Writing in "Montage and Architecture" (1938), Eisenstein located the theoretical pedigree of this editing process in Choisy's illustrations. He emphasized the significance of moving sequentially on the Acropolis past shifting points of view as a close approximation of film's ability to depict spatial motion. To Eisenstein, the Greeks left us "the most perfect examples of shot design, change of shot, and shot length."[32] "Victor Hugo called medieval cathedrals 'books in stone' (see *Notre Dame de Paris*)," he argued, so that "the Acropolis of Athens has an equal right to be called the perfect example of one of the most ancient films."[33] As ancient filmic architecture, the Acropolis's sequencing of processional views from the *Dipylon* Gate (or even as far away as the port of Piraeus) to steps of the Parthenon nuances episodic sequences. The path of the Panathenaic festival unfolds into a process of circumambulation that cues the cognitive assimilation of multiple cuts of shifting perspectival moments into an architectural film.

This sequential analysis of the Acropolis was equally important to Le Corbusier, as demonstrated by his publishing of Choisy's plan in *Vers une architecture* (*Towards an Architecture*, 1923). Choisy keyed a panoramic view taken from the threshold of the *Propylaea*, which depicted the Greek positioning of the Erechtheion and the Parthenon slightly calibrated to display two sides of each edifice. Le Corbusier transformed the multifocal pathway Choisy illustrated into a general principle of movement through built form called the *promenade architectural*. This procession is manifest most clearly at his Villa Savoye outside of Paris, whose cinematic path Pierre Chenal documented in his 1931 film *L'architecture d'aujourd'hui* (*The Architecture of Today*). Le Corbusier also referenced the sequencing of views when stating that "Arab architecture has so much to teach us" because it "is appreciated while on the move, with one's feet; it is while walking, moving from one place to another, that one sees how the arrangements of the architecture develop."[34] At the Villa Savoye, Corbusier claimed to be "dealing with a true architectural promenade, offering constantly varied, unexpected, sometimes astonishing aspects." Choisy's analyses of the Acropolis resulted in spatial epiphanies for Eisenstein and Le Corbusier, both of whom offered models for exploring the intersections of architecture and cinema, models that Tschumi published in *The Manhattan Transcripts* (1981) and built into his design for the *Parc de la Villette* in Paris (1982).

With his design of the new Acropolis Museum, Tschumi draws from the site's physical context through the cinematic lenses that Eisenstein and Le Corbusier derived from Choisy in order to arrive at a critical reframing of

Figure 4.30
**Bernard
Tschumi,
Acropolis
Museum
(Athens,
2001–2009),
site plan
and section,
courtesy
of Bernard
Tschumi
Architects**

the Panathenaic frieze. Located on the southeastern slope of the Acropolis near the Parthenon, on a site inhabited by sensitive archaeological ruins such as houses, shops, and baths, the museum houses a collection of antiquities discovered on the citadel. Tschumi organized the building into the three disjunctive layers of base, middle, and top, which have been slightly rotated from each other much like an archaeological dig may display the palimpsest of conflicting stratigraphy and multiple layers of inhabitation. The first layer appears at the archaeological level of existing ruins, above which hover galleries whose floors have been cut with apertures to view the artifacts below. The second layer contains the main galleries and orients itself to the existing street pattern

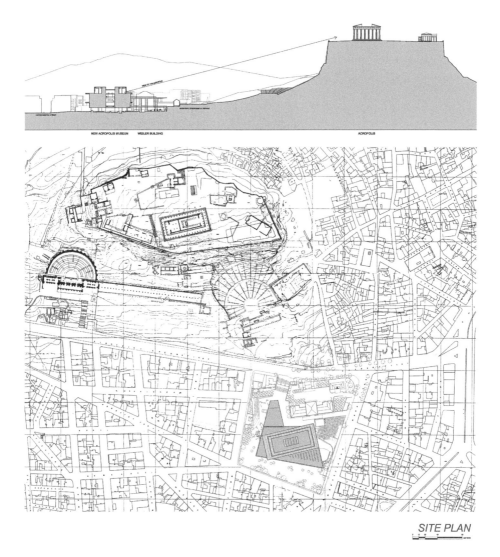

SITE PLAN

of modern Athens. The third layer rotates to perfectly align with the Parthenon and reproduces the temple's footprint as an abstract twin floating in space and time.

Tschumi notoriously considers spaces as independent of what happens in them to the extent that, for example, "Yesterday I cooked in the bathroom and slept in the kitchen" because sequences of events and spatial sequences can form independent systems, "with their own implicit schemes of parts."[35] Notorious because this approach to design subverts the conventional relationship between a space and the activities it contains into one of

Figure 4.31
Lawrence Alma-Tadema,
Phidias Showing the Frieze of the Parthenon to His Friends
(1868), Birmingham Museum and Art Gallery

Figure 4.32
Bernard Tschumi, Acropolis Museum (Athens, 2001–2009), Parthenon frieze, courtesy of Bernard Tschumi Architects, photo © Christian Richtrs

Figure 4.33
**Bernard
Tschumi,
Acropolis
Museum
(Athens,
2001–2009),
exterior view
with the
Acropolis in the
background,** ©
Peter Mauss-
ESTO

collisions, accidents, and similar disjunctions that heighten our participation in architecture as a serial event.

Tschumi describes the sequential movement through this building as narrating a spatial experience from the city to different time periods through "an architectural and historical promenade" that extends from the archeological layer to the Parthenon frieze.[36] The circulation path from entrance to summit produces "a family of spatial points linked by continuous movement of spatial experiences."[37] The Panathenaic way and Choisy's analysis of it are pulled into the loop of metaphorically ascending the slope of the Acropolis on a glass ramp through which it is possible to view ancient ruins below. Arriving at the topmost layer, the visitor discovers the Parthenon frieze framed in direct proximity to views of its origin at the Doric temple on the sacred rock.

This level contains the museum's critical and curatorial apogee in displaying the frieze suspended at eye level, but also with approximately half of its pieces rendered as plaster copies due to the originals remaining in England as the so-called "Elgin Marbles." Thomas Bruce, 7th Earl of Elgin, was a British diplomat and art collector who visited Greece (then under Ottoman rule) from 1802 to 1812. Elgin had obtained permission from Turkey to record and remove Greek antiquities on the Acropolis with the justification that these artifacts would be irreparably damaged by Greek and Turkish conflict. In what, even at that time, was interpreted as an act of vandalism, Elgin removed about half of the sculptures from the Parthenon, as well as artifacts from the Propylaea and Erechtheum. He shipped them back to England and sold them to the British Museum in 1816, where they remain on display today.

Greece has repeatedly requested the restitution of these significant pieces of artistic patrimony, but the argument against returning them has rested on Athens not possessing a museum with the proper standards of preservation required to properly maintain them. The new Acropolis Museum therefore needed to convince public opinion to pressure the British Museum to return the marbles. In response to this imperative Tschumi reasoned that: "The frieze is a narrative story, where the movement of your own body is a means of reading it as an experience in one place. In this sense, the building has a lot of reasons—both on an artistic level as well as on a political level—to exist."[38] The Parthenon frieze's absent presence in this display proffers a forceful request to return the missing pieces by prominently displaying their copies and aligning the gallery with the temple from which they were taken.

Demonstrating that highly articulate architecture may offer more than one reading, Tschumi's positioning of the Panathenaic frieze as the finale of the museum's circulation models the idea of architecture in response to context from the previous chapter and architecture as a tool of cultural critique in the next chapter. It condenses the broad implications of architectural scenography as it encompasses several conceptual positions linking gardens, narrative, and cinema through the sequential unfolding of experiential space. In this instance, as well as with picturesque architecture, asymmetry and irregularity become intentional compositional tools, a building can tell a story or express a mood, architecture ought to elevate moral conduct, the viewer's subjectivity is part of the design equation, ruins serve as powerful tools for evoking collective memory, and peripatetic views anticipate sequentially driven architecture.

Negative assessments of the picturesque focus on arbitrary compositional principles, irrational caprice, eclecticism, reducing architecture to scenography, and, perhaps most significant of all, subordinating architecture to an external narrative content. As art forms illustrating classical literature, both landscape paintings and picturesque gardens remained subservient to the larger fictions authored by those such as Virgil. When proclaiming "ut pictura poesis" ("as is painting so is poetry") in his *Ars Poetica* (19 BCE), Horace established a parallel between the arts as sharing common traits, aims, and content. Writing in *Laocoön: An Essay on the Limits of Painting and Poetry* (1766) Gotthold Ephraim Lessing offered the counter-argument that paintings and poems are not at all alike and their ontological status is fundamentally different. Poems work diachronically as time-base narrative while paintings operate synchronically in space. Eventually, this entire discussion will encumber the proposition that each different kind of artistic expression should focus on exploring its intrinsic operations and the production of architecture should likewise emphasize its autonomous disciplinary role in the production of form and space.

Notes

1   Alessandra Ponte, "Desert Testing," in *Architecture and Sciences: Exchanging Metaphors* (New York: Princeton Architectural Press, 2003), p. 90.

2   Daniel Libeskind *Marking the City Boundaries – Groningen*, ed. Andreas C. Papdakis (London: Academy Editions, 1992).

3   "Preface," in *Works in Architecture of Robert and James Adam, Esquires* (1773–1778), ed. Robert Oresko (London, Academy Editions: 1975), p. 45–46n, emphasis added.

4   Ibid.

5   Ibid.

6   Jurgis Baltrušaitis, *Aberrations: An Essay on the Legend of Forms*, trans. Richard Miller (Cambridge, MA: MIT Press, 1989), p. 139.

7   Yi-fu Tuan, *Topophilia: A Study of Environmental Perception, Attitudes, and Values* (Englewood Cliffs, NJ: Prentice Hall, 1974), p. 127.

8   Robert M. Craig, "Essay: Elder Brother Rock," in *A World History of Architecture* eds. Michael Fazio, Marian Moffett, and Lawrence Wodehouse, 2nd ed. (Boston: McGraw-Hill, 2008), p. 97.

9   Ji Cheng, *The Craft of Gardens*, trans. A. Hardie (New Haven: Yale University Press, 1989), p. 39.

10 E. V. Gatenby, "The Influence of Japanese on English" *Studies in English Literature 1* (1931), pp. 508–520; and S. Lanh and Nikolaus Pevsner, "Sir William Temple and Sharawadgi" *Architectural Review 106* (1949), pp. 391–392.

11 Baltrušaitis, *Aberrations*, p. 139, from R. L. Gerardin (Marquis de Girardin), *De la composition des paysages au des moyens zi'embellir la nature autour des habitations en joignant l'agrt.able a l'utile* (Geneva, 1775), p. 4.

12 Ibid.

13 Allen S. Weiss, *Mirrors of Infinity: The French Formal Garden and 17th-Century Metaphysics* (New York: Princeton Architectural Press, 1995), p. 41.

14 Dialogue from the film.

15 Weiss, *Mirrors of Infinity*, p. 13.

16 Massimo Scolari, *Oblique Drawing: A History of Anti-perspective*, trans. Jenny Condie Palandri (Cambridge, MA: MIT Press, 2012), p. 6.

17 Jan Krikke, "Axonometry: A Matter of Perspective" *Computer Graphics and Applications IEEE 20*, no. 4 (July/August, 2000), p. 7.

18 Mark Laird, *The Flowering of the Landscape Garden: English Pleasure Grounds, 1720–1800* (Philadelphia: University of Pennsylvania Press, 1999), p. 45.

19 George Hersey "Associationism and Sensibility in Eighteenth-Century Architecture" *Eighteenth-Century Studies 4* (Fall 1970), p. 72.

20 Ibid.

21 Lord Henry Home Kames, *Elements of Criticism: Volume 2* (New York: Scott and Seguine, 1819), p. 329.

22   Johann Joachim Winckelmann, "Reflections on the Imitation of Greek Works in Painting and Sculpture," in *The Art of Art History: A Critical Anthology*, ed. Donald Preziosi (Oxford: Oxford University Press, 1998), p. 35.

23   Edmund Burke, "A Philosophical Enquiry into the Origins of Our Ideas of the Sublime and Beautiful," in *The Writings and Speeches of Edmund Burke: Volume I: The Early Writings*, eds. T. O. McLoughlin and James T. Boulton (Oxford: Oxford University Press, 1997), p. 244.

24   Ibid.

25   Ibid, p. 246.

26   Etienne-Louis Boullée, *Architecture, Essay on Art*, ed. Helen Rosenau and trans. Sheila da Vallée (London: Academy Editions; New York: Harmony Books, 1976), p. 82.

27   Horace Walpole, *Anecdotes of Painting in England; Account of the Principal Artists* (London: W. Nicol, the Shakespeare Press, 1826), vol. IV, pp. xi–xii.

28   Harry Francis Mallgrave, *Modern Architectural Theory: A Historical Survey, 1673–1968* (Cambridge: Cambridge University Press, 2005), p. 192.

29   Ibid, p. 193.

30   DPZ firm profile: http://www.dpz.com/About/Profile.

31   Bernard Tschumi, *Architecture and Disjunction* (Cambridge, MA: MIT Press, 1994), p. 155.

32   Sergei Eisenstein, *Towards a Theory of Montage: Sergei Eisenstein Selected Works, Volume 2*, ed. and trans. Richard Taylor (Bloomington, Indiana: Indiana University Press, 1995), p. 60.

33   Ibid.

34   Le Corbusier, *Oeuvres completes* (Zurich: Editions d'architecture, 1964), vol. II, p. 24, as cited by Yve-Alain Bois, "A Picturesque Stroll around Clara-Clara*" *October 29* (Summer, 1984), trans. John Shepley, p. 56.

35   Tschumi, *Architecture and Disjunction*, p. 169.

36   Architect's website.

37   Tschumi, *Architecture and Disjunction*, p. 156.

38   http://archpaper.com/2009/04/02_new-acropolis-museum.

Chapter 5

Criticality

[T]he new spirit of capitalism has put to good use the artistic critique that was supposed to destroy it.[1]

—Bruno Latour

In 1986 Carlo Petrini started Slow Food in Rome, Italy to protest the siting of a McDonald's at the Spanish Steps. Beginning with the original aims of promoting regional gastronomic traditions, healthy eating patterns, and a slower pace of life, Slow Food has evolved into an international movement that "recognizes the strong connections between plate, planet, people, politics and culture."[2] Its manifesto seeks to restore the environmental equilibrium of food production and consumption through the guiding principles that good cuisine has flavor and aroma, is environmentally clean, and is produced in accordance with social justice. Grassroots movements such as Slow Food have yielded critiques of environmental exploitation, social inequity, or loss of regional identity.

The design and branding of global franchises such as McDonald's describes the architectural counterpart to the Slow Food manifesto, exemplified through the mass production of almost identical buildings whose designs are completed without reference to specific contexts. The term "McMansion" refers to mass-produced, super-sized houses that display a range of extraneous stylistic references, demonstrating how fast architecture has standardized and colonized the world. In his "Slow Manifesto" of 2009, Lebbeus Woods called for an architecture that resists rapid change, "even as it flows from it, struggling to crystallize and become eternal, even as it is broken and scattered."[3]

The idea of slow architecture offers an alternative approach to reading buildings that considers external pressures contributing to the design of form and space. It describes one avenue through which architecture operates as a vehicle for actively critiquing, rather than simply absorbing, a wide range of cultural contexts. Architecture's potential to comment upon and even transform its context relies on the simple question of "what is being critiqued?" Jane Rendell coined the phrase "critical spatial practice" so as "to describe both everyday activities and creative practices which seek to resist the dominant social order of global corporate capitalism."[4] In this section architecture may critique its engagement with exterior cultural pressures, socio-political forces, and its own disciplinary apparatus.

Beginning with the initial claim that architecture may resist repressive forces, this chapter reads buildings as critiques of the socio-political machinery that produces them—indeed, of the disciplinary mechanisms of architecture itself. This chapter explores reading architecture critically through buildings and spaces that restore socio-political agency, reveal hidden ideologies, and resist political assimilation. In terms of the latter category, one side of the debate surrounding architecture's very ability to perform in a critical capacity, due to its essential role as an abstract spatial art, questions the transformative social role of buildings in favor of apolitical, autonomous forms. We can understand the opposing trajectories of criticality in architecture as a debate between contextualism (responsiveness to site, culture, or contingencies) and autonomy (emphasis on formal inventiveness and design method). Arguably, architecture cannot solve non-architectural problems. But when considered as a space of inhabitation, as systems of boundaries, and as built work, criticality is unavoidable. Given that any built work of architecture necessarily engages its surroundings by the simple process of changing them, architecture either may offer unconscious or self-conscious commentary about its context, but it cannot not be critical of it.

Critical Contextualism

In 1981 Alexander Tzonis and Liane Lefaivre coined the term *critical regionalism* to emphasize the importance of "placeness," context, and history while avoiding the trap of imitation and wanton traditionalism.[5] In 1983 Kenneth Frampton published "Towards a Critical Regionalism: Six Points for an Architecture of Resistance" to emphasize architecture's inherent rootedness in a place as a viable response to modernism's messianic and destructive confrontation with context. With the operative term in his title being *resistance*, Frampton understood regionalism as blending modernism and vernacular building traditions into a practice of frisson and friction that reflects but also critiques its context. Frampton posited architecture as capable of maintaining a sustained critical practice that resists modernism's pressures of consumerism and homogenization through a self-conscious interplay between *gemeinschaft* and *gesellschaft*, between local culture and universal civilization. According to Frampton, architecture maintains the capacity to simultaneously cultivate resistant and culturally driven design solutions. He recommended limiting the expansion of cities into boundless megalopolises produced by the mathematics of abstract formulas. He censured modernism's tabula rasa approach to demolishing existing urban fabrics as "a technocratic gesture which aspires to a condition of absolute placelessness."[6] And finally, he considered the human body's capacity to tactilely read architecture as a way of resisting the domination of universal technology with regional building technologies. For Frampton, the rational grid organizing Jørn Utzon's Bagsvaerd Church (1976) near Copenhagen represents universal values that the arationality of its idiosyncratic concrete vault resists with multicultural references to other sacred spaces.

In another instance Frampton interpreted Luis Barragán's garden of *Las Arboledas* (1961) near Mexico City as staining the planar language of International Style modernism with the polychrome of Islamic architecture and memories of the architect's childhood pueblo. "My earliest childhood memories are related to a ranch my family owned near the village of Mazamitla," as Barragán explained, the earth's color was red and "in this village, the water distribution system consisted of great gutted logs, in the form of troughs, which ran on a support structure of tree forks, 5 meters high, above the roofs."[7] While Barragán's work is tactile, sensual, and earthbound, as Frampton wrote, it also offers hermetic spaces in which to withdraw from the industrialized world. Critical regionalism invites architects to explore culture and context as a form of resistance to commercial design formulas and in support of the sociopolitical transformation that buildings may enact.

Figure 5.1
**Jørn Utzon,
Bagsvaerd
Church in
Copenhagen,
Denmark
(1976), courtesy
of SEIER+SEIER**

With their home-office at 9/10 Stock Orchard Street (2001), Sarah Wiggelsworth and Jeremy Till demonstrate the ways in which architectural resilience, cultural critique, and formal sophistication may operate as mutually supportive interlocutors in a design conversation relying on the skills of a *bricoleur*, the handyman who patches things together improvisationally. Pieced together architecture from a diverse range of foraged resources and assembled with the cunning misuse of standard construction materials, the Orchard Street house stands as built bricolage. In response to a challenging site in London, the architects designed an L-shaped building whose orientation harvests solar energy, creates a semi-public courtyard, and screens public spaces from an adjacent railway line. The architects clad the building in an array of experimental materials: quilted fabric attached to the structure with eyelets, straw bales enclosed behind corrugated polycarbonate plastic, and sandbags filled with a combination of sand, lime, and cement permanently set in place through the alchemy of rainwater. The list of inventive energy-saving devices continues: living green roof, larder cooled by air flowing from a ventilation tower, repurposed window frames, rainwater harvesting, chicken coop, kitchen garden, and more. The project also demonstrates the social value of live-work housing that mitigates the carbon footprint of traveling to one's job and reconnects the separate spheres of employment and residence. While composting toilets and photovoltaic panels, in and of themselves do not constitute an architectural of resilience, the design tools of proportion, rhythm, and scale applied

Figure 5.2
Luis Barragán
***Fuente de Los Amantes* in Mexico City (1966)**

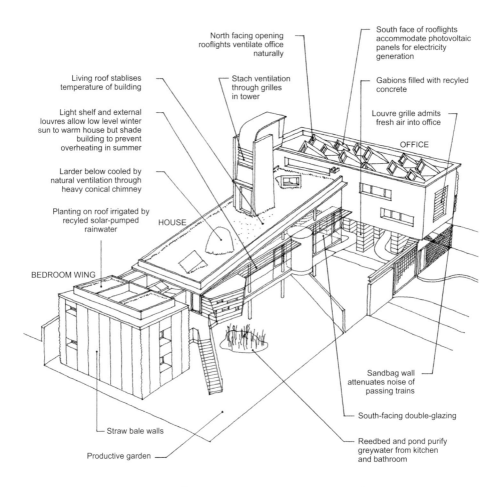

North facing opening rooflights ventilate office naturally

South face of rooflights accommodate photovoltaic panels for electricity generation

Living roof stablises temperature of building

Stach ventilation through grilles in tower

Gabions filled with recyled concrete

Light shelf and external louvres allow low level winter sun to warm house but shade building to prevent overheating in summer

Louvre grille admits fresh air into office

OFFICE

Larder below cooled by natural ventilation through heavy conical chimney

Planting on roof irrigated by recyled solar-pumped rainwater

HOUSE

BEDROOM WING

Sandbag wall attenuates noise of passing trains

South-facing double-glazing

Straw bale walls

Reedbed and pond purify greywater from kitchen and bathroom

Productive garden

Figure 5.3
Sarah Wigglesworth Architects, 9/10 Stock Orchard Street in Islington, north London (2001), courtesy of Sarah Wigglesworth Architects

to the stacking of cement sandbags, the silhouette of ventilation towers, and the L-shaped plan do. The Orchard Street house develops a critical position concerning the ways in which architectural experimentation with 360-degree life cycle strategies may deliver formal richness and complexity in its own right.

With the Ningbo Historic Museum in Ningbo, China (2007), Wang Shu of Amatuer Architecture offers an example of architectural bricolage that transforms historical debris into cultural tectonics. A building whose form was conceptually subtracted from a monolith, the Ningbo Museum references the surrounding mountains through metaphorical valleys, caves, sunken court-yards, and a lake. These artificial landscapes erode a prismatic volume whose form seems to have been sheared and sculpted by millennial forces. Wang explains this approach when explaining that, in traditional Chinese ink-and-wash landscape paintings, mountains represent "the place for Chinese people to find their lost and hidden culture."[8]

The museum's material surfaces resemble eroding cliffs of sedimentary rock in which momentary seismic upsurges have disturbed the repose of

horizontal stratification into irregular waves. Wang achieved stratigraphic textures through the regional construction technique of pouring reinforced concrete into bamboo formwork, a process that imprinted fossil-like channels of
bamboo in horizontal courses resembling eroded stone cliffs. He also used a
Chinese building technique called *wapan*, a sustainable vernacular construction
method that reincorporates debris left over from typhoons for rapidly building
walls during emergencies. Wang salvaged the remains of broken tile and brick
from the ruins of 30 villages the Chinese government razed in order to scrub
the site clean for a tabula rasa condition on which to build a new administration
center distributed along wide boulevards and empty plazas.

This erasure of thousands of years of inhabitation resulted in a zone local
inhabitants refer to as the "no memory area."[9] While Wang reinserted the
tectonic language of the lost villages into the museum, he also worked with
local craftsmen to preserve for posterity the important building technique of
wapan. In so doing he relinquished control over the surface pattern by inviting
craftsmen to randomly construct the aforementioned seismic upsurge of varie-
gated and unplanned strata. As Cole Roskam observes, this project oscillates
among China's complex dynamics between labor and development. Roskam
parses foreign responses to this project either as evidencing "architectural
dissidence" or as "a celebration of the [Chinese] government."[10] He positions
this architecture in a "rare domain that offers the potential for social critique
without directly opposing the ideological machinations of the state."[11] The
Ningbo museum participates in the architectural debate surrounding China's
struggle to reconcile ambitious modernization and expansion programs with

Figure 5.4
**Wang Shu
(Amatuer
Architecture),
Ningbo Historic
Museum in
Ningbo, China
(2005)**

the conflicting desire to preserve its national heritage. This project critiques China's demolition and construction campaigns through the incorporation of fragments of what had been destroyed in the walls of a building sponsored by the very same system that caused their destruction in the first place.

Institutional Critique

By examining the political resonances of the institutions sponsoring their shows, artists have developed useful models for reading architecture critically. Alex Bigman points out that "any critique of a museum exhibition must, to some degree, imply a coextensive critique of its architecture."[12] Art museums operate as particularly enticing sites for artists to critique their ambivalent relationship with institutions, offering spaces to display work that may convey strident socio-political commentary while simultaneously marketing it as neutral cultural capital. While proffering locations of artistic sovereignty, museums control who, what, and how art is displayed, rendering the work complicit with the generally conservative systems that sanction art's display. The museum's white walls may isolate a work of art from visual distractions while they also establish threshold conditions at entrances that filter artists and audiences alike. Institutional critique serves to reveal the latent structural power hidden among apparently benign systems such as the museum apparatus. Alexander Alberro explains that institutional critique was an artistic practice dating from the 1960s and 1970s that "confronted the institution of art with the claim that it was not sufficiently committed to, let alone realizing or fulfilling, the pursuit of publicness that had brought it into being in the first place."[13] As a critique of institutions, this art necessarily concerns the architecture of these spaces. When architecture performs as a hand-maiden to power structures, through invisible negotiations with financial institutions, property ownership, or permitting processes, institutional critique offers the potential to reveal these clandestine forces.

Hans Haacke's art installations offer overtly architectural forms of cultural contestation. Haacke worked for about 20 years producing "Shapolsky et al. Manhattan Real Estate Holdings, A Real Time Social System, as of May 1, 1971," acting in the capacity of a detective documenting and exposing the seedy real-estate activities of one of New York City's largest slumlords. His detailed maps, charts, photographs, and didactic panels presented information revealing heretofore hidden data linking numerous transactions and holdings to the Shapolsky family. Scheduled to exhibit this work in 1971 at New York's Solomon R. Guggenheim Museum, the museum's director Thomas Messer canceled "Hans Haacke: Systems" and ultimately fired the curator Edward Fry just six weeks before the opening. Messer offered the alibi that the proposed show "violates the supreme neutrality of the work of art and therefore no longer merits the protection of the museum."[14] As it turns out, Haacke's work implicated one of the museum's trustees whose business was tied to Shapolsky and the show was closed due to concerns over liability. But there is more to consider here. Haacke's project would have inserted the slum housing of Harlem into a high-art institution located on the Upper East Side of Manhattan, placing the urban outsider position of economic disparity in the heart of an elite, white museum enclave.

Where the Shapolsky project implicates museums as political spaces, Haacke's installation of "Germania" at the 1993 Venice Biennale actively engages the German Pavilion as a site for transforming architecture into an object of political critique. Originally built in 1909 according to Daniele Donghi's designs, in 1938 Ernst Haiger renovated the pavilion according to modifications Adolf Hitler proposed after his 1933 visit to Italy. Hitler requested that marble slabs replace the existing parquet floor—with stone symbolizing the duration of a regime destined to last centuries and to fall into beautiful ruins. Haacke implemented the latter scenario by smashing the marble paving into pieces and leaving the rubble on a floor across which visitors were allowed to walk, accompanied by amplified Hitler speeches.

Just five years after Haacke's dismissal from the Guggenheim show, Gordon Matta-Clark displayed "Window Blow-Out" for the 1976 exhibition "Idea as Model" at the Institute for Architecture and Urban Studies (IAUS), a forum for architectural discussion founded by Peter Eisenman. Clark was scheduled to display black-and-white photographs depicting the broken windows of vandalized modernist housing projects in the South Bronx. Instead, he borrowed an air gun from Dennis Oppenheim and shot out all the gallery windows from the inside while ranting: "These were the guys I studied with at Cornell, these were my teachers."[15] Matta-Clark earned a Bachelor of Architecture degree from Cornell University in 1968, which placed him in close contact with architects who participated in the IAUS and were in the show. It also placed him in the instrumental position of being an insider able to critique the underpinnings of architecture's role in structuring exclusionary cultural practices. As an

Figure 5.5
Hans Haacke, "GERMANIA," installation view at the German Pavilion, Venice Biennale (1993) from Bernd Heinz / vario images and Alamy

experiment with inclusionary practices, Matta-Clark helped found *Food* (1971), an artist-operated restaurant at the corner of Prince and Wooster Streets that was part event and part sustenance. The kitchen was exposed to the dining area, the meals conflated food with sculpture, the restaurant employed and fed struggling artists, and the entire process implicitly critiqued the concept of art as commercial consumption in the *terroir* of New York asphalt.

The mid-1970s in Manhattan was an era when the US economy was in decline and punk rock music was in ascent. Matta-Clark's actions were contemporaneous with bands such as the Ramones that expressed a form of artistic self-destruction that had yet to be completely absorbed into a system of mass consumption. Having grown up in New York's Greenwich Village, Matta-Clark was close to the disastrous planning policies of post-war modernism and community activist responses such as Jane Jacobs's *Death and Life of Great American Cities* (1961). Protests against Robert Moses's proposal to extend Fifth Avenue through Washington Square Park galvanized groups such as the Village Independent Democrats and the *Village Voice*. The counter-culture dynamics of the 1970s combined with Matta-Clark's Cornell training contributed to his concept of *Anarchitecture*, a position claiming that architecture acts as an environment with "metamorphic gaps and leftover spaces."[16]

The violence of "Window Blow-Out" parallels Matta-Clark's practice of cutting through abandoned buildings to reveal sectional views and interconnected perspectives, which in turn produced radically new kinds of architectural spaces. In *Splitting: Four Corners* (1974) he cut a house in half and tipped one side slightly upward to further expose the chasm. In *Conical Intersect* (1975) he cut a large cone-shaped hole through two seventeenth-century buildings about to be demolished to make room for the new Centre Georges Pompidou in Paris. With *Bingo* (1974), he moved the façade of a condemned house along the Love Canal in Niagara Falls to Artpark in Lewiston, New York. In so doing he drew attention to the plight of approximately 950 families evacuated from their homes due to Electrochemical's (Hooker Chemicals and Plastics) leaking of pesticides and dioxin into the groundwater. In producing highly influential spatial experiments, which destroyed, venerated, and generated architecture at the same time, Matta-Clark tore down walls between private spaces and public art, revealing spatial politics through a building's messy materiality.

The challenge for architects navigating spatial critique is to question institutional practices without directly undermining the institutional resources that make it possible to build in the first place. Architecture is the physical embodiment of the institution it houses. While it is possible to cut and probe its physiognomy or expose its apparatus of authoritative control, challenging the political affiliations of clients may result in no building at all. To navigate institutional critique from the position of architecture requires a deft hand at allowing socio-political forces to inflect built form while framing scenarios where the reverse may occur, where built form inflects socio-political forces.

Lina Bo Bardi's *Museu de Arte de São Paulo* (MASP or São Paulo Museum of Art, 1968) in Brazil exemplifies the potential for architecture to participate in

Figure 5.6
Gordon Matta-Clark, *Conical Intersect*, **Detail, 27–29 rue Beaubourg, Paris (1975), from Repro-photo: Philippe Migeat, Musee National d'Art Moderne, Centre Georges Pompidou, Paris, courtesy of Art Resource**

institutional critique. Bardi reconciles modern universalism with local culture in a building that affirms architecture's capacity to restructure society. Her grand gesture at MASP was to suspend the main galleries in the air from two 243-foot-long beams attached to four monumental columns, constructing the longest span in the world at the time. She levitated a glass box containing exhibition spaces in order to make room for a public plaza. This *belvedere* (a structure with a beautiful view) terrace inserted a semi-open public space in the center of the project, an urban room for the staging of social, cultural, and political events. Upon seeing MASP while riding along the Avenida Paulista, American avant-garde poet and musician John Cage asked the driver to stop the car, got out, walked from one side of the belvedere to the other, raised his arms, and exclaimed: "It is an architecture of freedom!"[17]

Bardi selected the belvedere site, designed the building, and established innovative programming to invigorate MASP from the perceived role that museums had become little more than tombs for dead art. Her substitution of white walls with glass and her inclusive approach to curatorial practices located diverse cultures front and center of the gallery space, all the while positioning art and architecture in direct proximity to the empowerment of subaltern groups. At MASP, as Esther da Costa Meyer observes, "transparency

Figure 5.7
**Lina Bo Bardi,
Museu de Arte
de São Paulo
(São Paulo
Museum of Art,
1968)**

has acquired a new, transitive meaning, a sort of reciprocity, more appropriate to a collective building than to a private one…, as the museum opens itself up to the scrutiny of the city and in turn becomes a huge belvedere."[18]

Bo Bardi's curating of the *pinacoteca*, the main gallery space, equally explored the power of transparency to transform. She suspended paintings between glass panels, attached to freestanding floor bases, with didactic material placed on the back side of artwork whose framed canvases often remained exposed as a reference to artist's easels. Both the building and the art it contains float in a transtemporal space of collage and superimposition, the first with works of art collapsing into each other in floating glass frames and the second with the city being squeezed into the space of a gallery through floating glass walls.

"Architecture and architectural freedom," as Bardi asserted "are above all a social issue that must be seen from inside a political structure, not from outside it."[19] In producing what she referred to as a "museum that belongs to the people," Bardi expanded the conventional limits of this institution's boundaries.[20] She curated the gallery through a lens that treated all cultural production equally, without hierarchical distinctions between style, chronology, or geography. In this way she vigorously integrated Brazil's regional art production with the art of Western Europe in a project that resisted modernity's colonizing impulses. For Gabriela Campagnol and Stephen Caffey, Bardi completely liberated "the museum from its function as a treasury-reliquary-mausoleum conceived to address, valorize and reassure cultural elites."[21] She rendered all works of art egalitarian by making them equally accessible to both the initiated and the uninitiated. Bardi experimented with what she referred to as *arquitetura pobre*, translated into English as *poor architecture* but referencing Italy's *arte povera* movement from the 1960s, exploring the potential of found objects and commonplace materials to critique the museum's capacity to separate life from art. According to her: "I feel that in the São Paulo Art Museum I eliminated all the cultural snobbery so dearly beloved by the intellectuals (and today's architects), opting for direct, raw solutions."[22] Rough concrete, exposed ducts, industrial rubber floors, and an elevator whose machinery is visible through its glass shaft establish the vocabulary for *arquitetura pobre*.

MASP articulates the premise that architecture is inherently political and unavoidably personal. Influenced by Paulo Freire's emancipatory teaching philosophy, MASP provides space for São Paulo's highly diverse population to participate in the city's main cultural institution. Freire was a Brazilian educator who developed the concept of "critical pedagogy" and published *The Pedagogy of the Oppressed* in 1970. Early in the 1960s, Brazil officially implemented his instructional programs as a way to educate and liberate the country's poor and illiterate citizens. Rather than conform to existing systems of oppression, Freire's process sought to empower students by confronting their stark reality from a position of criticality. He argued that "no pedagogy which is truly liberating can remain distant from the oppressed by treating them as unfortunates and by presenting for their emulation models from among the oppressors. The oppressed must be their own example in the struggle for their redemption."[23] MASP takes clues from Freire's pedagogy as a site holding the potential to democratize knowledge. Roger M. Buergel summarizes the institutional critique MASP makes explicit: "Learning from Bo Bardi today entails conceiving of institutions in terms of their self-perforation, their own undoing."[24]

Critical Architecture

In "Why Has Critique Run out of Steam? From Matters of Fact to Matters of Concern," Bruno Latour recognizes that "a certain form of critical spirit has sent us down the wrong path, encouraging us to fight the wrong enemies and, worst of all, to be considered as friends by the wrong sort of allies because of a little mistake in the definition of its main target."[25] While critical thinking entails most design processes, producing critical objects remains a challenge that leads architecture into the cul-de-sac of biting the hand that feeds it. Can architecture be critical and, if it can, is it then possible for built work to resist being assimilated by the very forces it purports to critique in the first place?

The "Deconstructivist Architecture" exhibition, which opened in 1988 at the Museum of Modern Art (MOMA) in New York, is an example of the commercial appropriation of critical work. Assembling seven emerging architectural luminaries under one roof—Frank Gehry, Daniel Libeskind, Rem Koolhaas, Peter Eisenman, Zaha Hadid, Bernard Tschumi, and the firm of Coop Himmelb(l)au— the show coined the neologism of *deconstructionism* by combining Jacques Derrida's philosophy of *deconstruction* and the Russian avant-garde art movement of *Constructivism*. The exhibition and its accompanying catalog branded a loose collection of practitioners into a coherent stylistic alliance accessible to MOMA's select museum-going public and to students of architecture interested in learning about the ways in which theoretical inquiry might inform design processes. Their press release for the show describes deconstructivist architecture as "obsessed with twisted shapes, warped planes, and folded lines" that "intentionally violate the pure forms of modern architecture."[26] The initial exhibition and its ensuing publications distilled complex and often antagonistic theoretical positions regarding the production of architecture into digestible formats for consumption by specifying its imitable stylistic attributes. Gordon Matta-Clark's work was absorbed into this process. The introductory essay to the exhibition catalogue published his *Splitting: Four Corners* as an antecedent to a movement characterized by architecture breaking apart from inside its own spatial logics, returning this work back to the rarefied architectural milieu Matta-Clark critiqued in the first place.

Digging into the ways architecture critiques its own disciplinary apparatus, Mark Jarzombek summarizes that in the heady era of the 1980s and 1990s critical practices largely confined themselves to "the history-theory wing of the discipline," when "having a critical practice meant that one formulated questions about architecture's theoricity (often with Martin Heidegger and Jacques Derrida in the background), or that one related architecture to issues of historicism, gender, culture and fashion."[27] Architectural theory from this time period introduced a spectrum of design perspectives across the divide between extrinsic and intrinsic criticality, between architecture that responds to socio-political pressures and one that strategically retreats into its own formal language as a path of resistance, between contingent and autonomous responses to cultural and political influences.

The latter approach drew its polemical stance from architecture's ability to eschew external cultural influences in favor of autonomous form making. This self-referential method of looking inside architectural design processes, in fact, emerged from outside of the discipline, from philosophy, art criticism, and critical theory. The argument for extracting politics from architecture drew from theories that advocated focusing on formal design processes as a way of remaining politically autonomous. The term "critical theory" emerged from the Frankfurt School, a group of thinkers in 1930s Germany including Theodor Adorno, Max Horkheimer, and Walter Benjamin, who developed the writings of Karl Marx and Sigmund Freud into tools for confronting invisible forces of repression, otherwise known as ideology. As Horkheimer stated, the goal was to "to liberate human beings from the circumstances that enslave them."[28] With regard to the question posed at the beginning of this chapter, of "what is being critiqued," it was the way in which ideology and the mechanisms of the culture industry fostered false consciousness. The critique concerned the ways in which totalitarian propaganda or capitalist merchandizing systems turned the liberating dimension of art against itself.

In *Aesthetic Theory* (1970) Adorno offered the strategy of *autonomy* as a way for art "to turn critically against itself and break through its illusory imprisonment."[29] He posited the two criteria of an artwork either to act as an autonomous object or to respond to social phenomena. As autonomous art turns its back on the world, it is then able to withdraw into the work itself, focusing on its integral organization. Architecture relies on enough self-absorption and formal involution to position autonomy as part of its critical modality. Between autonomous architecture that looks internally for its essential structure and contingent architecture that looks externally for its methodical impetus, two important directions emerge regarding architecture's critical thrust. If contingency critiques the world but hazards complicity, autonomy's retreat into the realm of pure form risks irrelevancy.

Joseph Godlewski, who develops the distinction between these terms, explains that artistic autonomy was "characterized by a critical disciplinary stance, tended to be academic, and had an affinity for theory."[30] Conversely, he writes, contingency was inter- or extra-disciplinary, "dealt with the 'real' world, and was aligned with practice."[31] He contends that the autonomous direction of critical architecture "slowly transmogrified into an elitist, self-interested (and often self-referential) formalist discourse hell-bent on preserving 'the discipline.'"[32] In contrast, K. Michael Hays argues that strategies for resistance based on contingency potentially reduce architecture to "an epiphenomenon, dependent on socioeconomic, political, and technological processes for its various states and transformations."[33]

This all goes to distinguish between a binary of contingent architecture, where buildings emerge in response to context and culture, and of autonomous architecture, where buildings derive from self-referential form generation. When architecture is a mere medium through which a cultural imaginary flows, it potentially becomes an unwitting accomplice to existing power structures. In this case, resistance is futile. And yet, when architecture withdraws into a set of autonomous operations accountable only to its internal logic, the resulting apolitical form paradoxically renders it into a marketable commodity. In this case too, resistance is futile. When expressed as an either/or choice between context and form neither position may offer a satisfying strategy for resistance. However, they may be approached across a path that navigates the outer limits of contingency and autonomy and resistance is located in an architecture that derives from the logic of its own formal system, but is precisely inscribed within its context.

The buildings in this publication mediate critical positions between autonomous form and contextual contingency to the extent that they are legible and offer a high degree of interpretive potential. As previously mentioned, every built addition to a context, regardless of whether or not it simply reproduces neighboring styles verbatim or radically opposes them, critiques its site by transforming it. Even a building made entirely of reflective glass critiques its environment by mirroring it from some views and erasing it from others. Such is the case with Ludwig Mies van der Rohe's 1921 unbuilt design for the Friedrichstrasse Skyscraper competition project in Berlin. Hays describes this project as a "surface qualified no longer by patterns of shadow on an opaque material but by the reflections and refractions of light by glass."[34] Mies inserted a drawing of this daring new tower into a photograph of an historical context featuring eclectic buildings, producing a radical contrast with the proposed sparkling architecture that scrapes the sky. Mies's montage depicts an abstract shard of glass in a critical relationship with the existing city by means of a reflective surface that mirrors, distorts, and re-forms the urban context. Mies's montage demonstrates that a confrontation between existing and new buildings can be understood as a position of criticality, regardless of whether or not the designer intended for the project to ask a critical question. Hays threads the needle of critical architecture when placing Mies's work in the center of these tensions. He argues that Mies's architecture is critical insofar

Figure 5.8
Ludwig Mies van der Rohe, Friedrichstrasse Skyscraper Project, entry in the Friedrichstrasse skyscraper competition (Berlin, 1921), courtesy of the Museum of Modern Art

as it resists "the self-confirming, conciliatory operations of a dominant culture" and yet remains "irreducible to a purely formal structure disengaged from the contingencies of place and time."[35]

Hays writes about Mies's German Pavilion constructed for the 1929 International Exposition in Barcelona, Spain: "a participant in the world and yet disjunctive with it, the Barcelona Pavilion tears a cleft in the continuous surface of reality."[36] It operates in oscillation between the construction of space and site, developing a critical resistance to both politics and formalism within this fissure. As an example of autonomous architecture, the building was designed to act as a *repräsentationspavillon*, a representational pavilion that lacked any substantive program aside from serving as a receiving room for the King and Queen of Spain to sign a "Golden Book" and officially open the exposition. As an ostensibly functionless form, the pavilion models the autonomy of self-referential generative operations through its floating planes and projecting lines.

Josep Quetglas identifies the contingent dimension of this project in a row of eight, freestanding Ionic columns, found in period photos, that describe the pavilion as critical of and resonant with its immediate surroundings. In choosing the site himself, Mies also claimed the columns located in parallel alignment to the front of his building as part of his design. The appropriation of the classical columns parallels his having located Georg Kolbe's statue of *Alba* (*Dawn* or *Sunrise*) in the pavilion's reflecting pool, a reference to the statue of Athena standing inside the Parthenon's cella. For Quetglas, who interprets the pavilion as a modern incarnation of a Doric temple: "To disregard the row of columns because it is not Mies's work would be tantamount to disregarding Kolbe's statue."[37] Both reference the classical precedents infusing this project with relational and with abstract formal principles.

Figure 5.9 Ludwig Mies van der Rohe German Pavilion (Barcelona Pavilion) constructed for the 1929 International Exposition in Barcelona, Spain, courtesy of the Museum of Modern Art

Mies conceptually redistributed the eight freestanding Ionic columns from the existing colonnade into the eight cruciform columns holding up his temple. *Alba* complements the tactile and colorful Onyx Dore marble wall whose quarried dimensions generated the building's proportional system. She also marks a moment of architectural self-critique wherein the atavistic figure of a dancing maenad stains the relentlessly abstract space with mythological forces looking backward to architecture's origins, across the street to the colonnade, and inward to the metamorphosis of Greek classicism into the language of steel.

George Dodds offers a lucid summary of the way in which the Barcelona Pavilion evinces architectural criticality by analyzing readings of it as both contingent and autonomous. Dodds distills the numerous interpretations of this project to arguments that consider the pavilion as an autonomous object that could be located anywhere and those that consider it to be a highly site-specific project. "Although it was the vanguard of what Hitchcock and Johnson called the International Style," he continues, "it is also characterized as a critique of the foundations upon which that movement was based."[38] Wolf Tegethoff similarly sees the pavilion as a propyleum to the Spanish Village above, wherein existing steps leading up the Montjuïc hillside, the axis of the fairgrounds, and the existing road operated as important contingencies.

The Barcelona Pavilion was conceived and constructed in under a year, dismantled a year after its construction, and eventually reconstructed in 1986,

Figure 5.10
Ludwig Mies van der Rohe German Pavilion (Barcelona Pavilion) constructed for the 1929 International Exposition in Barcelona, Spain with Georg Kolbe's statue Alba ("Dawn"), photograph by David Wayne Hall

years after Mies's death in 1969. It therefore might not appear to be a good candidate for the idea of slow architecture proffered at the beginning of this chapter. But Mies wrote: "Architecture depends on its time. It is the crystallization of its inner structure, the slow unfolding of its form."[39] The pavilion's temporal trajectory transcends its short life and posthumous resurrection. Rather, it stretches back to the enduring marbles Mies selected as building materials, the Greek temples that provided classical precedents, the Egyptian and Roman folding stools that formed models for the Barcelona chair, his training as the son of a stonemason, and his apprenticeship with Peter Behrens, while it projects forward into its site, new building technologies, and timeless minimalism. Indeed, achieving such minimalism is a slow process. As Blaise Pascal wrote: "I would have written a shorter letter, but I did not have the time."[40]

Notes

1   Bruno Latour, "Why Has Critique Run Out of Steam? From Matters of Fact to Matters of Concern" *Critical Inquiry 30*, no. 2 (Winter 2004), p. 231.

2   http://www.slowfood.com/about-us/our-history.

3   https://lebbeuswoods.wordpress.com/2009/01/07/slow-manifesto.

4   Jane Rendell, "Critical Spatial Practice," http://www.janerendell.co.uk/wp-content/uploads/2009/06/critical-spatial-practice.pdf.

5   Cf. Alexander Tzonis and Liane Lefaivre "The Grid and the Pathway: An Introduction to the Work of Dimitris and Suzana Antonakakis," in *Architecture in Greece* (Athens, 1981).

6   Kenneth Frampton, "Towards a Critical Regionalism: Six Points for an Architecture of Resistance," in *The Anti-aesthetic: Essays on Postmodern Culture*, ed. Hal Foster (Port Townsend: Bay Press, 1983), p. 26.

7   Emilio Ambasz, *The Architecture of Luis Barragàn* (New York: Museum of Modern Art, 1976), p. 9.

8   Till Wöhler, "Ningbo Museum by Pritzker Prize Winner Wang Shu," *Architectural Review*, March 1, 2010, https://www.architectural-review.com/buildings/ningbo-museum-by-pritzker-prize-winner-wang-shu/5218020.article.

9   Brendan McGetrick, "Ningbo History Museum" *Domus* 922/February 2009, https://www.domusweb.it/en/from-the-archive/2012/03/03/ningbo-history-museum.html.

10 Cole Roskam, "Structures of Everyday Life," *Artforum International*, November 2013, https://www.questia.com/read/1G1-349225154/structures-of-everyday-life.

11 Ibid.

12 http://www.artpractical.com/feature/architecture_and_the_museum.

13 Alexander Alberro, "Institutions, Critique, and Institutional Critique," in *Institutional Critique: An Anthology of Artists' Writings* (Cambridge, MA: MIT Press, 2009), p. 3.

14 http://ewaneumann.com/websites/haacke/shapolsky.html.

15 Gordon Matta-Clark, "Window Blow-Out," 1976, quoted in Pamela M. Lee, *Object to Be Destroyed: The Work of Gordon Matta-Clark* (Cambridge, MA: MIT Press, 2001), p. 116.

16 Gordon Matta-Clark, "Interview with Avalance (1974)," in *Land and Environmental Art*, ed. Jeffrey Kastner (New York: Phaidon, 2010), p. 273.

17 Gabriela Campagnol and Stephen Caffey, "Pepper the Walls with Bullets: Lina Bo Sardi's Museu Arte de Sao Paulo," Proceedings of the 2010 Creating Making Forum (University of Oklahoma College of Architecture / Division of Architecture), p. 145.

18 Esther da Costa Meyer, "After the Flood," *Harvard Design Magazine No. 16 / HARDSoft CoolWARM… Gender in Design*, http://www.harvarddesignmagazine. org/issues/16/after-the-flood.

19 As cited by Barry Bergdoll, "Foreword," in *Lina Bo Bardi* (New Haven: Yale University Press, 2013), p. ix.

20 Campagnol and Caffey, "Pepper the Walls with Bullets," p. 146.

21 Ibid, p. 148.

22 Da Costa Meyer, "After the Flood."

23 P. Freire, *Pedagogy of the Oppressed*, trans. Myra Bergman Ramos (New York: Continuum, 1970), p. 54.

24 Roger M. Buergel, "'This Exhibition Is an Accusation': The Grammar of Display" *Afterall 26* (Spring 2011), http://www.afterall.org/journal/issue.26/this-exhibition-is-an-accusation-the-grammar-of-display-according-to-lina-bo-bardi.

25 Latour, "Why Has Critique Run Out of Steam?", p. 231.

26 https://www.moma.org/docs/press_archives/6965/releases/MOMA_1991_0094_67-4.pdf?2010.

27 http://www.tandfonline.com/doi/abs/10.1080/13264820209478451?journalCode=ratr20.

28 Max Horkheimer, *Critical Theory Selected Essays* (New York: Continuum, 1982), p. 244.

29 Theodor Adorno, *Aesthetic Theory*, eds. Gretel Adorno and Rolf Tierfermann, trans. Robert Hullot-Kenter (London: Bloomsbury, 1997), p. 160.

30 Joseph Godlewski, "The Absurd Alibi" *The Plan Journal 7–14* (2016), p. 8.

31 Ibid.

32 Ibid., p. 11.

33 K. Michael Hays, "Critical Architecture: Between Culture and Form" *Perspecta*, vol. 21 (Cambridge, MA: MIT Press, 1984), p. 16.

34 Ibid., p. 19.

35 Ibid., p. 15.

36 Ibid., p. 25.

37 Josep Quetglas, *Fear of Glass: Mies van der Rohe's Pavilion in Barcelona*, trans. John Stone and Rosa Roig (Basel: Birkhäuser, 2001), p. 41.

38 George Dodds, "The Body in Pieces: Desiring the Barcelona Pavilion" *Anthropology and Aesthetics 39* (Spring, 2001), p. 172.

39 Ludwig Mies van der Rohe, "Technology and Architecture" (1950), in *Programs and Manifestoes on 20th-Century Architecture*, ed. Ulrich Conrads, trans. Michael Bullock (London: Lund Humphries, 1970), p. 154.

40 Blaise Pascal, *Provincial Letters: Letter XVI* (4 December 1656).

Introduction to Part 3
Inside-Out Architecture

I like to find something in between. Not only nature and architecture but also inside and outside. Every kind of definition has an in-between space. Especially if the definitions are two opposites, then the in-between space is more rich.[1]

—Sou Fujimoto

In "Quasi-infinities and the Waning of Space" (1966) Robert Smithson compares Frank Lloyd Wright's Guggenheim Museum to the human body: "No building is more organic than this inverse digestive tract. The ambulatories are metaphorical intestines. It is a concrete stomach."[2] Had it been painted pink, as one of Wright's renderings of this suggests, then this interpretation would resonate as even more visceral. Vitruvius's analogy between a well-built male body and architectural proportions, and Smithson's comparison of the Guggenheim Museum's continuous spiral circulation ramp and a gastrointestinal organ evince just two of numerous comparisons possible between bodies and buildings. To the extent that bones may act as structure, respiratory systems as ventilation, nervous systems as electricity, digestive systems as plumbing, pulmonary systems as hearth, skin as enclosure, and so on, building systems may be broken down into analogous physiognomic categories. The palpable relationship between buildings and bodies describes architecture's interior as filled with organs and living systems that pulse and vibrate dynamically. The shifting location of a structural system either as an exoskeleton or an endoskeleton introduces a biomorphic analogy that includes animals, insects, and plants among its potential models. Reading architecture from the inside out requires turning, rotating, and reversing normative interpretive models of architecture as solid objects through a dynamic process of vivisection that cuts through static spaces to reveal the living networks pulsing within.

As architecture and engineering become increasingly sophisticated in constructing hermetically sealed environments to compensate for our postlapsarian status outside of the Garden of Eden, the garden and its inhabitants become engineered. Instead of our inhabiting controlled environments, controlled substances may inhabit us. Hans Hollein's *Non-physical Environment (Architekturpille)* (1967) appears as a psychoactive pill that alludes to the insertion of exterior atmospheres into the deepest interior space of our consciousness. Between cyclopean manifestations of mechanical systems and microscopic performances of thermodynamic materials, this section explores architecture's interior purchase through environmental controls, material performances, and routine inhabitation.

To locate the form inside of performance offers a more pliable and specific way to read a building than Louis Sullivan's indelible slogan of form-follows-function. Insofar as a building's primary function could range from expressing its symbolic value to lowering its carbon footprint, or both simultaneously, the phrase operates as a slippery evaluative criterion leading to discordant rebuttals such as form follows folly, form follows finance, form follows fancy, or even form follows form.

Shaping interior space is a primary objective of architecture designed from the inside out. The 19th-century German art historian August Schmarsow inaugurated approaching architecture primarily as a spatial art. As Schmarsow wrote, "Our sense of space and spatial imagination press toward spatial creation; they seek their satisfaction in art. We call this art architecture; in plain words, it is the creatress of space."[3] In *Architecture as Space: How to Look at Architecture* (1957), Bruno Zevi located this concept squarely in the 20th century, offering that "the façade and walls of a house, church, or palace, no matter how beautiful they may be, are only the container, the box formed by the walls, the content is the internal space."[4]

The inhabitant's movements, rituals, and diurnal and nocturnal activities also shape interior spaces in response to patterns of use. Reading from the inside focuses on building systems, artificial environments, and human inhabitation as they govern exterior form and as they construct a world of their own, unencumbered by exterior exigency. The three chapters that follow, "Atmosphere," "Tectonics," and "Inhabitation," explore the inflection of space through mechanical systems, building materials, and human activity.

Figure P3.1
Hans Hollein,
Non-physical
Environment
(Architek-
***turpille)* (1967),**
photograph by
Roland Krauss,
© Privat
Archive Hollein

Notes

1   https://www.dezeen.com/2013/10/28/movie-sou-fujimoto-sctructures-between-nature-architecture. Ben Hobson, October 28, 2013.

2   Robert Smithson, "Quasi-infinities and the Waning of Space" (1966), in *Robert Smithson: The Collected Writings*, ed. Jack Flam (Berkeley: University of California Press, 1996), p. 35.

3   As cited by Harry Francis Mallgrave, *Modern Architectural Theory: A Historical Survey, 1673–1968* (Cambridge: Cambridge University Press, 2005), note 22, p. 198.

4   Bruno Zevi *Architecture as Space: How to Look at Architecture*, ed. Joseph A. Barry, trans. Milton Gendel (New York: Da Capo Press, 1993), p. 24.

Chapter 6

Atmosphere

Good architecture is associated with good weather.[1]

—*Mark Wigley*

In 1817 the English ornithologist, malacologist, conchologist, entomologist, and artist William Swainson discovered the *Cattleya labiate* or "corsage orchid" (also known as the *Crimson Cattleya* or *Ruby-lipped Cattleya*) growing wild in the Brazilian state of Pernambuco. He sent a specimen to the horticulturalist William Cattley, from which the flower finds its eponymous name, who nurtured its tendrils into blossoms. This discovery stimulated cross-fertilization between botany and the arts, producing a world in which the hybridization of orchids would come to symbolize nineteenth-century architectural aesthetics through the technology of hothouses. In 1822 Charles Darwin predicted that certain moths pollinize an epiphytic orchid from Madagascar, named Darwin's orchid (a.k.a. Christmas orchid or Star of Bethlehem orchid). In 1881 Joris-Karl Huysmans characterized the decadent aesthete Jean des Esseintes in *À rebours* (*Against Nature* or *Against the Grain*) through an adulation of orchids: "so delicate and charming, at once cold and palpitating, exotic flowers exiled in the heated glass palaces of Paris…"[2] From J. J. Grandville's *Les Fleurs Animées* to Charles Baudelaire's *Fleurs du mal*, from *Flowers Personified* to *Flowers of Evil*, exotic plants such as the orchid required artificial environments for their survival.

The German biologist Ernst Haeckel coined the term *ecology* to describe the relationship between an organism and its environment, developing a concept that eventually would come to influence architectural thinking about building performances. Haeckel discovered and documented thousands of new species, publishing 100 lithographs of them in *Kunstformen der Natur* (*Art Forms in Nature*, 1904)—including *Orchidae* (orchids), *Desmonema annasethe* (jellyfish), *Actiniae* (sea anemone), and *Radiolaria* (minute, marine protozoa). His research provided models for Art Nouveau architecture's zoomorphic forms. The gateway to the *Paris Exposition Universelle* (1900) that René Binet designed, for example, closely resembles Haeckel's illustration of coral structures. Of particular importance for architecture were Haeckel's finely detailed drawings of Radiolaria, forms of plankton that display crystalline shapes with

Figure 6.1
J. J. Grandville,
"Aubépine"
(Hawthorn
Flower), from
*Les Fleurs
Animées
(Flowers
Personified,
1847)*

curvilinear contours and whose complex exoskeletons have inspired research into bio-constructed buildings.

Hothouses

Although 19th-century architects had yet to develop the inhabitable plastic bubbles or pneumatic architecture of today, they did control atmospheres within sealed envelopes. The Victorian penchant for collecting, importing, and cultivating exotic butterflies, birds, horticulture, and humans relied on colonizing new worlds such as Haeckel's Mediterranean sea and Swainson's Pernambuco forest. The age of discovery filled encyclopedias, exhibition halls, conservatories, museums, and libraries with specimens brought back from the interiors of Africa, Asia, and South America. The hothouses necessary to support the artificial paradises needed to grow exotic species like the *Cattleya labiate* offered architects a design opportunity to manipulate interior atmospheres.

Figure 6.2
**Ernst Haeckel,
Radiolarians,**
*Kunstformen
der Natur
(Art Forms of
Nature,* **1904)**

Charles Fowler's design for the great conservatory at Syon House marks a significant English contribution to the development of greenhouses. Dating from 1830 and designed to house the Duke of Northumberland's tropical plants, it features a remarkable 38-foot-diameter-wide dome of glass made of panes held together by gunmetal frames to produce a transparent, curvilinear surface that shimmers in the sun like a soap bubble. As head gardener at the Chatsworth estate, Joseph Paxton furthered Fowler's work in the design and environmental control of the greenhouses he built for the Duke of Devonshire's tropical plants.

Figure 6.3
René Binet,
Triumphal
Gateway,
*Exposition
Universelle,*
Paris (1900)

A prized species in this collection was the *Victoria amazonica* (a.k.a. *Victoria regia*), a giant water lily found in the Amazon River that could grow to a diameter of four and a half feet. The internal ribs forming the plant's leaf structure offered a model for Paxton's great "stove" or conservatory, a large greenhouse enclosed by a transparent system of ridge-and-furrow glass, faceted to capture sunlight and drain water off of the surfaces. In order to produce an artificial environment that simulated warm tropical climates, he connected underground boilers to seven miles of water pipes that heated the space during winter. This structure catalyzed the transformation of environmental enclosures leading from small orangeries, where fruit trees were stored for the winter, to colossal curvilinear buildings entirely clad in glass.

In order to complete the design and construction of an enormous building in less than eight months for London's 1851 Great Exhibition of the Works of Industry of All Nations, Paxton turned to the Chatsworth conservatory as a model for a structure that came to be known as the Crystal Palace. The final result of Paxton's design consisted of two floors of exhibition spaces flanking a three-story-tall atrium, entirely made of glass and cast-iron. The building was strategically sited in Hyde Park so that a 168-foot-tall barrel vault intersected the main atrium in order to soar above an existing elm tree. The Great Exhibition attracted participants from all over the world to display national products of culture and industry that were collected under one roof covering a footprint of over 770,000 square feet, making it the largest cast-iron and plate-glass building in the world at the time.

Paxton met the impossibly tight deadline by deploying assembly line construction processes, using prefabricated modular materials, and inventing new

Figure 6.4
Charles Fowler, the Great Conservatory at Syon House in west London (1827)

Figure 6.5
Joseph Paxton, the Crystal Palace in London for the Great Exhibition of 1851

building technologies. The Crystal Palace marks a watershed in architecture's inexorable move toward the axiom of environmental performance becoming a dominant paradigm and for the construction of a building entirely clad in the transcendent building material of glass. Paxton's incipient assembly line construction techniques transformed architecture into an enclosure composed primarily of glass "skin" and iron "bones." Its existence opened the door for Paul Sheerbart to hypothesize in 1914 that if we wish to raise our culture to a higher level, we are forced to transform our world "through the introduction of glass architecture that lets the sunlight and the light of the moon and stars into our rooms not merely through a few windows."[3] Its sparkling glass vaults promulgated the metaphor of truth in transparency and the metaphysical properties of crystalline solids to which modern architecture would subscribe. Observing the significance of glass and crystal to the 19th-century architec-tural imaginary, Isobel Armstrong explains that crystal returns architecture to a world of geology, vapor, minerals, and subterranean charms. It demands to be seen as much as seen through. For Armstrong, "the 'tremulous scintillations' of crystal facets, glass against glass, declare crystal's apparent nearness to the natural world of cave and grotto."[4] As she posits, glass is a congealed liquid with its own micro-atmosphere that may approximate the magical qualities of crystal, a material that "constitutes a living representation of the faceted multiplicity of convergent times and spaces."[5]

From the thousands of small iron and glass building components to interior temperatures to the items on display or the number of daily visitors, the Crystal Palace demonstrates reading architecture through the calculus of numbers. Paxton's prefabricated building systems resulted in 1,000,000 square feet of interior space, 900,000 square feet of glass, 3800 tons of cast-iron, 700 tons of wrought iron, and finished dimensions of 1851 feet long by 128 feet high. To facilitate on-site production methods, Paxton attached construction trolleys to cast-iron rails and used steam engines to drive the machinery. Other innovative processes of mass production transformed individual plate glass panes into repetitive units, the combination of which allowed for infinitely expandable ridge and furrow surfaces that doubled as rain channels. It hosted six million people coming to view 14,000 exhibits of 100,000 objects displaying machines such as steam hammers, Bessemer pumps, and boilers alongside fine silks, satins, rare wood, suits of armor, perfumes, tobaccos, exotic foods, and orien-tal carpets. It also manifested the sway of world colonization when displaying tableaux such as Ethiopian "Serenaders" or a "Nubian Court" as part of the exhibition.

Without proper ventilation and shading, glass conservatories became suffocating and sweltering environments. For a building that could accommo-date as many as 90,000 visitors per day, each of whom would have radiated body heat in addition to the sun's warming rays, interior temperatures reached as high as 97°F. Paxton strove to mitigate solar heat gain by providing oper-able louvers, canvas shades, and hand-operated fans blowing across fabric saturated with water. Regular monitoring of interior temperatures resulted in a systematic post-occupancy report compiled by the Commissioners of the Great Exhibition that critically and scientifically evaluated the building's environmental performance. Despite the inadequacy of Paxton's solutions to deliver a perfectly controlled environment, the Crystal Palace established an important precedent for sealing interior spaces with atmospheres indifferent to exterior climates. In what will emerge as part of modern architecture's exploration of natural daylight and its canon of hygiene, as Henrik Schoenefeldt observes, "Paxton's proposals resonated with concerns about atmospheric pollution, [and] insufficient ventilation."[6]

By the middle of the 19th century, numerous European cities had been transformed into a labyrinthine network of public arcades piercing deeply into the interior of city blocks with iron and glass roof systems that provided natural light to illuminate the luxury goods displayed in store windows below. As cultural critic Walter Benjamin argued in his *Passagenwerk* (*Arcades Project*, 1927–1940), the arcades defined the ur-phenomena of modernism with skylights illuminating a material history of architecture and of bourgeois culture. While a number of these arcades still remain in cities such as Paris, London, and Milan, the emergence of large department stores—where diverse products of mass production could be purchased together in one location—helped to promote the demise of the specialty shop.

The process of pouring of liquid metal into molds of just about any shape allowed cast-iron architecture to seamlessly bind ornament and structure, producing a new stylistic species known as Art Nouveau, which exhibited sinuous curvilinear forms referencing Haeckel's illustrations of flowers and insects. Benjamin captured the spirit of this work when describing Art Nouveau as a line-language that expresses "the flower as the symbol of naked, vegetal nature confronting a technically armed environment."[7] The cast-iron structures Hector Guimard designed as entrances to Paris's Métro stations appear to metamorphose into the shapes of orchid stamens, dragonfly wings, and praying mantis eyes that blur into each other as a lyrical ornamental program transmuting architecture into nature. Exotic plant specimens in glass conservatories became flowers grown from out of cast-iron, insofar as Art Nouveau described a microscopic architectural interior found in the cross-section of iron-carbon alloys that melt into prescribed shapes when exposed to high temperatures.

The 19th century's international expositions, arcades, and department stores constitute building types that emerged in order to display consumer goods, offering generic components for the design of contemporary regional shopping centers with open plans covered by glass atria that can be extruded indefinitely in any direction to produce an infinitely long building that may grow over time. Peter Sloterdijk considers the Crystal Palace to be the first "hyper-interior that offers a perfect expression of the spatial idea of psychedelic Capitalism."[8] He sees these self-contained spaces as prototypes for later theme-park interiors and event architectures that abolish any contact with of the outside world. Inventions as prosaic as heating, ventilating, and air conditioning systems (HVAC) allowed for the construction of the hermetically

Figure 6.6
**Hector
Guimard,
entrance to the
Père Lachaise
Métro station
in Paris (1903)**

sealed spaces Sloterdijk interprets as both literal and metaphorical spheres and bubbles.

It comes as little surprise then, given architecture's ability to produce artificial weather systems inside buildings, that the first regional shopping mall in the United States opened in Edina, Minnesota, a part of the country with an extreme temperature differential between hot summers and cold winters. The key to the success of Victor Gruen's Southdale Center (1956) was air conditioning. This technology allowed consumers to shop in comfort 12 months out of the year in a space *Time* magazine called a "pleasure-dome-with-parking."[9] Having emigrated from Vienna to Los Angeles, Gruen's vision for Southdale derived from European models of public space and urban design. The mall was planned to form part of a neighborhood center surrounded by apartment buildings, houses, schools, a medical facility, a park, and a lake. While this larger vision was destined to remain on paper, the mall itself initiated a formula for architecture to manufacture environments and experiences whose performances are evaluated more in the dollars and cents people spend inside than on their actual comfort or wellbeing. As the shopping mall evolved into a perfect machine for consumption, it was also acting as a machine of production, fostering new desires along with the spaces and products accompanying them.

Along with air conditioning, early shopping malls relied on skylights, escalators, indoor planting, simulated streets, convenient parking, and a comforting suburban location. Cagier strategies to capture consumer dollars describe how this building type performs as a perfect desiring machine, offering glimpses into the way in which corporations read architecture as an instrument of market capital. Recessed skylights reduce the glare on windows displaying goods. Transparent handrails allow for the continuous viewing of potential destinations. Fixed food court seats prevent lingering. Storefronts without walls invite consumers to enter without having to open

a door. Escalators located at each end of the mall ensure that consumers walk the entire circuit. As Margaret Crawford observes: "In the film *Dawn of the Dead*, both zombies and their victims are drawn to the mall, strolling the aisles in numb fascination, with fixed stares that make it difficult to tell the shoppers from the living dead."[10] Crawford introduced the technical term "Gruen Transfer" to designate "the moment when a 'destination buyer,' with a specific purchase in mind, is transformed into an impulse shopper, a crucial point immediately visible in the shift from a determined stride to an erratic and meandering gait."[11]

Figure 6.7
Victor Gruen,
Southdale
Center in Edina,
Minnesota
(1956), courtesy
of Gruen
Associates

The shopping mall has grown up and out since Southgate, with projects such as Rick Caruso's Americana in Glendale, California taking the lid off the atrium and opening the interior to the sky. While subtly sealing the mall's edges with atmospheric music, Caruso reconciles consumer nostalgia for small-town band shell parks with the polish of old world glamour in a project replete with its own trolley, pseudo-Eiffel Tower, dancing fountain, and residences. Staking the claim that "shopping is arguably the last remaining form of public activity," Rem Koolhaas collaborated with students and faculty from Harvard University's Graduate School of Design (GSD) to produce an 800-page tome entitled *Project on the City II: The Harvard Guide to Shopping* (2001).[12] A veritable treasure trove of shopping architecture, the publication considers subject matter as diverse as Trajan's Market in Rome (ca. 100–110 CE), the Royal Isfahan Bazaar (1585), Disneyworld, airport malls, escalators, air conditioning, and bar codes—revealing predatory strategies, such as customer tracking devices, that heighten consumer demand. As this publication demonstrates, the architecture of shopping maintains a rich formal history. It also identifies the mall's ability to affect behavior through mechanical systems that merits attention for revealing design's power to influence both human and building performances.

Conduit

Despite the overwhelmingly transformative impact of HVAC systems on modifying interior environments, their general role has been to remain closeted and silent servants to larger inhabitable spaces. Louis Kahn distinguished between served and servant spaces, designing buildings that celebrate mechanical systems as integral and even inhabitable parts of architecture. His work probes what it might mean to project oneself deeply inside of a building, in the sense of inhabiting plenums and systems. Scottish castles featuring auxiliary spaces nestled into thick exterior walls formed sources of inspiration for his exploration of inhabitable spatial pockets or *poché*. The 12th-century French use of *poché* translates directly as *purse* and *pocket*, but also referenced a poached egg because the yolk forms a pocket inside the white. These spatial pockets found their way into the language of architectural pedagogy as the name for the process of cross-hatching or filling in the thickness of walls on drawings to make them read more clearly (as introduced in Chapter 3). *Poché* also constitutes the inside of walls that may either be solid or inhabitable. The wall's thickness may or may not house more deeply interiorized spaces such as mechanical systems, water closets, stairways, servant's spaces, or secret rooms.

Kahn's design of the Richards Medical Research Laboratories at the University of Pennsylvania (1960) collects pipes and ducts in smaller servant spaces dedicated to supporting the larger served spaces of the research laboratories. Kahn located laboratories in three towers linked to a fourth central service tower containing mechanical systems, research animals, stairs, and elevators. Each laboratory also contains its own stairway and exhaust system located in spaces articulated as smaller brick towers pulled to the outside of the building, expressing their performative identity as auxiliary units serving the larger research space. Kahn's organizational system made it so that the air a person inhaled never came into contact with the air that was exhausted from these experimental laboratories.

In comparison with the Alfred Newton Richards Medical Research Laboratories, at the Jonas Salk Institute for Biological Studies located in La Jolla, California (1965), Kahn rotated the mechanical systems from vertical shafts of space into a horizontal plenum, the first building to use interstitial space as an integral part of the HVAC design. In order to make room for the inhabitation of service spaces necessary for operating the laboratory's heating and ventilating systems, Kahn alternated every other floor of this six-story building with a mechanical plenum whose 100-foot Vierendeel truss provides a column-free span across the building's width. He isolated the laboratories from individual study spaces by attaching them to the building's exterior, providing windows to view the Pacific Ocean.

Kahn's commitment to seeking expressive poetry in prosaic technologies inspired Reyner Banham to praise him, in *The Architecture of the Well-Tempered Environment* (1969), for giving "monumental external bulk to the accommodations for mechanical services."[13] Concomitantly, Banham commended Frank Lloyd Wright's Larkin Building in Buffalo, New York (1904) for its innovative

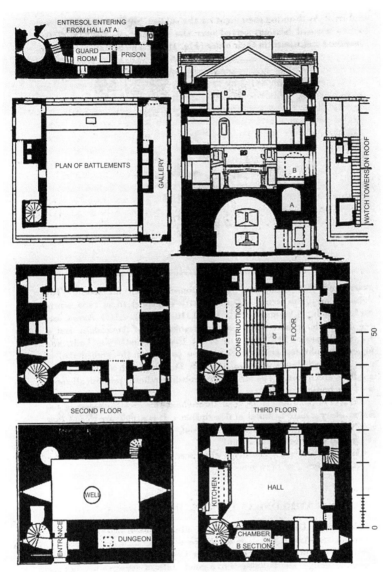

Figure 6.8
**Comlongen
Castle,
Dumphriesshire
Plan featuring
auxiliary
spaces, from
Vincent Scully,
Louis I. Kahn
(New York:
Braziller, 1962),
ill. #116**

external expression of mechanical services and for establishing an important precedent for Kahn's research: "Probably the first building designed to accommodate all the paraphernalia associated with modern air conditioning."[14] The Larkin Building was a simple rectangle containing five stories of office space surrounding an atrium with a glazed roof. Ducts running from basement to roof located inside of shafts adjacent to staircases and expressed on the building's exterior provided environmental conditioning. Wright described the Larkin Building "as a simple cliff of brick hermetically sealed."[15]

Figure 6.9
**Louis Kahn,
Alfred Newton
Richards
Medical
Research
Building
and Biology
Building at the
University of
Pennsylvania,
Philadelphia
(1965)**

Figure 6.10
**Sectional
diagram of
the interstitial
space of Louis
Kahn's Jonas
Salk Institute
for Biological
Studies in La
Jolla, California
(1965), drawn
by Hitisha
Kalolia**

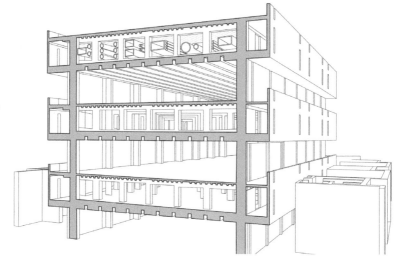

Banham also admired Franco Albini's design of a "technological building for an historical setting" with his *La Rinascente* department store in Rome (1961). The exterior massing borrows its cornice detail and proportions from the *palazzo* (palace) directly across the street. The exposed steel frame on the façade supports pre-cast corrugated concrete panels that provide channels up to three feet wide to house mechanical systems such as air-trunking and pipe-runs that descend from plant-rooms under the roof. The entire system ornaments the façade with accordion folds whose dimensions vary in relation

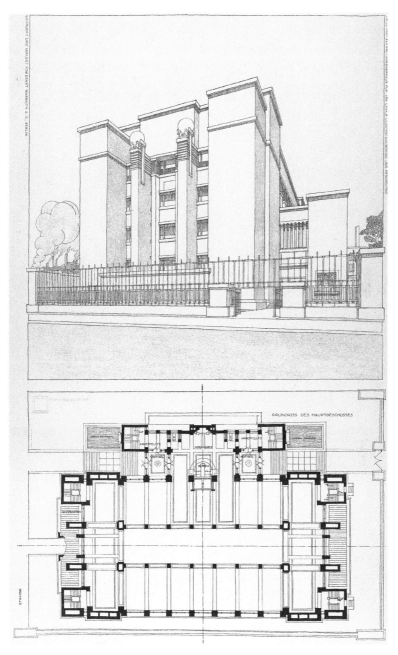

Figure 6.11
Frank Lloyd Wright, the Larkin Administration Building in Buffalo, New York (1906, demolished), from the Wasmuth portfolio (1910)

to the systems they house. Further underscoring the significance of this building's ability to merge contextual and mechanical responsiveness, as Kay Bea Jones clarifies, Albini's "architectural expression consisted of aestheticized technologies that are ordinarily concealed, even denied."[16]

Figure 6.12
Franco Albini,
La Rinascente
**department
store in
Rome (1960),
photograph by
Kay Bea Jones**

The Centre Georges Pompidou (1977) offers a spectacular expression of mechanical systems defining a building's exterior, dramatically expressing the truss system that spans the entire 196-foot width of the building to provide column-free space for flexible art galleries. Located in Paris's historical center on a site called the Plateau Beaubourg (hence the building's nickname of "Beaubourg"), the Centre Georges Pompidou completes the project of turning architecture inside out that 19th-century paleotechnological experiments in iron and glass initiated in this city. The team of Renzo Piano, Richard Rogers, and the Ove Arup Partnership won an international competition from out of 681 entries for a large-scale project that concluded in the building of approximately 1,111,965 square feet (103,305 square meters) of space

enclosing a *Bibliothèque publique d'information* (Public Information Library), the *Musée National d'Art Moderne,* and a center for musical and acoustical research.

The architects responded to the competition requirement for publicly accessible and flexible interior spaces with a massive exoskeleton of cast-steel gerberettes (small, cantilevered girders) attached to the large trusses. As the building clearly externalizes its structural virtuosity, it also suggests a kind of architectural exhibitionism by exposing its private mechanical systems to the public street. The architects showcased vertical circulation and exposed structure on the west elevation, while on the east they displayed brightly colored ducts and pipes. The gerberettes support a thick "extrastitial" zone that produces a highly three-dimensional façade animated by horizontal walkways and exposed escalators that allow for visitors to participate in the dynamic movement this part of the building orchestrates.

Creating an outdoor urban theater, the plaza performs as an auditorium gently sloping to the animated west façade, acting as a *scaenae frons*, the permanent background of an ancient Roman stage. With the project opening just 11 years after Paris's May, 1968 civil unrest, the large public plaza symbolized the potential for public space to make room either for social liberation or political unrest. The Beaubourg is more than simply a museum for the display of rarified art; it serves as a national symbol for the post-1968 regeneration of the public sphere in Paris, where information, education, and public debate were placed at the center of everyday life. The mechanical and structural systems in the Beaubourg, then, also work as social critique. With a façade that operates as a dynamic work of public art used to disseminate museological programs through public information systems, the building's porous envelope begins to

Figure 6.13 Richard Rogers and Renzo Piano, the Centre Georges Pompidou (Paris, 1977), elevation from the competition entry illustrating the concept of the building as an interactive billboard, image courtesy of Fondazione Renzo Piano and Rogers Stirk Harbour & P.

erode the often-daunting threshold between institutions of high culture and the average person.

As Simon Sadler observes, the Beaubourg reflects the radical architectural experimentation of Archigram, an avant-garde team of architects instrumental in the English counterculture movement of the 1960s. Founding member Peter Cook developed the conceptual project of *Plug-in City* (1964) as a megastructure combining modular housing, supermarkets, an environmental balloon inflated during bad weather, schools, and more, all of which could be moved through a rooftop "craneway" that facilitated a condition of permanent change. The Pompidou similarly expresses *Plug-in City*'s diagonal exoskeleton, escalator tubes, supply tubes, and general aesthetic of exposed colorful systems. It operates as an icon of hi-tech architecture built by iconoclasts. It provides for the possibility of spontaneous activities in the public realm that cannot be programmed by official, top-down planning. Rogers and Piano responded to the competition's requirement for an information, entertainment, and cultural center by proposing large screens on the building's west façade to be used for projecting changing information about news, information, events, art work, and games. To this end,

Figure 6.14
**Plug-In City,
Typical Section,
Peter Cook,
© Archigram
1964, image
supplied by the
ARCHIGRAM
ARCHIVES 2019**

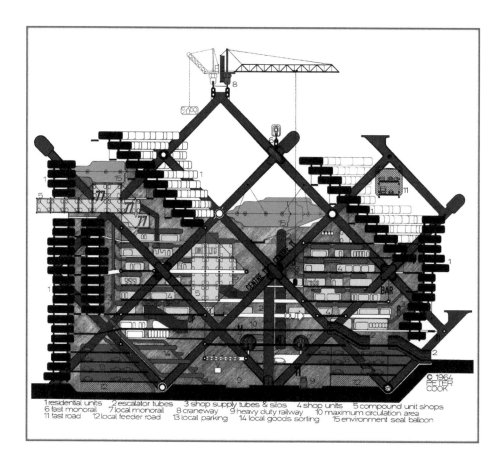

1 residential units   2 escalator tubes   3 shop supply tubes & silos   4 shop units   5 compound unit shops
6 fast monorail   7 local monorail   8 craneway   9 heavy duty railway   10 maximum circulation area
11 fast road   12 local feeder road   13 local parking   14 local goods sorting   15 environment seal balloon

President Valéry Giscard, who replaced Georges Pompidou in 1974, shut down the proposed screen-façade by claiming it to be "a political weapon."[17]

Applying Peter Sloterdijk's philosophy to the intended screens, his idea of interfacial spheres or bubbles of intimacy suggests reading this communication system as maintaining the potential to participate in a network of urban façades that implode the exclusive museum structure upon itself as they explode culture, art, and information into the city. The Beaubourg offers the possibility for telegraphing interactive data, moods, events, and artwork onto the public surfaces of other sites around Paris or the globe. It offers an alternative model to the principal use of computers as the generators of form, one that seeks performative parallels between buildings and information technologies to act as giant, interconnected communication systems with urban-scale façades providing access to each other and transforming cities into networked communication devices.

Indeed, the architects envisioned the building as a dynamic information system that could be deployed throughout France. The idea was for it to support constantly fluctuating programs inviting public participation in a design concept, according to the architects, located somewhere "between an information-orientated, computerized Times Square and the British Museum."[18] In this version of the project, the Beaubourg would act as cyclopean computer screen or urban brain manipulated through public access, symbolizing France's commitment to open debate, advanced telecommunications infrastructures, and technological expertise. It offers an ideal model for considering design through performative informational systems that portend architecture's shift from technology to technocracy.

Ewan Branda contextualizes the Beaubourg's engagement with digital technologies, observing that during the 1960s computers and information networks entered the public imagination. But by the end of the 1970s, as he concludes, they started to appear in workplaces, schools, and even homes, relegating their status to "only the most mundane of tasks, one from which they would emerge only two decades later."[19] In contradistinction to this normalization, Branda places the Beaubourg at the center of a conversation in which the changing nature of information technology exacted "new modes of architectural thinking that destabilized the traditional discursive function of the machine underpinning modern architecture."[20] According to Henri Lefebvre, the Centre Georges Pompidou was "a colossal information center, an immense 'computer' for receiving, breaking down, and redistributing all information concerning the industry of culture."[21]

Bubbles

As Le Corbusier wrote: "The soap bubble is completely harmonious, if the breath in it is spread equally, and well regulated on the inside. The outside is the product of an inside."[22] Architecture's experimentation with glass enclosures as a near-seamless interpenetration of outdoors and indoors somewhat paradoxically delivered the opposite result of creating environmentally sealed

Figure 6.15
**Nicholas
Grimshaw, the
Eden Project
in Cornwall,
England (2001)**

containers separating inside from out. Transparent buildings rely on the production of interior weather as a way to protect against their own vulnerability
to extreme differentials of heat loss and gain or to inhabit hostile exterior
environments, anticipating the increasingly immanent scenario that climate
change may render verdant landscapes into lunar deserts. Bubble architecture
is a transparent enclosure that isolates the world outside in order to construct
an alternative reality.

Nicholas Grimshaw designed the Eden Project (2001) in Cornwall, England
as eight interlinked, geodesic "biomes" that provide 23,000 square meters
of enclosed environments, one of which shelters the world's largest indoor
rainforest. Located on South Biosphere Road in Oracle, Arizona, Biosphere 2 is
a 3.14-acre glass enclosure inside of which eight "Biospherians" sealed themselves for two years, starting in 1991, on a mission "to test survivability and to
see whether a small group of humans could develop and live in a self-sustaining
colony, as one might imagine on some distant planet in outer space."[23] Locked
inside transparent and translucent enclosures, they produced their own food,
recycled water and their own waste, and conducted ecological research.

When exploring architectural efficiencies for the design of his lightweight
membrane-construction, Frei Otto famously studied the tensile systems of
soap bubbles as pneumatic structures found in nature. In 1971 Otto worked
with Ewald Bubner, Kenzo Tange, and Arup to envision Arctic City, an artificially
controlled environment in the Arctic Circle covered by a transparent, two-kilo-
meter-wide pneumatic dome to support the inhabitation of 40,000 people. Otto
also examined radiolarian micro-organisms as structural optimization models
that he developed into structural systems for the contoured roof he designed

for West Germany's pavilion at the 1967 World's Fair in Montreal, Canada. R. Buckminster Fuller remains the most significant advocate of bubble architecture, one who provocatively asked "How much does your house weigh?"[24] He designed the US pavilion for the 1967 World Fair Expo in Montreal, Canada as a 250-feet diameter sphere composed of a geodesic dome built out of structural steel and enclosed with acrylic cells. The Montreal pavilion gave built expression to Fuller's 1960 proposal, in collaboration with architect Shoji Sadao, to cover Midtown Manhattan in a two-mile-wide geodesic dome that would produce a controlled environment.

Figure 6.16 **Buckminster Fuller and Shoji Sadao,** *Dome Over Manhattan,* **1960**

Banham diagramed the difference between campfires and tents when advocating for an environmentally responsive architecture unrestrained by the weight of massive and immobile walls. Campfires radiate heat and light to produce a warm glow that brings people together. In contrast, the tent's membrane deflects wind and excludes rain but also segregates people.[25] Banham identified the campfire's ability to create community and produce space through gradient heat patterns instead of parietal walls. The campfire describes an architecture produced by environmental rather than structural systems, offering a model for experimental enclosures that relies on radiation and air movement.

In what appears as both a critique and celebration of architecture's utopian impulse to dwell naked in the Garden of Eden, the architecture collaborative of Superstudio, founded by Adolfo Natalini and Cristiano Toraldo di Francia in 1966, filmed a series of collages entitled *Supersurface—An Alternative Model for Life on the Earth* (1972). This project implicitly critiques the ubiquitous glass

Figure 6.17
Superstudio,
Supersurface—
An Alternative
Model for Life
on the Earth
(1971), courtesy
of Cristiano
Toraldo di
Francia

grid of corporate architecture for its potential to enfold the entire natural environment in an anonymous wrapper. The celebratory dimension dwells in the potential for the glass surface to operate as a giant solar collection system that provides a renewable source to power a universal energy and communication network into which nomadic encampments may plug. The possibility of living without permanent, three-dimensional structures and the potential for free energy could allow people to wander the earth while wearing a tent-backpack and plugging into this artificial campfire.

Fuller's Manhattan Dome, Archigram's Suitaloon, or Hans Hollein's inflatable Mobile Office, as Amy Kulper summarizes, exemplify experimental uses of bubbles from the 1960s, suggesting "that the potential elasticity of bubbles facilitated anything from the individual abode to the annexation of large portions of the city."[26] According to Kulper, Fuller coined the phrase "environment bubble" that Banham used in the 1965 essay "A Home is Not a House."[27] François Dallegret designed a bubble enclosure and environmental machinery to illustrate this essay, producing iconic and fanciful visions of architecture's future. In an interview with Dallegret, Alessandra Ponte mentions that "the text was created at the same time as the drawings," forming a fluid dialogue between work and image.[28] "Anatomy of a Dwelling" and "Transportable Standard-of-Living Package" articulate a trajectory away from architecture encapsulating atmospheres and toward architecture as atmosphere. The "Anatomy" drawing

The Environment-Bubble

Transparent plastic bubble dome inflated by air-conditioning output

depicts seemingly inhabitable ductwork interpenetrating a rabbit warren of plumbing, telephone cables, radio antennae, kitchen appliances, and more. Banham prophesized architecture's disappearance into systems, observing that this "baroque ensemble of domestic gadgetry epitomizes the intestinal complexity of gracious living."[29] As he put it in 1960s colloquialism, "this is the junk that keeps the pad swinging."[30] For the "Living Package" he and Dallegret appear naked in an environmentally controlled, transparent bubble replete with television, stereo, and refrigerator all powered by solar energy.

Figure 6.18 François Dallegret, "The Environment Bubble," photomontage drawing for Reyner Banham's "A Home Is Not a House" (1965), courtesy of François Dallegret

Vitreous Surfaces

In a strikingly kaleidoscopic expression of fluid, curvilinear surfaces at the Toledo Glass Pavilion in Toledo, Ohio (2006), Kazuyo Sejima and Ryue

Nishizawa of SANAA fold the exterior wall into interstitial zones much like the digestive tract Robert Smithson saw in Wright's Guggenheim Museum where "the ambulatories are metaphorical intestines."[31] The building's glass enclosure, coupled with glass interior walls, reflects its program to house glass artifacts. Sandwiched between a thin roof and floor, a single story of vitreous space squeezes into an ethereal zone that seems to float without the support of its invisibly thin steel columns. Pellucid glass partition walls enclose fluid curvilinear spaces floating within the larger glass enclosure, describing the museum as bubbles within bubbles that perform numerous environmental tasks.

Kiel Moe determines that the pavilion's thermally active surfaces produce three primary energy zones: an interstitial thermal buffer that exists as an air gap between the exterior glass enclosure and the interior dividing walls, a hot zone that the glass production facility produces, and individual gallery spaces that require controlled air temperature and humidity. Radiant heating and cooling systems in the floor and ceiling of the interstitial zone buffer differential interior and exterior temperatures and prevent condensation from forming on the glass surfaces. A hydronic floor slab recovers heat produced in the glass production facility and redistributes it elsewhere in the facility. The cool air the galleries require is recycled to reduce the heat of the glass production zone. Where the *New York Times* critic Nicolai Ouroussoff considers the pavilion to be a "diaphanous maze," Moe complements this assessment by describing it as "a prime example of the maximal within the minimal" that displays "a tendency for every component, every surface to perform multiple functions."[32]

Weather Architecture

In a world where television and thermostats produce space, according to the installation artist Olafur Eliasson, "the weather forecast is our mediated experience."[33] Television's flickering light draws architecture into the glow of screens that substitute for walls and offers the potential to liquefy surfaces into ephemeral environments. To this end, Eliasson installed *The Weather Project* in the Tate Modern Museum's enormous turbine hall in London (2003), a work of art simulating the presence of the sun. He did so with the aid of an illuminated circular disc radiating light through an artificially foggy atmosphere produced by a fine mist of sugar and water atomized through a humidifier. He also installed a mirror on the ceiling of this space, "emphasizing the megalomaniacal ambition of the architects" as well as the need for Londoners to enjoy just a bit of sunshine, even if artificially produced.[34] As Eliasson explains, "the mirror, not the sun," is what people stared at, "so the work is not so much the general spectacle of a fake sun, but a person's individual encounter with his own reflection."[35]

In his installation *Amplification* for the *Gen(h)ome Project* exhibition (2006) at the MAK Center for Art and Architecture at Rudolf M. Schindler's House in Los Angeles, Sean Lally constructed six miniature conservatories to house botanical gardens filled with orchids. These small gardens acted as living models for what could be larger, inhabitable self-sustaining interior spaces where rain, humidity, and condensation transition into one another as in a glass terrarium. Lally's work explores the potential for transforming natural forces—electromagnetic, thermodynamic, acoustic, or chemical—into architecture. His work relies on the use of heating devices, fans, lights, and fluorescent dyes to produce the heat, water vapor, and condensation for controlled

Figure 6.20
Olafur Eliasson,
The Weather
Project,
installation
at the Tate
Modern
in London
(2003–2004)

Figure 6.21
Sean Lally,
"Amplification,"
for *The*
Gen[H]ome
Project **at**
the MAK
Center in West
Hollywood
(2006–2007),
courtesy of
Sean Lally

Figure 6.22
François Roche,
"I'm Lost in
Paris: View
from Rear
Windows"
(Paris, 2008),
courtesy of
François Roche

microclimates. In *The Air from Other Planets, A Brief History of Architecture to Come* (2013) he argues that energy possesses the potential for material expression that the spaces and shapes of architecture may capture. He probes the adversarial boundaries between a building and its situated environment by exploring the potential for perimeters "that are represented not by a single line but instead through gradients of energy intensities nested within their surroundings."[36] His work closes the loop from *fin de siècle* decadence to bioclimatic technocracy that the orchid induces.

Working at an equally small scale to produce big effects, François Roche of R&Sie(n) grew 1200 hydroponic *dryopteris filix-mas* ferns in 300 hand-blown glass beakers to provide a leafy building envelope to entirely cover a house he designed called "I'm Lost in Paris" (2008). The house's glass surfaces benefit from the shading and privacy the ferns provide, as they also camouflage the residence under the appearance of an enormous garden hedge. The ferns live off of nutrient enriched rainwater that fills the glass beakers. Oscillating between the green of sustainability and the black of avant-gardism, Roche explains: "It takes off from a typically ecological approach, but goes beyond that. People are always curious when they walk by but sometimes they find the system creepy, or even dangerous to some; it is a game of attraction and repulsion."[37]

For their winning entry to the Bauaustellung (IBA) competition in Hamburg, Germany (2013) Sheila Kennedy and J. Frano Violich designed the IBA Soft House, where they shifted the conventional living wall of plants from outside to inside as a way of harvesting vegetables growing from out of a vertical wall illuminated by skylights and windows. While the entire design of this live/work row house demonstrates low carbon design innovations and ecologically responsive modes of inhabitation, the three-story air convection atrium that illuminates the living wall also allows daylight to penetrate deeply into the ground floor. This light, in turn, produces a differential between warm and cool air that a system of interior curtains modulate. As the architects write

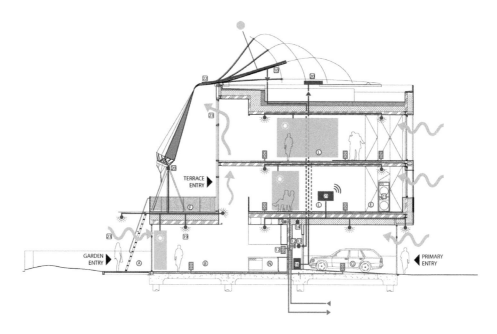

about this kinetic fabric, "the design expands the traditional role of the house-hold curtain, creating a new multi-tasking soft infrastructure which can be moved into instant 'rooms' that concentrate zones of heating or cooling from the radiant floor."[38] This smart interior textile parallels the flexible photovoltaic textiles, called "Twisters," that Kennedy and Violich located over the building's exterior glass surfaces and whose shape adapts and deforms according to the sun's movement.

Where Kennedy and Violich compress the traditional dividing wall to the thinness of a curtain that may adapt to variant climactic conditions, for an installation at the 2008 Venice Biennale called *Digestible Gulf Stream*, Philippe Rahm entirely removed any physical divides between spaces whose differ-ence is produced through the physics of convection flow. Rahm's minimalist installation consists of an elevated horizontal plane heated to 28°C located near another elevated plane cooled to 12°C, the differential of which forces the natural convection of air to produce a miniature Gulf Stream that divides the two spaces. In "Architecture as Meteorology" Rahm claims that architects should no longer build spaces, "but rather create temperatures and atmos-pheres."[39] Seeking to produce interpenetrable zones across which structure dissolves into meteorology, he arrives at the objective of Banham's gradient campfire.

In a game of smoke and mirrors, the work of artists who explore artificial environments dialogues with the work architects have completed in producing interior atmospheres. For *Condensation Cube* of 1963–1965, Hans Haacke built a transparent acrylic box filled with a small enough amount of water to produce a weather system where it conceptually rains inside. From 1968 to

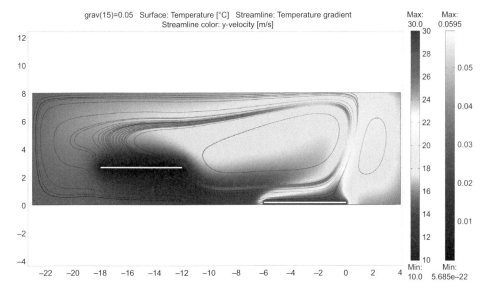

grav(15)=0.05 Surface: Temperature [°C] Streamline: Temperature gradient
Streamline color: y-velocity [m/s]

1971, Robert Rauschenberg developed a dynamic sculpture called *Mud Muse*, a mixture of clay and water that had been poured into an aluminum-and-glass display case and spit bubbles when sound-activated sensors triggered a compressed-air system. Amplifying Haacke's project to an inhabitable scale, Experiments in Art and Technology (E.A.T.) faceted a geodesic dome for the Pepsi Cola Pavilion on display for the Expo '70 in Osaka, Japan that featured

Figure 6.24
Philippe Rahm Architects, *Digestible Gulf Stream,* **International Exhibition of Venice Biennale (2008), courtesy of Philippe Rahm**

Figure 6.25
Fujiko Nakaya's "Fog Sculpture" for the Pepsi Pavilion by Experiments in Art and Technology (E.A.T.) at Expo '70 Osaka, Japan

179

a roof covered by Fujiko Nakaya's "Fog Sculpture," a mist shroud capable of producing a 150-foot diameter cloud that complemented a kinetic sound and light installation and a walk-in spherical mirror.

Referencing Hans Haacke's condensation cube and the Pepsi Cola Pavilion while delivering a liquid version of Banham's architecture without walls, the Blur Building dissolves architecture into pure atmosphere. Working with Nakaya as a consultant, the firm of Diller Scofidio + Renfro designed a media pavilion for the Swiss EXPO 2002 in Yverdon-les-Bains, located in Lake Neuchatel, with a giant floating cloud as its primary enclosure. The structure, based on Fuller's tensegrity system, consisted of a frame that cantilevered off of four concrete piles rising up from the lake bottom. To produce an enclosure consisting of nothing more than fog, the building drew lake water through a system of 35,000 high-pressure nozzles to produce a fine mist. Shifting climatic conditions that could impact the cloud are regulated through a smart weather system that monitors temperature, humidity, wind speed, and wind direction. "Contrary to immersive environments that strive for visual fidelity in high-definition," as the architects explain, "Blur is decidedly low-definition."[40] Featuring a bar that serves different types of water from around the world, in this pavilion "the public can drink the building."[41]

Working in collaboration with Steffen Reichert, Achim Menges exhibited *Hygroscope–Meteorosensitive Morphology* at the Centre Pompidou (2012), capturing the dynamic form of a radiolarian. A variable humidity control system in a sealed glass box connected to sensors registered the climatic transitions that regularly occur in Paris's exterior environment. The mechanism produced an artificial atmosphere for a biomimetic and meteorosensitive architecture

Figure 6.26
Diller Scofidio + Renfro, Blur Building for the Swiss EXPO 2002 in Yverdon-les-Bains

derived from the dimensional instability of wood that changes shape when exposed to moisture. As with an exotic tropical flower, the Hygroscope's wooden "petals" form and deform according to changing humidity levels. In another simulated flower project, Doris Sung harvested the sun as the morphological shape-shifter for *Bloom*, a full-scale installation she exhibited at the open-air Materials and Applications exhibition space in Silver Lake,

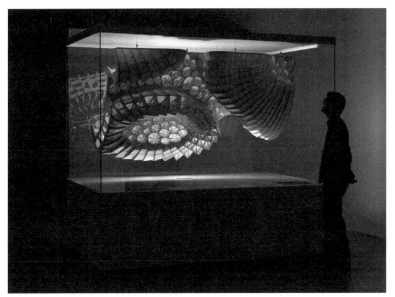

Figure 6.27
Achim Menges,
Hygroscope–
Meteoro-
sensitive
Morphology
displayed at
the Centre
Georges Pom-
pidou in Paris
(2012), courtesy
of Achim
Menges, © ICD
University of
Stuttgart

Figure 6.28
Doris Sung,
Bloom,
installation at
Materials &
Application
Gallery in Los
Angeles (2011),
courtesy of
Doris Sung

181

California. Sung joined 14,000 pieces of thermobimetal into an inhabitable flower that blossomed in response to sun angles and temperatures. Two thin sheets of metal with different thermal expansion rates are laminated together to produce a material that, due to their differential response rates, curls up when the temperature rises and flattens when it cools. Bloom transforms the hothouse of emerging technologies into a solar-kinetic architectural flower.

While transforming atmospheres into buildings, architects also assemble architecture into natural forms—creating hybrid gardens from robotic plants that grow natural flowers. Between biomorphic and biodynamic architecture, imitating either the shape or the performance of natural forms, architects are able to grow tectonic gardens indoors and without natural light. Atmospheric design processes redirect architectural priorities away from purely formal obsessions and towards scientific experimentation. With the expansion of architecture into experiential environments such as shopping malls and biospheres, terminology too begins to shift from program and function to event and performance. Performance in architecture concerns what a building does and how it does it, its use and the means by which it activates this use. Architecture designed to house performances—such as concerts (theaters), sporting events (stadiums), and science experiments (laboratories)—often exhibits innovative operational solutions to the questions of structure, acoustics, lighting, ventilation, and more. Architecture designed to perform in and of itself engages dynamic building systems that vibrate, make sounds, produce lighting effects, and control the air, much like a rock concert. This is a future Peter Eisenman envisions in which multimedia experiences liberate architecture from its static adherence to enclosed spaces and site specificity. As he puts it, we attend rock concerts to become part of an environment composed of light, sound, and movement: "this kind of event structure is not architecture standing against media, but architecture being consumed by it."[42] Architecture no longer mediates only between nature and technology—it creates its own environmental *gesamtkunstwerk*, a total work of art, that defines space through the more ephemeral condition of weather, acoustics, social media, light, and air.

Notes

1   Mark Wigley, "The Architecture of Atmosphere" *Daidalos 68* (1998), p. 20.
2   Joris-Karl Huysmans, *Against the Grain* (Jovian Press, 2017), p. 133.
3   Paul Sheerbart, "Glass Architecture" (1914), in *Programs and Manifestoes on 20th-Century Architecture*, ed. Ulrich Conrads, trans. Michael Bullock (Cambridge, MA: MIT Press, 1970), p. 32.
4   Isobel Armstrong, *Victorian Glassworlds: Glass Culture and the Imagination 1830–1830* (Oxford: Oxford University Press, 2008), p. 151.
5   Henrik Schoenefeldt, *The Building of the Great Exhibition of 1851—An Environmental Design Experiment* (Cambridge: Cambridge University Press, 2008).
6   Ibid.

7   Walter Benjamin, "Paris, Capital of the Nineteenth Century," in *Reflections: Essays, Aphorisms, Autobiographical Writings*, trans. Edmund Jephcott (New York: Schocken Books, 1978), p. 155.

8   Peter Sloterdijk, 'Talking to Myself About the Poetics of Space," *Harvard Design Magazine: No. 30/ (Sustainability) + Pleasure, Vol. I: Culture and Architecture*, interview, http://www.harvarddesignmagazine.org/issues/30/talking-to-myself-about-the-poetics-of-space.

9   Steven Miles, *Spaces for Consumption* (Thousand Oaks: Sage, 2010), p. 105.

10   Margaret Crawford, "The World in Shopping Mall," in *Variations on a Theme Park: The New American City and the End of Public Space*, ed. Michael Sorkin (New York: Hill and Wang, 1992), p. 14.

11   Ibid.

12   http://oma.eu/publications/project-on-the-city-ii-the-harvard-guide-to-shopping;   and Chuihua Judy Chung, Jeffrey Inaba, Rem Koolhaas, Sze Tsung Leong, and Tae-wook Cha, Harvard University, Graduate School of Design, and Harvard Project on the City, *Harvard Design School Guide to Shopping. Project on the City, 2* (Cologne: Taschen, 2001) front cover facing.

13   Reyner Banham, *The Architecture of the Well-Tempered Environment* (London: Architectural Press; Chicago: University of Chicago Press, 1969), p. 12.

14   Ibid.

15   David Arnold, "The Evolution of Modern Office Buildings and Air Conditioning: The First Century of Air Conditioning" *ASHRAE Journal* (June 1999), p. 43.

16   Kay Bea Jones, *Suspending Modernity: The Architecture of Franco Albini* (Farnham: Ashgate, 2014), p. 202.

17   https://www.dezeen.com/2017/01/31/renzo-piano-richard-rogers-photography-centre-pompidou-paris-40th-anniversary.

18   *Encyclopedia of Contemporary British Culture*, eds. Peter Childs and Michael Storry (New York: Routledge, 1999), p. 460.

19   Ewan Branda, *The Architecture of Information at Plateau Beaubourg* (Los Angeles: UCLA, 2012), "Abstract," http://www.escholarship.org/uc/item/0ww309s3.

20   Ibid.

21   As cited and translated by Branda, p. 3. From Jean-Pierre Seguin, *Comment est née la BPI: Invention de la médiathèque* (Paris: Bibliothèque publique d'information, Centre Georges Pompidou, 1987), p. 126.

22   As cited in ibid. From Le Corbusier, *Vers une Architecture*, 1923.

23   http://blogs.britannica.com/2011/09/years-glass-biosphere-2-mission.

24   Matilda McQuaid (ed.), *Envisioning Architecture: Drawings from The Museum of Modern Art* (New York: Museum of Modern Art, 2002), pp. 64–65, https://www.moma.org/collection/works/804.

25   Reyner Banham, *Architecture of the Well-Tempered Environment* (Chicago: University of Chicago Press, 1969), pp. 18–20 passim.

26   Amy Kulper, "Ecology without the Oikos: Banham, Dallegret and the Morphological Context of Environmental Architecture" *Field 4*, no. 1 (2011), p. 24.

27   Ibid.

28   https://appareil.revues.org/1765.

29   Robert M. Rubin, "Unveiling the Unhouse," http://www.artinamericamagazine.com/news-features/magazines/unveiling-the-unhouse.

30   Ibid.

31   Robert Smithson, "Quasi-infinities and the Waning of Space" (1966), in *Robert*

Smithson: The Collected Writings (Berkeley: University of California Press, 1996), p. 35.

32   Nicolai Ouroussoff, "Glass Pavilion at the Toledo Museum of Art" *New York Times*, August 28, 2006; and Kiel Moe, *Integrated Design in Contemporary Architecture* (New York: Princeton Architectural Press, 2008), p. 106.

33   Olafur Eliasson, "Think with Me About Your Extension of Now" *Cabinet: Issue 3 Weather* (Summer 2001).

34   Michael Kimmelman, "Art: The Sun Sets at the Tate Modern" *New York Times*, March 21, 2004.

35   Ibid.

36   Sean Lally, excerpt from *The Air from Other Planets: A Brief History of Architecture to Come* (Zürich: Lars Müller, 2014) in *ArchDaily*, April 13, 2014, https://www.archdaily.com/495586/the-air-from-other-planets-a-brief-history-of-architecture.

37   "Lost in Paris" house, by R&Sie Architects, February 6, 2009, https://www.wallpaper.com/architecture/lost-in-paris-house-by-rsie-architects#Lmfz4ABzcowrMZfA.99.

38   http://www.kvarch.net/projects/87.

39   http://www.philipperahm.com/data/projects/digestiblegulfstream/index.html.

40   https://dsrny.com/project/blur-building.

41   Ibid.

42   Peter Eisenman, *Written into the Void: Selected Writings, 1990–2004* (New Haven: Yale University Press, 2007), p. 13.

Chapter 7

Tectonics

Ornament is the figure that emerges from the material substrate, the expression of embedded forces through processes of construction, assembly and growth. It is through ornament that material transmits affects. Ornament is therefore necessary and inseparable from the object.[1]

—*Farshid Moussavi*

In 1851, the year in which the Great Exhibition opened in London, German architect and theorist Gottfried Semper published *Die vier Elemente der Baukunst* (*The Four Elements of Architecture*), a book where he divided architecture into the four fundamental components of mound, hearth, roof and supports, and non-structural enclosure. He divided these elements into the two basic procedures of *tectonics*, or the lightweight and linear system of a frame, and *stereometrics*, the massive and volumetric system of earthworks.

Semper designed the Crystal Palace's Turkish, Canadian, Swedish, and Danish exhibitions, during which time he closely studied the full-scale reproduction of a bamboo dwelling unit from the Caribbean Island of Trinidad. The "Caribbean hut" provided him with a convincing model of the four elements sufficient enough to evince his theories and to supplant earlier models of architecture's singularly classical origins with a global precedent. His deceptively simple yet highly prescient separation of structure and enclosure anticipated the curtain wall—a façade whose only structural capacity is to support its own weight. This separation also forestalled the idea of a free plan, the separation of structure and enclosure. His identification of textile design as non-structural enclosure locates the origins of architecture among the techniques of weaving, a domestic art with which women are frequently identified. Including weaving and textile design among the four elements also presented them as intrinsic architectural components linked to design details and the tying of knots. Indeed, the German *naht*, meaning a joint or seam, ties directly to *nähen*, meaning to sew.[2] Semper therefore opened architectural theory to seriously considering the importance of diverse precedents. As Kenneth Frampton observes, through Native American Mandan houses, the Gogo houses from Tanzania, the boulder footings of the traditional Japanese house,

Figure 7.1
**Gottfried
Semper,
drawing of
Caribbean Hut
from Trinidad
on display
at the Great
Exhibition
of 1851 in
London, in**
*Der Stil in den
technischen
und
tektonischen
Künsten, oder
praktische
Äesthetik*
(*Style in the
Technical and
Structural Arts,
or Practical
Aesthetics,*
1860–1863)

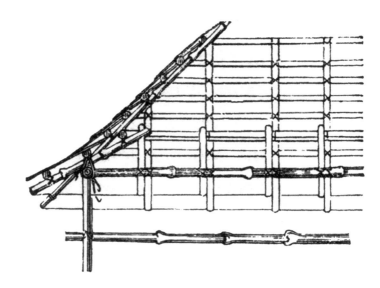

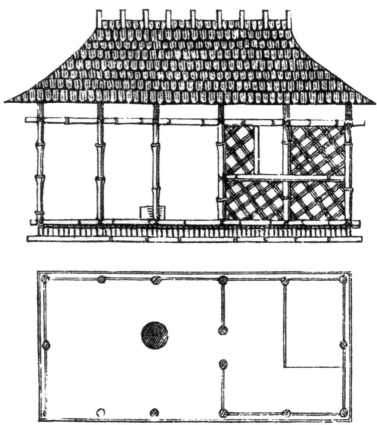

and traditional construction from the towns of M'zab in Algeria, "the general validity of Semper's *Four Elements* is borne out by vernacular building throughout the world."[3]

The hut represented architecture's *ursprüngliche Gebilde* (original formations) strongly enough for Semper to include it as an illustration in his later publication *Der Stil in den technischen und tektonischen Künsten, oder praktische Äesthetik* (*Style in the Technical and Structural Arts, or Practical Aesthetics*, 1860–1863). Semper described the Italo-Roman primitive hut, an originary edifice found in treatises by Vitruvius and Marc Antoine Laugier, as "a figment of the imagination."[4] He substituted in its place the Caribbean bamboo hut displayed at the Great Exhibition as "a highly realistic example of a wooden structure taken from ethnology."[5] In this later iteration of his theory he presented five essential categories for making artifacts: masonry (involving building with stone for hearth, walls, piers, etc.); carpentry (providing essential structures of timber, especially walls, partitions, and roofs); weaving (producing textiles and patterns); molding (creating pottery from clay); and metallurgy. The table below shows the combined systems of four elements and five techniques.

Four elements	Five techniques
Mound	Stereotomy (Masonry)
Roof + Supports	Carpentry
Non-structural Enclosure	Textile + Weaving
Hearth	Ceramics
	Metallurgy

Pairing the techniques Semper lists in *Der Stil* with the components from *The Four Elements* offers a useful rubric for reading buildings through tectonics, one that readily applies to the production of contemporary architecture. Semper's theory of two procedures, four elements, and five techniques offers a pliable model for reading architecture through a range of technologies that did not necessarily exist in the 19th century, but nonetheless exemplify the strength of his arguments.

Paleotectonics

A brief excursus into the multiple etymological trajectories of *tectonic* serves to enunciate the subtler connotations this approach to reading architecture elicits. Emerging from 19th-century lexicons as a term referencing the general notion of construction techniques, the theoretical pedigree of *tectonic* owes much to the concepts of storytelling, detailing, and weaving, and even, as discussed in Chapter 3, context. Along with *tectonic*, words such as *technique* and *technology* find their roots in the ancient Greek *techne*, a term that originally referenced a carpenter's knowledge about crafting wood. In

Studies in Tectonic Culture Kenneth Frampton traces the term to 5th-century Greece, where it evolved from meaning something specific and physical, such as carpentry, "to a more generic notion of making, involving the idea of *poesis*."[6] Frampton tempts architecture with the promise that technology may be poetic.

What precisely is the relationship between *techne* and *poesis*, two terms that at face value might seem to be unrelated if not entirely divergent? *Techne* derives from the Greek τέχνη, a term generally translated as art, but also meaning "craftsmanship" or "craft." *Poïesis* stems from ποίησις, meaning poetry, but also refers to "creation" or "production" while connoting such concepts as "making" and "fabrication." *Techne* references the skill, craft, technique, or method by which a work is achieved or created. *Poïesis* may be understood as its creative impetus, especially for a work of art. In short, *techne* refers to the craft and technique of producing art, while *poïesis* engenders its creative production. From *techne*'s art of making to *poïesis*'s making of art, these two terms merge in the final production of a work that displays both technique and creative inspiration.

The origins of *architect*, in turn, derives from *tectonic*. The Greek *arkhitekton* means master builder or director of works, deriving from *arkhi* (chief) and *tekton* (builder/carpenter). *Tectonic* enjoys an array of linguistic affiliations including craft, make, web, structure, weave, net, interlace, roof, house, plaster, coat of paint, and texture. *Texture*, in turn, references the Latin *textura*, meaning web, texture, or structure, as well as *texere*, meaning to weave, fabricate, and make wicker or wattle framework. Text, texture, and context relate to tectonics. To read the most specific architectural text is to examine its tectonics.

Mound

Semper's mound references the ground or foundations supporting the hut. As an element that absorbs numerous architectural modes of expression from masonry to poured-in-place concrete, it alludes to structural systems that have been extracted from and added to the earth. Frank Lloyd Wright's design of Fallingwater, the Kaufmann Residence in Bear Run Pennsylvania (1935), offers an optimum example of architecture emerging from a mound. Wright sited the house directly above a waterfall and on top of a rocky outcropping where the Kaufmanns spent time sunning themselves and swimming during vacations at their cabin. His signature pinwheel floor plan resulted in extroverted interior spaces and substantial reinforced concrete terraces that cantilever off of each other, echoing the pattern of rock ledges below. In the main living space a hearth set on a large boulder left in situ serves as the fulcrum for the implied rotation. This room is floored with waxed rocks left standing in their original positions on the hill and protruding upward as much as a foot. A tower made of stone quarried at the site projects directly upward from the hearth/mound, rotating the plan into a three-dimensional space.

Figure 7.2
**Frank Lloyd
Wright,
Kaufmann
House (Falling
Water) in
Bear Run,
Pennsylvania
(1939)**

Roof and Supports

Carpentry begins where the tree ends. This is especially true with Stave churches (*stavkirke*) that offer clear expression of Scandinavian architecture's attachment to wood. Not only do these churches express a tree's formidable strength but they also reference Nordic shipbuilding and Viking structures. Sited in the pristine landscape of *Sogn og Fjordane* county in Norway, within earshot of the *Lustrafjorden* (Luster fjord) and dating back to 1130, Urnes Stave Church serves as a paradigmatic example of wood construction techniques. In general, these structures are composed of massive load-bearing posts know as staves (*staver* in Norwegian) that rise up vertically from the corner of square sills, which in turn rest upon a continuous boulder foundation. The stone substructure engenders greater durability than inserting the posts directly into the ground. The square sill and corner columns produce a central space, or nave, that evokes the large gathering spaces of Viking great halls.

With the central space of a Christian basilica called a *nave*, Frampton notes the "curious etymological connection in which the Latin word for ship, *navis*, is also commonly applied to the principal volume of a church."[7] The traditional wood detailing found in Stave churches adopts the technique of crafting joints without nails—such as mortise and tenon or dovetailing. G. Ronald Murphy offers an even more granular reading of the affinity between Stave churches and Viking shipbuilding techniques, observing that both used the details of knees and fishing. Stronger than timber sawn in the shape of an arc, knees are cut from the part of the tree where the roots curve to become the trunk. Fishing joints are similar to botanical grafting where two pieces of wood are joined on an angle.

Figure 7.3
**Urnes Stave
Church in Sogn
og Fjordane
county, Norway
(12th century)**

Japanese architecture also demonstrates sophisticated wood joinery and construction techniques that express the material's strength. The Himeji Castle (also *Hakuro-jo* or *Shirasagi-jo,* meaning "white Heron") is a feudal fortress located in the Hyōgo prefecture dating from 1601 to 1614 with a main donjon (the Dai-Tenshu) that exemplifies these properties. Strategically located on the summit of a hill, the donjon sits on a large stone base that supports seven stories of white plastered earthen walls rising to a height of 147 feet at the ridgepole. Multiple layers of expressive flared hipped roofs and decorative dormers covered with ceramic tile rest on undulating wood gables. As if built around trees, two massive, continuous 80-foot-tall wood columns support the structure in the middle, running from the foundation to the seventh story.

While numerous parts of the world dramatically explore wood's potential to express monumentality, complexity, and permanence, the use of this material in the United States responds to quantity and expedience. The 1830 US census counted the nation's population at 12,860,702 people, while just 40 years later the 1870 census records shows it jumping to 38,558,371. This rapidly rising population needed homes and they needed them to be built quickly, leading to the development of pre-cut, wood construction technologies that evolved from European timber framing construction techniques such as the German *fachwerk* house, to Braced Frame, to Balloon Frame, to Platform Frame. Braced frame construction relies on heavy post and beam timber generally held together with mortise and tenon joinery and strengthened by diagonal wood supports attached to corner posts. Balloon frames, which emerged in around 1830, use multiple, lightweight wood studs

Figure 7.4
Himeji Castle in the Hyōgo Prefecture of Japan (1601–1609)

nailed together and rising about two stories tall from sill to roof. Platform frames, the dominant structural system still used to build wood houses today, developed as a variant of the balloon frame with studs only rising one floor at a time and with a platform acting as the base of the second floor.

Technological advancements in lumber manufacturing witnessed new techniques such as machined nails, increasingly efficient sawmills, and eventually the introduction of drywall to replace plaster and lathe wall-building techniques. In around 1830, standardized wood components sized at 2 inches by 4 inches allowed for the development of lightweight framing to produce tectonic structures built of wood studs spaced 12–16 inches on center. These combined innovations made for faster, cheaper, and more transportable building systems than what had formerly been constructed by skilled carpenters. Dimensional lumber established a set of design conventions wherein doors, windows, trim, floor heights, and more were standardized into what would become off-the-shelf consumer goods.

Moreover, the portability of standardized pre-cut wood inspired the design of kit houses that could be mail ordered, along with the dreams and aspirations of a rising middle class, through catalogues such as those that Sears, Roebuck, and Co. produced. "From the elaborate multistory Ivanhoe, with its elegant French doors and art glass windows, to the simpler Goldenrod, which served as a quaint, three-room and no-bath cottage for summer vacationers," 447 different house styles and about 70,000–75,000 mail-order homes were designed and sold from 1908 to 1940.[8] Dimensioned lumber resulted in the standardization of house design exemplified by the planned communities of Levittown located in New York, Pennsylvania, and New Jersey. Starting in 1947, these mass-produced suburbs gathered together affordable houses with nearly identical designs and distinguishing names such as the "Lookout," the "Mariner," or the "Snug Harbor." The transformation of home building into suburban enclaves in the United States pivoted on the development of framing systems and mass-produced building components such as dormers, doors, and windows. Due to its ubiquity and variety of stylistic manifestations, the wood frame remains architecture's most prevalent structural system for housing in North America.

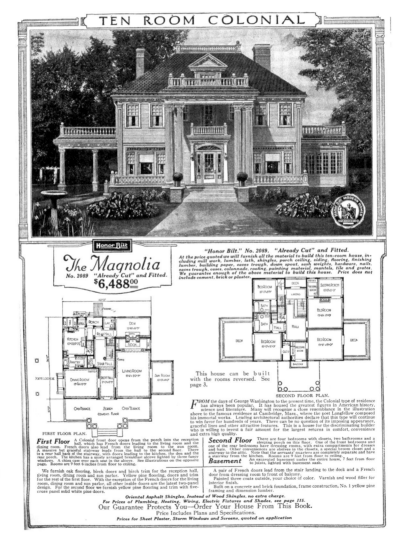

Figure 7.5
Catalog image and floorplan of Sears Magnolia kit house model (1921)

Hearth

Semper's hearth, the heart of his four elements, also forms the center of the home and of architectural origins as it gathers people around a warm fire. As a tectonic category, it references the process of firing earth into ceramics, a plastic building material that can be shaped simply by squeezing one's hands. Malleable, durable, strong, affordable, reproducible, and offering intrinsic ornamental properties, ceramics and unfired clay remain uniquely expressive architectural materials. Numerous buildings around the world are constructed from sun-dried mud bricks covered in a coat of mud or plaster. Indigenous architects in areas lacking abundant supplies of wood have turned to working with the earth by hand in order to sculpt dwellings and even entire cities with a material that can be shaped into complex curvilinear geometries with undulating wall thicknesses and vaults. Writing in *Architecture for the Poor* (1976), Hassan Fathy published a wall painting from the mortuary tomb of Queen Hatshepsut in Egypt dating to the eighteenth dynasty that depicts her making the kind of mud bricks he would use for the design and construction of walls for the village of New Gourna in Egypt (1946–1952).

The Walled City of Shibam in Yemen is composed of apartment buildings rising up to 11 stories high and dating to the 16th century, all built of mud brick. Also composed of sun-baked earth bricks, the Djenné Mosque in Mali, displays large timbers projecting from its surfaces that are used as permanent scaffolding for the annual process of replastering. Thought to date from between 1000 and 1450 CE, the Taos Pueblo near Taos, New Mexico is home to the Taos Indians and is considered to be the oldest continuously inhabited community in the United States. Made from sun-dried bricks composed of water, straw, and earth, the adobe walls are several feet thick and provide a thermal mass that mediates Taos's differential temperature changes. The abandoned city of Chan Chan (Sun Sun), capital of the Chimú kingdom (ca. 1100–1470 CE) located in the Moche Valley of Peru, features elaborate adobe walls finished with soft mud facilitating the carving of ornamental bas-reliefs on their surfaces. Rammed earth buildings similarly evidence the process of treating architecture as an inhabitable clay jar. In this process a series of layers of damp earth are poured into a temporary frame in the shape of a wall and then compressed to about half of their height, with the sequential layers often producing a stratified pattern. And finally, deriving inspiration from the kiln itself, Iranian-American architect Nader Khalili developed the Geltaftan Earth-and-Fire system as a way of constructing a house out of clay and then firing it from the inside to add strength and durability.

Antonio Gaudí implemented Rafael Guastavino's "Tile Arch System," based on the Catalan vault (also referred to as a timbrel vault). This system is thought to have descended from 14th-century Moorish building techniques that provided for lighter, more affordable, and more complex vaulting systems than conventional stone would allow. Guastavino's system, patented in the United States in 1885, used thin ceramic tiles laid flat in multiple layers bonded with rapid-setting mortar, resulting in a pliable, strong, and integrated structural

Figure 7.6
**The Walled
City of Shibam,
Yemen**

Figure 7.7
**The Great
Mosque of
Djenné, Mali,
courtesy of
Ruud Zwart**

system that could assume the shape of numerous geometries. Gaudí's Sagrada Familia church in Barcelona, Spain consists of thin Catalan vaults used to construct his signature catenary curves, hyperbolas, and parabolas.

Gaudí resourced regional Catalan traditions when cladding complex surfaces with locally produced ceramic tile. The material application of ceramic tile describes the widespread use of architectural clay that ornaments and protects the surfaces it covers. Used extensively inside and outside of Islamic architecture, buildings such as the Shah Mosque in Isfahan (1629) display shimmering and colorful surfaces of ceramic tile that homogenize disparate geometries into a continuous, fluid surface while they often communicate sacred verses written on this material. Referencing the millennial old tradition

Figure 7.8
Taos Pueblo, Taos, New Mexico

Figure 7.9
Chan Chan near Trujillo, Peru (capital of the Chimor empire 900–1470 CE)

of ceramic tile architecture in Asia, the office of Rodolfo Machado and Jorge Silvetti enveloped the Center for Asian Art (2015), an addition to the John and Mable Ringling Museum of Art in Sarasota, Florida, with over 3000 deep green, three-dimensional ceramic tiles whose variable and irregularly folded patterns shine under the Florida sky. Similarly, Amanda Levete reinterpreted Lisbon's calçada-tile pavements as three-dimensional ceramic tiles on the façade of the Museum of Art, Architecture and Technology in Lisbon (MAAT, 2016).

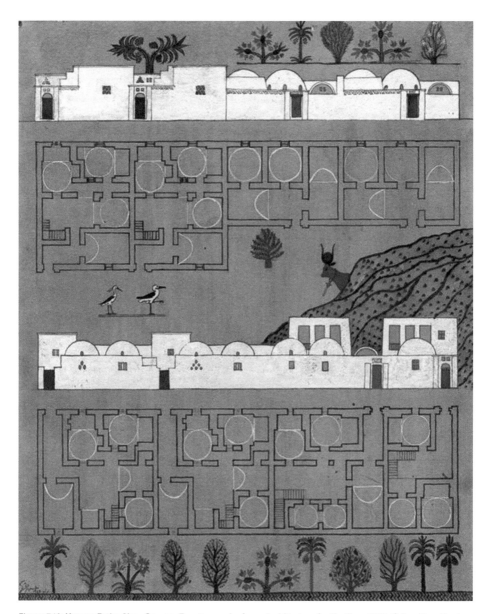

Figure 7.10 **Hassan Fathy, New Gourna, Egypt gouache from *Architecture for the Poor*, 1969,** © Aga Khan Trust for Culture/Hassan Fathy

Eladio Dieste pioneered structural tile in Uruguay with a number of single-layer shell structures constructed with funicular shapes. At the Iglesia de Cristo Obrero y Nuestra Señora de Lourdes in Estación Atlántida, Uruguay (Church of Christ the Worker and Our Lady of Lourdes, 1958–1960), also known more simply as Iglesia de Estación Atlántida, Dieste combined Gaussian vaults

Figure 7.11
**Nader Khalili,
Geltaftan
Earth-and-
Fire system
in Hesperia,
California,
courtesy of
California
Institute of
Earth Art and
Architecture**

and vertical ruled surfaces (*superficies regladas*) to transform humble brickwork into self-supporting systems of undulating walls and roof. Built of thin-shelled, single-brick thickness, Gaussian vaults derive stiffness and strength from the geometry of catenary arches that curve in two directions. Ruled surfaces begin as straight-line segments whose ends evolve into sinusoidal paths. Translated into the walls of the church, the curves are generated from straight lines at ground level that expand into conoidal waves as they rise to the top. Walls and roof meet at the intersection of two sets of parabolic curves, creating a flowing interior volume composed of undulating brick surfaces. Structures such as Félix Candela's thin undulating shells at the restaurant of the Hotel Casino de la Selva in Cuernavaca, Mexico (1956), Pier Luigi Nervi's ribbed dome at the Palazzetto dello Sport in Rome, Italy (1960), Paul Revere Williams' intersecting hyperbolic paraboloid of thin-shell concrete for the La Concha Motel in Las Vegas, Nevada (1961), or Antti Lovag's bubble rooms at the Palais Bulles in Cannes, France ("Palace of Bubbles," 1989), introduce reinforced concrete into the conversation of malleable earthen building materials, expanding the field of inquiry infinitely to the potential of radical curvilinear forms defined by superbly thin enclosures that offer the experience of inhabiting an ancient Greek terracotta pithos.

Metallurgy

The tower Gustave Eiffel designed for the 1889 Paris Exposition Universelle—commemorating the hundred-year anniversary of the French Revolution—is a decorative structure that symbolized the exposition's theme of "Utopia

Figure 7.12
**Rafael
Guastavino
vault patent
(1910)**

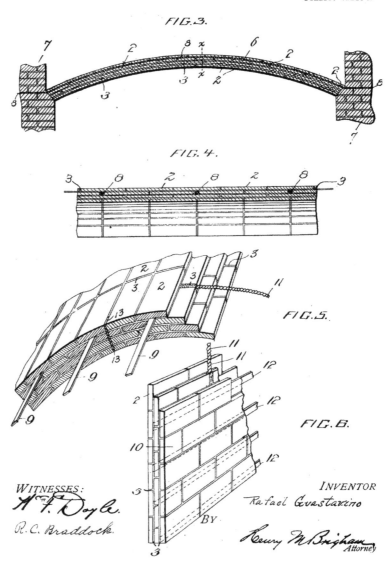

R. GUASTAVINO,
MASONRY STRUCTURE.
APPLICATION FILED JULY 31, 1908.

947,177.

Patented Jan. 18, 1910.
2 SHEETS—SHEET 2.

FIG.3.

FIG.4.

FIG.5.

FIG.6.

WITNESSES:

INVENTOR
Rafael Guastavino

BY

Henry M. Brigham
Attorney

Achieved." The Eiffel Tower's naked skeleton describes it as an ideal site for considering the performance of metallurgy unencumbered by the other four techniques of masonry, carpentry, weaving, and ceramics. Standing at 300 meters
tall, with 2.5 million rivets and a construction time of about 14 months, the
tower signifies both the city of Paris and the transformation of engineering into

Figure 7.13
Shah Mosque
(also known
as Masjed-e
Jadid-e Abbasi,
Royal Mosque,
or Imam
Mosque) in
Isfahan, Iran
(dating from
1611)

Figure 7.14
Machado
Silvetti, Asian
Art Study
Center at the
John and
Mable Ringling
Museum of Art
in Sarasota,
Florida (2015),
courtesy of
Machado
Silvetti, ©
Anton Grussi /
Esto

Figure 7.15
**Amanda
Levete, AL_A,
the Museum
of Art,
Architecture
and Technology
in Lisbon,
Portugal
(MAAT, 2016),
© Hufton and
Crow**

Figure 7.16
**Eladio Dieste,
Church in
Estación
Atlántida,
Uruguay (1952)**

Figure 7.17
Construction
of the concrete
roof of the
Palazzetto dello
Sport in Rome,
Italy for the
1960 Summer
Olympics by
the architect
Annibale
Vitellozzi and
the engineer
Pier Luigi
Nervi, courtesy
of Ministero
dei beni e
delle attività
culturali e del
turismo

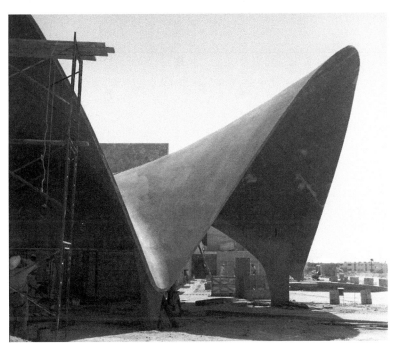

Figure 7.18
Paul Williams,
La Concha
Motel in
Las Vegas,
Nevada (1961),
permission and
credit courtesy
of Nevada
State Museum,
Las Vegas

Figure 7.19
**Antti Lovag,
Palais Bulles
("Palace of
Bubbles")
in Cannes,
France (1989),
courtesy
of Archives-
pierre-cardin**

architectural form. Sigfried Giedion observed that it "mastered the assembly of precisely dimensioned parts, so that the rivet holes of the factory-made members of the Eiffel tower could coincide to the tenth of a millimeter when being erected on site."[9] The first structure Eiffel's engineers Maurice Koechlin and Émile Nouguier designed simply relied on horizontal floors supported by shallow trussed arches. But in order to transform the tower into a gateway for the exhibition and underscore its sense of structural stability, they inserted a grand ornamental arch resembling Eiffel's 1882 design of the Garabit Viaduct, a bridge over the Truyère River in France, whose 541-foot-wide arch supports an 1854-foot-wide railway span. The addition of a decorative arch, in combination with almost no substantive function, emptied the tower of structural and programmatic demands. Ultimately its function has become to index the elasticity of steel structural systems, operate as an icon of the city, and perform as a symbol of French scientific advancements.

Giedion's description of the tower expresses the *poesis* of its *techne*: "the airiness one experiences when at the top of the tower makes it the terrestrial sister of the aeroplane" and, to a previously unknown extent, "the interpenetration of outer and inner space."[10] For Giedion, "the interpenetration of continuously changing viewpoints creates, in the eyes of the moving spectator, a glimpse into four-dimensional experience."[11] Although it may be hard to fathom, given Giedion's exuberance, at the time of its completion the tower for the Universal Exhibition was not universally appreciated. As Roland Barthes wrote: "Maupassant often lunched at the restaurant in the Tower, though he didn't care much for the food: It's the only place in Paris, he used to say, where I don't have to see it."[12] In considering the symbolic value of a structure that is almost impossible to avoid seeing from vantage points all over the city, Barthes understood that its significance remains intangibly linked to having absolutely no purpose at all. As he wrote, "even before it was built, it was

Figure 7.20
Preliminary
drawing of the
Eiffel Tower
by Maurice
Koechlin,
including size
comparison
with other
Parisian
landmarks
such as Notre
Dame de Paris,
the Statue of
Liberty, and
the Vendôme
Column

blamed for being useless, which, it was believed at the time, was sufficient to condemn it."[13] This is because "it was not in the spirit of a period commonly dedicated to rationality and to the empiricism of great bourgeois enterprises to endure the notion of a useless object."[14] Indeed, so vehement were reactions against this pure expression of technology that a Committee of Three Hundred signed a petition in 1887 protesting "against the erection ... of this useless and monstrous Eiffel Tower."[15]

The contradiction that the tower offers, between purposeless function and the purposeful expression of structure, merits analysis through Charles

Sanders Peirce's linguistic system of symbol, index, and icon. Peirce's terms operate as a system of signification wherein symbols attach linguistic meaning to the objects they describe through the process of established rules, indexes through traces of their performances, and icons through resemblance. The Eiffel tower symbolizes the city of Paris. As an index it meters out, one bolt at a time, the power of structural frames to distribute loads, resist lateral forces, and soar to great heights. And as an icon, it references triumphal arches and other ceremonial gateways. Due to its ability to measure actions, as a footprint in sand indicates the weight of the body, indexicality has emerged as an important operative term for architecture concerned with performance.

The tower materializes architecture's role in experimenting with innovative technologies, visualizing new conceptions of space, isolating design from programmatic requirements, producing a visual spectacle, and undressing steel frames. In comparison with the Eiffel Tower's naked structure, the Statue of Liberty, whose interior support Eiffel also engineered, is dressed. Auguste Bartholdi clothed the structure in an exterior envelop of folded and hammered copper plates to create the statue's flowing stola. The dressing of stone columns found in classical architecture compounds this vestimentary metaphor insofar as Vitruvius recounts that Ionic fluting, the sunken channels on a column's shaft, resembles the folds of a matron's garment. In comparison to the statue's voluminous gown, the Eiffel Tower offers a naked expression of the power of engineering to renew architecture through the truthful aesthetics of exposed structures. During its incipient use, according to Michael Adcock, "iron was merely a structural element, best kept hidden beneath more 'noble' materials such as a stone facade." As Adock hypothesizes: "The idea of constructing a building in which the inner elements were also the outer elements must have seemed as outlandish then as the 'inside-out' design of the Pompidou Centre seemed in our own time."[16]

The science of statics allowed engineers to complete precise calculations of structural forces to more closely determine material tolerances as buildings grew taller, thinner, and lighter than previous bearing-wall construction would allow. Steel is ductile, meaning that despite its strength, it is able to flex and stretch under pressure before actually breaking. The "moment frame," which relied upon a stiff or rigid (hence the name "rigid frame") connection, was often made with additional steel plates riveted between a beam and a column to prevent it from moving or rotating under dynamic forces. It translates structural forces through the entire system, thereby eliminating the need for extraneous supports such as bracing. Moment frames allow steel buildings to perform at a high capacity with the simple clarity of columns and beams for support. The three-dimensional grid system it generated would surface in varying degrees of synchronization across the façades of tall buildings, eventually metamorphosing into a structural diagrid enveloping buildings such as the Swiss Re Tower in London (see Figure 2.8).

The combination of elevator, steel frame, fire sprinklers, and curtain wall, incentivized by escalating real estate prices in Manhattan and Chicago, allowed buildings to attain previously unimagined heights. Heretofore, buildings had been limited to the number of floors a person could feasibly climb and the amount of weight a bearing wall could support. At 17 stories tall, the brick walls enclosing and supporting Daniel Burnham and John Wellborn Root's 1892 Monadnock Building in Chicago reached an unprecedented high of 215 feet. While the exterior masonry walls, augmented by a cast-iron cage structure, could have climbed higher, the challenge was that they had to grow proportionally thick at the base in order to support themselves at the top. The building's standing six-foot-thick walls at ground level squeezed out valuable commercial space.

Figure 7.21
Burnham and Root, north half of the Monadnock building in Chicago, Illinois (1891), courtesy of B. O'Kane / Alamy Stock Photo

Standing at ten stories tall and reaching a height of 138 feet, William LeBaron Jenney's Home Insurance Building in Chicago (1885) was the first steel-framed skyscraper supporting a curtain wall. Despite being a good 35% shorter than the Monadnock Building, it resolved the tectonic question of how to register the interior structure on the exterior elevations, while simultaneously allowing the curtain wall to express its non-structural capacity. The masonry skin registers its non-load-bearing capacity though large windows, larger than would be possible on a load-bearing structure. Indeed, the proportions of these windows align themselves with the dimensions of the steel grid beneath, with structural columns and beams expressed through projecting columns and spandrels. Despite this innovation, the building looks backward to the load-bearing ancestor of a typical Renaissance *palazzo* (palaces) such as Michelozzo di Bartolomeo's Palazzo Medici-Riccardi in Florence, Italy (1484). As with the Home Insurance Building, Renaissance *palazzi* are characterized by the five features of a courtyard, *piano nobile* (the "noble floor" usually at the second level), representational balcony (a central projection from which important dignitaries would greet the crowds below), a rusticated base, and a projecting cornice. The primary distinction between the original and its modern incarnation is the size of the window openings, offering an important tool for reading architecture as a manifestation of its interior structural logic.

Non-structural Enclosure

Among Semper's four elements and five techniques, woven mats, rugs, and complex knots locate architectural origins as coinciding with the beginning of textiles. For Semper, animal pens made of woven fences composed of tied sticks and branches introduced the earliest architectural constructs. The carpets that originally attached to supporting structures as enclosing membranes maintained vestiges of this role as hanging tapestries. For Semper, clothing referenced fabric enclosures through the German language's rich linguistic connotation of the words *Wand* or wall and *Gewand* or garment. He also pointed out that the term *Bekleidung* or cladding also references *Kleiden*, meaning to clothe or to dress. Semper's theory that textiles clothe buildings, expressed as his *Bekleidungsprinzip* or "dressing principle," recalibrated previous theories of architectural origins in terms of global references and traditionally feminine arts.

Renzo Piano's design for the Centre Culturel Jean-Marie Tjibaou in the southwest Pacific Ocean's island cluster of New Caledonia (1998) derives inspiration from traditional Melanesian Kanak chiefs' houses and other Kanak building techniques, taking Semper's argument full-circle. Combining industrially produced materials such as glass, aluminum, and steel with traditional wood and stone, Piano referenced Kanak woven vegetable fiber huts through a series of pavilions wrapped in porous walls made of wooden ribs and slats. The exterior enclosures of these buildings configure high-performance passive

Figure 7.22
**William
LeBaron Jenney,
Home Insurance
Building in
Chicago, Illinois
(1885), from
the United
States Library
of Congress's
National
Digital Library
Program under
the digital ID
mhsalad.250058**

ventilation systems, with resultant forms also evoking images of inhabitable parabolic baskets whose woven walls remain in a state of permanent completion. And finally, Bernard Cache and Patrick Beaucé of *L'atelier Objectile* translated the *Bekleidungsprinzip* into the digital language of contemporary architecture with their "Semper Pavilion" (1999). They transposed Semper's *bekleidungsprinzip* into software applications to facilitate the computer milling of two-dimensional wood panels forming a topology of interlacing digital knots.

Shigeru Ban dematerialized the enclosure of his unconventional "Curtain Wall House" (1995) in Tokyo, Japan with a pair of two-story-tall curtains free to blow in the wind. Hanging off of a cantilevered roof, these curtains may be

Figure 7.23
**Shigeru Ban,
Curtain Wall
House in
Tokyo, Japan
(1994–1995)**

Figure 7.24
**Renzo Piano,
Centre Culturel
Jean-Marie
Tjibaou near
Nouméa, the
capital of New
Caledonia
(1998), courtesy
of Renzo Piano
Architects and
Centre Culturel
Jean-Marie
Tjibaou,
photograph
courtesy of
Pierre Alain
Pantz**

drawn open or closed, allowing inhabitants to control the amount of privacy they require for a house located on the corner of two streets. An exemplar site for exploring Semper's concept of non-load-bearing woven enclosures remains the conventional curtain wall, a building system that carries within its own nomenclature the idea of pliable and lightweight fabric. In turn, the primary

Figure 7.25
**Bernard
Cache, "Digital
Semper,"**
*Anymore
Technology*
**(2009),
courtesy of
Bernard Cache**

site for considering the curtain wall's most pronounced architectural impact are early skyscrapers, offering a building type whose ability to reach soaring heights relied on the separation of structure and enclosure. A curtain wall may be any kind of enclosure—glass, brick, concrete panels, metal panel, fabric, etc.—that hangs off of a supporting structure. While it may be composed of any building material, the glass curtain wall in particular offered the advantage of articulating almost perfect transparency with the underlying structural system while opening up entire building floors to the unobstructed panoramas a tower's increased height would reveal.

Skeuomorph

The knots and textile patterns Semper transferred into the concept of *Bekleidung* provide a model for architectural ornaments forming the residue of what once were structural details. Semper describes the metamorphoses of details in response to the emergence of new materials with the concept of *Stoffwechsel*, meaning metabolism or material transformation. Henry Francis Mallgrave explains *Stoffwechsel* as "the process by which artistic forms undergo changes of material but carry forward vestiges or residues of their earlier material styles in later forms, symbolically alluding as it were to the materials used in the past."[17] The evolutionary tectonics of *Stoffwechsel* closely parallel the concept of *skeuomorph*, a term stemming from the Greek *skeuos*, meaning container or implement and *morphē* or form. A *skeuomorph* is an object that retains atavistic traces of its original identity through ornamental vestiges of components that previously functioned but are no longer of use. Think of stitching or bolts on plastic cases, the sound computers make when dragging an item into the "trash" or "recycle" bin, or the stamped wood grain on the metal siding of houses. A *skeuomorph* may perform as a transitional signifier between past and future technologies that helps negotiate unfamiliar systems through a more familiar representational language. When applied to architecture, past technologies surviving alongside new ones eventually register their tectonic history as ornaments.

How might this work? Reading Henri Labrouste's Bibliothèque Sainte-Geneviève in Paris (1838–1850) hinges on a single, salient detail to open the stone exterior to its cast-iron interior across the space of a wall's thickness. The library's façade features decorative *paterae* punctuating the spandrel spaces between stone arches that operate as *skeuomorphs* marking a transition from classical details to cast-iron building materials. Often featuring a bulbous knob called an *omphalos* or "bellybutton" projecting upward from the center, *paterae* served as libation bowls for making offerings to ancient Greek deities. As with much of the language of ritual that found its way into the ornamental program of Greek temples, *paterae* most frequently appeared on the friezes of Doric temples, alternating with bucrania, ox skulls with horns decorated with garlands. *Paterae* eventually entered the standard repertoire of architecture and the decorative arts as circular or oval ornaments with concentric rings often decorated with leaves and petals. They appear in a wide range of locations, including ceiling moldings, ornamental china, table legs, and the corner blocks of doorframes. Instead of using miter joints to frame two pieces of wood at 45-degree angles to form corners around doors, carpenters would insert a corner block often featuring a *patera*. Among the numerous details carpenters developed to join wood without messy visible connections, such as pelleting corners or slot screwing brackets, *paterae* offered an ornamental cover for visible screw joints. In this move from marble to wood and from sacred applications to decorative motifs, *paterae* smoothed architecture's transition away from literal classical uses.

At the Bibliothèque Sainte-Geneviève, cast-iron *paterae* bearing the library's monogram appear on the ground floor draped in wreaths and on the second floor, as iron discs encircled by ornamental leaves. Their appearance on the second floor, however, translates the sacred ornamental language of Greek

TRANCHE DE LA FAÇADE PRINCIPALE.　　　　COUPE.

Figure 7.26 Henri Labrouste, Library of Sainte-Geneviève (Paris, 1838–1850), partial elevation and section from *Revue générale de l'architecture et des travaux publics* (Paris: Ducher et cie., 1852, vol. 10, plate 23)

Figure 7.27
Henri Labrouste, reconstruction drawing of the Temple of Hera I, Paestum, 1828–1829, engraving by André Soudain (from Henri Labrouste, *Les Temples de Paestum: Restauration exécutée en 1829,* **1877)**

temples into the tectonic performance of holding the building together. They augment architecture's transition from stone to iron with a familiar gesture that seamlessly metamorphoses from one technology into another. In order to support a vaulted interior above the main reading room, Labrouste developed a structural system of prefabricated, cast-iron arches bolted together where a keystone normally would be placed in conventional stone arches. Meeting in the center, these "branches" spring from cast-iron columns running down the center of the space and from stone brackets on the walls. In order to securely attach the half-arch to the supporting stone corbel, Labrouste inserted tie-rods through the supporting walls, covering the structural scars left on the outside of the building with *paterae*.

During his time in Rome as a *pensionnaire* of the *Académie des Beaux-Arts* Labrouste completed drawings documenting temples located in the recently discovered Greek colonial city of Paestum (originally named Posedonia), Italy—the Temple of Hera I (ca. 550 BCE), the Temple of Hera II (ca. 460–450 BCE), and the Temple of Athena (500 BCE). The Temple of Hera I was referred to as a "Basilica" due to its unprecedented row of seven columns dividing the interior cella in half and making it appear to be a utilitarian public building instead of a temple. Giovanni Battista Piranesi produced the most celebrated drawings of the Paestum temples (1778–1779), displaying highly contrasting chiaroscuro that depicts the monuments as saturated with chthonic forces. Appropriate to the tectonics of stone trabeation, the columns on this Doric temple exhibit a muscular entasis, the perspective correction of parallel lines through a slight bulge towards the middle. The ionic order, on the contrary, was more appropriate for translating thick stone columns into the slender cast-iron versions Labrouste designed. Most importantly, both temple and library display the structural system of columns running down the center of these spaces.

The library explicates Labrouste's dialogue with Victor Hugo, who was then questioning architecture's ability to perform as a text that he would raise in *The Hunchback of Notre-Dame*. Neil Levine's intrepid research indicates that this building was "the first significant architectural response to the issues raised by Hugo."[18] While Hugo was working on *Notre-Dame de Paris* (later to become *The Hunchback of Notre-Dame*), Labrouste agreed to critique sections of the manuscript concerning architecture. This is the publication that initiated a quarrel between the book and the building discussed in Chapter 1, resulting in the apocalyptic statement of *Ceci tuera cela*: "This will kill That; The book will kill the building." As a form of architectural writing, Labrouste engraved the names of 810 scholars on the exterior façades to communicate its role as a library. Almost as if looking through a glass wall, the three columns of names located underneath the arches on the façades register the three sections of book stacks directly behind them inside the main reading room.

Placed in the context of Hugo's book, Labrouste's writing on walls of stone argues for architecture's continued cultural relevance as an enduring form of communication that in fact preserves books. In other words, books require libraries for their basic survival. For Levine, who describes the building as a *machine à lire* (a machine for reading), "the analogy of the printed book allowed architecture to break out of the confines of classicism and develop a functional form of expression."[19] As this project attests, architecture's tectonic narrative resides in the transition from ornament to details. Even when a building is visibly devoid of extraneous decoration derived from historical references such as *paterae*, highly wrought details are in fact sublimated ornaments.

Detail

Although Aby Warburg coined the phrase "God lies in the detail" as a foundation for his iconographical method for reading art, Ludwig Mies van der Rohe is most often credited with its enunciation. Let us not forget that the devil, too, lies in the detail. The condition of ornament disguised as detail is made especially clear in Mies's work where an articulate assemblage of tectonic components disguises its ornamental status. At the Seagram Building in New York City (1958), Mies expressed the idea of structural steel columns, which actually are hidden within concrete fireproofing, by attaching small bronze "I" sections to the exterior of the building as ornamental keys to unlock the larger structural concept hidden within. Transforming the idea of ornament from a cover applied to conceal the imprecise joining of materials into the detailing of

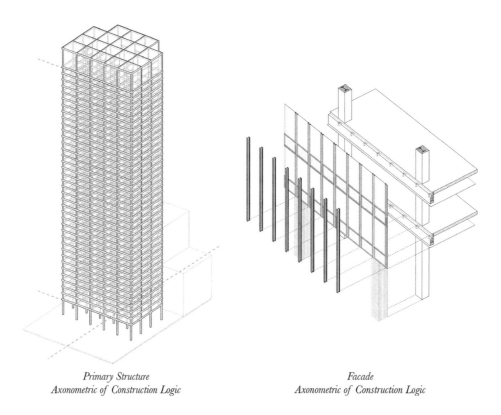

Primary Structure
Axonometric of Construction Logic

Facade
Axonometric of Construction Logic

**Figure 7.28
Diagram of
Ludwig Mies
van der Rohe's
Seagram
Building (New
York City, 1958)
by Paula Bizais
and Fallon
Walton**

materials precisely joined without any covering element expresses an ethos of Miesian modernism. The absence of ornamentation has become the ornament itself, located in the gaps, joinery, and studied connections of precise details.

Returning architecture to its vestimentary analogy, the term *detail* emerged in France around 1600 as *détail*: stemming from *detaillier* (to cut in pieces), *taillier* and *tailleur* (tailor), and *tailleor* (stone-mason), the person who cuts stone. Builders tend to saw before they hammer and quarry before they lay stone, describing the process of detailing as a material cut that architects mend or tailor. The way in which an architect closes or does not close this gap offers a defining moment of how to read a building from the position of *pars pro toto*, from the way in which a part describes its whole or a detail offers clues to unraveling the entire design narrative. Carlo Scarpa's architecture and Marco Frascari's interpretations of this work offer a striking instantiation of cut and sutured details. As Frascari illuminates us in "The Tell-the-Tale Detail," in Scarpa's work "each detail tells us the story of its making, of its placing, and of its dimensioning."[20]

A project that telescopes Scarpa's material details into a reading of his overall design concept is the Castelvecchio Museum in Verona, Italy (1958–1975). Scarpa transformed an existing medieval fortress, which had remained in use since its initial construction in the 12th century, into a museum of medieval, Renaissance, and 19th-century art. A public street leading to a bridge over the Adige River cuts through the middle of the site, creating a gap between its two wings and preventing Scarpa from connecting the museum at ground level. He responded to this challenge with an exterior bridge connecting the two existing second floors that reflects in macrocosm the microcosm of details found throughout the building. These details emphasize gaps between various materials. The bridge acts as a spatial hinge, with stairs circling around the focal point of the entire project, an equestrian statue of *Cangrande della Scala*, Lord of Verona between 1309 and 1329. The statue can be seen from a number of exterior viewpoints that lead visitors along a path that deposits them at the point of almost being able to touch it, but kept at a distance by a spatial gap. The statue punctuates the opening between the wings that

Figure 7.29
Carlo Scarpa,
*Museo
Civico di
Castelvecchio*
in Verona, Italy
(1959–1973),
photograph by
Paolo Monti

operates as a ceremonial detail, a gap in space that simultaneously separates and joins the two existing buildings. Frascari argues for "the conceptual identification of the detail with the making of the joint and the recognition that details themselves can impose order on the whole through their own order."[21] He approaches the joint as a fertile detail, the place where construction and the construing of architecture occur in the telling of a story that we may read as an essential part of understanding a building. He concludes this essay with a quotation from Louis Kahn, a strong admirer of Scarpa's work: "The joint is the beginning of ornament. And that must be distinguished from decoration which is simply applied. Ornament is the adoration of the joint."[22]

Cosmetics

Writing about "The Lamp of Truth" in *The Seven Lamps of Architecture* (1849), John Ruskin outlined three types of architectural deceits: "the suggestion of a mode of structure or support, other than the true one," "the painting of surfaces to represent some other material than that of which they actually consist," and "the use of cast or machine-made ornaments of any kind."[23] Ruskin's important concept of truth in materials has simultaneously influenced and limited the reading of architecture as necessarily expressing a tectonic of pure, unadulterated surfaces. When interpreting a building through Ruskin's abstinent lens, then, the way in which a material does or does not express its essential nature becomes a significant term of assessment. A brick must not be painted and should perform according the compressive forces inherent in its physics; wood grain only should appear on wood, *trompe-l'œil* surfaces are prohibited, and so on. In Ruskin's 19th-century milieu, when craftsmen were plentiful and materials natural, this position strikes a chord with the preservation of architecture's inherent identity of duration and stability. This position makes less sense in a contemporary world of commercial architecture where classical capitals are manufactured in fiberglass, exterior insulation and finishing systems (EIFS) stand in for actual plaster, plastic laminate imitates granite, or false window mullions are attached to the surface of glass. In these instances Ruskin's lamp of "truth" becomes one of "economy" as the costs of real materials and craftsmanship escalate. "Less costs more," as the saying goes. In these instances expressing the truth in materials is, in fact, to work with their essential fiction. Accentuating brick's decorative role as an applied panel or experimenting with plastic's ability to take on numerous forms and colors reveals the inherent beauty of truth as artifice.

Vitruvius's architectural triad of *firmitas*, *utilitas*, and *venustas* argues that a building should be solid, useful, and beautiful. This trinity has most commonly been translated into English as commodity, firmness, and delight, with the term *beauty* sequestered from the conversation.[24] However, the term *Vitruvius* used for beauty was *venustas*, letting loose the goddess Venus and her numerous pagan guises into architectural theory. This Latin term, as Peter Collins writes, literally represents the salient qualities possessed by the goddess Venus that "clearly implied a visual quality in architecture that would arouse the emotion of love."[25] Mario Perniola considers the plural implications of Venusian charm with her name referring to *Venenum*, which "also means dye, tint, color, and by extension makeup, 'maquillage.'"[26] He clarifies that the Venusian charm of *venenum*, which also signifies venum or poison, operates like the Greek term *pharmakon* introduced in Chapter 1, with a double meaning that can be used both positively and negatively.[27] The makeup and tints of cosmetics involves the art of beautifying while also invoking *techne*. *Cosmetic*, in turn, derives from the Greek *kosmetikē tekhnē* (κοσμητικὴ τέχνη), meaning the technique of dress and ornament, and from *kosmos*, meaning cosmos, order, and ornament. As applied beauty relating to processes like dyeing, tinting, coloring, and putting on makeup, cosmetics linger in the classical language of architecture with an understanding of beauty as only skin deep.

According to Mona Mahall and Asli Serbest, "for the Greeks kosmese meant the making-visible of a surface and the creating of an appearance."[28] For Semper, as Mahall and Serbest posit: "Architecture can be related to decoration in referring to the universal idea of the Greek word cosmos and its lexical meanings of ornament and world order."[29] In 1856 Semper offered a lecture in Zurich entitled "On the Formal Lawfulness of Ornament and Its Meaning as an Artistic Symbol" ("Ueber die formelle Gesetzmässigkeit des Schmuckes und dessen Bedeutung als Kunstsymbolik"), focusing on the Greek word *kosmos* as both cosmic order, cosmetics, and adornment.[30]

The relation of *kosmese* to cosmetics remains consistent with Greek temples whose white marble surfaces were painted in vivid, bright colors. It also describes chryselephantine (from Greek *chrysos*, meaning gold, and *elephantinos*, meaning ivory) statues—hollow bodies made of wood scaffolding to which would be attached various materials simulating a divinity dressed in full regalia. Thin pieces of ivory were carved and painted to stand in for faces and skin; sheets of gold leaf represented garments, armor, and hair; and glass or precious stones detailed elements such as eyes, jewelry, and weaponry.

Semper traveled to Greece and Rome studying classical polychromy, seeking traces of paint on sites such as the Parthenon and Trajan's Column. But he also drew from Antoine-Chrysostome Quatremère de Quincy's *Le Jupiter olympien, ou l'art de la sculpture antique considéré sous un nouveau point de vue* (*The Olympian Jupiter, or the Art of Antique Sculpture Considered Under a New Point of View*, 1814). Quatremère de Quincy was among the first scholars to argue for the use of polychromy in classical art and architecture, publishing colored illustrations of the chryselephantine statues of Zeus (Jupiter) at the sanctuary of Olympia and of Athena (Minerva) in the Parthenon, which Phidias constructed in gold and ivory. Quatremère de Quincy challenged the conventional reading of white marble as defining the quintessence of classical art and architecture, and, by extension, Western cultural identity. In addition to arguing for the use of polychromy on statues and temples, he further disrupted idealized canons of classical of purity when describing the encrustation of precious materials such as metals, enamels, and stones on architectural components such as stylobates, metopes, triglyphs, and acroteria. He argued that a combination of paint, stucco, and wax was used on temples in order to cover material imperfections, protect against weather and erosion, to break up

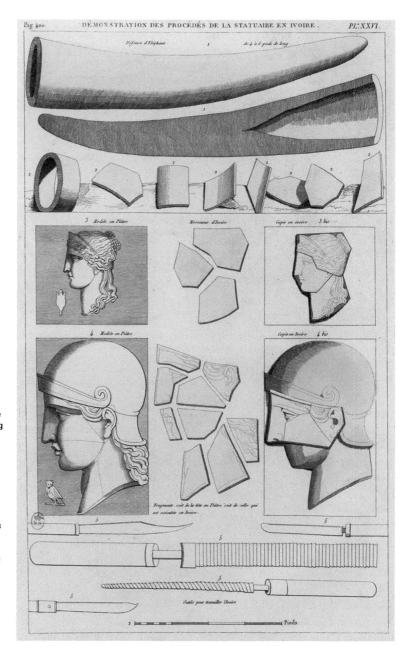

Figure 7.30
Antoine-
Chrysostome
Quatremère de
Quincy, making
ivory pieces
for the statue
of Minerva,
*Le Jupiter
olympien,
ou l'art de
la sculpture
antique
considéré sous
un nouveau
point de vue
(The Olympian
Jupiter, or the
Art of Antique
Sculpture
Considered
Under a New
Point of View,
1814)*

the monotony of whiteness, "or to provide some sort of trompe l'oeil without trespassing into actual painting."[31] As he wrote: "the use of marble by the ancients was so widespread that to leave it unadorned would have struck anyone who saw it as something rather cheap, especially in a temple. Colours were not merely used to make other materials look like marble, but to change the appearance of marble too."[32]

Semper picked up the debate, as Mallgrave reiterates, arguing that the first temples were staged platforms for communal rituals, "scaffolds upon which were attached decorative flowers, festoons, sacrificial animals, implements, shields."[33] Eventually these elements became permanent, colorful ornaments such as fillets, egg-and-dart motifs, arabesques, or rosettes. Mark Wigley makes the similar claim when stating that, for Semper, architecture begins with ornament. "It is not just that the architecture of a building is to be found in the decoration of its structure," he writes, "there is no building without decoration. It is decoration that builds."[34] As Wigley continues, this hierarchical reversal of ornament's role in architecture's origins also imposes itself on traditional spatial distinctions between inside and outside when textiles not only precede the construction of solid walls but also continue to organize the building when such construction begins.[35] Mahall and Serbest, following Wigley's hypothesis, argue that cosmesis allowed Semper to approach architecture as structural makeup, wherein: "Architecture is actually not to be found in its decoration but is structured by its decoration."[36] "By virtue of the inherent lawfulness that these processes impose on form making," as Mallgrave similarly offers, "architecture comes to be defined in its essence as an ornamental activity."[37]

Given the potential for architecture to be undermined by its own decorative program, it come as little surprise that Adolf Loos would struggle with ornamentation in his landmark essay "Ornament and Crime" (1910). In a piece of writing that has left the indelible expression in architecture that "ornament *is* a crime," Loos counters his own principle when acknowledging "the urge to ornament one's face, and everything within one's reach is the origin of fine art."[38] Loos's objection resided in his understanding that the ornament produced in his time bore no relation to the world at large.[39] Despite his protests to the contrary, built into architecture's most essential function as the *sine qua non* of the Vitruvian triad is the *venustas* of ornamentation that elevates mute buildings into expressive architecture. More importantly, by virtue of the concept that building is utilitarian and architecture requires an aesthetic supplement, architecture is inhabitable ornament. Nonetheless, pure and unadulterated ornamentation on buildings maintains the propensity to transgress architecture's proper boundaries as a source of aesthetic ambivalence.

Rem Koolhaas and OMA's "Haunted House," an exhibition space at Fondazione Prada's offices and permanent galleries in Milan, Italy (2008), is located in a renovated gin distillery dating from 1910. In order to distinguish this building from the other six existing on the site, the firm devised a compositional

strategy for this structure to stand out by cladding it in 24-carat gold leaf. The gold skin dematerializes form into pure shimmer, while it challenges conventional understandings of architecture's rootedness in truthful materials. Koolhaas, however, was not entirely innovative in using what might be considered an iconoclastic surfacing material. It should be remembered that Frank Lloyd Wright recommended gold leaf to cover the concrete exterior of Falling Water.

Notes

1   Farshid Moussavi, *The Function of Ornament*, eds. Michael Kubo and Fashid Moussavi (Barcelona: Actar, 2006), p. 8.

2   Thanks to Mikesch Muecke for pointing this out to me and for his book *Gottfried Semper in Zurich: An Intersection of Theory and Practice* (Lulu.com, 2005).

3   Kenneth Frampton, *Studies in Tectonic Culture: The Poetics of Construction in Nineteenth and Twentieth Century Architecture* (Cambridge, MA: MIT Press, 1995), p. 6.

4   Gottfried Semper, *Style in the Technical and Tectonic Arts, or, Practical Aesthetics Style*, trans. Harry Francis Mallgrave and Michael Robinson (Los Angeles: Getty Research Institute, 2004), p. 666.

5   Ibid.

6   Frampton, *Studies in Tectonic Culture*, p. 4.

7   Ibid, p. 249.

8   http://www.searsarchives.com/homes.

9   Sigfried Giedion, *Space, Time, and Architecture: The Growth of a New Tradition*, 3rd ed. (Cambridge, MA: Harvard University Press, 1954), p. 279.

10 Ibid, pp. 282 and 432.

11 Ibid, p. 284.

12 Roland Barthes, "The Eiffel Tower," in *A Barthes Reader*, ed. Susan Sontag (New York: Hill and Wang, 1982), p. 236.

13 Ibid, p. 239.

14   Ibid.

15 Giedion, *Space, Time, and Architecture*, p. 282.

16 Michael Adcock, "Remaking Urban Space: Baron Haussmann and the Rebuilding of Paris, 1851–1851" *University of Melbourne Library Journal 2*, no. 2 (1996), https://library.unimelb.edu.au/__data/assets/pdf_file/0008/1624850/adcock.pdf.

17 Harry Francis Mallgrave, *Modern Architectural Theory* (Cambridge: Cambridge University Press, 2005), pp. 136–136.

18 Neil Levine, "The Book and the Building: Hugo's Theory of Architecture and Labrouste's Bibliothéque Ste-Geneviéve," in *The Beaux Arts and Nineteenth-Century French Architecture*, ed. Robin Middleton (Cambridge, MA: MIT Press, 1982), p. 142.

19 Ibid, p. 173.

20 Marco Frascari, "The Tell-the-Tale Detail," in *VIA 7: The Building of Architecture* (Cambridge, MA: MIT Press, 1984), p. 29.

21 Ibid, p. 24.

22 Ibid, p. 29.

23 John Ruskin, *The Seven Lamps of Architecture* (New York: Wiley, 1849), p. 29.

24 According to David Brussat: "We owe the modern triad to Sir Henry Wotton, who translated (or paraphrased) the Vitruvian ideals in his 1624 work *The Elements of Architecture.* "*Commodity, Firmness, and Delight, or Toward a New Architectural Attitude.*" 12/13/2010. https://classicistne.wordpress.com/2010/12/13/commodity-firmness-and-delight-or-toward-a-new-architectural-attitude.

25 Peter Collins, "Commodity, Firmness, and Delight: The Ultimate Synthesis" *Encyclopedia Britannica*, https://www.britannica.com/topic/architecture/Commodity-firmness-and-delight-the-ultimate-synthesis. According to Collins, as the Latin term for beauty and the salient qualities possessed by the goddess Venus, *venustas* "clearly implied a visual quality in architecture that would arouse the emotion of love; but it is of interest to note that one of the crucial aspects of this problem was already anticipated by Alberti in the 15th century, as is made clear by his substitution of the word *amoenitas* ('pleasure') for Vitruvius' more anthropomorphic term *venustas*. Alberti not only avoids the erotic implications of the term venustas but, by subdividing *amoenitas* into *pulchritudo* and *ornamentum*, gives far more precise indications as to the type of visual satisfaction that architecture should provide. *Pulchritudo*, he asserts, is derived from harmonious proportions that are comparable to those that exist in music and are the essence of the pleasure created by

architecture. *Ornamentum*, he claims, is only an 'auxiliary brightness,' the quality and extent of which will depend essentially on what is appropriate and seemly. Both *pulchritudo* and *ornamentum* were thus related to function and environment in that, ideally, they were governed by a sense of decorum; and, since the etymological roots of both 'decoration' and 'decorum' are the same, it will be understood why, before 1750, the term decoration had in both English and French a far less superficial architectural implication than it often does today."

26   Mario Perniola, "'Venus' as Venom," in *Recoding Metaphysics: The New Italian Philosophy*, ed. Barbara Borradori and trans. Barbara Spackman (Evanston, IL: Northwestern University Press, 1988), http://www.marioperniola.it/site/dettag liotext.asp?idtexts=91.

27   Collins, *Encyclopedia Britannica*.

28   Mona Mahall and Asli Serbest, *How Architecture Learned to Speculate* (Stuttgart: Institut Grundlagen moderner Architektur und Entwerfen (IGMA), Universität Stuttgart, 2009), p. 39.

29   Ibid.

30   Mallgrave, *Modern Architectural Theory*, p. 136.

31   Paolo Bertoncini Sabatini, "Antoine Chrysostôme Quatremère de Quincy (1755–1849) and the Rediscovery of Polychromy in Grecian Architecture: Colour Techniques and Archaeological Research in the Pages of 'Olympian Zeus,'" in *Proceedings of the Second International Congress on Construction History* (Cambridge: Queen's College, University of Cambridge: 2006), p. 401, cf. A.-C. Quatremère de Quincy, *Dictionnaire historique d'architecture, comprenant dans son plan les notions historiques, descriptives, archéologiques, biographiques, théoriques, didactiques et pratiques de cet art; par M. Quatremère de Quincy, de l'Institut Royal de France (Académie des inscriptions et belles-lettres), et secrétaire perpétuel de l'Académie des beaux-arts* (2 vols, Paris, 1832), vol. 1.

32   Bertoncini Sabatini, "Antoine Chrysostôme Quatremère de Quincy." p. 404.

33   Mallgrave, *Modern Architectural Theory*, p. 132.

34   Mark Wigley, *White Walls, Designer Dresses: The Fashioning of Modern Architecture* (Cambridge, MA: MIT Press, 1995), p. 11.

35   Ibid, p. 12.

36   Mahall and Serbest, *How Architecture Learned to Speculate*, p. 39.

37   Mallgrave, *The Four Elements of Architecture and Other Writings*, p. 29.

38   Adolf Loos, "Ornament and Crime," in *Programs and Manifestoes in 20th Century Architecture*, ed. Ulrich Conrads (Cambridge, MA: MIT Press, 1971), p. 19.

Chapter 8

Inhabitation

It is the between that is tainted with strangeness. Everything remains to be said on the subject of the Ghost and the ambiguity of the Return, for what renders it intolerable is not so much that it is an announcement of death nor even the proof that death exists, since this Ghost announces and proves nothing more than his return. What is intolerable is that the Ghost erases the limit which exists between two states, neither alive nor dead; passing through, the dead man returns in the manner of the Repressed. It is his coming back which makes the ghost what he is, just as it is the return of the Repressed that inscribes the repression. In the end, death is never anything more than the disturbance of the limits. The impossible is to die.[1]

—*Hélène Cixous*

In *A Room of One's Own* (1929) Virginia Woolf considered the necessary solitude that a private space affords female writers to refine their creative processes. Woolf keenly understood the potential for women to be shuttered in spaces of domestic propriety and out of professional opportunity. In 1919 Woolf and her husband moved to Monk's House in East Sussex, England, where they built a "writing lodge" for her to work in. Reading the small space of this intimate room, the solitary desk positioned in the center allowed for Woolf to gaze through glass doors to infinite quietude as she composed her interior monologues. While rooms today may be locked and closed to keep prying eyes from looking in, closing the door to increasingly public access makes a room only of one's own the more exceptional space in which to dwell.

Reading architecture as a series of interior dialogues between rooms and those who inhabit them considers the ways in which space responds to lived experiences as they are handed down across generations, accrue individually over time, or learned on the spot. The bodily choreography required to poach an egg, plant a garden, or properly wash windows leaves a residue of the performance as permanent and impermanent traces on their responsive surfaces, the worn spot on the floor in front of the stove, the residue in a mudroom after a storm, or streaks left on the windows. As with fingerprints, which leave a

Figure 8.1
Virginia Woolf's writing lodge at Monk's House in East Sussex, England (from 1919), courtesy of National Trust Image / Andreas von Einsiedel

direct mark of a person's impression on an object, domesticity indexes the human body.

Architecture often strives to anticipate these traces spatially and materially. The sink Alvar Aalto designed for patients' rooms at the Paimio Sanatorium in Finland (1933) features an angle of repose that mitigates the noise of splashing water. The interior wood surface of Snøhetta's Norwegian Wild Reindeer Centre Pavilion (2011) merges computer and hand-crafted fabrication processes (shipbuilders' timber pegging and digital milling) to form multiple surfaces for diverse bodies. Undulating from ceiling to floor, it provides a series of stepped curves that form and deform into a variety of sitting positions, while producing an interior topography that seems to emerge from the natural context.

Gaston Bachelard contemplated the activities of dwelling and dreaming that architecture may summon in *The Poetics of Space* (1958). As Bachelard considered the house, it makes sense from the standpoint of architectural poetry "to say that we 'write a room,' 'read a room,' or 'read a house.'"[2] The ways in which architecture transforms inhabitation into poetry may involve sensorial delights such as the position of windows so that shadows of leaves sway on a curtain during an summer afternoon's breeze or the sun cracks into the bedroom on a crisp winter morning. The space of dreams may elicit incubi and succubi haunting one's sleep as they crawl out from the crevices of floor boards, closets, and one's darker imagination. Moving vertically from cellar to garret and penetrating the intimacy of drawers and wardrobes, Bachelard investigated how we experience houses from day to day, "on the thread of a narrative, or in the telling of our own story."[3] The sound of wolves sharpening their claws outside the cabin door on a stormy night only serves to heighten the pleasure of sitting inside to "listen to the stove roaring in the evening

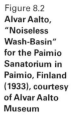

Figure 8.2
**Alvar Aalto,
"Noiseless
Wash-Basin"
for the Paimio
Sanatorium in
Paimio, Finland
(1933), courtesy
of Alvar Aalto
Museum**

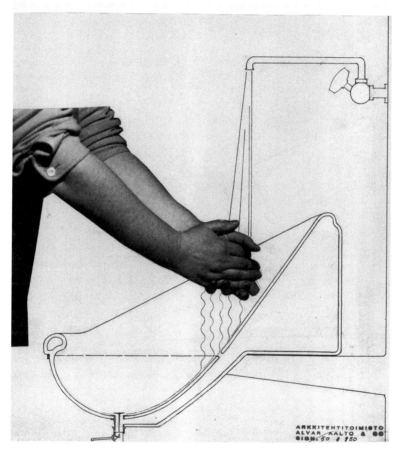

noiseless wash-basin

No noises, no water splashes when washing your hands in running water, because the basin-china is in position of 45 degrees.

stillness, while an icy wind blows against the house."[4] Bachelard elevated bodily knowledge above abstract logic, claiming "a house that has been experienced is not an inert box. Inhabited space transcends geometrical space."[5]

As a *locus* for reading the patterns of everyday life, the domestic interior compresses the multiple and often gendered performances of architecture—food preparation, personal hygiene, privacy, sexuality, financial management, domestic chores, cultural ritual, and more—into an *oikonomia* (with the Greek *oikos* referencing "household" and *nemein* meaning "management") as an economy of spatial patterns of inhabitation. Stemming from the Latin *inhabitare*, meaning "to dwell in," inhabitation maintains at its core the persistence

Figure 8.3
Snøhetta,
Tverrfjellhytta,
Norwegian
Wild Reindeer
Pavilion in
Hjerkinn,
Dovre, Norway
(2011)

of habits, something we do by nature and without thinking. The act of inhabitation results in embodied practices of everyday life, the performance of activities that often derive from quotidian rituals. The degree to which a space composes the gestures of everyday life or, conversely, adjusts to the movements and patterns of those who dwell within, offers tools for reading architecture through patterns of inhabitation.

Writing in *Outline of a Theory of Practice*, Pierre Bourdieu describes *habitus* as encompassing the social power of fundamental behavioral patterns and gestures inscribed in the body, shaping its most fundamental habits and skills.[6] The differences between eating a meal from a table or cross-legged on a floor, taking a bath or showering, cooking on a brazier or on a stove, or using a fork or a piece of bread as utensils all describe forms of *habitus* determined by the spaces and tools that inhabit us.

With respect to notions of privacy that emerged during the 19th century, Michael Dennis notes a transition during the 18th century, when a *res privata* eroded the *res publica* and "freestanding object buildings began to replace enclosed public space as the focus of architectural thought."[7] A conventional understanding of modern architecture identifies a drive to dissolve the distinction between interior spaces and the exterior world, as part of an attempt to introduce natural light and fresh air into stuffy and insalubrious Victorian rooms. This drive also did away with familial traces of inhabitation accumulated among the mementos and bric-à-brac that encrusted these rooms. The objects inhabiting the houses of our childhood, writes Jean Baudrillard, provide depth and resonance to our memories in a complex structure of interiority, and serve as boundary markers of the symbolic configuration of the home. "The caesura between inside and outside, and their formal opposition," he continues, "make this traditional space into a closed transcendence" where the objects that furnish it become household gods, "spatial incarnations of the emotional bonds and the permanence of the family group."[8] Sweeping away the psychological dust bunnies accumulated in the corners of domestic spaces became imperative. Modern police strategies offered a key to unlocking closed rooms and evacuating this dust. Psychoanalysis offered another. And the replacement of household servants with mechanical household appliances provided a third. Focusing on the subjects of the detective, the psychoanalyst, and the maid, these avenues of inquiry distill architecture's interior drives into characters of a fiction written for reading architecture as inhabitation.

The Detective

Let us begin by visualizing a room where a homicide has been committed. This room has been locked from within, but no one is inside and all the windows are sealed shut, leaving no means of entry or egress. How would you begin to analyze the scene of the crime? This is the enigma Monsieur C. Auguste Dupin faced when trying to solve the *Murders in the Rue Morgue* (1841), a short story by Edgar Allan Poe that initiated the genre of the detective novel. This tale also serves as a definitive moment for what has come to be called the locked-room dilemma, a puzzle no one can seem to solve except for the canny sleuth who uses logic and highly honed powers of observation to unravel the mystery. Locked-room mysteries have come to characterize a certain 19th-century anxiety regarding the distinction between exterior worlds and interior spaces. The locked apartment identifies the potential for a room to transform from a space of insulation against metropolitan chaos into a realm of shadows and secrets.

The shuttered rooms of Dupin's quarters in the Faubourg St Germain of Paris underscore an increasing unease regarding distinctions between 'inside' and 'outside' that Mark Madoff adduces in relation to the detective's interior *locus*, "a place of unexpected, inexplicable peril, of chaos which seems to sweep aside even the usual laws of physics."[9] As Jill Lepore maintains, 19th-century Americans were obsessed with physical boundaries marking privacy, "like the walls of a house, and, equally, with the holes in those walls, like mail slots cut into doors."[10] Lepore links sleuthing, architecture, and tectonics when explaining: "To detect is, etymologically, to remove the roof of a house."[11]

What of these locked doors and shuttered windows in terms of an increasingly chaotic exterior world? Luc Boltanski argues that detective fiction developed concurrently with the invention and description of a new mental illness that psychiatry labeled as paranoia. In this case: "The investigator in a detective story thus acts like a person with paranoia, the difference being that he is healthy."[12] The rising vocation of the professional detective augmented this anxiety. Poe based Dupin on Eugène François Vidocq—considered to be the father of modern criminology and the first private eye—a former criminal who founded the detective branch of the civil police force called the *Sûreté Nationale* in 1812 and the first private detective agency. This transition toward heightened social administration and state surveillance purportedly resulted in promoting the modern police societies that protected bourgeois property and sexual morality. In contrast to this normalizing system of control, Dupin was a counterculture figure or secret confidant who demonstrated Poe's concept of ratiocination, a method of analysis executed through logic and close observation. Dupin exercised the kind of resourceful imagination and unorthodox reasoning abilities, thoughtfulness and patience, which provide model methods for reading architecture through intimate details. "Here is the origin of the detective story," Walter Benjmain writes, "which inquires into these traces and follows these tracks."[13]

As Benjamin summarized, with "The Philosophy of Furniture" (1840) and "new detectives," Poe became "the first physiognomist of the domestic interior."[14] Benjamin's analysis also proffered clues for reading architecture from the inside of these 19th-century rooms through terms such as *étui*, traces, collections, and detectives. As souvenirs and mementos of the people living there, a proliferation of domestic objects came to form interior collections the inhabitant curated. Writing of Benjamin, Georges Teyssot notes: "It is during this period that his idea of 'dwelling' was established, with all the variations of meaning encompassed by the notion of habitation."[15] Traces accumulate on the domestic interior through the patterns of everyday use—the fingerprints and scuff marks, wear and tear, mends and amends that deposit a residue of human inhabitation and identify focal points for examining otherwise undetected details. The title of Naomi Schor's *Reading in Detail: Aesthetics and the Feminine* (1987) frames this approach to embroidering the finer points of interior spaces as "bounded on the one side by the *ornamental*, with its traditional connotations of effeminacy and decadence, and on the other, by the everyday, whose 'prosiness' is rooted in the domestic sphere of social life presided over by women."[16]

Fingerprints leave traces. The scientific analysis of identifying a person by the most unique and specific physiognomic detail codified in 1888, when Francis Galton developed a way to classify the ridges on our fingers as part of forensic science. This new approach to identification, necessary in the increasingly ugly and crowded metropolis, parallels the emergence of developing specific street addresses necessary to help the police locate a suspect's abode. The trajectory of this milieu eventually implicates modern architecture's preferred materials of chrome, glass, white walls, and polished marble as ideal surfaces for imprinting one's digits. Modernism's hygienic compulsions and open plans worked toward displacing *étui*, traces, collections, and corpses from its interiors, while making detection all that more accessible.

For Poe, the real crime was bad taste in decoration. In "The Philosophy of Furniture" he described an ideal room, elevating the practice of interior decoration to a literary conceit while instructing his audience on how to read a room. Gas-lit glass chandeliers represented the quintessence of false taste. Instead, to avoid the glare and glitter they produce, he proposed an oil lamp Aimé Argand patented in 1780 whose plain ground-glass shade cast uniform moonlight rays. Charles Baudelaire, who translated a number of Poe's works into French, wrote an introduction to "The Philosophy of Furniture," commenting "that the room which he offers us as a model of simplicity, is one which will seem to many a model of luxury."[17] Baudelaire drew from Poe's exegesis on interior decoration the sentiment that it is a delightful pleasure to imagine an ideal home as a place of dreams, described by silk, gold, wood, and metal, flickering in softened sunlight, or the brilliance of artificial lamps.

Characterizing the domestic imaginary of his time, Poe's detective novels elucidate rooms surrounded by doors disguised as bookcases, locked chambers, secret corridors, hidden drawers, and open keyholes. Wearied by the proximity of crowds, the inhabitant returns to her or his rooms inhaling an aroma of *parfum noire*, Baudelaire's allusion to the intermingling of sensations and memories a certain fragrance may elicit. Detective novels teach the reading of domestic interiors through a method of cryptography, a process of deciphering the secret writing of rooms facilitated by the close observation of traces, interior appurtenances, and clues hidden in plain sight.

Both a *locus* for daydreams and nightmares, the spaces of hidden cabinets, attics, and basements were to disappear from a modern architecture that attempted to sweep the unhealthy dust, clutter, and overwrought furniture from the domestic interior, and open rooms to fresh air, natural light, and good health. Traditional Japanese architecture became a fellow traveler to modern architecture's minimalist aesthetics, an antidote to those stuffy 19th-century rooms. Indeed, during the 19th century, Japanese woodblock printing influenced both the Impressionist movement and the architecture and decorative arts of Art Nouveau. The influence of Japanese wood joinery may be found in American Craftsman architecture such as the Gamble House in Pasadena, California, designed by Greene and Greene (1908–1909). Perhaps most importantly, Frank Lloyd Wright was an active dealer in *ukiyo-e* (picture of the floating world) prints that influenced his architectural renderings and conceptions of space.

Bruno Taut established a direct and reciprocal relationship between European modernism and traditional Japanese architecture. He emigrated from Germany to Japan in 1933, where he authored books on this subject, particularly *Fundamentals of Japanese Architecture* (1936) and *Houses and People of Japan* (1938), that located the 17th-century Katsura Imperial Villa (桂離宮 Katsura Rikyū, Kyoto, Japan) front and center in the attention of modern architects such as Walter Gropius and Le Corbusier. Even before this move, he included two examples of Japanese houses in *Die neue Wohnung. Die Frau als Schöpferin* (*The New House. Woman as Creator*, 1924): a room from the "Shinden of Sanboin" in Daigoji and one in the temple Shinju-an in Yamashiro. He expressed admiration for their restrained furniture, studied simplicity, harmonious materials, open plan, absence of decoration, and exposed wood. He also described the official picture niche or *tokonoma* and floors covered with mats called *tatami*. Summarizing the significance of this architecture, in a lecture from 1923, Taut quoted from Okakura Kakuzō's *The Book of Tea* (1906) writing of imperfection as a design strategy: "The dynamic nature of the (Taoist) philosophy laid more stress upon the process through which perfection was sought than upon perfection itself … Uniformity of design was considered as fatal to the freshness of imagination. True beauty could be discovered only by one who mentally completed the incomplete."[18]

Figure 8.4
View of the
pond from
the Geppa-rō
Pavilion at
the Katsura
Imperial Villa
(桂離宮 **Katsura
Rikyū**) in Kyoto,
**Japan, courtesy
of Raphael
Azevedo Franca**

Okakura claimed that *Teaism* is "founded on the adoration of the beautiful among the sordid facts of everyday existence."[19] For him, "only in the vacuum lay the truly essential. The reality of a room, for instance, was to be found in the vacant space enclosed by the roof and the walls, not in the roof and walls themselves."[20] It is finding value in imperfection, the art of "purposely leaving something unfinished for the play of the imagination to complete."[21] *Chashitsu* refers to buildings that house tea ceremonies, while the art of flower arranging, or *ikebana*, evolved into an aesthetic of minimalism that characterizes the accompanying spatial aesthetic. Tea houses generally consist of four basic components: (1) the tea-room proper, ideally accommodating five people; (2) the anteroom or *midsuya* where tea utensils are stored and cleaned; (3) the portico or *machiai* where guests wait until they are invited to enter the tea-room; and (4) the garden path or *roji* leading from the *machiai* to the tea-room. In pursuit of the simplicity and purity of Zen monasteries, the tea-house aspires to the condition of a humble cottage almost devoid of ornamentation, "an ephemeral structure built to house a poetic impulse."[22] It suggests a refined poverty that often costs much more than mansions because the arduous process of selecting the right materials and the precise workmanship to attain the perfect rustic note requires immense care and precision. Irregular pieces of wood and other materials exemplify the Japanese aesthetic principles of *wabi-sabi*, a term celebrating the unadorned and weathered simplicity of nature's imperfection and asymmetry.

The inside of a free-standing tea-room typically contains a low ceiling, a hearth built into the floor for boiling water, shoji screens, the *tokonoma* alcove for hanging scrolls and placing other decorative objects, and an ideal number of four-and-a-half tatami mats. Shoji screens, made of slender wooden frames filled with translucent paper, allow an even light to penetrate rooms when closed, while they may frame views to the outside world when opened. They economize space by sliding, eliminating the area required for door-swings. Made of rice straw, tatami mats cover floors in traditional Japanese rooms, forming a geometric ordering system of 2:1 so that they may be arranged to form a square.

Evoking Bourdieu's concept of *habitus*, their placement may determine how a person walks carefully across the space, paying attention not to disturb the arrangement of the mats. In a similar demonstration of the way in which architecture may affect bodily comportment, guests were required to remove their shoes before passing through the *nijiriguchi*, a small opening that required crawling "in on all-fours, placing one's clenched hands on the Tatami, and then sliding in on the knees little by little."[23] Whether a samurai, who would leave his sword outside, or a poet, who entered with memorized verses, entered the house, the *nijiriguchi* created a threshold that equalized guests through a rite of passage into a realm of peaceful contemplation and mutual trust.

Tea-rooms demonstrate the way in which quotidian actions of daily life may arise out of ritual practices, combining sacred and profane patterns of inhabitation. According to Okakura, in the 6th century, Rikiu (also known as Senno-Soyeki) created the first free standing tea-room, regularizing to a high state of perfection the formal tea-ceremony. The customs he instantiated derived from the ritual of Zen monks who laid the foundations of the tea-ceremony when they successively drank tea out of a bowl before an image of Bodhidharma. Eventually etiquette training for women included learning how to conduct a proper tea ceremony. While the Japanese use of tea dates back at least to the 9th century, imported by Chinese Buddhist monks where it

Figure 8.5
Guests seated to receive tea, print by Yōshū Chikanobu (1838–1912)

had been used from as early as the 4th century, the tea ceremony remains a significant part of Japanese culture, influencing the design of residential architecture that maintains the tradition of *tatami* mats and *tokonoma*.

They also record the means by which a sacred ritual may become *habitus*. A number of contemporary Japanese architects have translated the tea house's airy simplicity into experimental iterations of its basic components. Terunobu Fujimori's Takasugi-an (meaning "a tea house too high," 2003) is a tea-room in Chino, Nagano Prefecture, Japan. It is a small room suspended high on a structure consisting of two chestnut trees cut from a nearby mountain and accessed by free-standing ladders that replicate the *nijiriguchi*'s role of spiritual transition. The interior is covered with plaster and accommodates a maximum of four-and-a-half tatami mats. A large window in this small room frames a view of the town where Fujimori grew up, effectively replacing the *kakejiku* (picture scroll). The window provides contact with seasonal changes as well as the irreversible industrialization taking place in provincial towns like Chino. Kengo Kuma further reduces the traditional tea house to its most minimal materials with *Fu-an*, a "floating" tea-room installed at the World O-CHA (Tea) Festival (2007). Designed to cover a space of four-and-a-half tatami mats, a light cloth called "super organza" drapes over a large balloon filled with helium. As Kuma explains, lightness and impermanence define the space of a tea house because traditional Japanese thinking considers something light to be of superior cultural value to something heavy. Floating epitomizes lightness.[24] For Kuma, "a teahouse is after all a kind of device of virtual reality."[25]

The Psychoanalyst

The secret spaces of Poe's detective novels and the en-suite sequence of rooms in a typical French *Hôtel* parallel the psychological topology of space that Sigmund Freud developed in analogy with the unconscious. Freud compared "the system of the unconscious to a large ante-chamber" out of which opens another "smaller room, a sort of parlor, which consciousness occupies."[26] A watchman stands at the threshold, the space of liminality between the two rooms, censoring psychic impulses and making certain they cannot be seen by the conscious. Objects that pass the watchman's attention contain psychic value that the analyst deciphers.

Echoing Poe's words on this topic, Freud wrote: "to some people the idea of being buried alive by mistake is the most uncanny thing of all."[27] For the claustrophobic, a closed room may operate as a tomb bearing an uncanny resemblance to being buried alive. Freud explores the psychological experience of uncanny architecture through the German word *unheimlich*, meaning "familiar," "native," and "belonging to the home." The uncanny taps into realms that are homely and cozy but also frightening. It is the name for everything that ought to remain hidden and secret, but, according to Friedrich Shelling, have become visible. Poe's mysteries rely on the status of the house,

Figure 8.6
Terunobu Fujimori, the Too-High Tea House, Nagano, Japan, courtesy of Edmund Sumner-VIEW / Alamy Stock Photo

to borrow from Freud, "in relation to death and dead bodies, to the return of the dead, and to spirits and ghosts" that condensate in the countenance of haunted houses and shadowy interiors.[28] Anthony Vidler places Poe's *The Fall of the House of Usher* in the realm of the uncanny through the descriptions of "bleak walls" and "vacant eye-like windows."[29] Abandonment, decrepitude, and the disarray of broken objects left over in these spaces accelerate a reading of the domestic sphere through the lens of repressed trauma buried in the basement.[30]

Freud offered clues to solving the riddles of the psychological complexes he diagnosed through the innumerable objects he displayed in his study and analysis rooms. As Joel Sanders and Diana Fuss read Freud's office,

Figure 8.7
**Kengo Kuma,
Fu-an, a
"floating" tea-
room installed
at the World
O-CHA (Tea)
Festival (2007),
courtesy of
Kengo Kuma**

"the placement of articles on and around the consulting room couch—the heavy Persian rug hung vertically from the wall and anchored to the couch by a matching rug, the chenille cushions supporting the patient's head, neck, and upper back, and the blanket and porcelain stove warming the patient's feet—all create the impression of a protected enclave, a room within a room, a private interior space."[31] Freud's office at Berggasse 19 in Vienna served as the *locus* of his analytical practice from 1908 until his 1938 exile to London. It consisted quite simply of a consultation room, where he worked with patients lying on the famous analytical couch, and a study, where he interviewed future patients. Both rooms were encrusted with his collection of books, antiquities, plaster casts, oriental rugs, photographs, statuettes, paintings, and more. While these numerous and highly metaphorical visual stimuli augmented a patient's therapeutic process, many objects specifically referenced his clinical theories: the Oedipus complex displayed in a reproduction of Jean-Auguste-Dominique Ingres's painting *Oedipus and the Sphinx*, or a small bronze statue of Athena whose apotropaic chest emblem of Medusa alluded to his essay on this subject.

When Freud received patients in his study, as Sanders and Fuss observe, he seated them on a chair facing a small mirror hanging from a window that reflected their visage back to them. This mirror significantly invoked Freud's observation regarding a pattern among patients to transfer their focus toward the analyst instead of themselves: "The doctor should be opaque to his patients and, like a mirror, should show them nothing but what is shown to him."[32] The small mirror in the consultation room aligned Freud's chair, the patient's seat, and the window on an axis with each other. It initiated a series of substitutions where the mirror reversed the gaze from out of the window and back to the patient's reflection of themselves, a view that Freud's body would fill when he sat down in front of his desk. Beatriz Colomina expands upon the significance of the interrupted window when she recounts a story that Adolf Loos told Le Corbusier: "A cultivated man does not look out of the window; his window is a ground glass; it is there only to let the light in, not to let the gaze pass through."[33] In this particular instance, window glass is to be looked at and not through.

In comparison to Freud's desk cluttered with referential antiquities, as previously mentioned, modern architecture's curative drives tended toward antiseptic cleanliness, bare rooms, and glass walls. Reading interior architecture requires paying attention to the placement of mirrors and the performance of glass walls in relation to their oscillating transparency and reflectivity, particularly in light of modernist architecture that pivoted attention from inside to out. No longer chambers of refuge and secrets, walls dissolved into glass and opened onto one another as large flowing spaces. Insofar as glass walls may act as mirrors, particularly at night, their reflective capacity increases at intersecting corners and other adjacencies into an abyssal sequence of mirrored images.

When deciphering the collections in Freud's rooms at Berggasse 19, Natalija Subotincic meticulously reconstructed the placement of every artifact, piece of furniture, and interior surface. She based her forensic research on photographs of these spaces taken in 1938 by Edmund Engelman just before Freud's exile to 20 Mansfield Gardens in London. Freud would use his collection of archaeological artifacts to illustrate points, developing them to assist the patients' travel to their subconscious. Basing her research on photographs of these haunting rooms Subotincic's reconstructions painstakingly depict the thick threshold between the study and the consultation room, the numerous antiquities, the rugs, the herringbone wood floor, and the consulting couch. Her drawings of Freud's office traffic between objects and their display strategies, allowing us to construct domestic spaces as part-biography and part-dream, part therapy and part disease.

In contrast to the collection of associative objects Freud displayed, architectural therapy necessitated uncluttered rooms illuminated by transparent windows. But in removing the 19th-century closets, curiosity cabinets, basements, and attics from their houses, modern architects were not entirely able to quell the delusions of their inhabitants. Richard Neutra, who studied under Loos, did not share his teacher's philosophy of glass when liberally deploying floor to ceiling, operable window walls in the residential projects he completed in Los Angeles. As a close friend of Ernst Ludwig Freud, also an architect and the eldest son of Sigmund Freud, Neutra frequently visited the family home. When emigrating to Southern California to work for Frank Lloyd Wright and live communally with Rudolph Schindler at his King's Road House in Los Angeles, Neutra brought with him Freud's ideas about the unconscious and an interest in exploring architecture's psychological potential.

Figure 8.8
**Natalija
Subotincic,
reconstruction
of Sigmund
Freud's
consulting
room at
Berggasse
19, Vienna,**
courtesy
of Natalija
Subotincic

Neutra also imported the theories of Wilhelm Wundt, a founder of experimental psychology whose research, according to Barbara Lamprecht, "laid the groundwork for measuring physical sensation."[34] Lamprecht distinguishes between Wright's and Neutra's design emphases, with the former privileging the hearth as the center of the house and the latter focusing on the sliding wall dematerializing the boundary between the indoors and the open terrace. She points out that, for Neutra, "the architect was a physician who had to know his patient's history."[35] Sylvia Lavin further argues that Neutra, who wrote extensively on psychology, developed the house as "an active producer of new instruments for acting psychoanalytically on the physical environment."[36] As she observes: "These developments came to define the house as a mirror not of society or of the family, but of the self."[37] As with the *shoji* screens Neutra so admired, his architecture of sliding glass planes allowed walls to entirely disappear in a marriage between interior and exterior spaces. In order to further enhance the reflective dynamics of these planes, Neutra strategically placed mirrors adjacent to windows, multiplying "ad infinitum these elements of energetic ambiguity."[38]

Neutra's design of a house for Dr. Philip Lovell in Los Angeles (1929), as Maarten Overdijk notes, contained "an open-air fitness suite, rooms for sunbathing and sleeping out in the open, and various dietary and therapeutic services," forming a nexus of psycho-physical architectural elements.[39] "His aim was not a seamless connection of architecture and landscape, à la Frank Lloyd Wright," as Overdijk continues, "but an unlocking of the *mental* interior of the inhabitants."[40] As Neutra eroded the exterior wall, he destabilized the barriers separating the human psyche from physical boundaries and liberated psychic energy. A significant part of his commitment to constructing psycho-physiologically curative environments relied upon the rigid liquid of glass. His work makes explicit the therapeutic goal of modern architecture to transform its inhabitant's behavior and health into a catalyst for reform where the architect may stand in for the psychoanalyst.

If fear of being buried alive constitutes the architect's drive to do away with solid walls, then *poché* is the material of its inhumation. *Poché*, as discussed in previous chapters, numbers among a rich lexicon of architectural terms that identify a theoretical genealogy leading from the *Académie royale d'architecture* (1671–1793) to the post-revolutionary *Académie des Beaux-Arts*, which provided a formal education for architects and a language for reading spaces that remains in the parlance of design education.

Terms such as *dégagement*, *distribution*, *enfilade*, *marche*, and *parti* respectively mean the independence of separate parts of a building, the suitable arrangement of parts, the axial arrangement of doorways connecting rooms across a visual alignment, the analysis of a building imagined as if walking through it, and the building's conceptual disposition. This terminology contributes to a precise understanding of the *hôtel particulier*, a luxurious private residence located in French cities. A typical 18th-century *hôtel* would feature a principal residential block or *corps de logis*, an entrance court or

Figure 8.9
**Richard Neutra,
Lovell House
(a.k.a. Lovell
Health House)
in Los Angeles,
California
(1929)**

cour d'honneur, and would bridge the space *entre cour et jardin*, between the entrance court and a rear garden. When an *hôtel* was sited on an irregular block, which was often the case, the thickened space of the perimeter walls would negotiate the disjunction between the urban exterior and domestic interior. *Dégagement* allowed for the absorption of misalignment between exterior and interior volumes with smaller clusters of irregularly shaped rooms acting as *poché* and attaching to regularly shaped rooms, which would connect to each other through the *enfilade*.

Antoine Le Pautre's design of the *Hôtel de Beauvais* (1654–1657) for Catherine-Henriette Bellier, Baroness de Beauvais, models the way an *hôtel particulier* adapted to an oddly-shaped site. Straddling the Rue François Miron and the Rue de Jouy, the site forms a v-shaped footprint comprised of three lots that had previously been occupied by medieval houses, the foundations of which Le Pautre incorporated into his design. With little elbow room to negotiate the standard *hôtel distribution*, he placed the *corps de logis* on the edge of the Rue François Miron and developed an axis from this entrance to a u-shaped *cors d'honneur*, locating the garden element on the second level above the stables. This ingenious organization resulted in a perfectly symmetrical courtyard that negotiates the city's shifting grid with a masterful play between solid-void or figure-field.

The *hôtel particulier* evolved according to a highly structured sequence of increasingly private spaces distributed across an alignment of social hierarchy and etiquette. The house's master and mistress dwelled in their own separate suites of rooms referred to as *appartements*, the culmination of

Figure 8.10
**Antoine Le
Pautre, Hôtel
de Beauvais in
Paris, France
(1654–1657),
photograph
by Philippe
DEMARIA**

the sequence. Guests would first enter a vestibule and then, depending on how deeply they were allowed to penetrate the interior, proceed to the *anti-chambre*, and finally the *chambre de parade*—a large room from which the most privileged guests would be received *en lit*, or in bed. Privacy during this period succumbed to public ritual manifest most clearly at Versailles, where the royal bedroom was located on axis with the formal gardens and the ritual of the *Levee du roi*, the king's rising from bed, established the most coveted positions at court.

Writing in *Le génie de L'architecture; ou, L'analogie de cet art avec nos sensations* (*The Genius of Architecture; or, The Analogy of That Art with Our Sensations*, 1780), Nicolas Le Camus de Mézières outlined in great detail the *hôtel*'s spatial sequences and required decorum. For Mézières, every room should express a unique purpose and inhabitants should be able to deduce its use from the imprint of its *character*. One way to achieve a distinctive *character* for each room was to vary their shapes so that some would be square or rectangular, others round or oval, and still others octagonal or polygonal. The geometry of octagons, in particular, was useful for arranging doors and expanding reflections in mirrors. Each geometry potentially described a unique expression of character such that "in rooms where a serious character is desired, square forms will be chosen; round ones are more cheerful, and curves are more voluptuous."[41]

Outlining each room, Mézières also offered a window into the daily life of a French *hôtel*. He called for a salon to be proceeded by several anterooms— for servants, valets, and waiting callers—and the anteroom to be proceeded by a vestibule. To enhance the dining experience, "parterres, groves, fountains, waterfalls, will embellish the room at dinnertime; in the evening, the decoration will change, and chandeliers and candelabra will replace the beauties and

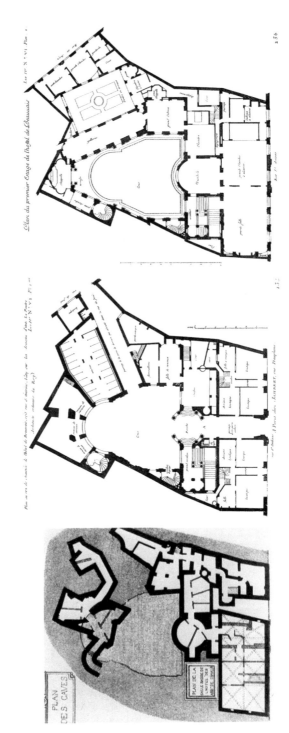

Figure 8.11 Antoine Le Pautre, Hôtel de Beauvais in Paris, France (1654–1657), from J. Marot, *Blondel, Architecture françoise* (1752)

splendors of nature."[42] Kitchens were highly elaborate, with numerous rooms and requirements for cleanliness, light, and fresh air. Whitewashed plaster walls with few projections to collect dirt describe spaces which included larders, a wood cellar, a roasting chamber, a pastry kitchen, a scullery, a servant's hall, a kitchen yard, pantries, a room for silver, lodging for the head cook, and more.

The bedchamber required its own dressing room, boudoir, and lodging for one or two valets or lady's-maids and a footman. The boudoir was the abode of delight where the Mistress "seems to reflect on her designs and to yield to her inclinations."[43] A private apartment should be "set aside for bathing, which ordinarily comprises a bathroom, a vapor bath, a lobby, and a water closet."[44] Because the technology was imported from England, the water closet was referred to as a *cabinet à l'Anglaise*. It contained marble troughs with running water that turned on with a faucet, located in a room hermetically sealed so odors would not escape. The *cabinet* was a rather sophisticated enterprise, offering "little conduits from which water springs when one desires to wash oneself."[45]

Mézières also described an intricate series of hidden spaces that allowed the master of the house to survey his domain from concealed locations and for servants to move about unseen. In order to pass from one end of the *hôtel* to the other invisibly, he recommended arranging a hidden passage way through the thickness of the walls. Another strategy for secret surveillance was to conceal a story between floors called an *entresol*, allowing the owner to spy on guests and servants through small concealed openings. The servants themselves performed in a world of concealed passages and sequestered rooms or actually lived in a part of the *entresol*.

The Maid

The *hôtel particulier* demonstrates that the servant's preferred comportment was to be silent and invisible. As large manor houses began to contract in size, so too did the number of household helpers, while appliances such as washing machines and refrigerators began to replace human labor. Real and virtual maids shared spaces in modern domestic architecture, which catered to clients requiring servants quarters but also, to borrow from Le Corbusier, demanded a vacuum cleaner.[46]

Writing in "Rationalization in the Household" (1927), Grete Schütte-Lihotzky questioned the backwardness of household management at that time, describing it as a severe impediment to the development of women and their families.[47] She lamented the status of middle-class women, who often had to run their houses without help of any kind, and of working-class women for being so over-burdened with chores that it negatively affected their general health. Her answer to domestic servitude was the Frankfurt Kitchen, designed for Ernst May's social housing project in Frankfurt, Germany, where some 10,000 units were integrated into new apartments. These kitchens condensed culinary space into compact rooms derived from standards of efficiency, ease of cleaning, hygiene, and compact workflow. Lihotzky applied the principles of Taylorism, the scientific management of human productivity, and used time-motion studies of women working to determine the most efficient ergonomic distances for the kitchen's shape, size, and cabinetry. As Georges Canguilhem puts it, with Taylor and other scientific studies of work-task movement, "the human body was measured as if it functioned like a machine."[48] Lihotzky included time-saving features such as a fold-down ironing board, swivel stool, glass-fronted cabinetry, gas stove, adjustable lighting, industrial sink, garbage drawer, and storage bins, all placed in optimal relation to each other and arranged "to coincide with the general order of tasks through which meals are made and cleaned up after" and "to maximize *das Existenzminimum* (the basic requirements for living)."[49]

Figure 8.12
**Margarete
Schütte-
Lihotzky,
Frankfurt
Kitchen in
Frankfurt,
Germany
(1926),
photograph
by Christos
Vittoratos**

While 19th-century ornamental details and cluttered bric-à-brac strained both detective work and housework, modern architecture maintained its own housekeeping challenges. Where the transparency of glass and the freeing of floor plans may have opened the shutters of dark rooms, these changes required maintenance to keep surfaces sparkling and rooms compositionally pure. The decay of traces of inhabitation that glass architecture yielded coincided with a parallel evaporation of coziness, a term, we might recall, that coincides with the idea of the uncanny and those suffocating spaces that make inhabitants feel buried alive. German art historian Adolf Behne declared "away with coziness" as an antidote to "the dull vegetative state of jellyfish-like comfort in which all values become blunted and worn."[50] No longer were fingerprints the sole nemesis of criminals; they also worried connoisseurs of modern architecture who demanded surfaces without smudges.

In Ludwig Mies van der Rohe's experimental design of Dr Edith Farnsworth's house, a weekend retreat built in Plano, Illinois (1951), he slid glass walls between the two floating planes of a floor and a roof to create a continuous volume of space. He achieved the prodigious accomplishment of reducing architecture to *beinahe nichts* or almost nothing. But for Dr. Farnsworth, living in glass box proved to be too much. Placing inhabitants permanently on display in a sealed container, the Farnsworth House in fact produced a jellyfish-like discomfort of living in an aquarium. Try, in this instance, to imagine living in a house whose exterior walls are made entirely of glass, though located on a remote rural site, where the bedroom is visible to outside views, and the only enclosed space occupies a small central core. Would you walk around undressed or leave dishes in the sink? For some people, this form of exhibitionism would be perfectly acceptable, even liberating. But for others, the need for coziness and expectations of privacy were not so easily deterred by the radical new forms of living European modernists explored in order to free inhabitants from their repressive drives and bourgeois values. With no screens to keep out insects, which were prevalent in the humid Illinois summers, Farnsworth's choices were to swelter inside a sauna or suffer mosquitos, eventually resulting in the installation of porch screens—despite the architect's protests.

In her design of E.1027 *Maison en Bord de Mer* (meaning "seaside house," 1926–1929), Irish furniture designer Eileen Gray built a house balancing on the edge between the transparency of modernism and the closed rooms of the French *hôtel*. She embraced the accumulated traces she quite literally inscribed on its surfaces. E-1027 exemplifies the shifting status of architecture as it began to replace domestic servants with mechanical appliances, but still maintained the vestiges of the more traditional location of the maid in a servant's chamber. The house's interior organization, in part, stems from the external pressures of its spectacular site on the cliffs above the Ligurian Sea at Roquebrune-Cap-Martin near Monaco. Gray mapped its solar envelope in order to locate rooms according to their relationship to the daily movement of the sun—with morning light streaming into bedrooms on the east and afternoon sun penetrating public

Figure 8.13
**Ludwig Mies
van der Rohe,
Farnsworth
House in Plano,
Illinois (1951),
photograph
by Paulette
Singley**

rooms facing south. Furthermore, the site was isolated from other residences, even lacking an access road, so that all building materials had to be wheelbarrowed in while she camped on the land during its construction. Along with responding to these external conditions, the house foregrounds the discreet intimacies and specificities of domestic inhabitation. As she put it, "the poverty of modern architecture stems from the atrophy of sensuality."[51]

At just about 2800 square feet, the house is organized around an L-shaped plan that terraces down a steep slope across two floors. One enters through a foyer at the second level, beyond which a living space or *salon* opens onto a panoramic view of the *Côte d'Azur*. This level also contains a kitchen tucked in the back, a large bedroom with its own bathroom, a sleeping alcove next to a second bathroom, and a laundry. A glass accordion wall facing the sea unfolds onto a large terrace whose moveable canopies provide shading devices for both summer and winter sun. A skylight located above a spiral staircase illuminates a stairwell wide enough to include shelves. It performs as a kind of fulcrum onto which the rest of the rooms attach themselves.

Pockets of closets, built-in furniture, and embedded passages expand the thickness of walls and provide a layer of spatial padding that lends this project its architectural sensuality. In the tradition of the *hôtel particulier*, the bed Gray placed in the salon merged private and public spatial practices, operating as a social centerpiece where one could greet visitors *en lit*. In another trace vestige of the *hôtel*, the master bedroom at E-1027 was separated into its own distinct realm of rooms clustered into a suite, or *appartement de commodité*. A private exit allowed for the possibility of departing undetected. Gray herself described the house in terms of a sequential seduction: "The desire to penetrate … a transition which still keeps the mystery of the object one is going to see, which keeps the pleasure in suspense … Entering a house is like the sensation of entering a mouth which will close behind you…"[52]

Gray's interior demonstrates the potential for design to reduce rather than enhance the work of cleaning and of organizing one's life through a series of domestic apparatuses that accommodate possessions and coziness, but resist collection-mania and suffocation. She choreographed innumerable gestures across the entire house from the perspective of someone accustomed to domesticity. As with Gray's design of freestanding furniture such as the Bibendum Chair, the Non Conformist Chair, and the E-1027 bedside table—a circular piece of glass suspended in steel tubing that can be lowered and raised to bring the tray to the desired height—the house became a piece of furniture where the opening and closing of doors, the pushing and pulling of walls, and the lifting of tables described a domestic environment where objects shift positions and change meanings.

No specific domestic need was left unattended. Upon entering, visitors may deposit their umbrellas in a specially designed stand or place their hats on top of loose-knit netting underneath task-lighting that replaced dark and dusty shelves. The living room offers the split condition of an opaque fireplace located against the transparent glass wall facing the sea. A glass shower in the bathroom at this level reflects the shape of the human body with a circular glass enclosure, while receiving natural light from a vertical slit in the wall that parallels the orientation of a standing body. The kitchen was modeled on regional habits of preparing meals outside in the summer and inside in the winter and opens to the outside through glass panels. Gray covered a foldable gate-leg tea table with a sheet of cork to reduce noise and protect glassware and installed pivoting drawers in the cabinets.[53] The headboard in the master bedroom featured a white reading light, a blue night light, an alarm clock, and outlets for an electric kettle and a foot warmer. A table that cantilevers from the bedside pivots and adjusts into a reading stand. The guest bedroom, with an exit directly onto the garden, contains a movable partition at the foot of the bed to protect against the Mistral wind and a cabinet concealing a writing desk. Gray designed a satellite mirror for the bathroom to magnify one's face for shaving and illuminated glass shelves in the wardrobes. A submerged square in the garden table doubles as a lounge for sun bathing and, with a table that could be lifted from the ground, a cocktail area. The house indicates the degree of precision and attention Gray gave to the subtle rituals and comfort of daily life.

The house is an architectural love letter. Gray wrote amorous secrets throughout it delivered in coded messages, beginning with the title of E-1027, cryptically uniting her and her partner Jean Badovici's names in its title; "E" for Eileen, 10 for the place in the alphabet of the letter "J" for Jean, 2 for "B" for Badovici, and 7 for "G," Gray. The word games continue with *Entrez lentement*, enter slowly, appearing on the entrance porch, followed by *défense de rire*, no laughing, in the entrance hall. On top of a nautical map of the Mediterranean that hangs above the salon bed, she inscribed the phrases *invitation au voyage* (invitation to voyage), *beaux-temps* (beautiful weather), and *vas-y-totor* (let's go,

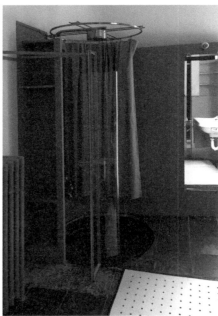

Figures
8.14–8.16
**Eileen Gray,
E.1027 Maison
en Bord de Mer
in Roquebrune-
Cap-Martin,
France (1929),
photograph
by Paulette
Singley**

Totor, her car's nickname). For Caroline Constant, the map was "an induce-
ment to travel farther afield, both luring the imagination and underscoring the
limited temporality of modern conditions of dwelling."[54] She wrote in the guest
room, "Madame petite et coquette" and "Monsieur qui aime se regarder la
nuque"—madame is small and pretty, monsieur likes to look at the back of

his neck. At the entrance to the service area, she wrote "SENS INTERDIT" (forbidden direction) and distributed other clues around the house such as *couverts* (table settings), *oreillers* (pillows), and *choses légères* (light things—above a soap dish). The place for the *chapeaux* (hats), *pour les dents* (literally "for teeth," meaning toothbrushes), *pyjama* (pajamas), *bidet*, *valise* (suitcases), and *peignoirs* (bathrobes) are all labeled with words, whether or not it was self-evident that this is where they went or what they were used for. In contrast to Corbusier's assertion that a house is a "machine-à-habiter" (a machine for living in), Gray's house operated as a "machine à lire" (a machine for reading).

E.1027 exhibits Le Corbusier's "Five Points Towards a New Architecture" published in *L'Architecture Vivante* of 1927, with the ground floor raised on "pilotis" or columns, an accessible roof "garden," an open plan allowing for the division of space with non-bearing walls, horizontal "ribbon" windows, and a free façade. Badovici invited Le Corbusier to stay there between 1938 and 1939, allowing him to paint eight large wall murals both inside and outside E-1027. When he "published the murals in his *Oeuvre complète* (1946) and in *L'Architecture d'aujourd'hui* (1948), he referred to E-1027 as "a house in Cap-Martin" and omitted Gray's name as the architect to the extent that he received credit for its design and some of its furniture.[55] After losing a bid to purchase the house itself, in 1951 Le Corbusier purchased a piece of property, directly encroaching from above, where he built a small cabana for himself. He also built five holiday cabins for Thomas Rebutato directly above the house, a small restaurant called *Étoile de Mer* (Starfish), and a detached studio, completing what constitutes a small village of buildings surrounding E-1027. Gray was forced to abandon the house during the Second World War, after which German soldiers used the walls for target practice. She departed with her maid, Louise Dany, who had become her companion—a woman with whom she shared almost fifty years of her life from 1927 to 1976.[56]

Notes

1   Hélène Cixous, "Fiction and Its Phantoms: A Reading of Freud's *Das Unheimliche* (The 'Uncanny')" *New Literary History 7*, no. 3 (Spring, 1976), p. 543.

2   Gaston Bachelard, *Poetics of Space*, trans. Maria Jolas (Boston: Beacon Press, 1994), p. 14.

3   Ibid, 5.

4   Ibid, 47.

5   Ibid.

6   Cf. Pierre Bourdieu, *Esquisse d'une théorie de la pratique, précédé de trois études d'ethnologie kabyle* (1972), published in English as *Outline of a Theory of Practice* (Cambridge: Cambridge University Press, 1977).

7   Michael Dennis, *Court and Garden: From the French Hôtel to the City of Modern Architecture* (Cambridge, MA: MIT Press, 1986), p. 1.

8   Jean Baudrillard, *The System of Objects*, trans. James Benedict (New York: Verso, 1996), p. 16.

9   Mark S. Madoff, "Inside Outside and the Gothic Locked-Room Mystery," in *Gothic Fictions: Prohibition/Transgression*, ed. Kenneth W. Graham (New York: AMS Press, 1999), p. 50.

10   Jill Lepore "The Prism: Privacy in an Age of Publicity" *New Yorker*, June 24, 2013, http://www.newyorker.com/magazine/2013/06/24/the-prism.

11   Ibid.

12   Luc Boltanski, *Mysteries and Conspiracies: Detective Stories, Spy Novels and the Making of Modern Societies* (Cambridge: Polity Press, 2014), p. 13.

13   Walter Benjamin, "Paris, Capital of the Nineteenth Century," in *Reflections: Essays, Aphorisms, Autobiographical Writings*, trans. Edmund Jephcott (New York: Schocken Books, 1978), p. 245.

14   Ibid.

15   George Teyssot, *A Topology of Everyday Constellations* (Cambridge, MA: MIT Press, 2013), p. 84.

16   Naomi Schor, *Reading in Detail: Aesthetics and the Feminine* (New York: Methuen, 1987), p. 4.

17   Charles Baudelaire, "Preface to the Philosophy of Furniture," in *Histoires Grotesques Et Sérieuses* (Paris: Michel Lévy, 1865) in *Baudelaire on Poe Critical Papers*, trans. and ed. Lois and Francis E. Hyslop, Jr. (New York: Dover).

18   Manfred Speidel, "Japanese Traditional Architecture in the Face of Its Modernisation: Bruno Taut in Japan," in *Bruno Taut, 1880–1880*, ed. Winfried Nerdinger and M. Speidel (Milan: Mondadori Electa, 2001), p. 101.

19   Okakura Kakuzo, "III. Taoism and Zennism," *The Book of Tea* (1906), http://www.sacred-texts.com/bud/tea.htm, p. 1.

20   Okakura Kakuzo, "III. Taoism and Zennism," *The Book of Tea* (1906), http://www.sacred-texts.com/bud/tea.htm.

21   Ibid, p. 31.

22   Ibid, p. 30.

23   http://japanese-tea-ceremony.net/chashitsu.html.

24   http://www.nbm.org/about-us/national-building-museum-online/kengo-kumas-floating-tea-1.html.

25   http://kkaa.co.jp/works/architecture/floating-tea-house.

26   Sigmund Freud, "Introductory Lectures on Psychoanalysis. Lecture XIX: Resistance and Repression," http://www.gutenberg.org/files/38219/38219-h/38219-h.htm#LEC-TURE_19.

27   Sigmund Freud, "The Uncanny" (*Das unheimliche*), in *The Standard Edition of the Complete Psychological Works of Sigmund Freud*, vol. XVII, trans. James Strachey and Anna Freud (London: Hogarth Press, 1917–1917), p. 244. Writing in "The Premature Burial" of 1844, Poe remarks: "To be buried while alive is, beyond question, the most terrific of these extremes which has ever fallen to the lot of mere mortality."

28   Ibid, p. 241.

29   Anthony Vidler, *The Architectural Uncanny: Essays in the Modern Unhomely* (Cambridge, MA: MIT Press, 1992), p. 19.

30   Cixous, "Fiction and Its Phantoms…" p. 543.

31   Joel Sanders and Diana Fuss, referencing Sigmund Freud's *Papers on Technique, Recommendations to Physicians Practicing Psychoanalysis* in "Berggasse 19: Inside Freud's Office," in *Stud: Architectures of Masculinity*, ed. Joel Sanders (New York: Princeton Architectural Press, 1996), p. 124, available at: http://joelsandersarchitect.com/berggasse-19-inside-freuds-office-with-diana-fuss.

32   Sanders and Fuss "Berggasse 19."

33   Le Corbusier, *Urbanisme* (Paris, 1925), p. 174, as cited by Beatriz Colomina, "The Split Wall: Domestic Voyeurism," in *Sexuality & Space*, ed. Beatriz Colomina (New York: Princeton Architectural Press, 1992), p. 74.

34   Barbara Lamprecht, *Richard Neutra, 1892–1892: Survival Through Design* (Los Angeles: Taschen, 2004), p. 9.

35   Ibid, p. 11.

36   Sylvia Lavin, "Open the Box: Richard Neutra and the Psychology of the Domestic Environment," in *Assemblage* no. 40 (Cambridge, MA: MIT Press, 1999), p. 8.

37   Ibid, p. 11.

38   Ibid, p. 18.

39   Maarten Overdijk, "Richard Neutra's Therapeutic Architecture," https://www.failedarchitecture.com/richard-neutras-therapeutic-architecture.

40   Ibid.

41   Nicolas Le Camus de Mézières, *Le génie de L'architecture; ou, L'analogie de cet art avec nos sensations* (*The Genius of Architecture; or, The Analogy of That Art with Our Sensations*, 1780), ed. Werner Szambien (Los Angeles: Getty Center for the History of Art and the Humanities, 1992), p. 108.

42   Ibid, p. 137.

43   Ibid, p. 115. See also Jean-Francois de Bastide's *The Little House: An Architectural Seduction*, trans. Rodolphe El-Khoury (*La petite maison*, 1879; New York: Princeton Architectural Press, 1997).

44   Ibid, p. 122.

45   Ibid.

46   Le Corbusier, *Towards a New Architecture*, trans. Frederick Etchells (New York: Dover, 1986), p. 123.

47   First published as "Rationalisierung im Haushalt" *Das neue Frankfurt 5* (1926–1927), pp. 120–120.

48   Georges Canguilhem "Machine and Organism," in *Incorporations*, eds. Jonathan Crary and Sanford Kwinter (New York: Zone Press, 1992), p. 63.

49   http://www.nybooks.com/daily/2011/01/21/when-modernism-entered-the-kitchen.

50   As cited by Karina van Herck, "Modern Architecture and the Suppression of Coziness," in *Negotiating Domesticity: Spatial Productions of Gender in Modern Architecture*, eds. Hilde Heynen and Gülsüm Baydar (New York: Routledge, 2005), p. 124.

51   https://www.theguardian.com/theguardian/2001/jul/21/weekend7.weekend5.

52   As cited by Peter Adam, *Eileen Gray: Her Life and Work* (London: Thames & Hudson, 2006), p. 217.

53   Cf. Caroline Constant, *Eileen Gray* (London: Phaidon, 2000).

54   Ibid, p. 95.

55   On August 27, 1965, Le Corbusier went swimming in the sea below his cabin at Roquebrune-Cap-Martin, the one overlooking E.1027, where he suffered a heart attack and died.

56   Cf. Katarina Bonnevier, *Behind Straight Curtains: Towards a Queer Feminist Theory of Architecture* (Stockholm: Axl Books, 2007), p. 76.

Introduction to Part 4
Out-and-Out Architecture

*After this he put to death Procrustes, as he was called, who dwelt in what was known as Corydallus in Attica; this man compelled the travellers who passed by to lie down upon a bed, and if any were too long for the bed he cut off the parts of their body which protruded, while in the case of such as were too short for it he stretched (*prokrouein*) their legs, this being the reason why he was given the name Procrustes.*[1]

—Diodorus Siculus

Having considered methodologies for reading architecture in the previous two parts of this book that emphasized exterior and interior forces influencing the configuration of a building, this part focuses on reading architecture through the space in between that involves the intrinsic logics of *sui generis* form generation. Reading architectural form, in part, relies on being able to visualize the abstract concept of *space* as an invisible yet finite material, a malleable clay that architects mold and shape into contained volumes. This reading privileges stereometric above tectonic interpretations of architecture where form is seen as an almost fluid continuum of space as opposed to constructed and joined pieces. It also privileges syntax over semantics, that is, the reading of compositional strategies comes before any potential meanings they may convey.

Evidencing space as form, Luigi Moretti's plaster cast of the interior space of Guarino Guarini's Santa Maria della Divina Provvidenza (1662) in Lisbon renders the spatial void of this church as a stereometric solid. Architectural space is a pliable entity, a plastic material that may be stretched or squeezed into varying degrees of depth and flatness. Interior space, as Bruno Zevi contended, provides the aesthetic basis for judging a building, to the extent that everything else is "always subordinate to the spatial idea."[2] With "House," a temporary public sculpture completed in East London on October 25, 1993, Rachel Whiteread gave full-scale, built expression to the solidification of space Moretti expressed in his plaster models by spraying 2 cm of concrete over the entire inside surface of a three story Victorian terraced house to produce the image of a monolithic solid when the exterior walls were removed.

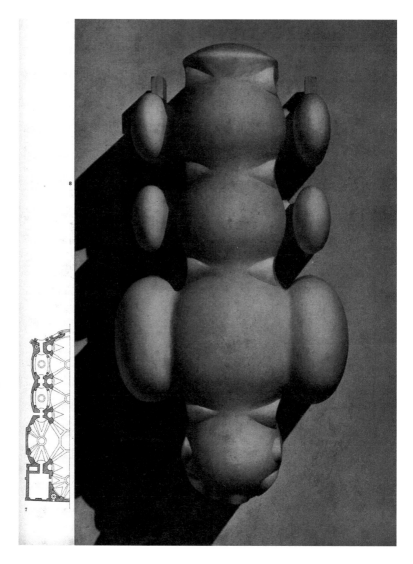

Figure P4.1
Luigi Moretti, plaster cast of the interior space of Guarino Guarini's Santa Maria della Divina Provvidenza (Lisbon, 1662), from Luigi Moretti "Strutture e sequenze di spazi," *Spazio* (IV: 7), 1952–1953

Reading architecture formally requires an ability to identify the invisible spaces located between thick and thin layers, to consider the registration between solid and void, and to evaluate part-to-whole relationships as belonging to an evaluative process that develops the analytical tools of comparison, composition, and convolution discussed in the following chapters.

This book places out-and-out architecture, at the end of a series of meditations on context and content as a way of stripping a building of everything it does in order to isolate form in the realm of what it does not do performatively. In this section architectural design is bounded by an invisible frame that severs it from the external world. Whether it is the sheet of vellum upon which a Renaissance draughtsman would refine a detail, the tracing paper where a modern architect would project an abstract composition, or the edges of a computer screen where contemporary designers puzzle through complex software, it is possible to partition the design process away from so-called real-world contaminants and explore the production of a form whose only destination is a museum wall.

In works such as "The Pilot's Planit House" (1924) and "Contra-Construction Project" (1923), Russian Supremacist Kazimir Malevich and de Stil founder Theo van Doesburg, in collaboration with Cornelis van Eesteren, respectively, explored the iterative progression of form in models and drawings that had neither sites nor specific programs, articulating a conceptual position that liberated architecture from the exterior and interior pressures of

Figure P4.2
Rachel Whiteread, "House" (London, 1993)

253

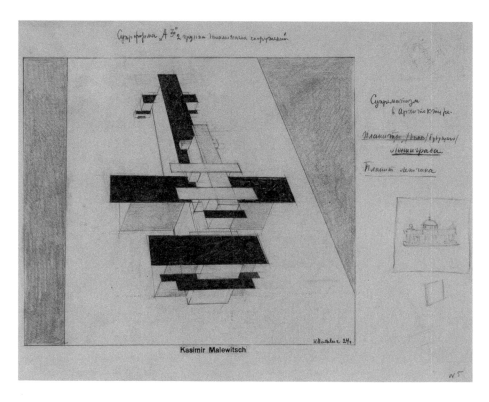

Kasimir Malewitsch

Figure P4.3
**Kazimir
Malevich, "The
Pilot's Planit
House" (1924),
courtesy of
the Museum
of Modern Art,
New York**

context and performance. Such exploration of an architecture delimited by a bounding frame separating it from the physical world translated well onto a computer screen that portrays form in a continuum lacking gravity, structure, or scale—where objects float in a digital vacuum filled only by splines and vectors.

This part provides a set of compositional tools for engaging the properties of type, form, and enclosure, in order to assess architecture through the variable principles of abstraction, geometry, and complexity. Verbs emerge as operative vehicles for translating design processes into the properties of formal analyses. The discipline-specific steps once deployed for producing abstract forms drawn by hand such as rotate, superimpose, project, or offset have matured into the more abstruse parlance of computer commands such as scale, loft, plot, divide, extrude, pipe, explode, cluster, and more. These terms describe an action, but do not necessarily establish a *raison d'être* beyond their own set of self-prescribed rules. This part intends to demonstrate that there are reasons behind the rules and, in fact, there is no such thing as empty form. An image of a procrustean bed, of functions being forced to fit uncomfortably into a predetermined form, comes to mind when considering the way in which an architect may stretch or amputate programs to conform to exotic shapes. For the projects appearing in the next three chapters, however, the shape of the bed-building itself retains interpretive priority.

Figure P4.4
**Theo van
Doesburg,
"Contra-
Construction
Project" (1923),
courtesy of
the Museum
of Modern Art,
New York**

Notes

1   Diodorus Siculus, *Bibliotheca historia* IV 59.5 (1st century BC). Library of History,
    Book IV, 59–85 (end) published in vol. III of the Loeb Classical Library edition, 1939,
    http://penelope.uchicago.edu/Thayer/E/Roman/Texts/Diodorus_Siculus/4D*.html.
2   Bruno Zevi, *Architecture as Space: How to Look at Architecture*, trans. Milton
    Gendel (New York: Horizon Press, 1974), p. 28.

Chapter 9

Type

While the revival of the notion of type through Antoine-Chrysostome Qua-tremère de Quincy corresponded with a return of architectural theory to Platonic ideals, the introduction of the term typology *put into circulation ideas that originated in nineteenth-century ethnography and criminology.*[1]
—Georges Teyssot

While composing this chapter, I am typing. The buttons I strike on my keyboard correspond to innumerable fonts of different shapes and sizes, each of which communicates the essential form of a single letter. Thus, an **A** and an *A* correspond to each other, even though they are rendered with highly diverse inclinations and embellishments. As with the legibility of different fonts for the same letters in the alphabet, from Trajan Pro to Edwardian Script, architectural "typing" similarly operates by classifying similarities among variants of the same form located in diverse times and places. Architects often describe buildings in terms of letters such as "H," "L," "T," and "O." Entire alphabets have been drawn by designers, such as Johann David Steingruber's *Architektonisches Alphabet* (*Architectural Alphabet*, 1773), Antonio Basoli's *Alfabeto Pittorico* (*Pictorial Alphabet*, 1839), or Steven Holl's *Pamphlet Architecture 5: Alphabetical City* (1980), enticing architects to write giant words with buildings. Basoli took the writing of architectural alphabets to a highly alliterative level when depicting fantastical scenes in lithographs that contain numerous figures whose names all begin with the letter he is spatializing. When an "A" is represented by an Arabian building, it also happens to be an *aranceria*, an orangery. These alphabetical architectures get to the heart of how form may operate independent of any primary function, elevating the symbolic performance of letters to emerge as the dominant interpretive strategy. As with different fonts for the same letter, an architectural type tolerates substantial modification to the point of almost complete dissimilarity among the different variants.

The basic premise that an abstract and pliable template maintains consanguinity between forms while allowing them to register significant differences from each other neatly summarizes the idea of "type" in architecture. Rafael Moneo succinctly clarifies type as "a concept which describes a group of objects characterized by the same formal structure."[2] Insofar as typing

Figure 9.1
Antonio Basoli,
*Alfabeto
Pittorico* **(1839)**

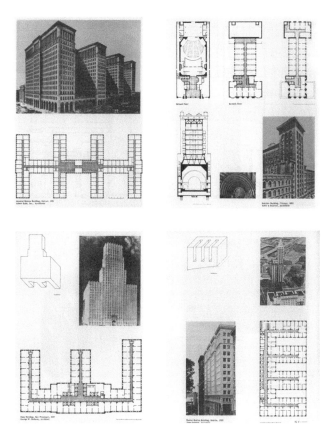

Figure 9.2
General Motors Building in Detroit (1921), Albert Kahn, Inc., Architects; Schiller Building in Chicago (1892), Adler & Sullivan, Architects; Russ Building in San Francisco (1927), George W. Kelham, Architect; and Dexter Horton Building in Seattle (1922), John Graham, Architect, from Steven Holl, *Alphabetical City Pamphlet Architecture #5* (New York, 1980)

architecture posits an approach to reading buildings in terms of serial legibility, architectural types operate as conveyors of meaning that occurs relationally with other members of the series, where each form corresponds to an abstract idea of an original archetype. *Type* refers to morphological similarities shared among buildings, languages, or living organisms, with terms such as "archetype," "prototype," "genotype," or "stereotype" always returning to the essential etymon of *type* as the comparative, reproductive, or originary moment of typing. It offers tools for encrypting architecture with a formal language of composition, developing a hermetic approach to design processes that architects often deploy as a point of departure that potentially eschews a building's context and content. Reading architecture as a type initiates the process of understanding architecture as form. Although type-driven design methodologies often begin with a precedent, generally inspired by programmatic or contextual similarities, these references may submerge into the abstraction of pure form as a project develops. Type also inserts a scientific corollary into the process of reading buildings to the extent that it parallels the systematic placement of natural elements into taxonomical series of like genuses and species in order to determine their shared characteristics.

While an architectural type may align with specific programs or activities, just as often it does not. In contradistinction to building types, which fix relationships between form and program, design types may operate independently of functional specificity. We should therefore distinguish between an "architectural type," a seminal form-finder, and a "building type," a concept Nikolaus Pevsner codified in *A History of Building Types* (1976) to identify the correspondence between a building's general use and certain standard architectural responses to this use. In this respect, the rapid development in the 19th century of new institutions and industries to accommodate an increasingly urban population witnessed the emergence of new programs, such as public schools, prisons, hospitals, factories, train stations, libraries, theaters, slaughter houses, stock exchanges, and more, forging architectural types into a bond between similar functions and their respective forms. And to a large extent this reading still holds, wherein the shape of transportation buildings, hospitals, religious edifices, etc. signify the activity they house.

But just as often as not, like a false cognate in a foreign language, buildings do not house what the exterior form suggests. That a building initially might be constructed for one purpose and then successfully accommodate another for which it was not originally intended clarifies how architectural types or typologies describe form without function. As with the hermit crab that can find shelter by squeezing itself into almost any shape, architects may deform programs to fit into a variety of predetermined shells. A building that starts out as a chapel may alternatively enclose a library, a nightclub, a clothing store, or an artist's studio—even to the betterment of the architectural experience than purpose-generated spaces. This formal pliability largely accounts for the success of adaptive reuse projects that take a building designed for a function that is no longer viable and repurpose it for an activity it was not intended to house. Alongside the resilience of preserving building materials and the aesthetic patina of cast-off tectonic systems, the spatial slippage between form and program that often accompanies adaptive reuse projects may produce rich spatial tensions not always derived from conventional design processes.

"The School of Athens"

An important question initiates this discussion: precisely what is the abstract and pliable template that triggers a typological series? An architectural type may begin from a built precedent that dates back to some long-lost antecedent. Or it may begin as an ideal concept, an archetype, that wends into a physical manifestation of this ideal. Both origins, the physical and the ideal, offer formal models or paradigms for architects to adapt, transform, reinterpret, hybridize, and proliferate. Raphael Sanzio's fresco "The School of Athens" (1509–1511), located in the Vatican's *Stanza della Segnatura*, illustrates an instrumental distinction between a metaphysical type and its physical manifestation in architecture. Raphael depicts Plato and Aristotle walking together among a group of philosophers: Plato's academy in Athens transfigured

Figure 9.3
**Raphael
Sanzio, "The
School of
Athens"
(Vatican, Italy,
1509–1511)**

into the architecture of Renaissance Rome. Raphael's depiction of a debate between Plato and Aristotle begins to tease out these complementary schools of thought as design processes deriving either from archetype or prototype. As Plato points upward to the drum of a magnificent dome framing the sky and heavenly ideals, his student Aristotle gestures toward the ground and real-world pragmatics, to the actual ground in fact upon which St Peter's was built. This scenario positions architectural types as deriving from ideal forms that may result in the bricks and mortar of architecture's very foundations.

Bramante's design for rebuilding Old St Peter's Basilica, a late-Roman edifice that had fallen into disrepair, featured a centralized plan surmounted by hemispherical dome. To summarize a long but relevant building history, in 318 CE, the Roman Emperor Constantine ordered the construction of a Christian basilica on the Vatican Hills where St Peter was purportedly entombed. The Constantinian plan took the form of a Latin cross, similar to the letter "†" or to the shape of the wood apparatus used for crucifixions. Pope Julius II initiated a building campaign to demolish the old church and build a new one, appointing Bramante to design an edifice that reflected the humanist revival of classical antiquity. Bramante proposed a Greek cross plan in the shape of a plus sign or "+," the crossing of which he intended to cover with the hemispherical dome depicted on a cast bronze medal from 1506. His design formally references the placing of the Pantheon on top of the Basilica of Maxentius and Constantine, a building near the Roman Forum whose typology paralleled that of ancient Roman baths. In so doing he substituted the Pantheon's continuous supporting wall with the basilica's structural piers, allowing him to superimpose the spherical diameter of a dome onto an open cross plan.

Figure 9.4
Cast bronze medal of Pope Julius II commemorating the building of St Peter's depicting Donato Bramante's design for St Peter's Basilica (attributed to Cristoforo Caradosso Foppa, 1506)

After Bramante's death in 1514, at which point the four central piers intended to support the dome had risen up to the level of the cornice, Raphael took over the project, eventually to be followed by a number of other architects including Baldassarre Peruzzi and Antonio da Sangallo the Younger. By the time Sangallo was in charge of the project, Bramante's original piers had begun to display cracks indicating serious structural instability. In 1547 Michelangelo Buonarroti became the building's new "Capomaestro," or master builder, during which time he stabilized Bramante's design by thickening the piers and exterior walls enough to support the 137.7-foot-wide diameter dome he designed to span the crossing. Eventually Counter-Reformation religious philosophy compelled the church to provide a more linear liturgical space and a larger urban presence, thereby returning the church to a conventional Latin cross basilica configuration. This required Carlo Maderno to extend the Greek cross by three bays and design its present monumental façade. The process of changing plans back and forth heralded an entirely new building type, that of a dome surmounting a Latin cross plan. From Constantine's original basilica, to Bramante's centralized church, and then to Maderno's extension to a Latin cross plan surmounted by Michelangelo's dome, the transformation of St Peter's sponsored a plethora of typological descendants, among which includes St Paul's Cathedral in London and Sainte-Geneviève in Paris.

The basilica features a rich stratigraphy of archeological layers that includes traces of the Circus of Nero and Caligula at the lowest level, foundations of the Constantinian church above, and the current Renaissance edifice that rises over these footings. These layers also determine how the term *basilica* evolved from nomenclature describing a generic building type in ancient Rome, which housed law courts and other public functions, to its present meaning of *church*.

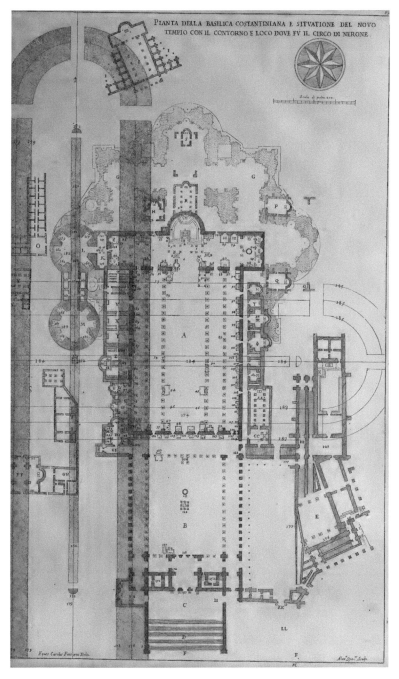

Figure 9.5
**Carlo Fontano,
Plan of
St Peter's
depicting
palimpsest
of layers,
including
Constanian-
era basilica
and Circus of
Nero/Caligula
from *Il Tempio
Vaticano e
sua origine:
con gl'edifitii
più cospicui,
antichi e
moderni, fatti
dentro e fuori
di esso* (Rome:
Ex typographia
Jo: Francisci
Buagni, 1694)**

Figure 9.6
Carlo Fontano, Plan of St Peter's depicting Carlo Maderno's extension of Michelangelo's plan from *Il Tempio Vaticano e sua origine: con gl'edifitii più cospicui, antichi e moderni, fatti dentro e fuori di esso* (Rome: Ex typographia Jo: Francisci Buagni, 1694)

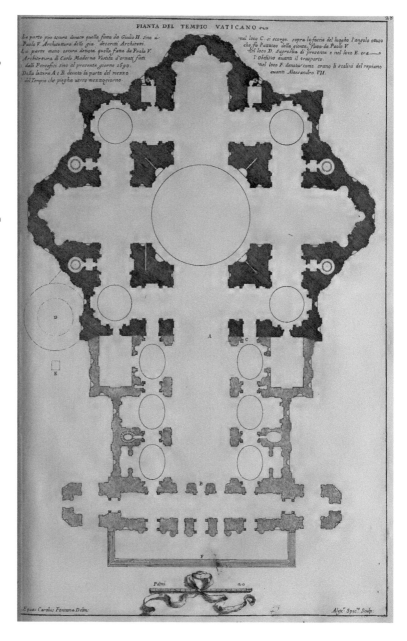

Constantine's edifice on the Vatican hills, as did most Christian churches at the time, adopted the Roman basilica type of a simple rectangular building with a shed roof, central nave, aisles on each side, and a semi-circular apse terminating one end. Early Christian architects borrowed this typology and its name, establishing an architectural space for communal worship that offered

PROSPETTO DEL TEMPIO VATICANO   CON SVOI FONDAMENTI

Figure 9.7
**Carlo Fontano,
Elevation of
St Peter's
depicting Carlo
Maderno's
façade and
Michelangelo's
dome from**
*Il Tempio
Vaticano e
sua origine:
con gl'edifitii
più cospicui,
antichi e
moderni, fatti
dentro e fuori
di esso* **(Rome:
Ex typographia
Jo: Francisci
Buagni, 1694)**

a humble counterpoint to the monumental temples of ancient Rome, which housed colossal statues of gods but excluded a congregation. Bramante and Michelangelo transformed the type, but not the name, into a building plan in the shape of a Greek cross, included a dome at the crossing, and merged the

Figure 9.8
**Carlo Fontano,
section and
elevation of
Old St Peter's**
from *Il Tempio
Vaticano e
sua origine:
con gl'edifitii
più cospicui,
antichi e
moderni, fatti
dentro e fuori
di esso* (Rome:
Ex typographia
Jo: Francisci
Buagni, 1694)

centralized Roman temple type with the basilica type. Although Greek cross basilicas with domes had existed from the time of Hagia Sophia (530s CE) in Constantinople and St Mark's in Venice (11th century), Maderno's extension of the Greek cross into a Latin cross plan synthesized the paradigm of a basilica with a dome. Moreover, each of these iterations describes our contemporary understanding of a *basilica*.

Centralized Types

In 1963 Giulio Carlo Argan's essay "Tipologia" was published in English as "On the Typology of Architecture," where he asserted that "typological series

VUE DU PETIT TEMPLE DE BRAMANTE ET D'UNE PARTIE DE L'ÉGLISE, ET DU COUVENT DE S PIETRO IN MONTORIO

Figure 9.9
Paul-Marie Letarouilly, perspective of Donato Bramante's San Pietro in Montorio (1502, a.k.a *tempietto*) from *Edifices de Rome Moderne Édifices de Rome moderne: ou recueil des palais, maisons, églises, couvents, et autres monuments publics et particuliers les plus remarquables de la ville de Rome (1840–1855)

do not arise only in relation to the physical function of buildings but are tied to their configuration."[3] Argan provided architects with an argument to initiate building design from the position of precedents, a form of research many modern architects had abandoned, but that would become a clarion call for postmodernism's historical turn. Part of the critique against typological design processes, which tend to begin with a formal precedent, stems from the concern that it limits invention, prescribes sterile formulaic responses, or compels architects to look backward instead of forward. Argan argued instead for type's ability to generate hybrid combinations and evolve new forms. He considered St Peter's centralized plan surmounted by a dome as a model of typological hybridity. He also identified Bramante's church of San Pietro in Montorio (1502, a.k.a *tempietto* or small temple) for having adapted the peripteral Vesta temple type, a circular plan with columns surrounding the exterior, into the Renaissance ideal of centralized church plans that his design of St Peter's made emblematic.

Andrea Palladio published numerous examples of centralized buildings in *I quattro libri dell'architettura* (1570, *The Four Books of Architecture*) and in so doing provided an essential conduit between ancient buildings, Renaissance interpretations of these sources, and future generations of architects who would come to derive inspiration from this book. He published illustrations of centralized buildings such as the "Temple of Jupiter" (an ancient Roman nymphaeum also called the Temple of Minerva Medica), a Vesta temple on the Tiber River (Temple of Hercules), the Baptistery of Constantine, Bramante's Tempietto, the Pantheon, the "Temple of Bacchus" (Santa Costanza), and the Temple of Vesta at Tivoli. By including the Villa of Paolo Almerico in his treatise, later known as the Villa Capra but more familiarly referred to as *La Rotonda*, Palladio disseminated his adaptation of the centralized temple typology into a private residence. In so doing he secularized a sacred form and pushed the type into a new arena of architectural expression.

In order to emphasize the prodigious impact of Palladio's treatise on the history of Western architecture, we must imagine a time before cameras and the internet, when the dissemination of architecture relied on travel sketches, paintings, and books filled with detailed woodcuts or engravings of buildings from afar. While Palladio's built work clearly merits attention for the breadth and depth of his oeuvre, his published woodcuts provided for the widespread diffusion of ideas that ignited an international design movement.

Figure 9.10
Andrea Palladio, Villa Rotonda (a.k.a Villa Almerico Capra Valmarana) in Vicenza, Italy (begun 1567), photograph by Jeffrey Balmer

Due to the rapid dissemination of Palladio's treatise, with Giacomo Leoni being the first to publish an English translation of *The Architecture of A. Palladio, in Four Books* (1716–1720), the Villa Rotonda and numerous other examples of Palladio's work have served as primary prototypes for dozens of villas, garden pavilions, houses, and mansions that derived their forms from images in the *Quattro Libri*.

The Rotonda both responds to and ignores its immediate context. As a bilaterally symmetrical pavilion with a dome surmounting a central, circular hall, it could be located almost anywhere as a spatial abstraction that responds

Figure 9.11
Andrea Palladio, front view of the Villa Foscari (Malcontenta, Mira, Italy, 1560), photograph by Hans A. Rosbach

Figure 9.12
Andrea Palladio, rear view of the Villa Foscari (Malcontenta) in Mira, Italy (1560), photograph by Haros Gallery

only to its internal geometry. Palladio designed an ideal form of architecture that transcends its immediate site as a free-floating type that rotates the Pantheon three times about its center, sacrificing frontality and site specificity for an ideal geometry. The four identical façades stand out as an aberrant and willful denial of context and function in favor of perfect form. Taking as a counter-example his Villa Foscari or *Malcontenta* (1560), the front and rear façades of this building differ significantly, demonstrating a more site-specific approach than that of the Rotonda's unflinching symmetries. And yet, the Rotonda served as both a pleasure retreat and a working farm, demonstrating site-specific responses to its location on top of a hill, commanding distant views, and attracting cool breezes while surveying the pastoral landscape of fields afar. It offers the archetypal model of several villas Palladio designed in the area of the Veneto that maintain formal kinship with each other through variations of the nine-square grid (a square divided by a grid of nine equal parts) that organizes these building plans.

Among the considerable litany of buildings that derive inspiration from the Villa Rotonda, Palladio's student Vincenzo Scamozzi initiated the process of mutation with the Villa Rocca Pisana in Lonigo, a nine-square plan surmounted by a centralized dome but now featuring only one projecting portico. In 18th-century England, where Palladio's influence is most pronounced, the Chiswick House (1729) numbers among the more significant variations of the Rotonda type. Designed by Richard Boyle, 3rd Earl of Burlington (Lord Burlington) and William Kent, the Chiswick House offers a compelling example of Neo-Palladian architecture that evolves its typological predecessor into experimental geometries. Burlington traveled to Italy to study Palladio's work in situ, returning to England with the formal vocabulary necessary to transform his estate at Chiswick into an ideal villa and garden. He metamorphosed the

Figure 9.13
Vincenzo Scamozzi, Villa Rocca Pisana in Lonigo, Italy (1574), from Scala/Art Resource New York

Figure 9.14
**Richard Boyle,
3rd Earl of
Burlington
(Lord
Burlington)
and William
Kent, Chiswick
House in
Chiswick,
England (1729)**

Rotonda's central hall from a circle into an octagon surmounted by a dome and inserted perfect squares, circles rectangles, and octagons into the eight remaining rooms of the nine-square grid. A pedimented portico projects from the front façade while two others appear on the side façades as superimposed layers of one surface upon another.

Figure 9.15
**Thomas
Jefferson,
Monticello in
Charlottesville,
Virginia (1796),**
photograph
by Martin
Falbisoner

Longitudinal Types

The *Quattro libri* provided a compendium of architectural types that made Palladian architecture available for Thomas Jefferson to export to North America. Jefferson derived inspiration from the Rotonda for his own villa at Monticello (1796), the name he gave to his Virginia plantation. In 1819, he founded the University of Virginia, designing its campus with a central library that resembles the Pantheon in Rome. As minister to France from 1784 to 1789, Jefferson imbibed the visionary architectural theories espoused at this time in Paris by architects such as Claude Nicolas Ledoux, Etienne-Louis Boullée, and Charles-Louis Clérisseau. On Clérisseau's advice, with whom he collaborated, Jefferson modeled his design for the Virginia State Capitol on the *Maison Carrée* (Square House), a classical Roman temple located in Nîmes, France. This ancient longitudinal type engendered a near-exact copy in Richmond, the first neoclassical building in the United States.

Attributed to Marcus Agrippa, the Maison Carrée was built in 16 CE according to models of temples dedicated to Apollo and Mars Ultor in Rome. But during the 18th century, it was thought to have been a Greek temple. Demonstrating that a type does not necessarily register a specific function, while the Maison Carrée began as a pagan temple, after the fall of the Empire, it was purportedly used as a Visigoth palace, a consular house, stables, apartments, and a church. The Virginia State Capitol adopted the Maison Carrée more as a specific model to duplicate and less as an abstract idea to manipulate. Conversely, the collection of teaching pavilions bordering the lawn fronting the library at the University of Virginia exemplify the transformation of the

Figure 9.16
**Maison Carrée
in Nîmes,
France (16 CE),
photograph
by Paulette
Singley**

272

rectangular temple type into a series of experimental buildings framing the central space of this academic village. With each of the pavilions Jefferson mixed and mingled sources to produce an iterative building sequence that speaks to creative freedom and mixed architectural components.

Jefferson profoundly understood that public education was essential to maintaining democratic values and therefore built a campus that both literally and metaphorically located architecture at the center of teaching and learning. With the residential teaching pavilions alternating with one-story dormitories, the very structures the students and faculty inhabited served as didactic architecture. In order "to serve as specimens for the architectural lecturer," as Jefferson wrote, no two pavilions are identical.[4] Regarding his use of various models that reference diverse political architectural origins, from ancient Greece to French neoclassicism, Richard Guy Wilson relates that Jefferson symbolically responded to the "splintering of knowledge through the growth of science and specialized expertise" by architecturally rendering "the educational system as an assemblage of functions, differentiated but coordinated."[5]

Rational Types

An 18th-century Jesuit priest and architectural theorist, Marc-Antoine Laugier inaugurated the widespread architectural appreciation of the Maison Carrée, deriving inspiration for his theory on architectural origins from this building. Laugier admired the Maison Carrée for its simplicity and nobility, meanwhile establishing architecture's role in adopting the rational ordering systems of nature.[6] As Laugier narrated architecture's progression from sapling to the shelter of a *cabane rustique* (rustic cabin), early builders discovered four tree branches that happened to fall in the forest, lifted them up to serve as columns, and foraged branches to serve as beams to support a pitched roof covered with leaves. Laugier distilled Vitruvius's taxonomy of humanity's first dwellings (Book II, Chapter 1)—ranging from arbors constructed with the boughs of trees, caves excavated in mountains, and dwellings made of twigs interwoven and covered with mud or clay—into a tidier explanation of original settlements. In so doing, Laugier took early humans from out of the insalubrious and unstable cave and into fresh and rational wood shelters that theoretically metamorphosed into classical marble temples.

The term *type* would not appear in architectural theory until Antoine-Chrysostome Quatremère de Quincy authored his entry "Type" for the *Encyclopédie Méthodique*, vol. 3, pt. II (Paris, 1825). The term exemplifies its own linguistic genealogy in stemming, as Quatremère de Quincy demonstrated, from the Greek word *typos*, meaning "model, matrix, imprint, mold, mark, figure in relief, or bas relief" and from the Latin word *typus* which means 'figure, image, form, kind'."[7] In a significant distinction between the slavish imitation of ancient classical canons and more fluid interpretations of this architecture, Quatremère de Quincy posited that "the word 'type' presents less

Figure 9.17
**Frontispiece of
Marc-Antoine
Laugier's**
***Essai sur
l'architecture,***
**2nd ed., 1755,
by Charles
Eisen**

the image of a thing to copy or imitate completely than the idea of an element which ought itself to serve as a rule for the model."[8] He contrasts *model*, an object meant to be copied, with *type*, "an object after which each [artist] can conceive works of art that may have no resemblance" to each other.[9] As the object to be copied, French neoclassical design principles elevated the Parthenon in Athens to a paradigmatic position. Laugier's *cabane rustique*, also known as the "primitive hut," offered architecture its first theoretical exegesis on what Quatremère de Quincy would later describe as a type.

Although the word was introduced earlier in Chapter 7 regarding Semper's proposing of the Caribbean hut in *Der Stil* as an alternative archetypal building, it should be mentioned at this point that the term *primitive* carries with it certain negative connotations. Adrian Forty compares its use in architecture, "where people appear quite untroubled by the political and cultural objections to the word," with other disciplines, where "it tends to denigrate who or what is described by it, and implies an assumption of superiority in whoever uses it."[10] As Forty summarizes, "primitive exists among a whole constellation of words—'savage', 'barbarian', 'exotic', 'aboriginal', 'backward', 'uncivilized', 'naïve', 'instinctive', 'authentic', 'archaic', 'native', 'tribal', 'erotic', 'traditional', 'outsider'," while in architecture it also includes "'vernacular', 'anonymous', 'non-pedigree', 'spontaneous', and 'indigenous'."[11] While all of these verbal associations overlap with the idea of *primitive* as it is used today, Forty reminds us that until the late eighteenth century, it "had no other meaning than 'at the origins', or 'original'" and only in the nineteenth century, when social Darwinism determined African, Oceanic, and North American Indian societies to be the precursors of Western civilization did 'primitive' take on connotations of a supposed position regarding the early stages of human social development.[12] Indeed, Laugier referred to "l'homme dans sa premiere origine" (man in his first origin) rather than to the phrase Wolfgang and Anni Herrmann used in their translation: "man in his primitive state."[13]

Insofar as "all the splendors of architecture ever conceived have been modeled on the little rustic hut," this typology became a vehicle for Laugier to express his concept that "by imitating the natural process, art was born."[14] He argued for the reasonable imitation of architecture's rational response to natural forces, such as the inclination of a pitched roof to shed rain off of a minimal structure composed only of the essential parts of column, entablature, and pediment. The frontispiece Charles-Dominique-Joseph Eisen engraved for the 1755 edition of *Essai* depicts a rustic shelter as if having grown directly from nature, with living trees acting as the four supporting columns next to which classical ornaments, having been cast aside, lay on the ground as just so many old ruins.

While Laugier liberated architecture from supposed decorative frivolity, his rational approach to the design of external enclosures somewhat incongruously arrested form in a singular position unresponsive to the pressures of internal use. Indeed, use must adapt itself to this formative type. In an argument of *reductio ad absurdum*, Laugier's reasoned proposal for a structure lacking any enclosing walls does not actually function as viable shelter. His rationalism, in a sense, is not entirely rational. Responding neither to specific exterior nor to interior forces, the hut stands out as *a priori* and unreceptive to the architect's exploration of empirical solutions.

Laugier's writing marks an alliance between classicism's and modernism's shared ideals of timeless form. His argument concerning the origins of architecture prefigured the reasoning of design into a rigorous set of minimal and essential components that characterizes much of modernism. As he dispensed with what he perceived to be the overwrought and excessive ornamentation of Renaissance, Baroque, and Rococo architecture in favor of a pristine neo-classicism, he drew upon the clarity of ancient Greek temple construction as a means to transcend the idea of style altogether. In this respect, Mies Van der Rohe's Farnsworth House (1951) delivers a more uncompromising rendition of the *cabane rustique* than was technologically available to Laugier in his time. Composed of thin steel columns supporting floor to ceiling glass, Mies solves Laugier's lack of enclosure through the magic of transparent walls and reiterates the tripartite formula of column, entablature, and roof—now with a flat plane instead of a pitched slope. By constructing a modern explication of classical principles, Mies returns Laugier's origins to their rightful place in Greek classicism as a freestanding pavilion seen in the round where articulate columns translate the marble temple into modern steel (see Figure 8.13 in Chapter 8).

As an object to be copied for its ability to elicit the appearance of classical architecture, Laugier's hut also proved a powerful icon for the language of postmodern architecture wherein the pediment operates as the dominant signifier of a Greek temple. Aldo Rossi developed the *cabane rustique* and the circular temple as leitmotifs throughout his own work, in projects such as the Monument to the Resistance in Segrate, Italy (1965), the primary school in Fagnano (1972), the floating *Teatro del Mondo* (1979, *Theater of the World*), and even the "Tea and Coffee Piazza" (1983) he designed as an addition to Alessi's product line.

Figure 9.18
**Aldo Rossi,
*Teatro del
Mondo*
(*Theater of the
World*, 1979)
floating in front
of the Punta
della Dogana in
Venice, Italy**

By the mid-18th century, general knowledge about Greek architecture would have come from visits to the Doric temples at Paestum, publications on these temples by architects such as Giovanni Battista Piranesi, or from treatises such as James Stuart and Nicholas Revett's *The Antiquities of Athens and Other Monuments of Greece* (1762) or Julien David Le Roy's *Les Ruines des plus beaux monuments de la Grèce* (*Ruins of the Most Beautiful Monuments of Greece*, 1758). During and after his time at the French Academy in Rome from 1731 to 1738, Jacques-Germain Soufflot completed drawings of Paestum that Gabriel-Pierre-Martin Dumont published as engravings in his *Suite de plans de trois temples antiques à Paestum* (1764). Claude Mathieu Delagardette followed with *Les Ruines de Paestum ou Posidonia* (1799).

The first building in France to demonstrate the hybrid potential of Laugier's theory was Soufflot's church Sainte-Geneviève (currently called *Panthéon*), whose foundations were laid in 1758. It fused a Greek temple front, a dome indebted to Bramante's *Tempietto*, freestanding interior columns, and hidden flying buttresses into a new form of church design. Despite this hybridity but due to its classical temple front, Laugier praised Sainte-Geneviève as "the first model of perfect architecture."[15] As a synthesis of Greek, Roman, Renaissance, and Gothic elements, Sainte-Geneviève demonstrates the way in which recombinant precedent may result in entirely unprecedented architecture.

Around the same time Sainte-Geneviève was being completed, with construction lasting from 1758 to 1790, Claude-Nicolas Ledoux was building his designs for 50 tax-collecting offices called *barrières*, demonstrating serial typological transformations that exploded Sainte-Geneviève's neoclassical propriety into an accumulation of additive geometries. These tollgates levied taxes at goods entering the city through *le mur des Fermiers généraux*, the wall of the corporation of farmers that enclosed pre-revolutionary Paris. Calling

Figure 9.19
Soufflot, Le Panthéon (formerly church Sainte-Geneviève) in Paris, France (1790), photograph by Camille Gévaudan

them "les Propylées de Paris," the propylaea of Paris, Ledoux referenced monumental gateways, such as on the Acropolis in Greece, that had become an urban type for marking ceremonial thresholds. He designed each entrance as a separate and unique architectural entity derived from a variation of types that he fraternized and distorted into unprecedented forms. This work was revolutionary enough to provoke Quatremère de Quincy to proclaim that "almost all of these monuments seem to be amalgams of every bizarreness found or not yet found to the present, a new residue of combinations until now impossible."[16]

Figure 9.20
Claude-Nicolas Ledoux, Barrière d'Enfer (photograph by Coyau), Barrière de la Villette (photograph by Coyau), Barrière du Trône (photograph by Reinhard-hauke), Barrière de la rotonde de Chartres (photograph by Gregory Deryckère) in Paris, France (1758–1790)

Symbols of repression built by the *ancien régime*, a number of *barrières* were demolished during the French Revolution, even before the Bastille was stormed on July 14, 1789, while more were torn down in the 1850s and 1860s as part of Napoleon III and Baron Haussmann's expansion of Paris. The remaining four tollgates—the Barrière de la Villette, Barrière du Trône, Barrière d'Enfer, and Barrière de la rotonde Chartres—demonstrate Ledoux's vast range of stylistic references and the liberties he took with them. Similar to Palladio's Villa Rotonda, but lacking a dome, the Barrière St Martin is composed of a cylinder surmounting a bilaterally symmetrical square base with pedimented porticoes. The Barrière du Trône (or barrière de Vincennes) is a set of identical pavilions sited across the L'avenue du Trône that feature large semi-circular openings articulated with voussoirs that alternate between voids that subvert the arch's ability to perform as a compressive system. Another set of twins, at the Barrière d'Enfer ("Gate of Hell"), two pavilions

face each other across the Place Denfert-Rochereau. They display rusticated columns of alternating circular and square stone lozenges that stretch elastically into portions of walls. And, finally, the Barrière de la rotonde de Chartres references Bramante's *tempietto*, now rendered with disproportionately large Doric columns. Drums without domes, arches on columns, Greek orders on domed pavilions, these mix-and-match components bred an iterative and irreverent typological series.

Urban Types

Along with identifying a system for reading buildings, typological investigation provides a tool for categorizing and thereby responding to the shapes, forms, voids, and patterns of urban and suburban environments. Both in terms of identifying the formal structure of an existing urban fabric and of understanding the referential collective memories certain typologies absorb, architectural types and the spaces in-between them describe fruitful sites for reading architecture that extends this mode of inquiry beyond the scale of an individual building. It offers a methodology for inserting new architecture into various contexts so as to reference existing building patterns.

The *barrières* offered a model for a conceptual museum of architecture, mutating from one pavilion to another as unique but nonetheless sequential hybrid forms, which the academical village at University of Virginia similarly describes. Jefferson's design for the University of Virginia also provides a model for typological analysis that considers the voids between buildings as much as the solid architecture that forms these spaces. With historical precedents such as the original peristyle courtyard fronting Rome's Pantheon, Jules Hardouin Mansart's chateau and gardens at Marly-le-Roi (1679), and the College of William and Mary, where Jefferson studied from 1760 to 1762,

Figure 9.21
Thomas Jefferson, University of Virginia in Charlottesville, Virginia (founded 1819), photograph by Karen Blaha

Figure 9.22
Thomas Jefferson, University of Virginia Pavilion IX, photograph by John Neilson

Figure 9.23
Claude-Nicolas Ledoux, House for Marie Madeleine Guimard (Paris, France, 1770), *L'Architecture considérée sous le rapport de l'art, des mœurs et de la legislation* **(1768–1789)**

forming examples of architecture expressed as negative space, the University of Virginia's green lawn and axial library were to become the requisite identity of numerous collegiate campuses. For their master plan of Columbia University at Morningside Heights in Manhattan, McKim Mead and White located the Low Memorial Library (1895), a neoclassical pavilion crowned with a dome, on axis with the great lawn, creating an indispensable open space for

Type

an academical village set in an unrelentingly dense city. With the University of Virginia, as Mary Woods persuasively argues, Jefferson "was no longer the gentleman-architect who amused himself by designing a country house, but a modern-day architect and planner who anticipated the environmental, social, and symbolic ramifications of a complex institutional building type."[17]

Jefferson's lawn accomplished in a rural setting what numerous plazas, places, piazzas, and squares actualize in urban settings, a strong figural void within a dense urban fabric that acts as a roofless room in the city. Inigo Jones, who introduced Palladio's *Quattro libri* to England, as discussed in Chapter 4, completed an urban design for the Earl of Bedford's speculative housing quarter in London that included the public amenities of a church and a public plaza to incentivize living in the new row houses surrounding the square. Jones composed an arcade surmounted by a continuous wall of housing that enclosed a three-dimensional spatial volume. Jones located the church of St Paul's in Covent Garden (1633) on the plaza's central axis while introducing the language of classicism into the Perpendicular Gothic style of architecture prevalent at that time. He adopted the rustic order of Tuscan temples with four substantial columns supporting a billowing pediment. Spatial voids such as at Covent Garden and its precedent at the Piazza Grande in Livorno belong to a typological series of public spaces that have been carved out of an existing urban fabric, emerge from the foundations of previous layers of inhabitation, grow organically from patterns of use, or spring from urban design proposals.

Rossi theorized the significance of civic spaces in his seminal publication *L'architettura della città* (*The Architecture of the City*, 1966), where he posited the concept of the urban artifact, that is, a typology "whose function has changed over time or for which a specific function does not even exist."[18] As

Figure 9.24
The East Prospect of St Paul's Church, Covent Garden to the Great Square and the West prospect of Covent Garden invented by Inigo Jones (1640), after Colen Campbell, print made by Henry Hulsberg (London, 1715–1725)

281

an urban artifact endures, its form and location become steeped with customs and rituals that provide a community with a sense of longevity and identity. Saturated with both collective and individual memories, the meaning of these artifacts overshadows their functions, which quite often no longer serve a specific purpose. The urban artifact, as he explains, argues for architectural types wherein "form persists and comes to preside over a built work in a world where functions continually become modified."[19] His *Teatro del mondo* (Theater of the World, 1979) references both the abstract typological form of Laugier's *cabane rustique* and the mnemonic arts, the arts of memory that rely on topographic loci, or places, in order to recall long passages of literature. Recalling that Anthony Vidler gave him a copy of Frances Yates's *Theatre of the World* with the dedication "For A., from the theater of memory to the theater of science," Rossi mused that his earlier *Teatrino scientifico* [*Little Scientific Theater*, 1978] was a theater of memory in the sense of repetition while the *Teatro del mondo* preserved the cultural memory of the anatomical theater at Padua and Shakespeare's Globe Theatre among its typological references.[20]

Organic Types

Rossi cited Jean-Nicolas-Louis Durand's *Précis des leçons d'architecture données à l'école polytechnique* (*Summary of Lectures on Architecture Given at the École Polytechnique*, 1802–1805) to argue for the typological dialogue between buildings and cities: "Just as the walls, the columns, & c., are elements which compose buildings, so buildings are the elements which compose cities."[21] A student of Étienne-Louis Boullée, Durand was a pivotal figure in modernizing architectural theory to reflect the emerging scientific methodology of the 19th century. He proposed an infinitely variable system for addressing the urgent design needs of a rapidly changing metropolis with increasingly diverse building programs. He and Quatremére de Quincy were contemporaries—the former becoming professor of architecture at the École polytechnique in 1795 and the later acting as perpetual secretary to the Académie des Beaux-Arts from 1816 until 1839. As their respective names imply—the teaching of fine arts versus technical knowledge—the different emphases of these two Parisian schools parallels that of their primary envoys. The École Polytechnique was a technical school that specialized in science and engineering, in contrast to the École des Beaux-Arts's emphasis on fine arts and architecture. Where both theorists explored typological design principles, to return to the conceptual opposition set up at the beginning of this chapter, one could say that Quatremére de Quincy espoused a Neoplatonic argument leading back to architecture's metaphysical origins, while Durand's emphasis on a componential approach to generating built progeny responds to an Aristotelian position of exigency.

Indicative of the scientizing of type into an evolutionary theory of morphological change, in his *Précis des leçons*, Durand used the French *genre*—meaning genus, kind, sort, or style—instead of the Latin *type*. In *Recueil et*

parallèle des édifices de tout genre (*Compendium and Parallel of Buildings of All Kinds*, 1800), Durand developed a classification system for the significant historical typologies he diagrammed in plan, section, and elevation, drawn at the same scale as each other, and grouped according to function: theatre, stadium, market, etc. In *Précis des leçons d'architecture* he expounded ways to operate on these types in order to permute new hybrid architectures, which maintained the potential to become either normative or distorted species. Durand was influenced by Étienne-Louis Boullée's pure geometric forms, contemporary advancements in the natural sciences, and Gaspard Monge's descriptive geometry, combining their comparative taxonomical methods for both studying and producing architecture. As founder of the École Polytechnique, Monge explicated a precise drawing method that projected geometry through a system of points, lines, and planes onto the new medium of graph paper. Durand applied a similar metric of standardization to his architectural subjects by delineating them with gridded backgrounds and placing them on an axis like a biological specimen to be dissected.

Durand offered lessons for the production of new architecture based on the analysis of past buildings, innovating a design methodology that offered the appearance of scientific objectivity. He proposed compositional strategies based on the combinative arrangement of building parts—such as porches, vestibules, staircases, and courts—that could be dissected into repeatable and exchangeable components as a proto-digital solution for designs that self-generate according to a software application. "What is paradoxical

Figure 9.25 **Jean-Nicolas-Louis Durand, "Gothic and Modern Churches," from** *Recueil et parallèle des édifices de tout genre* (*Compendium and Parallel of Buildings of All Kinds*, **1800**)

283

Figure 9.26
**Jean-Nicolas-
Louis Durand,
"Combinaisons
Horisontales,
de Colonnes,
de Pilastres,
de Murs, de
Portes, et
de croisées"
("Horizontal
Combinations
of Columns,
Pilasters,
Walls, Doors,
and Crosses")
from *Précis
des leçons
d'architecture
donnés
à l'École
polytechnique
(Summary of
Lectures on
Architecture
Given at
the École
Polytechnique,
1802–1805)***

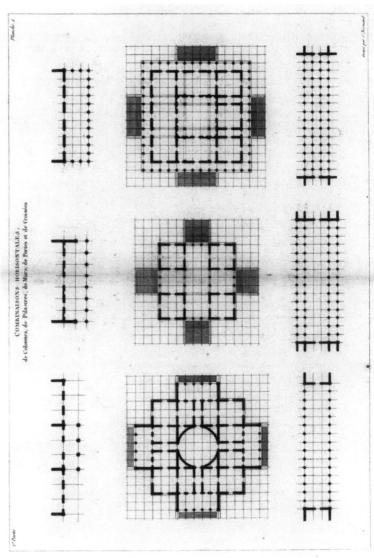

Part II. Composition in General

Plate 1

about Durand's system," Philip Steadman clarifies, is that "his compositional procedure is essentially a formal, geometrical one, and not in a certain sense functional at all."[22]

The analogies arising from the natural sciences that describe Durand's project coincide with emerging developments in 19th century biological theory, propelling discussions of type into both an aesthetic and functional study of organic form. Baron Georges Cuvier provided systematic analytical tools for architects to derive a building's conceptual *raison d'être* from scientific models. Cuvier, titular professor at the Jardin des Plantes in Paris, developed a system called the "subordination of characters" in which each animal could be categorized according to a fixed type of internal organ that distinguished it from other species. Cuvier's *Tableau élémentaire de l'histoire naturelle des animaux* (*The Animal Kingdom Arranged after its Organization; Forming a Natural History of Animals, and an Introduction to Comparative Anatomy*, 1798) organizes animals according to how their organs work, a concept called "functional integration" that could be compared to Durand's compendium for the systematic classification and visual analysis of architectural species. During the 19th century, according to Steadman, "we shall find biological taxonomy invoked explicitly as a model for classifying building and artifact types and styles."[23]

Cuvier's methodologies influenced Eugène Emmanuel Viollet-le-Duc, a colorful *dramatis persona* who eschewed study at the École des Beaux-Arts but emerged to be an influential theorist, architect, and preservationist. Viollet-le-Duc was a prolific writer who authored the *Dictionnaire raisonné de l'architecture française du XIe au XVIe siècle* (*Dictionary of French Architecture from the 11th to the 16th Century*, 1854–1868) and *Entretiens sur l'architecture* (*Discourses on Architecture*, 1863–1872). He strongly advocated against the architectural eclecticism then prevalent at the École des Beaux-Arts, claiming that "in the study of the arts of the past … we should observe a clear distinction between a form which is only the reflection of a tradition … and a form which is the immediate expression of a requirement, of a certain social condition."[24] He dedicated two chapters of *Histoire d'un dessinateur* (*Story of a Draftsman*, 1879) to comparative anatomy. His concept of organic architecture in the *Dictionnaire raisonné de l'architecture*, as Teyssot informs us, paralleled Cuvier's theory of the correlation of organs, "in which an organ existed only in relation to the whole, and each form could be explained only through its place in the system."[25] This scientific definition would offer a parallel to concepts of organic architecture.

In tracing this discussion to modernism, type became a tool for extricating architecture from an emphasis on origins to a developmental process paralleling the newly emerging biological sciences and genetic sequencing. Anthony Vidler positions the primitive hut as a form that was "both embedded in the classical tradition and newly adopted in the terminology of the natural sciences."[26] Eisen's frontispiece for the *Essai sur l'Architecture* similarly demonstrates the duality of architectural origins and natural organisms forming typological systems. While one interpretation of the rustic hut in the woods returns it to ancient Greece and the Parthenon, another sees it as anticipating architecture that grows from living, upright trees as an organic form of inhabitation. Laugier anticipates a movement in design practices that seeks to genetically program nature into habitable spaces, transcending mere biomimicry with emergent life forms in which buildings grow biodynamically from trees or other organic elements.

Figure 9.27
**Georges
Cuvier, skeletal
comparisons
of animals
from** *Tableau
élémentaire
de l'histoire
naturelle des
animaux* **(1798)**

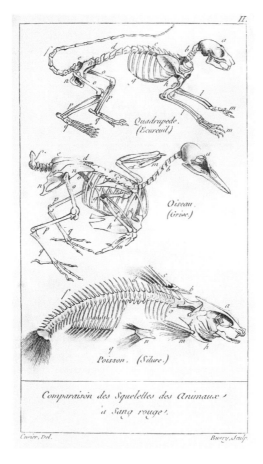

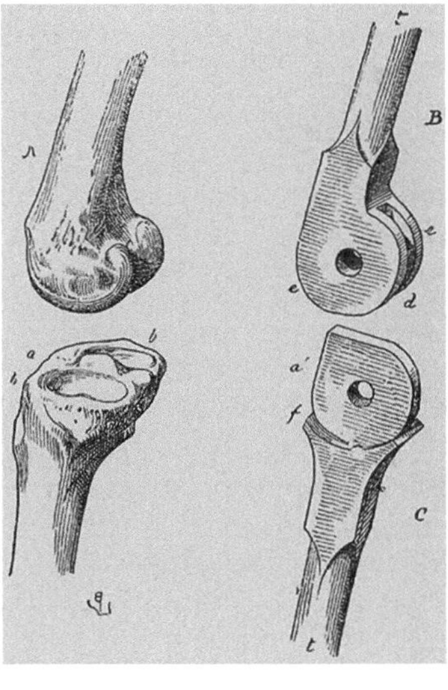

Figure 9.28
**Eugène
Emmanuel
Viollet-le-Duc,
application of
mechanical
joints,**
*Histoire d'un
dessinateur
comment on
apprend à
dessiner* (*Story
of a Draftsman,*
1879)

Figure 9.29
**Eugène
Emmanuel
Viollet-le-Duc,
design for a
concert hall
expressing
Gothic
principles
in modern
materials;
brick, stone
and cast iron,
*Entretiens sur
l'architecture
(Discourses on
Architecture,
1863–1872)***

Inspired by the structural clarity and integrity of Gothic buildings, Viollet-le-Duc argued for architecture to respond to the pressures of use and the models of nature over predetermined styles. He propelled type into an engagement with the new building material of iron. His drawings of iron trusses depicted skeletal forms that stylistically complemented the attenuated language of the imaginary Gothic architecture they supported, while they simultaneously echoed the paleontological displays in Paris's National Museum of Natural History, where Cuvier held a post.

Partially due to Henry van Brunt's translation of the *Entretiens* into *Discourses on Architecture* (1875) and partially due to Louis Sullivan, who was Frank Lloyd Wright's mentor and who had studied at the École des Beaux-Arts in 1874, a number of American architects such as Frank Furness, John Wellborn Root, and Wright himself fell under the spell of Viollet-le-Duc's rational reform of architecture. As Wright put it: "I believed the 'Raisonne' was the only really sensible book on architecture in the world. I got copies of it for my sons, later. That book was enough to keep, in spite of architects, one's faith alive in architecture."[27] Viollet-le-Duc espoused the theory that buildings should adhere to the functional laws of nature in order to develop organic logics, observing that: "The lilies of the field, the leaves of the trees, the insects, have style, because they grow, develop, and exist according to essentially logical laws."[28] For him: "We can spare nothing from a flower, because, in its organization, every part has its function and is formed to carry out that function in the most beautiful manner."[29] Wright would similarly claim that his "designs have grown as natural plants grow," while Sullivan would state: "Whether it be the sweeping eagle in his flight or the open apple-blossom, the toiling work-horse, the blithe swan, the branching oak, the winding stream at its base, the drifting clouds, over all the coursing sun, form ever follows function, and this is the law."[30]

Given the intellectual history of the term *organic*, indicating either the holistic performance of bodily organs in a part-to-whole system or the more general sense of design aesthetics derived from the external shapes and geometries found in nature, the theories of organic architecture Sullivan and Wright put forward fall into both the holistic and aesthetic lineage of 19th-century biologists such as Cuvier, Charles Darwin, Ernst Haeckel, and D'Arcy Wentworth Thompson. Sullivan's work exhibits energetic ornamentation that unfurls into the appearance of animate organic material momentarily frozen in place. At the Guaranty Building (1896, now the Prudential Building) in Buffalo, New York, this blossoming vegetal ornamentation is most pronounced. Sullivan and his partner Dankmar Adler covered every exterior surface of this building with lush terracotta ornamentation that explodes at the corners of the cornice into a system of leaves and vines that erode the building's structural silhouette and render it as an overgrown ruin.

Figure 9.30
Louis Sullivan and Dankmar Adler, Guaranty Building (now the Prudential Building) in Buffalo, New York (1896), photograph by Tom Fawls

Interwoven vines and tendrils insinuated themselves into Sullivan's architecture as ornamental contaminants of a broader analogy between design and nature he organically applied to the entire edifice. Given Sullivan's enthusiasm with naturally derived ornamentation, it may seem something of a contradiction that he coined the widespread motto "form follows function." Recalling Viollet-le-Duc's conviction that every part of a plant has a form that carries its function, Sullivan's verdant ornamentation provides a symbolic language for reading his architecture as the built expression of organic forms operating according to a set of natural rules but does not necessarily derive from a normative understanding of function as expressed through lack of ornamentation.

Considered to be the "Father of the Skyscraper," Sullivan defined the ethos of this new building type in the essay "The Tall Building Artistically Reconsidered" (1896), where the infamous "form ever follows function" statement originally appeared.[31] Sullivan conceptualized the ideal skyscraper as possessing the tripartite division of a base containing commercial spaces, a shaft of offices, and an attic story housing mechanical systems into a strategy he demonstrated at the Guaranty Building. However, as this building demonstrates, the skyscraper's function of providing a repetitious number of flexible floors does not necessarily offer considerable opportunity for formal expression. What, then, is a tall building's primary design function? As Sullivan well understood, the skyscraper's foremost objective is to stretch the economic value of a piece of land into the sky.

For Sullivan: "It must be tall, every inch of it tall. The force and power of altitude must be in it, the glory and pride of exaltation must be in it. It must be every inch a proud and soaring thing, rising in sheer exultation that from bottom to top…"[32] His simple argument that a tall building's function is to be tall is, in fact, quite nuanced. For in accepting the economic drivers of this new architectural type, he translated the rudimentary facts of commodity capital into the transcendental spirit of reaching to the sky, to the sublime heights of heaven expressed through the tectonics of verticality, which his bursting ornamentation announced. He identified architecture's ability to contribute ornamental beauty and the vertical aspirations for loftier goals onto a new type whose emergence had been driven by the calculus of speculative investment and the raw forces of market capital.

When he stated that "the design of the tall office building takes its place with all other architectural types made when architecture, as has happened once in many years, was a living art. Witness the Greek temple, the Gothic cathedral, the medieval fortress," he articulated a precise awareness that a heroic new architectural typology had been born, one whose role was not to imitate historical precedents, but to soar above them.[33] As a vertical shaft whose limitations were seemingly unlimited, its double and even conflicting role was to extend real estate vertically and to complete the spiritual transformation of architecture into modernity that its structural innovations broadcast. As Vincent Scully describes the Guaranty Building: "All the contrasting elements had been drawn into one continuous plastic unity, into a vertical body standing on legs, and stretching and swelling with muscular force … A new kind of giant stood high on his legs: mass man with steel muscle, tensile and springy."[34]

If Sullivan's verdant ornamentation remains petrified in stone and terracotta, then it finds living expression in Patrick Blanc's green wall designed for the river façade of Jean Nouvel's *Musée du quai Branly* in Paris. More recently, the biological application of type has metastasized into research concerning biomimetic architecture that remains indebted to 19th-century scientific treatises. The project of architectural emergence, which seeks to grow shelter from living cellular tissue, finds its origins in the conflation of architecture and organicism that emerged at this time.

Philip Beesley propels the organic analogy into animated biomimetic design practices, as if he has liberated Sullivan's ornamentation from terra cotta and cast-iron into the architecture of hylozoism, a Greek philosophical concept that matter is in some sense living. Beesley's "Hylozoic Ground," exhibited in Canada's Pavilion at the International Architecture Exhibition Venice Biennale of 2010, performs as an immersive, interactive, and responsive environment. Into what can best be described as artificial growth hanging from the pavilion ceiling, Beesley wove digitally fabricated shapes—what appear to be feathers, whiskers, and fishing lures—into transparent and translucent acrylic components that move and react to a series of touch sensors and shape-memory alloy actuators. When activated, the entire system surges in waves of quavering movement like a drawing of one of Haeckel's radiolarians come to life. "Hylozoic Ground" performs as a suspended geotextile that

slowly extracts hybrid soil from the surrounding air it breathes in a process that makes synthetic earth. Beesley describes this process: "empathic motions ripple out from hives of kinetic valves and pores in peristaltic waves, creating a diffuse pumping system that pulls air, moisture, and stray organic matter through the filtering Hylozoic membranes."[35] The final installation, part nature, part robot, resulted in a complex and intricate network of tens of thousands of digitally fabricated components, a cross between hypodermic needles, vials of a secret unguent, and synthetic feathers, that the architect animated with sensors to respond to movement.

Digital Types

A conventional understanding of modern architecture presents it as a paradigm shift that turned away from developing building precedents as generative models and toward other sources of inspiration. The aforementioned developments in the natural sciences, the products of civil engineering such as bridges and grain silos, objects of mass production, automobiles, airplanes, ocean liners, and the fine arts each in their own way contributed to the transformation of type as an architectural precedent into type as a component of mass production. The model of the typewriter offered at the beginning of this chapter returns, but now as a machine that can systematically reproduce form with minimal variation. Writing in "Typology and Design Method," Alan Colquhoun argued for a lingering presence of type in the modern movement, often thought to entirely have rejected this concept by replacing the idea of imitation with innovation. As Colquhoun demonstrates, embedded in the production of modern architecture is "a tension between two apparently contradictory ideas—biotechnical determinism on the one hand and free expression on the other."[36] The deterministic trajectory of machined buildings implies the complete abnegation of the designer's creative role, or agency, in order to enact an architecture that descends as a *deus ex machina*. In response to a Calvinist system, according to Colquhoun, seemingly rational modes of production, such as discipline and frugality, are elevated above intuitive creative expression insofar as design authorship often finds its alibi in the objective reasoning of the technological and scientific languages that constitute positivism.

Stemming from the 19th-century developments in biological and architectural theory we have just covered, the idea of primitive types plays an important role in developing the technologically advanced computational design practice that was introduced in Chapter 2 as scripting. When discussing the way in which to translate architectural form from inert architectural precedents to dynamic digital programs, William Mitchell understood that axiomatically driven primitives could generate geometric types in a manner "reasonably consistent with the influential early definition of architectural type that was given by Quatremère de Quincy in his *Dictionnaire historique d'architecture*."[37] Not only did Mitchell develop Quatremère de Quincy's idea of type into a programmable concept of formal resemblance, he also invoked Laugier's "primitive hut" as a universal architectural prototype that anticipated the primitives he developed in reconstructing Palladio's Villa Foscari (a.k.a. Malcontenta). "According to Laugier," Mitchell wrote, "in order to qualify as a true work of architecture, a building must, in some sense, instantiate the type represented by the primitive hut."[38] Durand's *Précis des leçons d'architecture* also provided Mitchell with the operative terms for transforming Palladio's architecture into software, illustrating the means by which digital form generation relies on cross-axes, grids, squares, and circles that are taken as primitive shapes.

While more recent computer-generated architectures may have eclipsed the conventional understanding of types as referencing either Palladio or other architectural paradigms such as centralized and longitudinal temples, biological and natural models nonetheless dwell within a series of generative forms that are beginning to organize themselves into typological categories determined by the DNA of their generative software. This begins to suggest a taxonomy of computer-generated shapes. Among these new typologies, certain architects have produced work emblematic of a larger body of formal responses to design intelligence: the tornado-torus found in Winka

Figure 9.32
Winka Dubbeldam, "Soundscapes" at the National Building Museum (2003), courtesy of Winka Dubbeldam and Archi-Techtonics

Figure 9.33
**Farshid
Moussavi and
Alejandro
Zaera-Polo of
Foreign Office
Architects
(FOA),
Yokohama
International
Passenger
Terminal in
Yokohama,
Japan (2002),
photograph
by Satoru
Mishima**

Figure 9.34
**Massimiliano
and Doriana
Fuksas, New
Milan Trade
Fair in Milan,
Italy (2005),
courtesy of
Studio Fuksas**

Dubbeldam's "Soundscapes" at the National Building Museum (2003), the artificial topography at Foreign Office Architects's Yokohama International Port Terminal in Japan (2002), or the arithmetic variations of craters and dunes in Massimiliano and Doriana Fuksas's and New Milan Trade Fair (2002–2005). These projects exemplify innovative typological models. They suggest, in an era when scientific experimentation seeks to manipulate technology and biology into robotically produced buildings or sentient, living architectures, that the architect's agency to evolve hybrid typologies through imaginative and creative research remains an essential dimension to enacting the future of robotic or animate architectures.

Notes

1   Georges Teyssot, *A Topology of Everyday Constellations* (Cambridge, MA: MIT Press, 2013), p. 31.
2   Rafael Moneo, "On Typology" *Oppositions*, vol. 13 (Cambridge, MA: MIT Press, 1978), p. 23.
3   Giulio Argan, "Sul concetto della tipologia architettonica," in *Progetto e destino* (Milan: Alberto Mondadori, 1965), reproduced in *Theorizing a New Agenda for Architecture: An Anthology of Architectural Theory 1965–1995*, ed. Kate Nesbitt (New York: Princeton Architectural Press, 1996), p. 244.
4   Ralph G. Giordano, *The Architectural Ideology of Thomas Jefferson* (Jefferson, NC: McFarland, 2012), p. 199.
5   Richard Guy Wilson, "Jefferson's Lawn: Perceptions, Interpretations, Meanings," in *Thomas Jefferson's Academical Village: The Creation of an Architectural Masterpiece*, ed. Richard Guy Wilson (Charlottesville: University of Virginia Press, 1993), p. 62.
6   Marc-Antoine Laugier, *An Essay on Architecture*, trans. Wolfgang and Anni Herrmann (Los Angeles: Hennessey & Ingalls, 1977), p. 13.
7   Antoine-Chrysostome Quatremère de Quincy, "Type," in *Oppositions Reader: Selected Readings from a Journal for Ideas and Criticism in Architecture (1973–1984)*, ed. K. Michael Hays (New York: Princeton Architectural Press), p. 618. See also Anthony Vidler, "Introduction to 'Type'," in *Oppositions Reader*, p. 617.
8   Ibid.
9   Ibid. Cf. *The True, the Fictive, and the Real: The Historical Dictionary of Architecture of Quatremère de Quincy*, trans. Samir Younés (London: Andreas Papadakis, 1999), p. 255.
10 Adrian Forty, "Primitive: The Word and Concept," in *Primitive: Original Matters in Architecture*, eds. Jo Odgers, Flora Samuel, and Adam Sharr (Abingdon: Routledge, 2006), p. 3.
11 Ibid, p. 4.
12 Ibid.
13 Ibid, p. 5.
14 Laugier, *An Essay on Architecture*, p. 12.
15 From the "Discours sur le retablissement de 1'architecture antique," Lyon, Academie des Sciences, MS 194.

16 Anthony Vidler, *Claude-Nicolas Ledoux: Architecture and Social Reform at the End of the Ancien Régime* (Cambridge, MA: MIT Press, 1990), p. 251.

17 Mary N. Woods, "Thomas Jefferson and the University of Virginia: Planning the Academic Village" *Journal of the Society of Architectural Historians 44*, no. 3 (October 1985), p. 267.

18 Aldo Rossi, *The Architecture of the City* (*Architettura Della Città*, 1966), trans. Diane Ghirardo and Joan Ockman (Cambridge, MA: MIT Press, 1982), p. 46.

19 Aldo Rossi, *A Scientific Autobiography*, trans. Lawrence Venuti (Cambridge, MA: MIT Press, 1981), p. 1.

20 Ibid, p. 68.

21 Rossi, *The Architecture of the City*, p. 35.

22 Philip Steadman, *The Evolution of Designs: Biological Analogy in Architecture and the Applied Arts* (Cambridge: Cambridge University Press, 1979), p. 29.

23 Ibid., p. 27.

24 Eugène-Emmanuel Viollet-le-Duc, *Lectures on Architecture*, vol. 1, trans. Benjamin Bucknall (New York: Dover Publications, 1987), p. 451.

25 Georges Teyssot, *A Topology of Everyday Constellations* (Cambridge, MA: MIT Press, 2013), p. 34.

26 As cited by Sam Jacoby, "The Reasoning of Architecture: Type and the Problem of Historicity" (London: Architectural Association Diploma Dissertation, 2013), p. 53, from Anthony Vidler, "The Idea of Type" (1977) in *Oppositions* and "From the Hut to the Temple: Quatremere de Quincy and the Idea of Type," in *The Writing of the Walls: Architectural Theory in the Late Enlightenment* (New York: Princeton Architectural Press, 1987), p. 147.

27 *Frank Lloyd Wright: An Autobiography* (New York: Duell, Sloan and Pearce, 1943), p. 75.

28 Donald Hoffmann, *Understanding Frank Lloyd Wright's Architecture* (New York: Dover Publications, 1995), p. 3.

29 Ibid.

30 Frank Lloyd Wright, "In the Cause of Architecture" (1908), in *Frank Lloyd Wright: Essential Texts*, ed. Robert Twombly (New York: W. W. Norton & Company, 2009), p. 95; and Louis Sullivan, "The Tall Building Artistically Reconsidered" *Lippincott's Magazine*, March 1896, p. 408.

31 Ibid.

32 Ibid, p. 406.

33 Ibid, p. 408.

34 Vincent Scully, *American Architecture and Urbanism* (San Antonio: Trinity University Press, 2013), p. 108.

35 Philip Beesley, *Hylozoic Ground: Liminal Responsive Architectures* (Toronto: Riverside Architectural Press, 2010), back cover.

36 Alan Colquhoun, "Typology and Design Method," in *Theorizing a New Agenda for Architecture: An Anthology of Architectural Theory, 1965–1995*, ed. Nesbitt, Kate (New York, Princeton Architectural Press, 1996), p. 254, first published in *Arena*, 1967.

37 William J. Mitchell *The Logic of Architecture: Design, Computation, and Cognition* (Cambridge, MA: MIT Press, 1990), p. 87.

38 Ibid, p. 90.

Chapter 10

Form

Tell me something about the villa that you cannot see.[1]

—Colin Rowe

While strong concern for rationality influences Eladio Dieste's work, he also claims to have "been guided by a sharp, almost painful, awareness of form."[2] If for Jean Prouvé "formalism is the negation of architecture," then for Christopher Alexander "the ultimate object of design is form."[3] Where Patrik Schumacher states that "Form delivers Function," Peggy Deamer will argue that "today, 'formalism' is a negative term to which it is almost embarrassing to refer."[4] Although these quotations have been extracted from their larger historical contexts, they nonetheless indicate that the role of formalism in architecture engenders powerful debate. For the purposes of reading architecture through form, however, this chapter adopts Judith Wolin's assertion that "if you're not a formalist, you're probably just asleep."[5] Simply put, *form* is the visible shape or configuration of an object, while *formalism* is the production or interpretation of objects independent of a search for any other meaning than the self-referential geometries and complexities they articulate. If forms and their formations abound in the world, from spoons to cities or from clouds to cupolas, then formalism is an essential tool for interpreting them.

Linear and Painterly

"We refuse to recognize problems of form," as Mies van der Rohe famously wrote, "but only problems of building."[6] For Mies: "Form is not the aim of our work, but only the result. Form, by itself, does not exist. Form as an aim is formalism; and that we reject."[7] But where Mies rejected formalism in word, he articulated it in deed. As discussed in Chapter 5 for its potential to be read in terms of criticality, the German Pavilion in Barcelona equally may be read as reckoning with internal logics that have little to do with context or program. Formal analysis suggests reading the Barcelona Pavilion as a synthesis of classicism and modernism, permanence and transience, centrality and displacement, or harmony and rupture. It locates the ionic portico of Karl Friedrich

Schinkel's Altes Museum in Berlin inside a canonical Der Stijl work such as Piet Mondrian's "Composition with Large Red Plane, Yellow, Black, Gray, and Blue" (1921) or Theo van Doesburg's "Counter-construction" (unbuilt, 1923). It gives built evidence to van Doesburg's observation that: "In contrast to frontalism, which had its origin in a rigid, static way of life, the new architecture offers the plastic richness of an all-sided development in space and time."[8]

Der Stijl eroded architecture's walls from the corners to produce, as van Doesburg wrote, a "ground-plan entirely different from the classical one, since inside and outside now pass over into one another."[9] The principles of Der Stijl that the Barcelona Pavilion demonstrates—the centrifugal explosion of a closed form into an open work—coexist simultaneously with the balanced symmetry of a Greek Temple—appearing in a rectangle defined by eight structural columns supported on a podium. Construction joints in the pavilion's travertine paving produce a ubiquitous grid that performs as a defining element without which the manifestation of modernism's universal space and infinite axes would lack precise articulation.

Colin Rowe pressed the limits of formal analysis when comparing Mies's Brick Country House (unbuilt, 1923) with Michelangelo Buonarroti's Cappella Sforza (Sforza Chapel) in the Basilica of Santa Maria Maggiore in Rome (1581)—claiming that each demonstrates a version of architectural Mannerism. Dating from about 1520 to 1600, architectural Mannerism served as a transitional movement between the Renaissance's recovering of classical canons, a clear expression of part-to-whole relationships, and the Baroque's dissolution of these rules into a fluid confluence of spatial movement between part and whole. As evidenced by figures such as Michelangelo, Giulio Romano, and

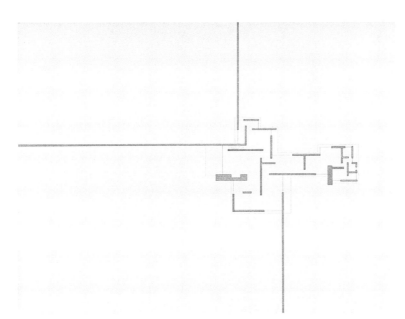

Figure 10.1
**Ludwig Mies
van der Rohe,
plan for a Brick
Country House
(unbuilt, 1923)
courtesy of
the Museum
of Modern Art,
New York**

Figure 10.2
**Michelangelo
Buonarroti,
Sforza Chapel
in the Basilica
of Santa Maria
Maggiore in
Rome, Italy
(1558), drawn
by Hitisha
Kalolia**

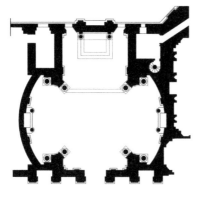

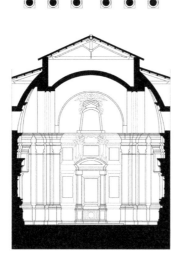

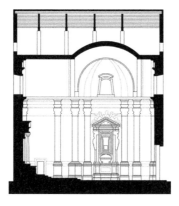

Baldassare Peruzzi, Mannerism relied on the codification of architecture's classical language in order to challenge these very systems by pushing and pulling classical proportions into experimental new forms that broke established orthodoxies. "While retaining the externals of classical correctness," according to Rowe, Mannerism "was obliged at the same time to disrupt the inner core of classical coherence."[10] Rowe's radical ahistorical pairing of the Cappella Sforza and the Brick Country House evidences his own unique Mannerist approach where he breaks the normative research methods of cause and effect analysis and chronology to identify formal ambiguity and deliberate complexity as a conversation between otherwise disparate epochs.

When analyzing a building's façade formally, Rowe compared Raphael's "School of Athens" with Bramante's Casa Caprini in Rome (from 1510 and where Raphael just so happened to live), offering an emblematic model of a building's ability to develop the illusion of thickness within the thin dimensions of an exterior wall. As he argued, "if the School of Athens celebrates the High Renaissance achievement of a deep space in which human figures and architectural detail move equipped with their own internal animation … then the Casa Caprini may be constructed as a representation of this deep space condensed within the limits of a façade."[11] Consider the difference between Rowe's description of Raphael's painting and the one I wrote in the previous chapter on type that emerged from the Italian Renaissance's specific intellectual and architectural milieu. Rowe focused instead on the painting itself to extract legible principles from its internal spatial composition as a point of entry for exploring broader priorities for interpreting architectural façades. His proclivity to approach architecture through art's mutually conversant compositional principles offers an important model for reading architecture as form.

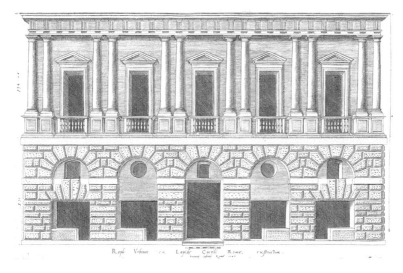

Figure 10.3
Donato Bramante, Casa Caprini in Rome, Italy (1510, demolished), drawn by Antoine Lafrery, from Gianfranco Spagnesi, *Progetto e architetture del linguaggio classico: (XV–XVI secolo)*

Swiss art historian Heinrich Wölfflin established the method of comparing two different artworks and in so doing contributed to the development of architecture's formalist orientation. Taken together, his two publications *Renaissance and Baroque* (1964; *Renaissance und Barock*, 1888) and *Principles of Art History: The Problem of the Development of Style in Later Art* (1932; *Kunstgeschichtliche Grundbegriffe*, 1915) irreversibly transformed the possibilities of reading architecture into a process that privileged intrinsic formal relationships over references to cultural contexts or recourse to functional determinism. Before the advent of digital images, which can be formatted in numerous ways while being projected from a single lens, generations of art and architectural history students would attend class in rooms equipped with two slide projectors, each one delivering an image of a different work in order to offer a close reading of their comparative forms. Through the use of separate "magic lanterns" (early slide projectors), Wölfflin pioneered the method of comparison following five pairs of objective oppositional concepts:

1. linear and painterly;
2. planar and recessional;
3. closed and open form;
4. multiplicity and unity;
5. absolute and relative clarity.

Wölfflin provided scholars with fundamental tools to apply formal analysis to built form, recovering Baroque art and architecture from near-anonymity after it had been cast aside by generations of historians who decried it to be bizarre, overwrought, and disturbed. In Wölfflin's schema, Renaissance art adheres to the first column of five attributes—linear, planar, closed, multiple, and absolutely clear—while Baroque art exemplifies the second—painterly, recessional, open, unified, and relatively clear.

A straightforward comparison between Renaissance and Baroque architecture demonstrates the value of Wölfflin's method. Although separated by about 150 years—Donato Bramante's Tempietto and Francesco Borromini's Sant'Ivo alla Sapienza (1642–1660) suggest distinctly alternative formal readings of these two centralized churches in Rome. Notably, the Tempietto occupies the center of a courtyard as a freestanding object, while St Ivo's circular dome emerges as a convex curve on a tangent with the concave end of a rectangular courtyard, distinguished between centripetal and centrifugal spatial forces. As if drafted with a sharp pencil, the Tempietto's cylindrical base, semi-circular dome, and colonnade of Tuscan columns suggest a more *linear* arrangement of parts in which all surfaces are relatively *coplanar*, centralized geometries operate as *closed* forms, and an additive assemblage of parts results in *multiple* solids whose articulation renders *absolute clarity*. In contrast, St Ivo's pilasters seem to blur into walls like the strokes of a *painter's* brush, producing a series of powerfully three-dimensional surfaces with

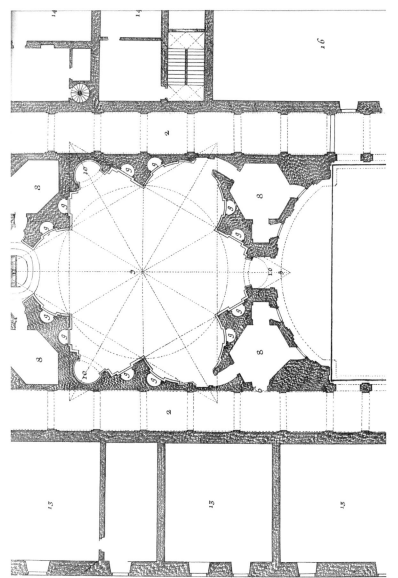

Figure 10.4
**Francesco
Borromini, plan
of Sant'Ivo
alla Sapienza
(1642–1660)
in Rome,
from *Opus
architectoni-
cum*, published
by Sebastiano
Giannini (1720
and 1725)**

projecting and *receding planes*. This geometric movement *opens* the composition outward toward niches and inward toward the center, producing a volumetric harmony across a *unified* and *relatively clear* silhouette. While these
readings are somewhat over-determined to make a point and the system does
not always translate smoothly from art to architecture, this exercise serves to
demonstrate the way in which formal analysis operates in architecture. It also
demonstrates how a building may be read without recourse to contextual,
performative, material, or historical references. The critique of this analytical

Figure 10.5
**Francesco Bor-
romini, section
of Sant'Ivo
alla Sapienza
(1642–1660)
in Rome,
from *Opus
architectoni-
cum,* published
by Sebastiano
Giannini (1720
and 1725)**

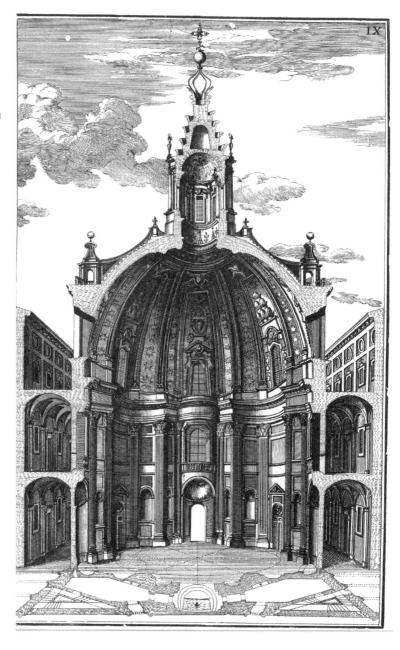

strategy is that it reduces the object of inquiry to a so-called empty vessel of
purposeless form. The counter-critique is that architecture's unique and essential role is first and foremost to define form, with all other influences remaining
subordinate to its discipline-specific role.

Scala di Palmi Romani

Figure 10.6
Francesco Bor-
romini, detail
of spiral and
flaming tiara
on Sant' Ivo
alla Sapienza
(1642–1660)
in Rome,
from *Opus
architectoni-
cum*, published
by Sebastiano
Giannini (1720
and 1725)

303

Nine-Square Grid

Wölfflin's system is pliable enough to accommodate a wide range of subject matter and commute into alternative modes of inquiry. Among them are Rowe's deceptively simple analyses that obliquely demonstrate seemingly empty form to in fact be "full." In his influential essay "The Mathematics of the Ideal Villa" (1947), he introduced heterodox comparisons between Palladio's and Corbusier's villas, refining Rudolf Wittkower's research published in *Architectural Principles in the Age of Humanism* (1949). Wittkower identified the diagrammatic geometry underlying each villa plan as a nine-square grid that paralleled Palladio's use of harmonic ratios inside each room and

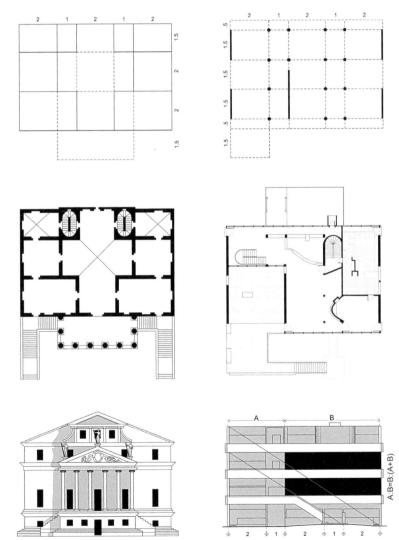

Figure 10.7
**Comparison
between Le
Corbusier's
Villa Stein in
Garches (a.k.a.
Villa Stein-de
Monzie or Les
Terrasses) and
Palladio's Villa
Foscari (La
Malcontenta,
1558–1560)
in Mira, Italy,
drawn by
Hitisha Kalolia
after Colin
Rowe**

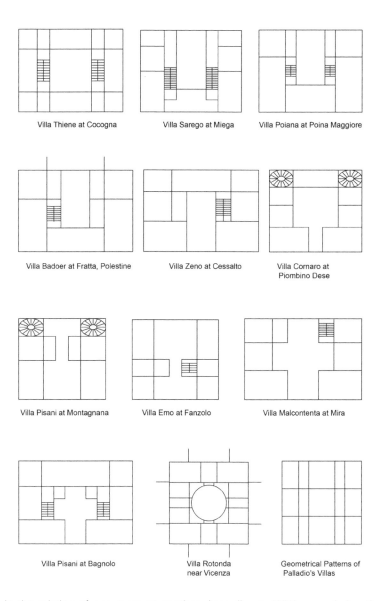

Figure 10.8
**Rudolf
Wittkower's
diagram of the
nine-square
grid prevalent
in the villas
of Andrea
Palladio, drawn
by Hitisha
Kalolia from
*Architectural
Principles in
the Age of
Humanism*
(1949)**

Villa Thiene at Cocogna

Villa Sarego at Miega

Villa Poiana at Poina Maggiore

Villa Badoer at Fratta, Polestine

Villa Zeno at Cessalto

Villa Cornaro at
Piombino Dese

Villa Pisani at Montagnana

Villa Emo at Fanzolo

Villa Malcontenta at Mira

Villa Pisani at Bagnolo

Villa Rotonda
near Vicenza

Geometrical Patterns of
Palladio's Villas

in the relation of one room to another. According to Wittkower, during the Renaissance architects planned rooms according to mathematical parallels between musical and spatial proportions.[12]

With the "Mathematics" essay, Rowe launched the nine-square grid into a comparison between Le Corbusier's Villa Savoye in Poissy (1928–1931) and Palladio's Villa Almerico-Capra (*La Rotonda*, 1570) in Vicenza and between Le Corbusier's Villa Stein in Garches (a.k.a. Villa Stein-de Monzie or *Les Terrasses*) and Palladio's Villa Foscari (*La Malcontenta*, 1558–1560) in Mira. By subordinating context and use to relationships between geometry and proportion, Rowe initiated the enduring academic exercise of manipulating the nine-square grid into a series of iterative and abstract cubic volumes that a designer may evolve into increasingly complex forms.

Rowe compared the descriptions that Corbusier and Palladio authored about each villa, a cursory reference to causal histories, describing them in Virgilian terms of a pastoral tradition that venerated bucolic country life. But this is just about as much historical data as Rowe provided to evidence his position.[13] In another atemporal comparison, between two villas separated by approximately 350 years, his identification of their identical core geometries was enough to suggest a historical continuum. His conjectural history, embedded in formal analysis, profoundly diluted the received view of modern architecture as having turned its back on history and precedents. While providing a systematic approach for how to read architecture from a formal perspective, he simultaneously demonstrated that a formalist approach may reveal spatial politics. He persuaded a generation of architects reading this essay that historical references dwell in modernism, that historical precedent was a potent design tool, and, perhaps more importantly, that form inherently holds content.

Plan libre and *Raumplan*

The Villa Stein's column grid liberates interior walls from having to perform structural work, providing for a generous exploration of the *plan libre* or free plan. Partition walls divide interior spaces into curved, beveled, and angled rooms that differ on each level, producing fluid and highly manipulated shapes that seem to emerge from one of Corbusier's paintings. But despite the rich spatial complexity this building exhibits, particularly in the subtracted volumes that result in exterior spaces, the sectional floor-to-floor heights remain uniform. Floors do not connect to each other through double height volumes on the inside of the building as they do on the outside. Instead, a discussion focusing on Corbusier's spatial complexity and double story volumes in section would consider the *Immeubles Villas* of 1922, a work that demonstrates the formal strategy of interior double-height spaces. The fundamental challenge of reading the Villa Stein as an expression of Corbusier's research into painting is that the expressive planimetric forms are less present in section. *Plan libre* does not necessarily equate to *section libre*.

In contrast, Adolf Loos's *raumplan*, loosely translated from German as "space plan," offers a sectionally complex diagram of diverse volumes interlocking as distinct spaces that break the standard pancake stacking of floors. The taciturn exterior of Loos's Villa Müller in Prague, Czech Republic (1928–1930) belies the level of spatial sophistication its interior contains. Recalling Wölfflin's categories, the Villa Stein represents an open form, with spatial volumes eroded primarily from the outside in, while the Villa Müller expresses a closed form, with spatial volumes clustering around a central stair, the steps of which allow each floor level to vary just a few feet in height. Adding to this sectional complexity, Loos provided for smaller rooms in plan to display

Axonometric Spatial Build-Up with Perspective Locations

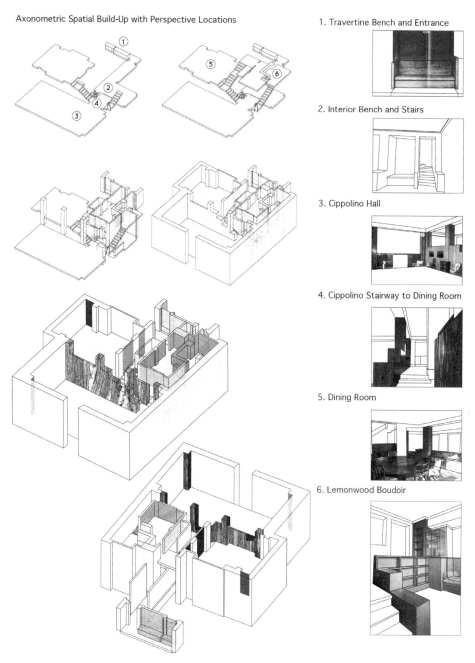

1. Travertine Bench and Entrance

2. Interior Bench and Stairs

3. Cippolino Hall

4. Cippolino Stairway to Dining Room

5. Dining Room

6. Lemonwood Boudoir

Figure 10.9 **Diagram of Adolf Loos's Villa Müller depicting a material palette wherein distinct colors and textures enhance a sequential journey through the house, by Amy Atzmon (2012)**

correspondingly smaller sectional heights. As Loos posited, "man will one day succeed in playing chess on a three-dimensional board, so too other architects will solve the problem of the three-dimensional plan."[14] The *raumplan* allowed him to solve the design challenge of providing individual proportions for each room, fitting them together as a three-dimensional chessboard comprising a stereometric whole.

Both Loos and Le Corbusier express the building's exterior envelope as pure prisms undisturbed by the pitched roofs, eaves, shutters, and flower boxes of typical vernacular houses built at that time and still today. And yet, their revolutionizing of space presents formal counterparts. Whereas Le Corbusier famously wrote:

> The Plan is the generator.
> Without a plan, you have lack, of order, and willfulness.
> The Plan holds in itself the essence of sensation.
> The great problems of to-morrow, dictated by collective necessities, put the question of "plan" in a new form.
> Modern life demands, and is waiting for, a new kind of plan.
> both for the house and for the city.[15]

Loos, in contrast, would claim:

> My architecture is not conceived in plans, but in spaces (cubes). I do not design floor plans, facades, sections. I design spaces … For me, there are only contiguous, continual spaces, rooms, anterooms, terraces etc. Stories merge and spaces relate to each other. Every space requires a different height…[16]

Despite the sizeable difference in planimetric and sectional approaches to the design of a house, from Le Corbusier's *plan libre* to Loos's *raumplan*, from the Villa Stein to the Villa Müller, the house as a rabbit warren of dark rooms and randomly additive spaces was displaced with intersecting geometries and interconnected volumes. Taken in tandem, these projects offer models for reading architecture as a series of complex spatial volumes and the ways in which they exert themselves on the exterior enclosure, either as deep space condensed into the façade as a legible imprint of interior ordering systems or as building elevations that mask the spatial complexity contained within.

Transparency

The ability to read a building's interior through its façade concerns architectural transparency. Rowe established criteria for interpreting transparency that extracts compositional information from otherwise mute form. Just as Rowe also supplemented the more normative comparison between buildings of the same time period to one between buildings from different periods, he also compared buildings and paintings. His studies on the affinity between art and architecture articulated the paradigm shift, mentioned in the previous chapter, of modern architects displacing typological models found in existing buildings to those found in the products of mass production, engineering, nature, and art.

In an essay he co-authored with the painter Robert Slutsky, "Transparency: Literal and Phenomenal" (1963), Rowe theorized modern architecture's spatial complexities of simultaneity, coincidence, ambivalence, projection, space-time, interpenetration, and superimposition found in Cubist painting. No longer the opaque, thick façades of Renaissance palazzi—where load bearing walls limit window sizes to small punched openings—the new architecture of structural steel and glass curtain wall required a system of analysis that could assess this work through an appropriately modern compositional lens. According to Henry Francis Mallgrave: "Rowe and Slutsky were essentially projecting an architectural theory of formal autonomy, that is, a kind of aesthetic formalism operating within its own inner sanctum of visual laws."[17]

As Rowe and Slutsky cite Gyorgy Kepes's *Language of Vision*, phenomenal transparency in painting occurs when two or more figures overlap and delineate geometries that "interpenetrate without an optical destruction of each other."[18] Literal transparency in painting coincides with glass objects, such as windows, wine bottles, or vases, which appear to be clear even though they are rendered on an ostensibly opaque canvas. Phenomenal transparency occurs in painting when the geometric outline of a background object registers on the surface of a foreground object, thereby rendering it cognitively transparent. Phenomenal transparency may be understood through the

Figure 10.10
László Moholy-Nagy, *Am 7 (26)* (Sprengel Museum, Hannover, Germany, 1926), courtesy of bpk Bildagentur and Art Resource, NY
© ARS, NY

overlaps of a Venn diagram where two conjoined circles produce the third intermediary geometry. The circles interpenetrate to produce a third space without any visual destruction of each other. László Moholy-Nagy's 1926 painting *Am 7 (26)* demonstrates this elegantly, with a gray circle superimposed upon three rotated polygons that reads as transparent because the corner lines may be seen to penetrate the circumference, while the smaller white circle on top appears as opaque because the lines of the polygon it covers cannot be seen. The application of this concept to reading architecture is clear: literal transparency involves surfaces through which it is possible to see, while phenomenal transparency involves the projection of background forms onto foreground forms, and vice versa, through the use of geometric alignments. In architecture, literal transparency relies on windows and phenomenal transparency corresponds to the ways in which a façade reveals and conceals a building's underlying compositional strategies.

In terms of Cubism's conversation with modern architecture, Rowe and Slutsky claimed that the "fusion of temporal and spatial factors" produced the "frontality, suppression of depth, contracting of space, definition of light sources, tipping forward of objects, restricted palette, oblique and rectilinear grids, and propensities toward peripheric development" that characterized this movement and contributed a vocabulary of formal operations to the lexicon of architecture.[19] One of Cubism's basic tenets is to depict a single form from simultaneous points of view as a way of introducing the dimension of time into pictorial space while removing the static dimension of Renaissance perspective from the composition. In traditional one-point linear perspective, shapes are distorted to simulate the foreshortening of vision, e.g. circles become ovals and squares become parallelograms. Cubism dispenses with such sleight of hand in order to explore form in its geometric purity, as figuration begins to give way to abstraction. Le Corbusier painted under his given name of Charles-Édouard Jeanneret, collaborating with Amédée Ozenfant to develop a critique of Cubism called Purism and to publish the 1917 manifesto *Après le cubisme* (*Beyond Cubism*). Jeanneret and Ozenfant embraced Cubism's geometric superimpositions, but rejected its indecipherable abstraction in favor of pure forms generated by everyday objects, the *objet type* or type-object. As Bernhard Hoesli has diagrammed them, these explorations of flattening three-dimensional space onto two-dimensional canvases and murals provided Le Corbusier with formal compositions that would insinuate themselves into his architecture. Insofar as Le Corbusier was "primarily occupied with the planar qualities of glass and Gropius with its translucent attributes," Rowe and Slutzky compared the façade of the Villa Stein with the glass corners of the workshop wing at Walter Gropius's Bauhaus (1926) in Dessau, Germany—providing respective exemplars of phenomenal and literal transparency. At the Bauhaus workshop, the glass corner of a highly transparent curtain wall erodes the structural presence of recessed columns that the building's projection above the base emphasizes as a floating form. At the Villa Stein, the subcutaneous organizing principles hidden behind the

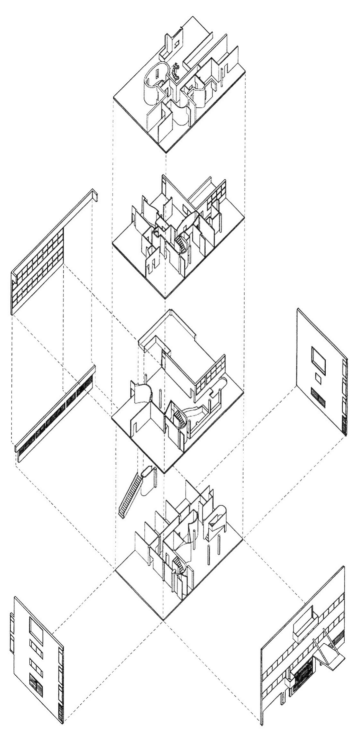

Figure 10.11
**Exploded
Axonmetric
Diagram of
Villa Stein by
Jodi Pfister
(2008)**

Figure 10.12
**Bauhaus
workshop
building
in Dessau,
Germany
(1926),
photograph by
Lucia Moholy,
courtesy of
Harvard Art
Museums/
Busch-
Reisinger
Museum, Gift
of Ise Gropius,
BRGA.20.37.1
© Lucia Moholy
Estate/Artists
Rights Society
(ARS), New
York/VG Bild-
Kunst,**

opaque façade telescope onto the front elevation as a composition of slightly protruding planes.

The formalist tradition finds its most influential apologist in Peter Eisenman. In his doctoral dissertation at the University of Cambridge (where he encountered Rowe), entitled "The Formal Basis of Modern Architecture" (1963), he analyzed the architecture of Le Corbusier, Alvar Aalto, Frank Lloyd Wright, and Giuseppe Terragni. Decades later, he published *Giuseppe Terragni: Transformations, Decompositions, Critiques* (2003), in which he further articulated the formal analyses initiated in Cambridge. In this book he synthesizes the abstract formal systems within Terragni's architecture, particularly through a series of axonometric drawings that delaminate the layers

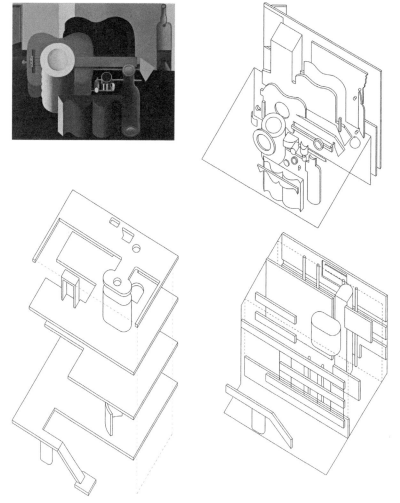

Figure 10.13
Le Corbusier
(Charles-
Édouard
Jeanneret),
Still Life (1920),
courtesy of
Museum of
Modern Art,
New York,
and Bernhard
Hoesli's
diagram of this
painting and of
Le Corbusier's
Villa Stein from
"Commentary"
Transparency
(Berlin:
Birkhäuser
Verlag, 1997),
drawn by
Hitisha Kalolia

of their exterior envelops. The brief descriptions of the drawings analyzing the Casa Giuliani-Frigerio, an apartment building in Como, Italy (1940), provide a panoply of approaches to reading a building formally: "circumscribed by a rectilinear volume," organized by "a lateral, or east-west, tripartite division articulated by the shear walls," and divided into "a tripartite division, with perpendicular grain in the left, northernmost segment and parallel grain in the center segment."[20]

Cardboard Architecture

Eisenman designed a series of houses in which he extracted domestic space from iterative axonometric drawings, the generative starting point of which

Figure 10.14
**Diagram of
Giuseppe
Terragni's Casa
Giuliani-
Frigerio in
Como, Italy
(1940), from
Peter Eisen-
man,** *Giuseppe
Terragni: Trans-
formations,
Decomposi-
tions, Critiques*
**(2003),
courtesy of
Peter Eisenman**

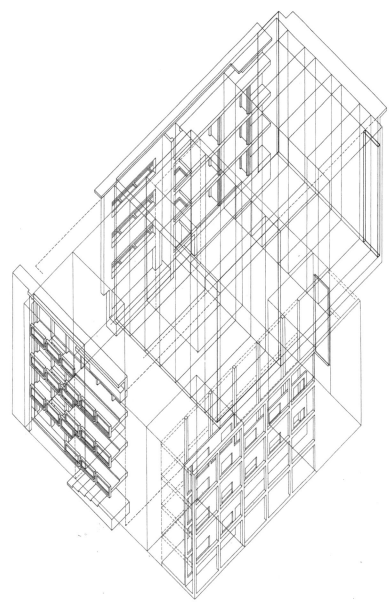

implied a nine-square grid. In so doing he developed a proto-computational design process that distanced architecture from both site and programmatic function—where abstract numbers displaced the client's names as conventional project titles. Of the four houses he completed from this series of investigations—House I for Mr and Mrs Bernard Barenholtz (1967–1968, Princeton, New Jersey), House II for Mr and Mrs Richard Falk

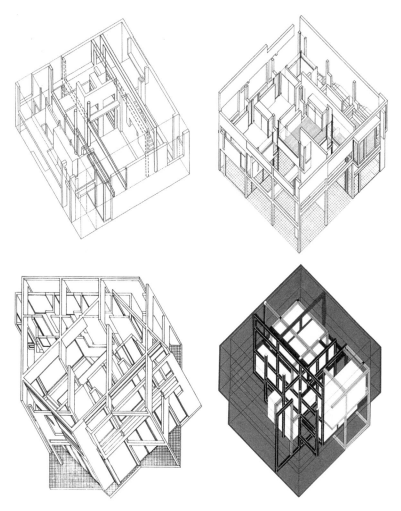

Figure 10.15
**Peter
Eisenman,
drawings of
House I (upper
left), House II
(upper right),
House III (lower
left), and House
VI (lower
right), courtesy
of Peter
Eisenman and
the Canadian
Centre for
Architecture**

(1969–1970, Hardwick, Vermont), House III for Mr and Mrs Robert Miller (1969–1971, Lakeville, Connecticut), and House VI for Mr and Mrs Richard Frank (1972–1975, Cornwall, Connecticut), the one with the notorious glass slice bisecting the bedroom—the planar geometries and experimental construction methods provoked criticism that his built work was precariously model-like. Turning a liability into asset, Eisenman arrived at the phrase "cardboard archi-tecture" to postulate the idea that design work existing only on paper may also constitute significant architecture. Both John Hejduk and Eisenman cata-lyzed architectural research expressed through drawings and models as ends in and of themselves. Cardboard architecture likewise retains architecture's disciplinary autonomy as pure research into the exploration of form that devel-ops from an internal set of criteria. It allows architects to work almost inde-pendently from the pressures of a market economy and to experiment with architectural form in an acontextual and potentially apolitical creative arena. As the manifestation of design operations that singularly reference architecture's inherent ordering systems, this autonomy offers a refuge into formal and aesthetic innovation removed from the exigencies of rapid commodification and assimilation.

And yet, as discussed at the beginning of this chapter, formalism remains a contested term. As Eisenman observes, "of all the terms in the architectural lexicon, or, for that matter, those of painting and sculpture, the one most laden with social and political opprobrium is formalism."[21] Eisenman's formalism describes a conceptual pursuit that seeks to distinguish architecture's unique aesthetic identity in contradistinction to other arts, one that explores the way in which form shapes space and vice versa. This position parallels Gotthold Ephraim Lessing's writing in *Laocoön: An Essay on the Limits of Painting and Poetry* (1766), introduced in Chapter 4, that the ontological status of each art form—from poetry to architecture—is fundamentally unique compared to any other and requires its own autonomous means of expression. Architecture's autonomous modality is the production of form. Evidenced most notably in the house series, Eisenman's use of axonometric drawings acts as a rational, objectifying device onto which a series of geometric operations—such as divide, rotate, and shift—have been neatly enacted. The design of a house acts as an alibi to explore the purely formal language of a building's basic components: plane, column, stair, and aperture. Meanwhile, the concept of "cardboard architecture" disabuses the discipline from a reductive functionalism and prioritizes the exploration of form as architecture's primary objective.

Convolution

From Eisenman's early manipulations of grids and planes in the house series to his curvilinear work at the City of Culture of Galicia (*Galician: Cidade da Cultura de Galicia*, 2011) at Santiago de Compostela in Spain, architectural design processes have evolved from iterative hand drawings to digitally generated parametric models. Parametricism relies on the ability of designers to write scripts with algorithmic codes, to set "parameters" for computers to perform a set of digital operations to produce complex, self-generating compound-complex geometries. Pre-digital precedents for these convoluted geometries, found in Eero Saarinen's Trans World Flight Center in New York City (1962), Berthold Lubetkin's Penguin Pool at the London Zoo (1934), and Oscar Niemeyer's constructed topography at the French Communist Party Headquarters in Paris (1965), demonstrate that complexity may anticipate digital form generation.

These buildings enter the conversation as examples of complex curvature in the built domain constructed before computer programs such as Maya, CATIA, and Rhino assisted the design and fabrication of an infinite variety of relational geometries. As a significant contribution to advancing digital design

Figure 10.16
**Eero Saarinen's
Trans World
Flight Center
in New York
City (1962)**

processes, Frank Gehry's highly expressive curvilinear buildings have relied on the synergy among physical models and building information modeling software to translate his forms into digital construction documents that allow for optimizing and fabricating experimental materials. Undulating and unfolding like the petals of a flower in the process of opening, the Guggenheim Museum in Bilbao, Spain (1993–1997) was made possible through digital design processes that could take a building all the way from concept to the thin detail of titanium sheets that clad the exterior.

Both parametric and Baroque architectures develop convoluted form in shapes that are intricately folded, twisted, or coiled. The complexity of Baroque architecture anticipates and at times eclipses its distant digital progeny in parametric design, offering eccentric examples of compound-complex curvatures that place form front and center of the discussion. Before its more recent ascendancy as a proto-parametric model, Baroque architecture was regarded as the pathological "result of an obsessive attraction to forms of monstrosity and to a vulgar taste."[22] The essential characteristic of Baroque architecture for Wölfflin was its painterly quality, wherein "the beauty of a building is judged by the enticing effects of moving masses, the restless, jumping forms or violently swaying ones which seem constantly on the point of change."[23] As with the comparison between Bramante and Borromini discussed earlier in this chapter, balanced and static forms gave way to masses that seemed to move, flow, and even breathe.

Treating Baroque architecture as a purely formal investigation is to willfully ignore its significant political and scientific underpinnings. While it is neither possible within the scope of this book nor entirely relevant when entertaining

Figure 10.17
**Oscar
Niemeyer's
constructed
topography
at the French
Commu-
nist Party
Headquarters
in Paris (1965),**
photograph by
Aaron Whelton

a discussion on form to fully consider the theological and scientific milieu culminating in Baroque architecture, it remains useful to briefly consider the Counter-Reformation and the significant discoveries in the natural sciences which were essential to stimulating this aesthetic upheaval. This brief segue serves to contrast a formalist method of inquiry with one that exclusively focuses on reading architecture through supplementary texts. The Roman Catholic Church inaugurated its Counter-Reformation with the Council of Trent (1545–1563), offering a response to the Protestant Reformation, which Martin Luther launched after posting *The Ninety-Five Theses* on the door of All Saints' Church in Wittenberg, Germany in 1517. The Counter-Reformation inculcated widespread religious renewal through the most literal re-form of church build-ing that resulted in Baroque architecture. New orders such as the Jesuits, Theatines, and Oratorians commissioned buildings in Rome—such as Chiesa

Figure 10.18
**Berthold
Lubetkin's
Penguin Pool
at London
Zoo (1934),
photograph by
Kenneth J. Gill**

Figure 10.19
**Frank Gehry,
Guggenheim
Museum Bilbao
in Bilbao, Spain
(1997)**

Il Gesù (Church of the Gesù, 1568) by Giacomo da Vignola, Sant'Andrea della Valle (Saint Andrew of the Valley, 1590) by Carlo Maderno, and the Oratorio dei Filippini (Oratory of Saint Phillip Neri, 1650) by Francesco Borromini—whose expressive architecture mediated an intense spiritual communion between the laity and the divine.

Publishing *Astronomia nova* (*New Astronomy*) in 1609, Johannes Kepler revised Nicolaus Copernicus's circular orbit of the earth with the sun into an ellipse. He offered a new model of space that focused attention on a geometry whose two foci describe a linear trajectory of movement in comparison with the circle's static, single center. Kepler unleashed cosmic momentum for the use of compound curvatures in architecture that the ellipse derived from the trajectory and velocity of objects in space. The ellipse and the oval became privileged geometries in Baroque architecture, further exemplifying Wölfflin's distinction between open and closed forms. In breaking with the classical models of harmony and proportional systems prevalent during the Renaissance and introducing movement to their design repertoire, Baroque architects exploited forms suggestive of motion to summon a corresponding sensory emotion.

Merging theological and scientific influences, the spiral holds a special place in Baroque geometry, appearing in helical columns patterned after those thought to have descended from the ancient Temple of Solomon in Jerusalem, appearing as the helicoidal staircase Borromini designed at the Palazzo Barberini in Rome, or springing into the spire of his church St Ivo alla Sapienza. Extensive analysis of St Ivo's iconographical program—in reference to its role as a church dedicated to St Yves, built for La Sapienza (meaning wisdom), University of Rome, and also patronized by the Barberini family— extracts allegorical value from its formal geometry. Two intersecting equilateral triangles overlaid in the shape of a hexagram or a six-pointed geometric star, with alternating concave and convex curvatures as the apexes of the star, is the geometric language describing St Ivo's plan. In section, the undulating accordion pleats this planimetric geometry produces are extruded vertically to the level of the cornice and the spring-point of a hemispheric dome, after which they curve to meet at a lantern that illuminates the space below. In comparison, an iconographical reading would interpret the hexagram as referencing the Star of Solomon that symbolizes wisdom. The center hexagon in the star plan also forms a honeycomb shape that is thought to allude to the heraldic flying bee located on the Barberini's coat of arms and imprinted on myriad surfaces of the ecclesiastical complex, a symbol of the family of Pope Urban VIII, who patronized the construction of St Ivo.

The chapel's iconography likewise suggests images Cesare Ripa published as illustrations for his *Iconologia overo Descrittione Dell'imagini Universali cavate dall'Antichità et da altri luoghi* (Rome, 1603), which depicts three elements found on St Ivo's spire: "the Holy Spirit" as the Dove, "Philosophy" as a spiral stair, and "Wisdom" (Sapienza) as a flaming crown. A spiraling spire with a dove resting on an orb projecting from the flaming crown of divine knowledge may also reference the three-tiered papal tiara rendered as a helix. John Beldon Scott fuses iconographic and formal analysis when positing that the spire references the conch shell or *cochlea*, a Greek term meaning *snail*. In Latin this species is named *mitra papalis*, "alluding to the papal mitre and tiara," while similar shells were referred to as the *corona papale* because "the volutes of its cone look like the turns in the crowns placed on the papal tiara"[24] (see Figure 1.7 in Chapter 1).

Much like the entablature supporting St Ivo's spire, the Temple of Venus in Baalbek, Lebanon (ca. 3rd century CE) displays the proto-Baroque geometry of

Figure 10.20
**Agostino
Veneziano's
engraving of
Suleiman the
Magnificent in
his Venetian
helmet (1535)
with four tiers
symbolizing his
imperial power
exceeding that
of the three-
tiered papal
tiara**

SVLIMAN·OTOMAN·REX·TVRC· X·

a scalloped entablature that curves into the six peripteral columns that support it. Closer to Rome, the Piazza d'Oro (Golden Court) at Hadrian's villa in Tivoli displays a hall with an undulating floor plan of convex and concave curves inscribed within a Greek cross plan. Further afield, the giant minaret of the Great Mosque of al-Mutawakkil in Samarra, Iraq (848/49–52 CE), constructed as a conical spiral, offers a cyclopean precursor to Borromini's spire. Completed under the caliph Al-Mutawakkil, the Samarra mosque features the Malwiya minaret that spirals 52 meters high. This minaret, in turn, recalls the stepped forms of Mesopotamian Ziggurats and Pieter Bruegel the Elder's interpretation of the "Tower of Babel" (1563).

Borromini's spire exhibits geometries that mathematics could not esti-mate at the time of its construction from 1642 to 1660. Only after Isaac Newton and Gottfried Leibniz developed the concepts and formulas of calculus to measure differential geometry could St Ivo's complex spiral be reproduced mathematically. Borromini's spire distorted a regular conical helix into one that displays differential curvature and increasing torsion towards the top. The way in which the hemispheric dome rounds off the volume of space extruded vertically from the plan also demonstrates complex geometric curvature. Pie-shaped, curved planes located between the cupola's interior ribs transition from a convex curve, located at the level of the drum, and then bulge inward to the center of the church, transitioning into a concave curve

Figure 10.21
**Temple of
Venus at
Baalbek,
Lebanon
(early 3rd
century CE),
photograph
by Jenny
Bergensten**

Balbek, temple circulaire de Vénus.   164.

Figure 10.22
**Piazza d'Oro
at Hadrian's
Villa in Tivoli,
Italy (ca. 128
CE), drawn by
Boyuan Zhang**

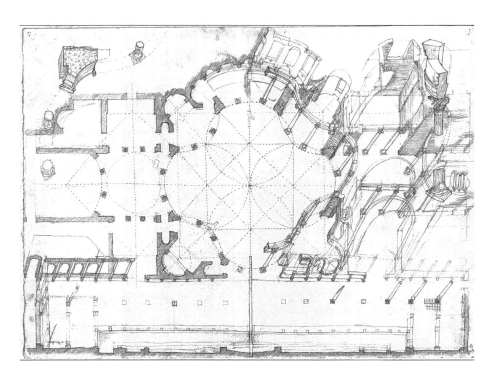

Figure 10.23
**Spiral Malwiya
Minaret of
the Al-Jami
Mosque at
Samarra in
Baghdad, Iraq
(9th century),
photograph by
David Stanley**

at the lantern that pushes outward toward the exterior. "In this fashion," as Staale Sinding-Larsen observes, "a convex surface is turning continuously, that is, differentially, into a concave one."[25] "The undulating wall of Borromini's invention," as Sigfried Giedion proffered, changes "the stone wall into an elastic material."[26] Giedion considered Borromini's work as paralleling modernism's inexorable drive toward a spatial revolution. He concluded that the cutting of pie-shaped curvatures from out of the perfectly circular dome, in order to continue the movement of the plan upward and treat structure as though it were flexible, "must have had the same stunning effect upon Borromini's contemporaries that Picasso's disintegration of the human face produced around 1910."[27]

Camillo-Guarino Guarini, *prepositus* or abbot of the Theatine order and a scholar, engineer, and mathematician, was also an architect whose domes erode their abstract spatial envelop into a series of ribbed arches the superimposition of which renders the plastic modeling of surfaces into stone filigree illuminated by a halo of light. Guarini's churches in Turin—Cappella della Sacra Sindone (1668–1694, Chapel of the Holy Shroud) and the Church of San Lorenzo (1668–1687)—demonstrate virtuoso performances in stone vaulting. Their minimal rib structures achieve the stereometric (the precise cutting of stone) sophistication of French Gothic cathedrals mixed with the geometric complexity of Islamic domes. At the Cappella Sindone, a series of six arches, which spring from a drum above the altar, support another six smaller arches that support yet another set of six smaller arches and so on to complete six levels in all, forming arches that merge semicircular domes with gothic vaults. Since the dome is constructed of interwoven masonry arches, the entire structure appears as an inverted stone basket through which natural light streams. At San Lorenzo, Guarini floated an eight-pointed star in a plan around which eight curves project inward from the exterior walls and intersect with vertical arches that support an eight-pointed ribbed dome above. Guarini published techniques for drawing plans, sections, and details of his complex three-dimensional forms in *Architettura civile* (1737),

Figure 10.24 Camillo-Guarino Guarini, Cappella della Sacra Sindone (Chapel of the Holy Shroud) in Turin, Italy (1668–1694), photograph by Antonio Filigno

Figure 10.25 Camillo-Guarino Guarini, Church of San Lorenzo in Turin, Italy (1668–1687)

Figure 10.26
Dome above
the Mihrab
inside the
Mosque-
Cathedral
in Córdoba,
Spain,
photograph
by Fernando
González Sanz

offering instructions to similarly delineate the projective geometric technique of earlier mathematicians such as Gérard Desargues. As the interlocking arches and star-shaped plans of Guarini's churches indicate and his travels evidence, he drew direct inspiration from Moorish mosques in Spain such as the vaults over the *maqsura* (an enclosure, a box or wooden screen) and *mihrab* (an element that frames the *qibla*, a mark that indicates the direction of Mecca) at the Great Mosque in Córdoba (833–988) which form a direct antecedent for San Lorenzo.

Rotational curves date back to the 3rd century BCE with Archimedes's Screw, named after the Greek mathematician who invented a machine to pump water vertically inside a pipe. The screw displays a two-dimensional curve that moves away from a fixed point with a radius vector rotating at a constant rate to produce a form that looks much like a corkscrew. This spiral may be constructed either with all dimensions fixed, as if inscribed in a cylinder, or with a radius vector that increases in size, as if inscribed in a cone. The geometry of Archimedes's spiral may respond to a number of geometric pressures in which differential curvatures and increasing torsion deform its pure geometry into parabolic spirals, hyperbolic spirals, and logarithmic spirals whose a helical surfaces twist and bend into three-dimensional volumes or intersect each other like the double helix spirals found in DNA. In these various manifestations, the spiral retains in its formal logic concepts such as dynamic movement, the cycle of time, springing tension, growth, a journey, or stored energy.

Geometry

The logarithmic spiral or *spira mirabilis* differs from the Archimedean spiral insofar as the distances between rotations accelerates. This geometry is found throughout nature as a repeating pattern—seen in nautilus shells, the spin of hurricanes, curved ram horns, and more—with a seemingly magical repetition across the physical world, providing it with something of a sacred aura. The logarithmic spiral's self-similar geometry and curvature fit within a Golden Rectangle—a polygon that can be segmented into a rectangle whose short side may be multiplied by 1.618 to produce its length. The golden section delimits ideal aesthetic proportions making appearances in the Parthenon in Athens and Notre Dame in Paris, as well as in work by Palladio and Le Corbusier. When curves are connected to the corners of the nesting squares, they inscribe a logarithmic spiral within the original rectangle. This mathematical system relates to the Fibonacci series, a formula where every number after the first two is the sum of the two preceding ones, as with the following sequence: 0, 1, 1, 2, 3, 5, 8, 13, 21, 34, etc.

Architects often seek objective design methodologies such as the Golden Rectangle to identify ideal proportioning systems for form generation that the careful observer may be able to detect. With theories of balance and symmetry deriving in part from Pythagorean proportioning systems, which relate to musical harmonies, Renaissance architects began to systematize

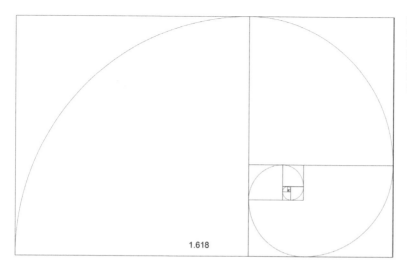

Figure 10.27
**Golden
Rectangle
(Golden
Section), drawn
by Hitisha
Kalolia**

1.618

preferred geometries as part of their formal repertoire. As Palladio wrote in the *Quattro libri*:

> The most beautiful and proportionable manners of rooms, and which succeed best, are seven, because they are either made round (tho' but seldom) or square, or their length will be the diagonal line of the square, or the square and a third, or of one square and a half, or of one square and two-thirds, or of two squares.[28]

Renaissance architects seeking to identify a basis for proportioning systems in classical architecture also could consult Vitruvius's *De architectura*, which recommended systems such as the following room proportions:

> In width and length, atriums are designed according to three classes. The first is laid out by dividing the length into five parts and giving three parts to the width; the second, by dividing it into three parts and assigning two parts to the width; the third, by using the width to describe a square figure with equal sides, drawing a diagonal line in this square, and giving the atrium the length of this diagonal line.[29]

With proportional recommendations such as these, architects enjoyed the benefits of a codified design rubric that they could apply on a rule of thumb basis without necessarily having to adhere to them as inflexible doctrine.

Other geometries stand out as carrying particular cultural or symbolic value or simply for providing generative ordering principles. The *Vesica Piscus*, meaning "bladder of a fish" in Latin and whose intersection symbolizes union, is a geometric ordering system that derives from the intersection

Figure 10.28
**Sebastiano
Serlio, vesica
piscus in**
*Tutte l'opera
d'architettura*
(1537–1575)

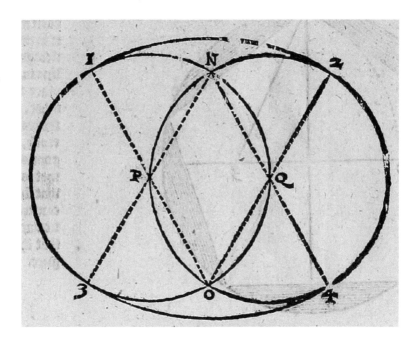

of two circles with the same radius, whose center-points coincide with the perimeter of the other circle. The resulting geometry, which generates numerous complex forms, produces a pointed arch and a proportioning system important to Gothic architecture as well as geometries found in Renaissance spaces. Marc Nevue considers Sebastiano Serlio's description of ovals from *Tutte l'opera d'architettura* (1537–1575) as describing the construction of a *Vesica Piscus* with the *ovato tondo* or *ova lo tondo*, the round oval. Beginning with two overlapping circles and using their two points of intersection to generate arcs, these tangent arcs transform the circles into an oval. "Connecting the endpoints of the line to one of the points where the circles intersect generates an equilateral triangle," as he explains the geometric proof that "is the basis of Euclidean geometry."[30] While Nevue explores the *Vesica Piscus* forming the plaza of the Prato della Valle in Padua, it appears most famously in the oval Gianlorenzo Bernini designed for St Peter's plaza in Rome.

To continue this conversation on formal geometries found in architecture, the five Platonic solids of tetrahedron, cube, octahedron, dodecahedron, and icosahedron are polyhedrons with the same number and shape of faces meeting at each vertex. In his *Mysterium Cosmographicum* (1596), Kepler constructed a model of the solar system based on the nesting intersections of these solids, with the first being the octahedron, followed by the icosahedron, the dodecahedron, the tetrahedron, and finally the cube. The Mandala, Sanskrit for "circle," is a sacred cosmic symbol used as a basic diagram for Hindu and Buddhist architecture that represents the universe though a concentric

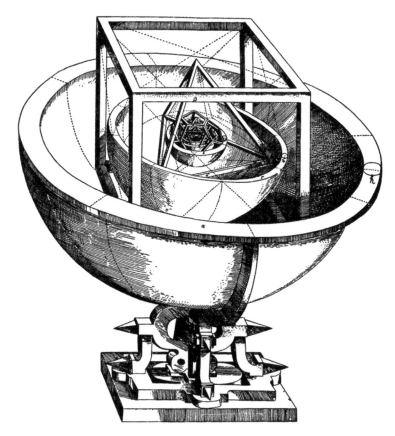

Figure 10.29
**Johannes
Kepler, nested
Platonic solids,
*Mysterium
Cosmograph-
icum (The
Cosmographic
Mystery,*Tübin-
gen, Germany,
1596/1621)**

configuration of geometric shapes, which often take on the form of a circle divided into four separate sections. In Islamic architecture, geometric patterning reaches its apogee with surface tile patterns mirroring in detail larger architectonic forms such as the star vault. Ideal forms such as these imprint sacred and celestial symbols onto architecture in a pattern that generally leads from a specific cultural meaning to abstract mathematics, insofar as what ended in secular geometric ornamental applications often began with sacred principles that were held in common.

Folds

Innovations in digital design processes have invigorated interest in Baroque complexity. A set of esoteric terms and their resultant forms, such as *asymptote*, *stochastic*, *Boolean*, *topology*, and *epigenetic*, offer a highly specialized vocabulary to describe architecture that has leaped across time from 16th-century Italy and into a neo-Baroque era of computational design. This is a dynamic world of drawing where vectors replace lines and dynamic splines substitute for inert curves. The Baroque also found its way into Gilles Deleuze's

Figure 10.30
**Mandala of
the forms of
Manjushri, the
Bodhisattva of
Transcendent
Wisdom (late
14th century),
Tibet, courtesy
of Rogers
Fund, 1977,
Metropolitan
Museum of Art,
New York**

Le pli—Leibniz et le baroque of 1988 (*The Fold: Leibniz and the Baroque*), where the author provides a conceptual armature for then-emerging practices in computational design's exploration of topology, complex geometry, morphology, and morphogenesis. In "The Fold, 'Pleats of Matter'"—from the 1993 issue of *Architectural Design: Folding in Architecture,* (edited by Greg Lynn)—Deleuze directly references Wölfflin's analysis of Baroque architecture as being marked by specific material traits. He writes that it displays the following attributes: flattening of the pediment, low and curved stairs that push into space, matter handled in masses or aggregates, the rounding of angles and avoidance of perpendiculars, the use of limestone to produce spongy and cavernous shapes, or the use of a vortical form put in motion by renewed turbulence, "which tends to spill over in space, to be reconciled with fluidity at the same time fluids themselves are divided into masses."[31]

The French title of *Le pli*, meaning the fold, is redolent with words such as *pliant* and *complicated*, encapsulating a remarkable constellation among French theory, Baroque geometry, and computational form-generation as a formidable

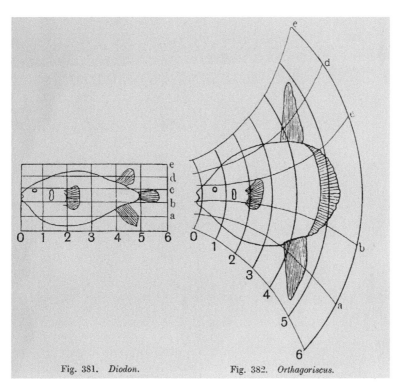

Figure 10.31
D'Arcy
Wentworth
Thompson,
Diodon
compared with
Orthagoriscus,
from *On
Growth and
Form*

Fig. 381. *Diodon.*   Fig. 382. *Orthagoriscus.*

approach to architecture that smoothed the highly radical philosophical activism of Deleuze and his writing partner, Félix Guattari, into purely formal applications. *Smoothing*, indeed, became an operational term. As Lynn explains, it "incorporates free intensities through fluid tactics of mixing and blending" that remain heterogeneous in content while homogeneous in shape.[32] Architecture incorporated the folds, pleats, ruching, and convolutions of Baroque art and architectural details into habitable spaces generated by software. Lynn introduced a viscous mixture of baroque curvature and animation software into architecture as he explored scientific form-generation based on the movement and action of René Thom's catastrophe diagrams, anexact geometry, embryology, and D'Arcy Thompson's stretched morphologies.[33]

Jürgen Mayer H. synthesized computational thinking in his Metropol Parasol covering the Plaza de la Encarnación (2011) in Seville, Spain, offering a topological model for public space that lofted forms characteristic of Baroque urbanism into a floating canopy. A significant contribution of Baroque architecture was to have exported complex, dynamic forms from inside of buildings out into the public sphere, transforming cities into a series of theatrical plazas built for public promenade. Michelangelo's *Ricetto*, the space he designed for the vestibule of the Laurentian Library in Florence, Italy, translated into built form from his 1524 sketch for this project, demonstrated the use of stairs to express a highly sculptural transition from one level to another. Characterized

Figure 10.32
**Michelangelo
Buonarotti,**
Ricetto,
**stairs for the
vestibule of
the Laurentian
Library in
Florence, Italy,
translated into
built form from
his 1524 sketch,
courtesy of
Images by
Sailko**

Figure 10.33 **Francesco de Sanctis and Alessandro Specchi, Scalinata (Spanish Steps), at the church of
Santissima Trinità dei Monti (Holy Trinity of the Mountains) in Rome (1725) at the Piazza di Spagna, depicted in
an engraving by Giovanni Battista Piranesi (***Vedute di Roma***Tomo I, tav. 23)**

Figure 10.34
Alessandro
Specchi, *Porto
di Ripetta* in
Rome (1704,
demolished), as
it was depicted
in an engraving
by Giovanni
Battista
Piranesi
(*Vedute di
Roma* Tomo I,
tav. 50)

Figure 10.35
Jürgen Mayer
H., Metropol
Parasol,
Plaza de la
Encarnación in
Seville, Spain
(2011), courtesy
of Jürgen
Mayer H.

as a lava flow of curves and rivulets pouring from out of the reading room, the *Ricetto* inaugurated the design of magnificent stairs that eventually will spill out into the public realm. Eventually structures such as the so-called Spanish steps, the Scalinata di Trinità dei Monti in the Piazza di Spagna and the demolished Porto di Ripetta, provided public stair models for displaying a warp and weft of curvatures that distinguished them from the existing urban fabric of rectilinear buildings.

Mayer's parasol adapts this tradition of animating the public sphere with dynamic radical forms to Seville, Spain by elevating a horizontal surface above the level of the plaza as an inhabitable structure standing at almost 30 meters high. Six columnar trunks of varying organic inclination support intersecting curves that translate the epic clouds painted onto the ceilings of Baroque churches into an explosion of space and form to produce what Mayer describes as a "cathedral without walls."[34] Reminiscent of the Cathedral of Seville's dynamic buttresses and pinnacles, and elevated above the level of the balustrade, as with the Spanish Steps, this is about as much as the parasol references the historical city. Rather, it offers a series of autonomous curves that float above a rectilinear context, an insertion of painterly shapes into the otherwise linear, vertical façades and an expression of convoluted form.

Notes

1   Cf. Peter Eiseman: "I remember my shock when traveling with Colin Rowe in Italy in the summer of 1961, after my first year of teaching at Cambridge. Rowe said to me in front of my first Palladian villa: 'Tell me something about the villa that you cannot see.' He did not want me to tell him about its three stories, about its material rustication, about its symmetrical window arrangement; these were obvious and seeable. But an architect must learn to see beyond the facts of perception. An architect must see as an expert." Peter Eisenman course syllabus for "Formal Analysis: Theories of Authority: Seeing as an Architect" Yale University School of Architecture (Fall, 2016), https://www.architecture.yale.edu/courses/13867-theories-of-authority-seeing-as-an-architect.

2   Eladio Dieste, "The Awareness of Form," in Stanford Anderson, *Eladio Dieste: Innovation in Structural Art* (New York: Princeton Architectural Press, 2003), p. 191.

3   "Video: Peek into the House of Jean Prouvé, the Pioneer of Prefabrication," https://architizer.com/blog/video-jean-prouves-house; and Christopher Alexander, *Notes on the Synthesis of Form* (Cambridge, MA: Harvard University Press, 1971), p. 2.

4   Patrik Schumacher, "Formalism and Formal Research" *ARKETIPO – International Review of Architecture and Building Engineering* #104, 2016, available at: http://www.patrikschumacher.com/Texts/Formalism%20and%20Formal%20Research.html; and Peggy Deamer, as cited by Hakan Anay, "(Epistemological) Formalism and its Influence on Architecture: A Concise Review" *ITU A|Z 9*, no. 1 (2012), pp. 70–85, from Peggy Deamer, "What is the Status of Work on Form Today?" in *Form Work: Colin Rowe*, ed. Cynthia Davidson (New York: Anyone Corporation, 1994), p. 60.

5   Judith Wolin, *ANY 7/8: Form Work: Colin Rowe*, ed. Cynthia Davidson, guest ed. R. E. Somol (New York: Anyone Corporation, 1994), p. 58.

6   Ludwig Mies van der Rohe *G*, No. 2, 1923, in Franz Schulze and and Edward Windhorst's *Mies Van Der Rohe: A Critical Biography* (Chicago: University of Chicago Press, 2012), p. 106.

7   Ibid.

8   Theo van Doesburg "Towards a Plastic Architecture" (1924), in Ulrich Conrads, *Programmes and Manifestoes on 20th-Century Architecture*, trans. Michael Bullock (London: Lund Humphries, 1970), p. 80.

9   Ibid, p. 79.

10   Colin Rowe, "Mannerism and Modern Architecture," in *The Mathematics of the Ideal Villa and Other Essays* (Cambridge, MA: MIT Press, 1987), p. 34.

11   Colin Rowe, "Grid/Frame/Lattice/Web: Giulio Romano's Palazzo Maccarani and the Sixteenth Century" *Cornell Journal of Architecture 4* (Fall 1990), p. 10.

12   Rudolf Wittkower, *Architectural Principles in the Age of Humanism* (London: A. Tiranti, 1952).

13   Colin Rowe, "The Mathematics of the Ideal Villa" (1947), in *The Mathematics of the Ideal Villa, and Other Essays* (Cambridge, MA: MIT Press, 1976), p. 2.

14   Quoted from Yehuda Safran, "Adolf Loos: The Archimedean Point," in Safran and Wilfried Wang, *The Architecture of Adolf Loos: An Arts Council Exhibition* (London: The Arts Council, 1985), p. 28.

15   Le Corbusier, *Towards a New Architecture*, trans. Frederick Etchells (New York: Dover Press, 1986), pp. 2–3.

16   *Adolf Loos*, Stenograph of a conversation between K. Lhota and A. L., Plzeň, 1930, http://en.muzeumprahy.cz/raumplan.

17   Henry Francis Mallgrave, *Modern Architectural Theory: A Historical Survey, 1673–1968* (Cambridge: Cambridge University Press, 2005), p. 396.

18   Colin Rowe and Robert Slutzky, "Transparency: Literal and Phenomenal" *Perspecta 8* (1963), p. 50.

19   Ibid, p. 46.

20   Peter Eisenman, *Giuseppe Terragni: Transformations, Decompositions, Critiques* (New York: Monacelli Press, 2003), p. 162.

21   Peter Eisenman, "[Bracketing] History" foreword to Anthony Vidler's *Histories of the Immediate Present: Inventing Architectural Modernism* (Cambridge, MA: MIT Press, 2008), p. vii.

22   Gregg Lambert, *On the (New) Baroque in Modern Culture* (© Gregg Lambert). An earlier version was published as *The Return of the Baroque in Modern Culture* (London: Continuum, 2004), p. 3.

23   Heinrich Wölfflin, *Renaissance and Baroque*, trans. Kathryn Simon (Ithaca, NY: Cornell University Press, 1964), p. 30

24   John Beldon Scott, "S. Ivo alla Sapienza and Borromini's Symbolic Language" *Journal of the Society of Architectural Historians 41*, no. 4 (1982), p. 307.

25   Staale Sinding-Larsen, "Operational Determination: Math in Buildings and Math Statements About Them" *Early Modern Culture Online 2*, no. 1 (2011), p. 5.

26   Sigfried Giedion, *Space, Time and Architecture: The Growth of a New Tradition* (Cambridge, MA: Harvard University Press, 1966), p. 113.

27   Ibid, p. 115.

28   Andrea Palladio, *The Four Books of Architecture* (New York: Dover Press, 1965), p. 27.

29   Marcus Vitruvius Pollio, *The Ten Books on Architecture*, trans. Morris Hickey Morgan (New York: Dover Press 1960), Chapter III, Book 6, p. 177.

30   Marc Neveu, "Prato della Valle, Reconsidered," in *Chora: Intervals in the Philosophy of Architecture*, eds. Alberto Pérez Gómez Alberto and Stephen Parcell (Montreal: McGill-Queen's University, 2011), vol. 6, p. 172.

31   Gilles Deleuze, *The Fold: Leibnitz and the Baroque*, trans. Tom Conley (New York: Continuum, 2006), p. 4.

32   Greg Lynn, "Architectural Curvilinearity: The Folded, the Pliant and the Supple," in *AD Profile 102: Folding Architecture* (London: Academy Editions, 1993), p. 24.

33   D'Arcy Wentworth Thompson, *On Growth and Form* (Cambridge: Cambridge University Press, 1917). Thompson writes of these diagrams: "Fig. 381 is a common, typical Diodon or porcupine-fish, and in Fig. 382 I have deformed its vertical co-ordinates into a system of concentric circles, and its horizontal co-ordinates into a system of curves which, approximately and provisionally, are made to resemble a system of hyperbolas. The old outline, transferred in its integrity to the new network, appears as a manifest representation of the closely allied, but very different looking, simfish, Orthagoriscus mola. This is a particularly instructive case of deformation or transformation."

34   Ethel Baraona Pohl, "Waffle Urbanism" *Domus 947* (May 2011), https://www. domusweb.it/en/architecture/2011/05/10/waffle-urbanism.html.

Chapter 11

Enclosure

Views of (the outside) and views from (the inside) can contradict each other. Every window offers a new angle on the surroundings, and the site itself is sucked into the kaleidoscope.[1]

—Lucy Lippard

The Basilica of San Lorenzo in Florence, Italy dates back to 393 CE when the earliest church to occupy this site was consecrated. It served as the city's cathedral before the bishop's seat was transferred to the present location of Santa Maria del Fiore (the Duomo, or Florence Cathedral). With church construction beginning in 1419 according to Filippo Brunelleschi's designs, San Lorenzo is considered to be one of the first expressions of Renaissance architecture in Italy. As part of the larger monastic complex and the parish church of the Medici family, San Lorenzo connects to the Laurentian Library with Michelangelo's design for the *Ricetto*, the Sagrestia Vecchia (Old Sacristy, begun 1421) by Brunelleschi, and the Sagrestia Nuova (New Sacristy, begun 1510) that houses Michelangelo's tombs for Giuliano and Lorenzo de' Medici. Separated by nearly 100 years, Michelangelo's Sagrestia Nuova complements and refines the revival of classical canons Brunellschi initiated in the Sagrestia Vecchia. Such distinguished spaces, both for their artistic merit and historical significance to the Medici family, designate San Lorenzo as a highly freighted church in Florentine history.

Despite this constellation of important buildings, San Lorenzo remains strikingly incomplete, standing in its piazza naked without a façade, and leaving the city of Florence with a building curiously unfinished in rough stone and brick striations that evoke the image of an archaeological trench. Having remained incomplete at the time of Brunelleschi's death, eventually the Medici Pope Leo X entrusted the design of the façade to Michelangelo. Due to a combination of financial and time constraints, work on the design did not progress beyond drawings and a highly detailed wood model. As the model demonstrates, Michelangelo's design to cover what was undoubtedly viewed as an eyesore in this increasingly Renaissance city is significant for having proposed a rational grid system of engaged columns and pilasters that form a rhythmical pattern of A-B widths, and for the extension of

Figure 11.1
**Basilica of
San Lorenzo
in Florence,
from Images by
Sailko**

Figure 11.2
**Michelangelo
Buonarotti,
wood model of
façade design
for Basilica of
San Lorenzo,
from Images by
Sailko**

these columns into projections on the entablatures as a nascent Baroque detail.

This model illustrates the idea of a wall that is able to stand free of the building it was intended to cover, exemplifying an enclosure that operates as a design element that remains substantially autonomous from its interior spaces and exterior context.[2] Likewise, this building, which stands up independently from this detachable surface, does not necessarily require a cover in order to perform its duties as a church. Michelangelo's design acts as a rectangular billboard that masks the triangular roof of a traditional basilica and offers a quintessential example of a façade, a term referencing both the principal front of a building and a deceptive outward appearance. As Denis Hollier observes architecture's ability to operate as a cultural metaphor, "the term façade generally indicates 'concealing some sordid reality.'"[3] Just as "the creator's unified plan is a secret architecture, a pillar may signify the pillar of a community or a church, and 'keystones' prevent systems (whether political, philosophical, or scientific) from collapsing," architecture "always represents something other than itself from the moment that it becomes distinguished from mere building."[4] Hollier contends that architecture is representational because it explicitly contains metaphorical value. The façade, in this sense of a false front, acts as architecture's most representational feature.

Giulio Romano's interior courtyard of the Palazzo del Te in Mantua, Italy (1534) offers an equally compelling and self-referential demonstration of a Mannerist façade that subverts classical notions of architectural stability. Mannerist architecture, in this instance, may be understood as further developing the Renaissance's revival of classical language to the extent that canons had become codified and absorbed enough for architects to begin to manipulate and subvert these very standards. With exaggerated keystones interrupting the structural reading of pediments, missing stone courses dematerializing the rusticated walls, and triglyphs slipping off of their entablatures, Romano destabilized architecture's sense of stability while revealing the walls to be composed of a removable ornamental surface. Architectural enclosures, such as Michelangelo's and Romano's façades, may operate as aesthetic masks whose role remains independent of a building's exterior context and interior performance.

Quite often it is possible to read a building's enclosure as a reflection of its interior use. In the case of a typical Los Angeles "Dingbat" apartment, the size of windows index the amounts of privacy needed in the spaces behind them. The living room generally features the largest window size, the bedroom the medium size, and the bathroom the smallest size. Similarly, the outside of multistory buildings often indicates the location of stairs through windows that step up as they mark the angle of ascent. At Preston Scott Cohen's Nanjing Performing Arts Center (2008) on the new Nanjing University Campus in Xianlin, the dynamic angular geometry of stairs feature prominently as part of the envelope, with one wrapping around a tower as an additive element and another seeming to slice into the side elevation of the lower auditorium building as a subtractive cut. For the Stairs Office Building in Addis Ababa, Ethiopia (2008) by Zeleke Belay Architects, a stair deeply carves into the exterior surface of a five-story-tall tower, rendering the exterior walls as thin sculptural surfaces punctuated by red walls appearing from behind where the exterior skin has been pulled back to make way for the void this vertical circulation

Figure 11.3
Giulio Romano,
Palazzo del Te
in Mantua, Italy
(1524–1534)

produced. And in a final example, the exterior roof enclosing the commercial space of Farshad Mehdizadeh Architects' Termeh Office Commercial Building in Hamedan, Iran (2015) twists from horizontal to vertical orientation while it simultaneously pixelates into the material scale of bricks to form stairs leading up to the office spaces. Subtractive, additive, and morphologically dynamic vertical circulation systems expressed on the building's exterior offer design opportunities to produce legible form on highly expressive surfaces.

Figure 11.4
Gerard
Smulevich,
"A Dystopian
Dingbat Piazza
Del Popolo"
(in Culver
City, California
on Overland
Avenue, 2010),
courtesy
of Gerard
Smulevich

Figure 11.5
**Zeleke Belay
Architects,
Stairs Office
Building in
Addis Ababa,
Ethiopia (2008),
courtesy of
Zeleke Belay
Architects**

Figure 11.6
**Preston Scott
Cohen, Nanjing
Performing Arts
Center on the
new Nanjing
University
Campus
in Xianlin
University City,
Nanjing (2008),
courtesy of
Preston Scott
Cohen, Inc.**

341

Just as often as not, a building's enclosure may confound exterior readings of interior spaces. In the Villa Snellman in Djursholm, Sweden (1917), Erik Gunnar Asplund designed windows on the south façade of this country house that ever so slightly shift off of their centerlines to create a staccato rhythm on the exterior, while there is no obvious evidence in plan as to why this subtle displacement occurs. Formal surface preoccupations such as this may display applied patterning that rejects interior use and relational positioning, operating as a decorative wrapper disguising the contents of a gift box as it distinguishes itself from its architectural adjacencies. Lorcan O'Herlihy's Vertical House in Venice, California (2005) prioritizes the pattern of an external wrapper above internal use and external relationships. Located on a small infill lot, O'Herlihy wrapped the three-story house with a series of vertical panels that alternate in a loose checkerboard pattern between opaque and transparent surfaces that ignores the proximity of neighbors' adjacent windows located just feet away. The openings occur continuously as they wrap around the building, ignoring specific programmatic alignments or any distinction between the floors. The interior spaces feature surprising and unintended intersections between elements such as windows opening onto floor slabs or bathrooms segmenting pieces of the inhabitant's body in the framing of domestic space—a foot may mysteriously appear in the lower corner aperture of a bedroom or a torso may be cut by a vertical window rising only halfway up the room.

In contrast to the idea of a gift-wrapped enclosure whose material patterning operates in disjunction from the rest of the architecture, a number of forces exert themselves on exterior surfaces to render even the most

Figure 11.8
Erik Gunnar Asplund, Villa Snellman in Djursholm, Sweden (1917)

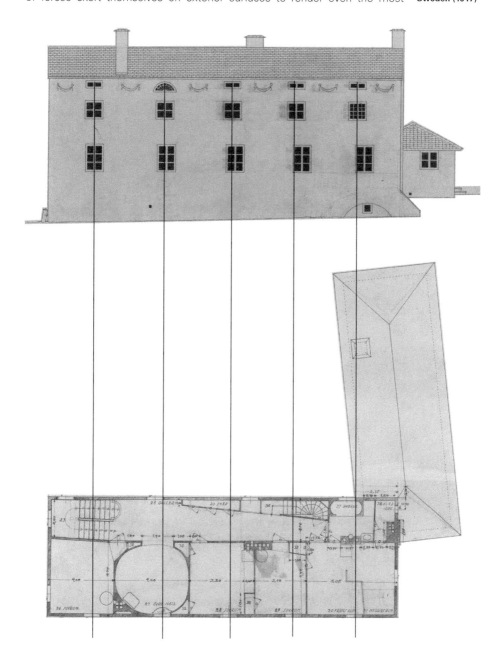

Figure 11.9
**Lorcan
O'Herlihy
Architects,
Vertical House
in Venice,
California
(2005), courtesy
of Lorcan
O'Herlihy
Architects**

decorative of enclosures as dynamic and responsive. Gravity, thermodynamic differentials, lateral forces, weather, and more cause architecture's exterior surfaces to expand, bend, and flex as living entities. Ned Kahn's façade for the Swiss Science Center in Winterthur, Switzerland (2002) demonstrates at a macro-scale what occurs on a building façade at a microscopic level. Kahn designed a surface composed of thousands of small aluminum panels that respond to air currents and form kinetic ripples that operates as a decorative enclosure.

Elevation, façade, skin, envelope—these terms are often used inter-changeably to describe a building's enclosure, a zone of space that may ignore internal or external exigencies to arrive at an expression of "out-and-out" architecture. As the part of a building that negotiates contextual alignments, such as framing views, with internal performances, such as day-lighting spe-cific tasks, the enclosure absorbs the tension between these two pressures

while inflecting to the architect's specific design strategy. Just as interior and exterior views may contradict each other, to borrow from Lucy Lippard, a building envelope may oscillate in response to divergent inside and outside forces. While the architect mediates these diverse pressures, the potential also exists to prioritize the design of the envelope as a formal entity with its own set of internal logics. The anthropomorphic analogy of façade and skin used to describe enclosures suggests that buildings may display facial affect or elastic membranes. A formal reading of these terms examines how an enclosure metaphorically, rather than dynamically, may cover a building as a face or an epidermis. Conversely, while elevation and envelope indicate performative surfaces, a formal reading of architectural enclosures through these terms foregrounds their compositional attributes. To conclude the analytical system put forward at the beginning of this book, this chapter considers out-and-out architecture as expressed in a building's enclosure by favoring formal composition above interior and exterior responsiveness.

Figure 11.10
Ned Kahn,
façade for
the Swiss
Science Center
(Winterthur,
Switzerland,
2002)

Elevation

In Book I, Chapter 2 of *De Architectura* Vitruvius summarized the essential tools an architect may use when designing a building as (1) *ordinatio* (order),

(2) *dispositio* (arrangement), (3) *eurythmia* (proportion, harmony of the parts), (4) *symmetria* (symmetry), (5) *decore* (décor, suitably), and (6) *distributio* (distribution, placement).[5] *Dispositio*, as he put it, is divisible into the three components of *ichnography* (plan), *orthography* (elevation), and *scenography* (perspective).[6] In particular, orthography combines the ancient Greek *orthos*, meaning correct or right, with *graphein*, meaning to write, into the concept of "correct writing." In contemporary drawing practice, orthographic projection means the two- or three-dimensional drawing of objects and spaces.

As a function of orthographic projection, *elevation* stems from *elevare* and implies the action of lifting up or elevating the building's vertical planes, or walls, from its horizontal planes, or floors. A form of delineation, elevation implies the drawing and design of a building's exterior as an action of projecting information from one surface to another, similar to the process of axonometric drawing. Introduced in Chapter 4, "Scenography," axonometric drawings provide for the orthographic projection of a two-dimensional shape, such as a square, into a three-dimensional form, such a cube, by extending vertical lines upward from the corners of the square, rotated at an angle from horizontal, until they reach the height necessary to form the sides of the cube and then connecting those points in space to form its top. Both the square and its corresponding cube may be drawn to scale so that they maintain the same geometric proportions and mathematical dimensions as each other. Elevations also include the roof plane or top portion of a cube as part of the designed surface, in contrast to façades which tend to operate primarily as vertical enclosures. At the Santa Catarina Market in Barcelona, Spain (2005), Enric Miralles and Benedetta Tagliabue exploited the fifth elevation when they covered an undulating roof

Figure 11.11 Miralles Tagliabue EMBT, Santa Caterina Market on Barcelona, Spain (2005), photograph by Roland Halbe, courtesy of Miralles Tagliabue EMBT

with a colorful tile pattern that would provide visual interest to the apartments looking down on what otherwise would be leftover space.

Given that axonometric drawing provides for the design of a building's elevation by projecting the plan onto the enclosure, the technique develops a synchronous reading between plan, section, and elevation in a geometrically accurate drawing that allows an architect to design apertures and surfaces in specific relation to the spaces they enclose. The ability to precisely measure a building's enclosure through the process of orthography explains one reason why axonometric projection operated in parallel with the modernist practice of registering interior spaces on exterior forms and the explosion from inside to outside that ensued. This technical tool provides for the projection of structural systems onto the elevation, allowing for columns and beams to appear on exterior surfaces as an abstract grid. This is a process implicit in the Office for Metropolitan Architecture's (OMA) design of the China Central Television (CCTV) Headquarters in Beijing (2012). Here they scored the exterior surfaces with a rotated grid of lines representing the building's structural forces that became more "dense in areas of greater stress, looser and more open in areas requiring less support."[7] As with the CCTV building, the elevation has the potential to map onto its surface a complex set of invisible interior pressures as compositional devices (see Figure 2.9 in Chapter 2).

Axonometric drawing also may allow for calibrating each surface of that imaginary square differently as a cartography of contextual conditions such as solar orientation or site alignments. Giuseppe Terragni's Casa del Fascio (1936), a building that once housed the Fascist Party headquarters in Como, Italy, exemplifies a building with four elevations that abstractly inflect to contextual and performative pressures. The front elevation references the culturally specific typology of an Italian *palazzo* (palace) with a central courtyard, regularly spaced window openings, and a vestigial defensive tower expressed as a solid plane. The double height, central gathering space inside the Casa del Fascio opens to the sky above the second floor and projects onto top of the front elevation as an exposed frame proportioned to the geometry of the Golden Section. The expressed structural frame forms a grid that comes into relief as the façade is carved away to reveal windows and balconies behind. Where each of the three other elevations vary the Golden Section proportions and ratio of solid to void in relation to interior use, nothing protrudes from the stretched datum of the perimeter on a building where all surface articulation is accomplished through the process of subtraction.

In contrast, Terragni's Casa Giuliani-Frigerio (1940), the apartment block also in Como discussed in the previous chapter, suggests a series of projections and overlapping planes across a set of operations that leave vestiges of the design process on the finished surfaces. The thin vertical windows on the corners of the front elevation reveal a frame that seems to have been pulled like a drawer from out of the interior volume, while the columns supporting the roof cornice on this side operate in the same way, as if pulled from up and out of the vertical plane. The projected corner renders the vertical wall,

Figure 11.12
**Giusepe
Terragni, Casa
del Fascio
(now Casa
del Popolo)
in Como,
Italy (1936),
photograph
by Giuseppe
Albano**

perforated with rectangular windows, into a freestanding plane that seems to have slid into place.

Façade

Demonstrated at the Villa Savoye, Le Corbusier's "Five Points Towards a New Architecture" (1926) are: (1) the use of *pilotis* or structural columns instead of walls; (2) a free plan that operates independently from the structure; (3) a free façade liberated from the need to support the building with walls; (4) ribbon windows that stretch horizontally across the length of the façade; and (5) a roof garden.[8] Liberated from its structural burden as a load-bearing wall, the free façade may adapt to any form of enclosure the architect chooses, from providing liberal apertures to allow for light and views to cladding the building in a solid screen projecting a digital image of windows on an otherwise opaque surface. *Façade* emerges in 16th-century French, deriving from the Italian *facciata*, meaning "the front of a building" and from the Latin *faccia* or "face."[9] Anthony Vidler recounts that the philosopher and mathematician Jean le Rond d'Alembert "put the problem most concisely when he defined architecture as the 'embellished mask of our greatest need.'"[10] From the transparency of reading interiors through affect, an outward expression of interior moods, to the opacity of disguising them with veils or masks, the building façade operates as architecture's representational veneer, able to project manifold intentions detached from purely utilitarian drives. "The term, *facade*, as applied to architecture," as Thomas L. Schumacher summarizes, "has taken on the same negative connotation that it has when applied to people."[11] While the modern movement shunned the façade in favor of the skeleton or the skull, as he writes, postmodernism's mask emphasized rhetorical façades and hyperbole. Michelangelo's design for San Lorenzo, Luigi Moretti's Casa Girasole in Rome (1950), and its progeny at Robert Venturi's Vanna Venturi House in Chestnut

Figure 11.13
**Luigi Moretti,
Casa Girasole
in Rome,
Italy (1950),
photograph
by Paulette
Singley**

Figure 11.14
**Robert Venturi,
Vanna Venturi
House in
Chestnut Hill,
Pennsylvania
(1964),
photograph by
David Turnbull**

Hill, Pennsylvania (1964) all operate as façades which suggest detachment from the buildings they efface. As Venturi so acutely demonstrated in the Vanna Venturi House: "Designing from the outside in, as well as the inside out, creates necessary tensions, which help make architecture. Since the inside is different from the outside, the wall—the point of change—becomes an architectural event."[12] For Venturi, "Architecture occurs at the meeting of interior and exterior forces of use and space. Architecture as the wall between the inside and the outside becomes the spatial record of this."[13]

"A window without shutters is an eye without eyelids," as Eileen Gray considers architectural enclosures.[14] Given that the windows and front door of a building may suggest eyes and a mouth, it is no coincidence that the term *façade* describes the face of a building. *Vestibule* similarly references both an anteroom and bodily cavities, such as the space between the lips and the teeth. The operation of façade as face emphatically appears at the entrance to the late 16th-century Palazzo Zuccari in Rome, where the main door presents a gaping mouth into which the visitor is swallowed. Its distant cousin, located in the Monster Park at Bomarzo (Parco dei Mostri), Italy, features the giant head of an Orcus forming a pavilion with a gaping mouth and teeth bared ready to devour lost picnickers. If a façade is a face, as with the Orcus, then it also suggests architecture's ability to demonstrate various moods or affects, such as terror or awe.

In his *Cours d'architecture* (1771–1777), Jacques-François Blondel delineated a series of column capitals upon which he superimposed human profiles as a way of expressing a building's proper character. According to him, "one could exaggerate the projection of the dripstone of the corona, which represents the nose of the head, or pull down the upper cyma representing the forehead; and fortify with corbels [the part] representing the chin, if one wants to give to the profile of a cornice a very rustic expression, following the Tuscan order."[15] For him, the term *character* denoted a building's physiognomic ability to express an idea similar to the way in which a building façade represents a face, specifically outlining the affect that certain types of buildings ought to produce—"churches should cause emotions connected with decency (i.e. decorum), royal palaces with magnificence, public buildings with grandeur, fortifications with solidity"—and so on.[16]

George Dance the Younger's façades for Newgate Prison in London (1770) and Peter Speeth's design of the Women's Penitentiary in Würzburg, Germany (1809–1810) feature foreboding exteriors with rusticated bases and small apertures that render the countenance of dread. More recently, Herzog and de Meuron's Central Signal Box (1994), a railway utility building in Basel, Switzerland, is clad with twisted copper strips, horizontal slats that present the enigmatic visage of a vintage welding mask at the point where the banding becomes the most porous. The Signal Box's horizontal striation suggest the visor André Breton referred to—"A highly evolved descendant of the helmet"—in a caption published in *L'Amour fou* (*Mad Love*, 1937) for a photograph by Man Ray. Admun Studio's apartment house in Tehran, Iran,

Figure 11.15 **Federico Zuccari, Palazzo Zuccari in Rome, Italy (from 1590), photograph by Paulette Singley**

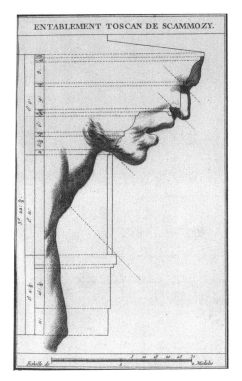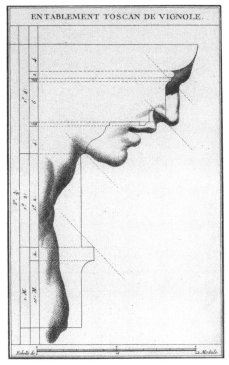

Figure 11.16 **Jacques-François Blondel and Pierre Patte, "Entablement Toscan de Scammozy; Entablement Toscan de Vignole" ("Tuscan Entablature by Scamozzi; Tuscan Entablature by Vignola"), in** *Cours d'architecture, ou Traité de la décoration, distribution & construction des bâtiments* **(Paris: chez Desaint, libraire, 1771)**

named Cloaked in Bricks (2015), rotates the horizontal graining of the Signal Box into a vertical exploration of the porosity of brick coursing. The rotated brick patterning of Cloaked in Bricks similarly describes a lattice façade with five oculi sliding to the left of the building behind, ever so subtly suggesting the mask some Islamic women wear to cover their faces, where only the eyes can be seen.

The ambiguous shape of Lars Spuybroek's D-tower, located in Doetinchem, the Netherlands (2003), displays a radical zoomorphic form that invites comparison with, perhaps, a giant squid or a walking protozoa. As an interactive public artwork, the 12-meter-high structure comes alive through an illuminated skin that changes color from green, to red, to blue, to yellow—according to information gathered from a public website calculating the emotional status of the city's participating population. Colors index public mood, with green representing hate, red love, blue happiness, and yellow fear, broadcasting whether the population is amorous or angry. Though not a façade per se, this project demonstrates how a building may convey feelings through a combination of social media and surface manipulation.

Just as cheeks blush or foreheads perspire when hot or emotionally charged, it is possible to read hidden psychologies through facial affect. As our bodies become increasingly mediated, the means of physiognomic communication also becomes augmented. Since "skin has become inadequate in interfacing with reality," according to the artist Nam June Paik, "technology has become the body's new membrane of existence."[17] If Times Square in New York is any indication, it has also become architecture's new façade, offering a mechanism to entirely erode the building's surface with information delivered on high-resolution screens that cover walls and surfaces with imagery that recalls Richard Roger's and Renzo Piano's competition proposal

Figure 11.17
Peter Speeth Women's Penitentiary in Würzburg, Germany (1809–1810), photography by James Steakley

Figure 11.18
**Herzog and
de Meuron,
Central Signal
Box in Basel,
Switzerland
(1994), courtesy
of Herzog and
de Meuron**

Figure 11.19
**André Breton,
"A Highly
Evolved
Descendant of
the Helmet"
from *L'Amour
fou* (*Mad
Love*, 1937),
photograph by
Man Ray**

Figure 11.20
**Admun Studio,
Cloaked in
Bricks in
Tehran, Iran
(2015), courtesy
of Admun
Studio**

for the Centre Georges Pompidou discussed earlier in Chapter 6. From face to interface to interfaçade, Lev Manovich posits that the overlaying of architecture with dynamic data produces "augmented space."[18] He speculates on the design opportunities involved with tangible interfaces, intelligent architecture,

Figure 11.21
**Lars
Spuybroek,
D-tower in
Doetinchem,
the
Netherlands
(2003),
courtesy of
Lars Spuybroek**

intelligent spaces, and context-aware computing that are rapidly transforming the built environment with "virtual layers of contextual information."[19] In
the scenario where information technology overlays surfaces as something
significantly other to building material, such as animated images or moving
texts, the screen supplants inhabitable form as architecture's primary role. The
counter-scenario of a hyper-surface delivering images of building materials suggests that hypo-materiality also exists, where images of "bricks and mortar"
façades project onto screens as ephemeral surfaces confounding architecture
with its own constructional imaginary. Consider the destabilizing potential of

a building's exterior surface onto which shifting pictures of concrete, glass, or even metal siding may be projected with a flickering image that both asserts and denies materiality.

Skin

Skin is the human body's largest organ and quite often a building's most important system. Rather than just a thin membrane with pigmentation, human and animal skin display a relatively thick sectional slice of numerous interactive components: sweat ducts, sweat glands, fat, hair follicles, glands, and nerves. As with architectural enclosures, skin protects the interior from the exterior, providing temperature control and moisture barriers. Patterning material behavior on the model of skin that grows back, recent technological innovation has resulted in self-healing building materials such as concrete that contains living bacterial aggregate to repair cracks. Nemesi & Partners (Michele Molè and Susanna Tradati) wrapped the Palazzo Italia pavilion at the Milan Expo 2015 in an engineered skin that extracts pollution from the air through biodynamic concrete panels. In 2013 students and professors from Stuttgart University's Institute of Building Structures and Structural Design (ITKE) designed the ArboSkin pavilion in Stuttgart, Germany from thermoformable sheets of bioplastic containing the renewable material Arboblend, composed of a combination of different biopolymers such as lignin, a by-product of wood pulping processes, and natural reinforcing fibers.[20] As architecture expands into the world of nanotechnology, the biological fabrication of living building skins becomes ever more viable.

This exploration of a building's epidermis as a pulsing biological building system works at both a functional and an aesthetic level, meaning that its

Figure 11.22
Nemesi & Partners (Michele Molè and Susanna Tradati), Palazzo Italia at the Milan Expo 2015, courtesy of Nemesi & Partners

Figure 11.23
**Institute
of Building
Structures
and Structural
Design (ITKE),
Stuttgart
University,
the ArboSkin
pavilion in
Stuttgart,
Germany
(2013),
photograph
by Manfred
Richard
Hommes,
courtesy of
ITKE**

discreet anatomical properties offer as many formal readings as they do performative readings. Its most powerful role in architecture has to do with the
metaphor of an architecture reduced to the components of skin and bones,
meaning enclosure and structure.

But where the phrase "skin and bones" frequently describes architectural
enclosures, what precisely does it reference? For Ludwig Mies van der Rohe,
it was axiomatic that early shelters were built from actual animal skins and
bones. In a 1923 lecture he described a typical Eskimo house in the following
way: "Moss and seal skins have here become building materials. Walrus ribs
form the roof structure." Consistent with his theory of *beinahe nichts* or almost
nothing, Mies van der Rohe translated this observation into an architecture of
hyper-thin enclosures where the wall almost disappears into a condition of
pure transparency that glass skin provides.

Despite the clarity of the metaphor between a building's glass epidermis
and its structural steel bones, the origin of this concept in seal skin introduces
the concept of pellicularity to architecture. Stemming from the Latin *pellis*,
meaning skin, the word *pellicular* has evolved to encompass such concepts as
leather, parchment, hide, film, scum, layer, fur, and plastic membrane. Through
the pliable meaning of pellicular, it becomes possible to explore architectural
enclosure as plastic wrap, that is, as a surface that is pliable, preservative,
and transparent. Pellucularity confounds foundational canons of classical purity
with oblique metaphors to substances that decay, as well as to questions concerning ornamentation and cosmetics. The dematerialized distinction between
inside and out that pellicular surfaces describe allows for differential interior
and exterior pressures to push, pull, and stretch the architectural enclosure
into spaces where these two realms nearly slip into one another like inter-
connecting soap bubbles. As with plastic wrap used for preserving food, their

potential to closely adhere to that which they protect acts as a prophylactic incubator breeding microbial environments between pellicular surfaces and the material they cover.

In contradistinction to the concept of thick and inhabitable *poché*—a term describing infill spaces that often is associated with the idea of substantial, inhabitable walls—pellicular zones may operate as hyper-thin spaces. They describe compressed atmospheres, condensation on surfaces, stretched and tensile wrappers, beguiling spatial conditions, and the pellucid dissolution of architectural space. As shiny and colored surface applications, they cover architecture with adherent ornament. Scum, paint, dyes, and cosmetics likewise describe pellicular zones as the thinnest and most pliable fusion of a material to the surface it covers. These peculiar pelliculars envelop architecture in spaces of otherness and intimacy with a thinness that dematerializes architecture's status as an inhabitable solid.

To a certain extent, any distinction between skin and envelope in common architecture parlance is nonexistent, as the terms are used almost interchangeably. One distinguishing factor in exploring skin as enclosure is that it introduces an array of physiognomic architectural metaphors to the conversation that open up the discussion to concerns of bodily ornamentation and identity. Tattooing, scarring, blemishes, wrinkles, beauty marks, freckles, pores, and pigmentation become part and parcel of a design vocabulary oriented around concepts of skin.

Vittoria de Palma and Jeffrey Kipnis consider the sensuous properties of Jacques Herzog and Pierre de Meuron's evanescent surfaces, teasing out the significance of allusive architectural membranes that glimmer with seductive properties. For de Palma, their work "exhibits an ongoing preoccupation with the status of the architectural surface," while for Kipnis it signals "an urbane, cunning intelligence and intoxicating, almost erotic allure."[21] Herzog and de Meuron's design for the Eberswalde Technical School Library (1999) demonstrates de Palma's and Kipnis's claims regarding the architects' slippery surfaces. As part of the design for the façades of this building, the firm collaborated with the photographer Thomas Ruff, who selected iconic images from his private collection of magazines to curate dot-screened pictures that were acid etched onto precast concrete panels or silkscreened onto glass panes, creating bands of representational strata on the library's exterior. As Gerhard Mack describes the library, "a simple cube of concrete and glass panels has been tattooed from top to bottom with a pattern of images—like the body of a Papuan."[22]

Compare this statement to the one that Adolf Loos wrote in "Ornament and Crime": "The modern man who tattoos himself is either a criminal or a degenerate."[23] And yet, Loos describes the origins of architecture as pellicular, writing: "In the beginning we sought to clad ourselves, to protect ourselves from the elements, to keep ourselves safe and warm while sleeping … Originally consisting of animal furs or textiles, this covering is the earliest architectural feature."[24] He expressed this sentiment most clearly in the bedroom

Figure 11.24
**Herzog and
de Meuron,
Eberswalde
Technical
School Library
in Eberswalde,
Germany
(1999), courtesy
of Herzog and
de Meuron**

he designed for his wife Lina, featuring a pale blue wall-to-wall carpet, covered with an Angora rabbit fur rug that curled up to the base of the bed. Lina's bedroom locates the animal skin of pellicular surfaces directly in the domestic interior.

Introducing a legible, specific socio-political content to the architectural surfaces of a library, Ruff curated the façade with images of Lorenzo Lotto's *Venus and Cupid*, Eduard Ender's painting of Alexander von Humboldt, a photograph of the Berlin Wall taken in 1961 showing a woman captured while trying to escape, another taken in 1989 showing the reunification celebration at the Brandenburg Gate, a *memento mori* still life with a skull by Pieter Potier, and so on. The process of transferring the images onto the concrete panels resulted in microscopic reservoirs of space. As Mack relates, the photographs were silkscreened onto a special plastic film that was covered with a concrete cure-retardant, instead of ink, and placed into the formwork. The amount of retardant used controlled the degree to which the surface of the concrete set. As he continues, "when the panel is taken out of the form work, and carefully washed with water and brushes, the concrete that has lain in contact with the retardant remains liquid and is rinsed away, leaving darker, rougher areas of exposed grey aggregate."[25] At a macroscopic level, as the architects state, "the imprint on the entire façade unifies the surface; the differences between concrete and glass seem to be annulled."[26] Any distinction between surface and ornament also disappears as the building becomes a canvas for the display of art and the architects relinquish agency on the articulation of the most visible part of their design.

At their Ricola-Europe SA, Production and Storage Building (1993), the architects choreographed the growth of ornamental surface scum they refer to as a "natural drawing."[27] They achieved this by enclosing the narrow elevations of this building with black concrete walls that direct water to fall from the roof down the sides into a deep bed of gravel. They also silkscreened translucent polycarbonate panels on the front façade with a repetitive plant motif based on photograph's by Karl Blossfeldt. Kipnis interprets these panels as introducing a new coherence to architecture's conventional polarity between ornamentalism and minimalism. As he writes, "when backlit, as seen in the interior during the day, the leaf pattern takes on an empty, numbing, camp fascination of a Warholian wallpaper," while on the exterior, "the images are rarely visible, emerging only fleetingly as hallucinations when hit at exactly the right angle by glancing light."[28] For Kipnis "this slick, eye-catching device belies the range and depth of technique HdM exercised in realizing the full cosmetic sophistication of the work."[29]

Extending the potential of glass fritting to augment the design of a transparent enclosure, MVRDV's (Winy Maas, Jacob van Rijs, and Nathalie de Vries) Glass Farm (2013) relies on a photographic collage of vernacular buildings to envelop a glass silhouette shaped in the form of a traditional Dutch farm building. In order to build a new structure in the town of Schijndel, on a site located between the church, the town hall, and the main street, the architects collaborated with the artist Frank van der Salm in creating the image of a fictional farm building compiled from photographs of actual structures found in the area. They produced an augmented history, a convincing imitation of a traditional building that they then applied as full-scale film attached to the skin of their new glass structure. Given that the applied image is substantially transparent and translucent, from the building's interior it is possible to inhabit its exterior surfaces and vice versa. In other words, when standing inside the building, one sees the exterior enclosure laminated onto the surface, while standing outside looking in, the interior spaces appear behind these surfaces. Inside is out and outside is in. Rough and smooth, transparent and opaque, solid and void, and inside and outside oscillate across the pellicular surface of this project where ostensibly dull brick appears as a glossy skin reflecting the context from behind a glass veneer, or thatched roofing seems to filter the sky when seen from inside, or pure glass corners emerge as if having had the brick scrubbed off them with a good cleaning.

At the Storefront for Art and Architecture gallery (2015) in New York City, Florian Idenburg, Jing Liu, and Sebastiaan Bremer of the studio SO-IL installed "Blueprint," a thin layer of white shrink-wrap film stretched across the exterior. As the folding panels of Vito Acconci and Steven Holl's original façade deform the plastic wrapper, the surface undulates with different levels of material tension. While Christo and Jeanne-Claude's wrapped buildings offer paradigmatic examples of the way in which a pellicular surface may engulf architectural form, SO-IL also invokes the more prosaic iconography and scale of a house being fumigated.

Figure 11.25
MVRDV (Winy Maas, Jacob van Rijs, and Nathalie de Vries), Glass Farm in Schijndel the Netherlands, (2013), courtesy of MVRDV

Figure 11.26
Florian Idenburg, Jing Liu, and Sebastiaan Bremer of studio SO-IL, "Blueprint," at the Storefront for Art and Architecture gallery (New York City, 2015), courtesy of SO-IL

Just as the image of a house swathed in a stripped vinyl tent, used to enclose gaseous pesticides necessary for fumigation, invokes the ordinariness of plastic wrapping, so too does the ubiquitous presence of house wrap in architecture. Demonstrating that pellicular architecture resides in the quotidian practices of commercial building as well as the hi-tech and avant-garde architecture discussed above, building wrappers dwell between exterior cladding

Figure 11.27
**Christo and
Jeanne-Claude,**
*Wrapped
Reichstag.
Berlin,
1971–1995,*
photograph by
Wolfgang Volz

and interior surfaces. Housewrap is the generic name for a synthetic material that performs as a weather-resistant barrier that prevents rain from penetrating the inside of walls while simultaneously allowing water vapor to pass through the enclosure, thereby preventing the growth of mold or rot. Tyvek is a brand name of this material, used in architecture as a protective barrier, providing an air pocket between the outer cladding of a structure, frame, and insulation. The significance is that these wrappers breathe, filtering in one kind of substance while blocking another.

Architectural skin operates physiognomically and analogically, with both interpretive systems (the literal and the abstract) intertwined among architectural performance and form, counterpoised in the depth of the surface. It goes without saying, then, that the metaphor of skin also carries with it the potential to reference human identity. David Adjaye's National Museum of African American History and Culture (NMAAHC, 2016), collaboratively designed with the Freelon Group and Davis Brody Bond, appears as a simple square volume wrapped in three tiers of perforated metal screen, known as the corona, that references the crown on a Yoruban statue from southwestern Africa located in the museum's collection. "The building is covered in metallic panels that morph from reddish gold to deep sepia in the changing light," according to Mabel O. Wilson, while the metal screen detail references wrought-iron construction

Figure 11.28
David Adjaye
with the
Freelon Group
and Davis
Brody Bond,
National
Museum
of African
American
History and
Culture in
Washington,
DC (2016),
photograph by
Tony Hisgett

frequently found on railings and balconies in New Orleans, Charleston, and other parts of the American South where "Most of that work was done by Black slaves who were, of course, not credited for their craftsmanship."[30] Because it represents the Smithsonian Institution advocating for an inclusive idea of black history in the United States and is located on the National Mall in Washington, DC, the NMAAHC is inherently situational and unavoidably symbolic. A contextual reading of the building notices that the negative space formed between the angle of the pyramid at the summit of the Washington Monument and the tiers of the façade share the same angle. Symbolically the tiered crown posits an image of upward mobility, Adjaye writes, as a "ziggurat that moves upward into the sky, rather than downward into the ground."[31] As much of a mask as a façade or crown, to mix the metaphors introduced at the beginning of this chapter, the cast aluminum bronze of the perforated screens also inserts the color Wilson describes as reddish gold to deep sepia onto the National Mall, a site whose cultural imaginary is dominated by white neoclassical buildings such as the US Capitol and the Lincoln Memorial.

Envelope

Just as a paper envelope wraps and seals a letter inside, a building's envelope acts as the separator between its interior and exterior that wraps around the entire structure, from foundations to roof. The model of a paper envelope evokes the image of a single surface folded inside itself to form a container. But, along with being a wrapper, in just as many ways, the envelope *is* the building. How then can we discuss this singularly important design element outside of its role as a building system? One tack is to focus on freestanding exposition buildings, such as the Eiffel Tower or the Blur Building discussed in earlier chapters, as a type of architecture that generally lacks a specific program and may be relocated from one site to another without entirely undermining its design integrity. Much like picturesque garden follies, freestanding exhibition pavilions often consist only of an enclosure, lacking mechanical systems or even a door, while emphasizing the production of experimental forms.

Thomas Heatherwick's UK Pavilion or "Seed Cathedral" for the Shanghai World Expo of 2010, themed "Better City, Better Life," eschews the normative architectural nomenclature of elevation, façade, or skin—performing as an envelope that wraps around space. Upon closer inspection, from what at a distance appears to be the bristly fur of an enormous Russian Ushanka-hat or Eva Hesse's *Accession* series of sculpture turned inside out, focuses into clarity as a building covered in 60,000 acrylic fiber-optic filaments rods projecting from inside to outside. The rods penetrate the pavilion's enclosing wall, forming a glowing and undulating interior space. The suspension of a single seed into each acrylic spine produces a politically freighted ornamental detail that references world hunger and increasingly precarious food sources.

Working with students from Yale University, the firm of FreelandBuck designed, fabricated and assembled the Yale Assembly Pavilion to operate as the information center for New Haven's 2012 summer International Festival of Arts and Ideas. What amounts to the warping of a triangulated pattern into a three-dimensional egg-crate structure, this self-supporting enclosure displays the parallax effect of appearing as a nearly opaque structure when viewed from one vantage point and an almost transparent wall from another as each of the over 1000 aluminum panels composing this pavilion are aligned to a single point in space. And with the WAVE/CAVE, for *Interni Magazine*'s 20th Edition Event called Material Immaterial, SHoP Architects designed a sculptural enclosure whose undulating form results from the different heights of a system of unglazed tile. While unprotected from the elements and programmatically open-ended, this envelope turns inside itself across the continuous surfaces of hollow tubes.

As with seal skin that may stretch across the substructure of whale bones without precisely attaching to it, an architectural envelope may perform as a pliant material that intermittently adheres to and detaches from the complex geometries of substructures. Of particular interest with respect to an envelope that privileges formal composition is the potential disconnect between an enclosure and the spaces it wraps, as if a single ribbon has tied the building up in a loose bow whose form remains independent from its primary interior volume. The principle that a gap may exist between a building's primary form and its enclosure allows for reading architecture through a series of variables that more precisely describe the relationship between enclosure and what is being enclosed as that of either a loose fit or tight fit.

A series of comparisons illustrate that a building's enclosure may be formally driven and that diverse envelopes may enclose similar uses. The 22 voluminous wood domes defining the silhouette of the Church of the Transfiguration in Kizhi Island, Russia, (1714), the billowing domes rising above the more shallow interior vaults of St Mark's Cathedral in Venice (1093), or the fantastical domes

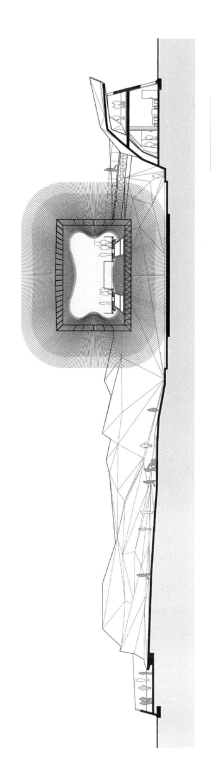

Figure 11.29 Thomas Heatherwick, section through UK Pavilion or "Seed Cathedral" for the Shanghai World Expo of 2010, courtesy of Thomas Heatherwick

Figure 11.30
Eva Hesse,
Accession II
(1968) © Eva
Hesse

Figure 11.31
FreelandBuck,
Yale Assembly
Pavilion for
New Haven's
2012 summer
International
Festival of
Arts and Ideas,
courtesy of
FreelandBuck

Triangulation Extruded through the Pavilion

Initial Structural Triangulation

Figure 11.32
SHoP
Architects,
WAVE/CAVE in
Milan (2017),
courtesy
of SHoP
Architects

forming the skyline of John Nash's Royal Pavilion in Brighton, England (1815) all display remarkable envelopes that enjoy a highly loose fit with the buildings they cover. This is particularly manifest when compared either with the domes of the Pantheon in Rome or the Hagia Sophia, a former Christian church turned into a mosque in Istanbul (537 CE), where the structure and the enclosure are synchronous. While both Coop Himmelb(l)au's BMW Welt building (2007) and Fernando Romero's Museo Soumaya in Mexico City (2010) display torsional geometries of twisted cylinders that seem to have been squeezed into the shape of a tight corset, the latter displays an introverted affect in comparison to the former's highly extroverted persona. The dome surmounting the Paris Panthéon, originally a church dedicated to St Geneviève discussed earlier in Chapter 9, features three domes nested inside each other. This triple shell strategy displays the idea of a second or even third skin as well as the potential for an enclosure to contain spaces within other spaces.

At the Asakusa Culture Tourist Information Center in Tokyo, Japan (2012), a building that contains multiple programs including a gallery and café, Kengo Kuma developed the strategy of stacking seven conceptual houses on top of each other, each with a different roof silhouette that creates diagonal, open air spaces between the floors. As Kuma explains this spatial strategy, "the center extends Asakusa's lively neighborhood vertically and piles up roofs that wrap different activities underneath, creating a 'new section' which had not existed in conventional layered architecture."[32] In contrast, Kazuyo Sejima and Ryue Nishizawa of SANAA designed their New Museum of Contemporary Art in

Figure 11.33
**Church of the
Transfiguration
in Kizhi Island,
Russia (1714),
photograph by
Matthias Kabel**

Figure 11.34
**John Nash,
detail of from
"A Cross
Section of the
Royal Pavilion
at Brighton"
(1815)**

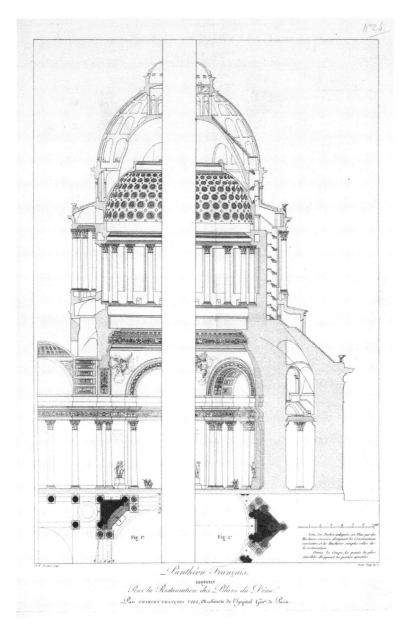

Figure 11.35
Charles-
François Viel,
"Section of
the Panthéon
with Viel's
plan for the
restoration of
the Piers of the
Dome, showing
proposed
reinforcement
of Jacques-
Germain
Soufflot's
original piers,"
in *Principes de
l'ordonnance
et de la
construction
des bâtiments*
(Paris:
Perronneau,
1797–1814)

Manhattan (2007) with seven stacked blocks, shifting horizontally as a way of allowing light to penetrate otherwise opaque gallery spaces and accommodating diverse programmatic requirements. Where for Kuma, the stacked blocks offer the opportunity to design a loose fit that is tightly assembled, for Sejima, the stack offers a strategy for incredibly close-fitting volumes to glide effortlessly past each other.

Figure 11.36
Wolf D.
Prix, Coop
Himmelb(l)
au, BMW
Welt building
in Munich,
Germany
(2007),
photograph
by Maximilian
Dörrbecker

Figure 11.37
Fernando
Romero,
FR-EE, Museo
Soumaya
in Mexico
City (2010),
photograph
by Carlos
Valenzuela

Studio Gang's Aqua Tower in Chicago (2009) and Reiser + Umemoto's O-14 commercial office tower in Dubai (2006) are two curvilinear structures that offer complementary approaches to stretching the skyscraper from out of its rectangular box. The Aqua Tower is an 82-story-tall mixed-use project containing a hotel, offices, rental apartments, and condominiums whose distinguishing characteristic is a series of floor slabs, each with a different curvilinear pattern that produces a ripple of horizontal lines across the envelope. While

Figure 11.38
**Kengo Kuma,
Asakusa
Culture Tourist
Information
Center in Tokyo,
Japan (2012),
courtesy of
Kengo Kuma**

the functional rationale for this vertical topography argues that the projecting curves produce balconies that facilitate community interaction among the tenants, provide shading from the sun, protect the building from Chicago's notorious winds, and help birds avoid it during flight, a formal reading focuses on its inspiration, as the office reports, from "the striated limestone outcroppings common in the Great Lakes area."[33]

Rather than developing projecting balconies to produce a curvilinear envelope, at the O-14 commercial tower Jesse Reiser and Nanako Umemoto develop curves in the form of a rectangular plan that has been slightly pinched in the middle, curved at the corners, and extruded vertically to the height of a 22-story-tall building standing on a two-story podium. A perforated concrete exoskeleton envelops an inner core, while it renders the building's exterior into a lace wrapper that belies the work it accomplishes as the primary vertical and lateral structure. The logics behind this enclosure explain it as allowing

Figure 11.39
Kazuyo Sejima and Ryue Nishizawa, SANAA, New Museum of Contemporary Art in Manhattan (2007), photography by Dean Kaufman

for column-free zones open to light, air, and views, as well as creating a one-meter-deep space between the shell and the main enclosure that shades these surfaces while producing a chimney effect to evacuate hot air. This is an environmentally considerate passive cooling system for an extremely hot climate that provides a vertical funnel for hot air to rise and, in so doing, to cool the surfaces of the glass windows behind the shell. The exterior shell operates as a diagrid, "the efficiency of which is wed to a system of continuous variation of openings, always maintaining a minimum structural member, adding material locally where necessary and taking away where possible."[34] The resulting pattern of lacey apertures, "a combination of a capillary branching field, gradients of vertical articulation, opacity, environmental effects, a structural field, and a turbulence field," appears to wrap the entire building in a screen whose perforations randomize rather than index specific programmatic activities within the building it veils.[35] Between the two projects, which respond to unique contexts and uses, the Aqua Tower's envelope produces an image of white foam waves crashing on the blue water of reflective glass, while O-14 appears as a porous wrapper that provides for cushions of space between it and the climatically enclosed spaces. But, as with the Aqua Tower, a preoccupation with abstract form generation also prevails.

Two buildings that express structure on their exterior surfaces, Skidmore, Owings, and Merrill's (SOM) John Hancock Center in Chicago (now 875 North Michigan Avenue 1968) and Neil Denari's HL23, a residential complex on the High Line in New York City (2012), demonstrate the means by which architects may distinguish thick and thin enclosures with subtle differences measured

Figure 11.40
**Studio Gang,
Aqua Tower in
Chicago (2009),
photograph
by George
Showman**

in mere inches or millimeters as a way of projecting their formal ideas onto
taut surfaces. In order to achieve the vertiginous height of 1127 feet for the
100-story-tall Hancock Center, chief architect Bruce Graham collaborated with
the engineer Fazlur Khan in deciding to explore a "trussed tube system" to
support the building with a reduced need for internal columns. Denari explores
similarly innovative structural technology at HL23, where a Steel Plate Shear
Wall System (SPSW) located at the elevator and stair core operates in
combination with a perimeter-braced frame system that provides structural
support for the reverse-tapered shifts, bends, and folds along the building's
south and east sides. Both projects rely on a trussed frame to complete
acrobatic structural feats, but go about expressing these feats of engineering
through thickly expressive or thinly deceptive envelopes.

At the John Hancock Center, X-braces appear on each side of the building's four exterior surfaces in six intervals, gathering into themselves multiple floors in each section while they slightly taper from the ground to the top as the building's volume decreases. The diagonal frame recedes ever so slightly from behind the expressed vertical columns while projecting forward from the horizontal spandrels, all uniformly covered in black aluminum cladding. This homogeneous cladding and the glare-proof, bronze glass windowpanes produce a building with a highly muscular enclosure flexing its structure above the city. From the face of the exterior columns to the windowpanes, five layers of architectural planes inhabit this relatively narrow zone, making the building read as a highly graphic, bas relief surface with shadows cast across the various projections.

HL23 is a 14-floor-tall condominium tower located at 23rd Street in New York's Chelsea arts district next to the High Line, an abandoned elevated railway that James Corner of Field Operations, landscape designer Piet Oudolf, and architects Diller Scofidio + Renfro retrofitted into a city park. With a small building footprint to work with, the building's volume increases as it moves vertically, with floors eventually cantilevering over the Highline Park as they grow in size. With just one residence per floor, the braced frame minimizes the number of columns interfering with the floor plans. It appears inside the units as angled, steel pipe columns located at the very perimeter of the floor plate.

Figure 11.42
Neil Denari, HL23, New York City (2012), courtesy of Neil Denari

Figure 11.43
**Skidmore,
Owings, and
Merrill's (SOM)
875 North
Michigan
Avenue
(formerly
John Hancock
Center),
courtesy of
SOM**

It appears on the exterior as oversized truss segments dramatically supporting clusters of three to four floors, signifying a substantial structural system necessary to support such a load. But, with a calculated sleight of hand, Denari deftly denies the muscularity of this structural system with a seemingly weightless envelope that hovers effortlessly above the park. He dematerialized the south elevation with a spandrel-free curtain wall system that displays floor-to-ceiling, single-pane windows articulated with white ceramic frit behind which the angled structural tubes appear, or rather disappear. As the tower dramatically bends and folds upward, the envelope reads as an enigmatically taut surface with a gravity-defying structural system.

If SOM expressed the muscularity of structure in 1969, then in 2012 Denari dematerialized it into a thin white frit on highly transparent glass that shimmers and sparkles across the building's fluid lines, as if in defiance of the laws of nature. Denari's slippery surfaces develop into a pellicular envelope that dematerializes architecture's status as an inhabitable solid on its two glass sides, while it reaffirms its gravitational status through metal panels on the third. As a merging of elevation, façade, skin, and envelope, this project synthesizes architectural enclosure in response to its context at the High Line and its residential content of inhabitation. It offers a refined and striking silhouette that stands out along a parkway that features several other significant buildings nearby, including Renzo Piano's Whitney Museum at Gansevoort Street, Ennead Architects's (formerly Polshek Partnership) the Standard Hotel, Amale Andraos and Dan Wood's (WORK AC) DVF Studio Headquarters (for Diane von Furstenberg Studio), Frank Gehry's IAC Building (InterActiveCorp Headquarters), Albert C. Ledner's Maritime Hotel, Jean Nouvel's condominiums 100 Eleventh Avenue, Zaha Hadid's Chelsea condos, and Diller Scofidio + Renfro's The Shed.

HL23 invites reading. Its form, siting, and tectonics offer interpretive clues to the stories it is telling. Its lean over the High Line becomes clear when looking down at the small footprint below and surmising that the building expanded its horizontal plane as it grew vertically in the service of a market economy. But it also inversely references New York City's 1916 Zoning Resolution, adopted as a way to keep light and air reaching the streets and that skyscraper architects generally interpreted as a series of stepped setbacks. The envelope indexes the public and private residential spaces with greater and lesser degrees of open and closed surfaces in response to the highly public adjacency of the Highline and prevailing views. Denari references the Highline's 19th-century industrial construction with cantilevers and x-bracing. And yet the form follows a set of internal logics and architectural research unique to Denari's practice of exploring fluidity and controlled curvilinearity. It resonates with the deft hand of a mannerist as the white fritting appears to stretch the structural capacities of x-bracing that simultaneously offers the second reading of a giant order three to four stories tall imposed upon the envelope.

Notes

1   Lucy Lippard, "Around the Corner: A Photo Essay," in *Site Matters: Design Concepts, Histories, and Strategies*, eds. Carol J. Burns and Andrea Kahn (New York: Routledge, 2005), p. 1.
2   Cf. Chapter 7 in this volume for more on indexicality.
3   Denis Hollier, *Against Architecture: The Writings of Georges Bataille*, trans. Betsy Wing (Cambridge, MA: MIT Press, 1989), pp. 21–31.
4   Ibid.
5   These definitions combine those of Granger Loeb, Morris Hickey Morgan, and a standard Latin dictionary; see also http://penelope.uchicago.edu/Thayer/E/Roman/Texts/Vitruvius/1*.html.
6   http://penelope.uchicago.edu/Thayer/E/Roman/Texts/Vitruvius/1*.html.
7   http://www.archdaily.com/236175/cctv-headquarters-oma.
8   Le Corbusier, "Five Points Towards a New Architecture," (1926) in *Programs and Manifestos in Twentieth Century Architecture*, ed. Ulrich Conrads (Cambridge, MA: MIT Press, 1970), pp. 99–101.
9   Italian translations of *De architettura* during the Renaissance initiated the humanistic application of anthropomorphic proportions to architecture, inspired by Vitruvius's comparison of human proportions of those of a circle and square delineated in Leonardo da Vinci's celebrated image of a male figure with outstretched arms.
10 Anthony Vidler, "Architecture's Expanded Field," in *Constructing a New Agenda: Architectural Theory 1993–2009*, ed. A. Krista Sykes (New York: Princeton Architectural Press, 2010), p. 322. Originally published in *Architecture Between Spectacle and Use* (Williamstown, MA: Sterling and Francine Clark Institute, 2008).
11 Thomas L. Schumacher "The Skull and the Mask" *Cornell Journal of Architecture: The Vertical Surface 3* (January 4, 1986), p. 5.
12 Robert Venturi, *Complexity and Contradiction in Architecture* (New York: Museum of Modern Art, 1966), p. 86.
13 Ibid.
14 As cited by Jasmine Rault in *Eileen Gray and the Design of Sapphic Modernity: Staying In* (Burlington, VT: Ashgate, 2011), p. 98.

15 Jacques-François Blondel, *Cours d'architecture* I (Paris, 1771), p. 262. As cited by Michael Hill and Peter Kohane, "'The Signature of Architecture': Compositional Ideas in the Theory of Profiles" *Architectural Histories: The Open Access Journal of the EAHN*, https://journal.eahn.org/articles/10.5334/ah.cu.

16 Jacques-François Blondel, *Cours d'architecture*, I (Paris, 1771), pp. 389–390. As cited by G. L. Hersey in "Associationism and Sensibility in Eighteenth-Century Architecture" *Eighteenth-Century Studies 4*, no. 1 (Autumn, 1970), p. 73.

17 https://www.vmfa.museum/mlit/nam-june-paik.

18 http://manovich.net/index.php/projects/the-poetics-of-augmented-space.

19 Ibid, p. 12.

20 https://www.dezeen.com/2013/11/09/arboskin-spiky-pavilion-with-facademade-from -bioplastics-by-itke.

21 Vittoria de Palma, "Blurs, Blots and Clouds: Architecture and the Dissolution of the Surface" *A.A. Files 54* (2006), p. 25; and Jeffrey Kipnis, "The Cunning of Cosmetics: A Personal Reflection on the Architecture of Herzog and De Meuron" *El Croquis 84* (1997), p. 430.

22 Gerhard Mack, "Building with Images: Herzog & De Meuron's Library at Eberswalde," in Gerhard Mack and Valeria Liebermann, *Eberswalde Library: Herzog & de Meuron, Architectural Landscape Urbanism 3* (London: AA Publications, 2000), p. 8.

23 Adolf Loos, "Ornament and Crime," in *Programmes and Manifestoes on 20th-Century Architecture*, ed. Ulrich Conrads and trans. Michael Bullock (London, Lund Humphries, 1970), p. 19.

24 Ibid, p. 22.

25 Jonathan Hill, *Immaterial Architecture* (New York: Routledge, 2006), p. 170.

26 https://afasiaarchzine.com/2013/07/herzog-de-meuron-20.

27 https://www.herzogdemeuron.com/index/projects/complete-works/076–100/094-ricola-europe-production-and-storage-building.html.

28 Kipnis, "The Cunning of Cosmetics," p. 432.

29 Ibid.

30 Mabel O. Wilson, "A Virtual Museum Tour" *Columbia Magazine* (Winter, 2016), https://magazine.columbia.edu/article/virtual-museum-tour.

31 https://www.smithsonianmag.com/arts-culture/q-and-a-with-architect-david-adjaye-18968512.

32 https://www.archdaily.com/251370/asakusa-culture-and-tourism-center-kengo-kuma-associates.

33 https://www.archdaily.com/42694/aqua-tower-studio-gang-architects.

34 Eric Goldemberg, *Pulsation in Architecture* (Fort Lauderdale: J. Ross, 2012), p. 220.

35 Ibid.

Index

Note: italic page numbers indicate figures; numbers preceded by n indicate chapter endnotes.

Aalto, Alvar 224, *225*, 312
Abhaneri (India) 62, *63*
Académie/École des Beaux-Arts 237, 282, 285, 287
Acconci, Vito 360
Ackerman, James 7
Acropolis, Athens 40, *41*, 121, 122–123, *122*, 124
Acropolis Museum, Athens (Tschumi) 120–127, *124*, *126*; and Elgin marbles 126–127; and Panathenaic frieze 122, 124, *125*, 126–127; stratigraphy of 124–125
Adam brothers 91, 110
Adam, Robert 102, *106*
Adcock, Michael 204
Adjaye, David 362–363, *363*
Adler, Dankmar 288
Admun Studio 350–352, *354*
Adorno, Theodor 142–143
advertising billboards 34, 35
aerial photography 2–4, *3*
Aerospace Research Center for IBM, Los Angeles (Noyes) *28*, 30
aesthetics 6, 7, 110, 120, 153, 204, 219, 260; and form 309, 316, 318, 326, 356–357; minimalist 229, 230; modernist/machine 32, 165, 168; of nature 110, 284, 288; Picturesque 89, 119
Agricultural Guard, House of (Ledoux) 26, *26*
Ahmedabad (India) 67
air conditioning 159, 160, 163, *173*, *see also* HVAC systems
Aitken, Doug 80

al-Mutawakkil, Great Mosque of (Samarra, Iraq) 321, *323*
Alba (Kolbe) 145, 146, *146*
Alberro, Alexander 136
Alberti, Leon Battista 24–25, 46, 221–222n25
Albini, Franco 164–165, *166*
Alexander, Christopher 296
Allen, Star 75–78
Alma-Tadema, Lawrence *125*
alphabets 15, 25, 257, *258*
Am 7 (Moholy-Nagy) *309*, 310
American architecture 33–37; Californian *see* California; housing 7–8, 33; and Palladianism 102; timber construction 190–192, *192*, 229; *see also specific American buildings/architects*
Americana, Glendale, California (Caruso) 161
Amiens Cathedral, France 35
Amun-Re, Great Hypostyle Hall of (Karnak, Egypt) 15–16, *17*, *18*
anamorphosis abscondita 94
Anarchitecture 138
Antiquities of Athens and Other Monuments of Greece (Stuart/Revett) 102, *105*
Aqua Felice (Rome) 61
Aqua Tower, Chicago (Studio Gang) 370–371, 373, *373*
aqueducts 61, 73
Arabic architecture 123, 193, 257, *321*, 323, 326, *see also* Islamic architecture
Arabic calligraphy 42–45, *44*, *45*
Aravena, Alejandro 32, *33*

ArboSkin Pavilion, Stuttgart (ITKE) 356, *357*

Arc-et-Senans (France) 25–26, *25*, *26*, *27*

arcades 62, 95, 159, 281

archaeology 1–4; and aerial surveys 2–4, *3*; and Freudian unconscious 61; and stratigraphy 61, 124–125

Archigram 168, *168*, 172

Archimedean spiral 326

architect: agency/authorship of 9–10, 47; and computer design 47, 72; emergence of profession of 24; etymology of 188; and quotidian inhabitation 32–33

architectural drawing/projection 72, 73–74, *73*, 283; axonometric 98–101, 312–314, 316, 346, 347; and elevations *see* elevations; orthographic 101–105, 346

architectural models 313–316, *315*, 337–339, *338*

Architecture considérée sous le rapport de l'art, des moeurs et de la legislation (Ledoux) 25–26, *25*, *26*

Architecture from the Outside (Grosz) 52–53

Architecture parlante 25–30, *25*, *26*, *27*, *28*, *29*, 36

Architecture Without Architects (Rudofsky) 67, *68*

architecture/building distinction 6–7, 260

Arctic City (Otto) 170

Argan, Giulio Carlo 266–268

Ariadne 1, 10

Aristotle 260–261, 282

Armstrong, Isobel 158

arquitetura pobre 141

art and architecture 6, 7, 25, 33, 131, 150, 188, 213; and autonomy 143–144; and Chinese art 102; and form 300, 301, 309–310, 312, *313*; and museums 136–137, 139, 140–141, 166, 167–169, 215; and natural world 153, 159, 175, 179, 182; origins of 275; and ornament 217, 219; and picturesque 90, 122, 127

Art Center College of Design, Pasadena, California (Ellwood) 85, *86*

art museums *see* museums

Art Nouveau 153, 159, 229

artefacts 61, 124, 127, 174, 235, 285; distribution of 4; five techniques for making 187; urban 281–282

Arup, Ove 166, 170

Asakusa Culture Tourist Information Centre, Tokyo (Kuma) 367–369, *371*

Asian Art Study Center, Florida (Machado/ Silvetti) 195, *199*

Asplund, Erik Gunnar 70–72, *70*, *72*, 342, *343*

associationism 109–110

astronomy 58–59, *59*

Athena 121, 145, 217

Athena Nikê, Temple of, Athens 121

Athens (Greece); Acropolis 40, *41*, 121, 122–123, *122*, 124; Erechtheion 121, *122*, 123, 127; procession through 121, 122, 123, 126; Propylaia 121, *122*, 123, 127; Temple of Athena Nikê 121, *see also* Acropolis Museum; Parthenon

Austria 38, *38*, 44, 116–117

autochthonous buildings 68

Autodesk 45–46

autonomy/contingency debate 131, 142–147

axonometric projection 98–101, 312–314, 316, 346, 347

Bachelard, Gaston 224

Bachot, Ambroise *101*

Bacon, Edmund 73

Bagsvaerd Church, Copenhagen (Utzon) 131–132, *132*

Baltrušaitis, Jurgis 91–92, 93

banality 8, 64–65

Banham, Reyner 162–163, 164, 171, 172, 173, *173*, 178, 180

Bank of England, London 114–116, *116*

Barcelona Pavilion (Mies van der Rohe) 145–147, *145*, *146*, 296, 297

Barcelona (Spain) 57, *58*, 73, *73*, 194, 346–347, *346*

Bardi, Lina Bo 138–141, *140*

Baroque architecture: and Counter-Reformation 318–319; and folds 329–330, 331; and geometry 317–326, 330; iconography of 21–22, *23*; and Mannerism 297–298; and Renaissance, compared 300–302, 317, 320; and science 318, 319–320

Barragán, Luis 132, *133*

barrières, Paris (Ledoux) 277–279, *278*

Barthes, Roland 7, 202–203

Bartholdi, Auguste 204

Bartolomeo, Michelozzo di 206

bas-relief 20, 193

BASCO Showroom, Philadelphia (Venturi/Scott Brown) 36–37, *37*

basilicas 19, 189, 212; evolution of 261–266, *262*, *263*, *264*, *265*, *266*, see also St Peter's Basilica; San Lorenzo, Basilica of

Basoli, Antonio 257, *258*

bathrooms 9, 125, 241, 244, 245, 339, 342

Baudelaire, Charles 153, 228–229

Baudrillard, Jean 226

Bauhaus workshop, Dessau, Germany (Gropius) 310, *312*

Beesley, Philip 290–291, *290*

Behne, Adolf 243

Behrens, Peter 147

Beijing (China) *29*, 30, 38–39, *40*, 347

Beijing Olympic Games Aquatic Center (PTW Architects) *29*, 30

Bekiroglu, Saffet Kaya 44–45

Bekleidung/Bekleidungsprinzip 206, 207, 209

Benjamin, Walter 8, 142, 159, 228

Bergisel Ski Jump, Austria (Hadid) 44

Bernini, Gianlorenzo 328

Bigman, Alex 136

billboards 34, 35, *167*

Binet, René 153, *156*

Bingo (Matta-Clark) 138

biology 153, 283, 284–285, *286*, 287, 288–289

biomimicry 50–51, *53*, 153–154, 156, *156*, 159, 180, 182, 290

Biosphere 2, Oracle, Arizona 170

"Bird's Nest", Beijing Olympic Games National Stadium (Herzog & de Meuron) *29*, 38–39

Black, Milton J. *29*

Blanc, Patrick 50, 290

Blondel, Jacques-François 350, *351*

Bloom (Sung) 181–182, *181*

Blossfeldt, Karl 360

Blue Mosque, Istanbul (Turkey) 42, 45

"Blueprint", Storefront for Art and Architecture, New York (SO-IL) 360, *361*

Blur Building (Diller Scofidio + Renfro) 180, *180*, 363

BMW Welt building, Munich (Coop Himmelb(l)au) 367, *370*

Boeri Studio 50, *52*

Boffrand, Germain 109–110

Boltanski, Luc 227

Books of Groningen, Netherlands (Libeskind) 89–90, *90*

Borromini, Francesco 300–302, *301*, *302*, *303*, 317, 320

Bosco Verticale, Milan (Boeri Studio) 50, *52*

botany see biology

Boudon, Philippe 32

Boullée, Étienne-Louis 13, 25, 111–112, 272, 282, 283

boundaries 6, 9, 16, 58, 131, 177; in homes 226, 227, 237

Bourdieu, Pierre 226

Bradford, John 2, *3*

Bramante, Donato 261–262, 265–266, 268, 277, 299, *299*; and Borromini, compared 300–302, 317

Branda, Ewan 169

Brazil 138–141, 153, 154

Bremer, Sebastiaan 360, *361*

Breton, André 350, *353*

Breugel, Peter the Elder 321

Brick Country House (Mies van der Rohe) 297–299, *297*

brise-soleil 66, 80

British Museum, London 127

Bruce, Thomas, 7th Earl of Elgin 126–127

Brunelleschi, Filippo 337

bubbles/pneumatic architecture 154, 169–173; and architecture as atmosphere 172–173, *173*; and campfires/tents 171–172, *172*; and soap bubbles 169, 170

Bubner, Ewald 170

Buddhism 67, 328–329

Buergel, Roger M. 141

building materials 50, 67, 68, 85, 150; ceramics see ceramics; glass see glass; iron/steel see metallurgy; new, and transformation 209–210; and truth 216, 220; wood see timber construction

building systems 149, 153–182, 208, 356, 363; and biomimicry 50–51, *53*, 153–154, *155*, *156*, 159, 180, 182; bubbles see bubbles/pneumatic architecture; conduits see mechanical systems; as *gesamtkunstwerk* 182; and performance 150, 153, 158, 159, 160, 161, 182; prefabricated/transportable 156, 158, 191; vitreous surfaces 173–175, *174*;

weather architecture *see* weather architecture
burial monuments 20–21
Burke, Edmund 110–111
Burlington, 3rd Earl of (Richard Boyle) 270–271, *271*
Burnham, Daniel 205, *205*

cabane rustique 187, 275–276, 282, 285, 292
CAD (computer-aided design) *see* computer design
Caffey, Stephen 140
Cage, John 139
California (US) *28*, 30, 161, 162, *164*; houses in 80, 83–86, *83*, *85*, *86*, *87*, 229, 237, *238*, 342–343, *344*
calligraphy 42–45, *44*, *45*
Calthorpe, Peter 120
Campagnol, Gabriela 140
Campbell, Colin 105–108
Campidoglio in Rome, (Buonarotti) 97, *99*
Canaletto, Antonio 97–98, *100*
Candela, Félix 197
Canguilhem, Georges 242
capitalism 34, 130, 142, 159
Capitol Records Headquarters, California (Naidorf/Welton Beckett) *28*, 30
Caracalla 19–20
carbon footprint 68, 133
cardboard architecture 313–316, *315*
Caribbean Hut (Semper) 185, *186*, 187, 275
carpentry 74, 187, 188, 189, 191, 198, 210
Carson, Rachel 69
Carter, Howard 2, 61
cartography 75
Caruso, Rick 161
Caryatids 40, *41*
Casa Batló, Barcelona (Gaudi) 57, *58*
Casa Caprini, Rome (Bramante) 299, *299*
Casa del Fascio, Como, Italy (Terragni) 347, *348*
Casa Girasole, Rome (Moretti) 348, *349*
Casa Guiliani-Frigerio, Como (Terragni) 313, *314*, 347–348
Castelvecchio Museum, Verona (Scarpa) 214–216, *215*
castles 162, *163*
Catalan vault 193–194
cathedrals 23–24, 123, 289
Cattleya labiate 153, 154

CCTV building *see* China Central Television Headquarters
Central Signal Box, Basel, Switzerland (Herzog & de Meuron) 350
Centre Culturel Jean-Marie Tjibaou, New Caledonia (Piano) 206–207, *208*
Centre Georges Pompidou *see* Pompidou Center
ceramics 57, 187, 193–196; and Gaussian vaults 196–197; and Guastavino's Tile Arch System 193–194, *198*; Islamic 194–195; sun-dried clay/bricks 193
Cerdá i Sunyer, Ildefons 73, *73*
Chan Chan (Peru) 193, *195*
Chand Baori stepped well (Abhaneri, India) 62, *63*
Chandigarh (India) 66–67, *66*
Chapel of the Holy Shroud, Turin, Italy (Guarini) 323–324, *324*
Chatsworth conservatory 155–156
Chaux (France) 25–26, *25*, *26*, *27*
Chenal, Pierre 123
Cheval, Ferdinand 53, *54*
chiaroscuro 110, 111
Chicago Tribune Tower (Loos) 42, *43*
Chicago (US) 204–206, *205*, *207*, *259*, 373–375, *376*; Aqua Tower 370–371, 373, *373*
Chiea Il Gesù, Rome (Vignola) 319
China 67, *68*, 134–136, *135*, 339, *341*, 364, *365*; modernization versus heritage in 135–136
China Central Television (CCTV) Headquarters, Beijing (OMA) 39, *40*, 347
Chinese art 97–98, *100*; axonometric drawing in 102
Chinese landscape gardens 92–93, *92*, 98, 112
Chiswick House, Chiswick, England (Burlington) 270–271, *271*
Choisy, Auguste 122–123, *122*, 126
Christo 360, *362*
Chrysler Building, New York (Van Alen) *27*, 30
chthonic 60, 212
Church of the Transfiguration (Kizhi Island, Russia) 364, *368*
churches 9, 23–24, 75, *76*, *283*; rock-cut 59–60, *60*, 61; Scandinavian Stave 189, *190*, *see also* basilicas
cinematic montage 120, 121, 123–124, 127

Cité Frugès (Le Corbusier) 32
City Planning According to Artistic Principles (Sitte) 116–117, *117*
Cixous, Hélène 223
cladding 80, 133, 206
Clarendon Tower, 200, Boston, US (Pei) 80, *82*
classical architecture: and modern architecture 26; Renaissance revival of 7, 19, 299, 339, 377n9
classicism 146, 213, 276, 281, 296
Clement XII 61
Clérisseau, Charles-Louis 272
climate control 156, 158–160; and weather architecture 175–182
Cloaked in Bricks, Tehran, Iran (Admun Studio) 350–352, *354*
close observation 2, 4
CNU (Congress for the New Urbanism) 120
Cohen, Preston Scott 339, *341*
collaborative process of architecture 9–10
Collins, Peter 216–217, 221n25
Colomina, Beatriz 1, 235
colonialism 154
Colquhoun, Alan 291
Columbia University, New York (McKim Mead and White) 280–281
columns 39–42, 62, 73, 145, 213; commemorative 19; Corinthian 39, *41*, 42; Doric *see* Doric columns; as exterior-interior screen 39–40; and human body 40–42, *41*; Ionic 39, *41*, 145, 204, 213; structural steel 213, *see also* Trajan's Column
commercial strip, architecture of 33
communication–function imperative 36–38
compass points 59, 63
compluvium 62
computer design 45–47, 72, 207, *209*, 224; and digital types 291–294, *292*, *293*; and form 300, 329–331; and Palladio's villas 47; and parametricism 316–317; and shape grammars 45, 46, 47
computer scripts 45–46
Concise Townscape, The (Cullen) 117–119, *118*
concrete 66, 67, 85, 135, 141, 164, 180, 188, 197
Condensation Cube (Haacke) 178, 179–180
conduits *see* mechanical systems

Congress for the New Urbanism (CNU) 120
Conical Intersect (Matta-Clark) 138, *139*
connotative value 39–40, 42
conservatories 153–159; biomimicry in 156; climate control in 155, 156, 158–159; and orchids 153, 154, 175–177, *176*, *see also* Crystal Palace
Constant, Caroline 70, 71, 246
Constantine 261, 262, 264
Constructivism 141
context 78–87, 143; and adjacencies 80, 85–86; and mirrored façades 80, *82*, *83*; and planning ordinances 80–85; root meaning of 79; and weathering 80, *81*
"Contra-construction Project" (van Doesburg) 253–254, *255*
convolution 316–326; and Baroque architecture 317–326; and science 318, 319–320
Cook, Peter 38–39, *38*, 168, *168*
Coop Himmelb(l)au 141, 367, *370*
Coopers, House and Workshop of (Ledoux) 25, *25*
Copernicus, Nicolaus 319
Corinthian columns 39, *41*, 42
Corner, James 375
cosmetics 216–220; etymology of 217; and polychromy 217–219, *218*
Counter-Reformation 262, 318–319
Covent Garden, London 281
Crawford, Margaret 161
Cretan labyrinth 1
critical pedagogy 141
critical regionalism 131–132
critical spatial practice 130
critical theory 142
critique, architecture as 130–147, 167–168; and autonomy/contingency 131, 142–147; and contextualism 131–132; and institutions 136–141; and modernization versus heritage 135–136; and reflective surfaces 143–144, *144*; and resilience 133–134; and resistance 131, 132, 142, 143, 145
Crystal Palace, London (Paxton) 156–159, *157*; Caribbean Hut at 185, *186*, 187; innovative construction of 156–158; and ventilation/shading 158–159
Cubism 309–310
Cullen, Gordon 80, 117–119, *118*

cultural institutions 5, 9, 141
"Curtain Wall House", Tokyo, Japan (Ban)
    207–208, *208*
curtain walls 185, 204, 206, 207–209,
    208, 376
Curtis, William 66, 67
Cuvier, Georges 284–285, *286*, 288
Czech Republic 306–308, *307*

D-Tower, Doetinchem, Netherlands
    (Spuybroek) 352, *355*
dado molding 8
d'Alembert, Jean le Rond 348
Dallegret, François 172, 173, *173*
Dance, George the Younger 350
Dante 21
Danteum, Rome (Terragni) 21
Dany, Louise 247
Darwin, Charles 153, 288
Davis Brody Bond 362–363, *363*
Davis, Ron 86
Dawn of the Dead (film) 161
de Palma, Vittoria 358
de Sanctis, Francesco *332*
De Stijl 297
Deamer, Peggy 296
Death and Life of Great American Cities
    (Jacobs) 69, 138
deconstructivism 141–142
"Deconstructivist Architecture" exhibition
    (MOMA) 141–142
decoration *see* cosmetics; ornament
Deleuze, Gilles 329–331
Denari, Neil 373–377, *375*
Dennis, Michael 226
department stores 159, 164–165, *166*
Derrida, Jacques 141, 142
Desargues, Gérard 326
Design with Nature (McHarg) 69
detail 213–216
detective fiction 227–232; and Japanese
    architecture *see* tea-rooms;
    and ratiocination/cryptography
    227–228, 229; and secret/hidden
    spaces 229
Dexter Horton Building, Seattle (Graham)
    259
Dictionary of French Architecture (Viollet-
    le-Duc) 285, 287–288
Dieste, Eladio 196–197, *200*, 296
Digestible Gulf Stream (Rahm) 178, *179*
digital types 291–294, *292*, *293*
Dilittanti, Society of 102

Diller Scofidio + Renfro 375, 376
"Dingbat" apartments, Los Angeles
    339, *340*
Diodon compared with Orthagoriscus
    (Thompson) *331*, 336n33
Diodorus Siculus 251
Discourses on Architecture (Viollet-le-Duc)
    285, 287, *287*
Divine Comedy (Dante) 21
Djenné Mosque (Mali) 193, *194*
Dodds, George 146
Dome of the Rock, Jerusalem 42
Donghi, Daniele 137
Doric columns 39, 40, *41*, 122, 212–213;
    Loos' design for 42, *43*
Doric temples 126, 145, 210, 212–213,
    277
Duany and Plater-Zyberk 119–120, *120*
Dubbeldam, Winka 292–294, *292*
duck/decorated shed paradigm 35–36, *36*
ducts 141, 162, 163, 164, 167, 173
Dughet, Gaspard 108
Dumont, Gabriel-Pierre-Martin 277
Durand, Jean-Nicolas-Louis 282–284, *283*,
    284, 292

E.1027 Maison en Bord de Mer,
    Roquebrune-Cap-Martin, France (Gray)
    243–247, *246*; domestic apparatuses
    in 245; and Le Corbusier 247; word
    games in 245–247
early architecture 187, 273, 275, 285, 292,
    see also archaeology
Earth-and-Fire system 193, *197*
E.A.T. (Experiments in Art and Technology)
    179–180, *179*
Eberswalde Technical School Library,
    Germany (Herzog & de Meuron)
    358–359, *359*
Eco, Umberto 6–7, 37–38
École Polytechnique, Paris 282, 283, *284*
ecology 153
Economist Newspaper buildings, London
    (Alison and Peter Smithson) 79–80, *81*
Eden Project, Cornwall (Grimshaw)
    170, *170*
Egypt 193, *196*
Egypt, Ancient 15–16, *17*, *18*, 35;
    hieroglyphs in 16–18
Eiffel, Gustave 197, 202, 204
Eiffel Tower 197–204, *203*, 363; reactions
    against 202–203; and symbol/index/
    icon 203–204

Eisen, Charles-Dominique-Joseph
275, 285
Eisenman, Peter 119, *119*, 137, 141, 182,
312–316, *315*, 334n1
Eisenstadt, Sandy 79
Eisenstein, Sergei Mikhailovich 123
elevations 345–348; axonometric
projection 98–101, 312–314, 316, 346,
347; and façades, compared 346;
orthographic projection 101–105, 346
Elgin Marbles 126–127
Ellwood, Craig 85, *86*
Elytra Filament Pavilion, Victoria and
Albert Museum (Menges) 50–51, *53*
enclosure: and elevation *see* elevations;
envelopes *see* envelopes; façades *see*
façades; gift-wrapped 342–343, *343*,
344; and interior use 339–343, *340*,
341, *342*; skins *see* skins; terminology
for 344–345
Ender, Edouard 359
energy-saving buildings 133
Engelman, Edmund 235
England 102, 270–271, *271*, 364–367,
368, *see also* London
English picturesque gardens 102,
105–110, *107*; and art 108–109, *108*;
and Associationism 109–110
engraving *see* text, architecture as
entresol 241
envelopes 69, 85, 167–168, 177, 308,
344, 345, 363–377; and freestanding
exhibition pavilions 363–364, *365*
environmental controls 150, 155
epistemological systems 6, 10
epitaphs 20–21, 30–31n6
Erechtheion, Athens 121, *122*, 123, 127
Escher, Frank 85
Esseintes, Jean des 153
Ethiopia 59–60, *60*, 61, 63, 339–340,
341
Evans, Arthur 61
excavation 59–61, *60*
exclusivity/inclusivity 52–53
Experiments in Art and Technology (E.A.T.)
179–180, *179*
Expo '70 Osaka (Japan) 179–180, *179*
exterior-interior adjacencies *see*
threshold

Fab Tree Hab (Terreform One) 51, *53*
façades 19, 25, 30, 66, 169, 299,
312, 337–339, 345, 348–356; and

elevations, compared 346; as
expressions of emotion 350–352; as
information system 35, 167–169, *167*,
352–356; mirrored 80
Fallingwater, Bear Run, Pennsylvania
(Wright) 188, *189*, 220
Farnsworth House, Plano, Illinois (Mies
van der Rohe) 243, *244*, 276
Farshad Mehdizadeh Architects 340, *342*
Fathy, Hassan 193
Fausch, Deborah 35–36
Fibonacci series 66, 326
fields 74–78; and figure, dynamic
between 75–78, *76*, *77*; and growth of
Great Mosque, Cordoba 78, *79*; and
optical illusions 75, *77*
figure-field analysis 75–78
fingerprints 223–224, 228
Flitcroft, Henry 105
"floating" tea-room (Kuma) 232, *234*
floating village (China) 67
Florence (Italy) 331–333, *332*, 337–339,
338, 348
FOA (Foreign Office Architects) *293*, 294
"Fog Sculpture" (Nakaya/Experiments in
Art and Technology) 179–180, *179*
folds 329–334
Fondazione Prada offices/gallery (Milan)
219–220, *220*
Fontano, Carlo *263*, *264*, *265*, *266*
Food (artist-run restaurant, New York) 138
foreshortening *see* perspective
form/formalism 6, 296–334; and
cardboard architecture 313–316, *315*;
and computer design 300, 329–331;
and convolution *see* convolution; and
five pairs of oppositional concepts
300; and folds 329–334; and function
14, 260, 289; and geometry *see*
geometry; linear/painterly 296–303;
and Mannerism 297–299; and
modernism 296–297; and nine-square
grid 304–306, *304*, *305*, 314; and
plan libre/raumplan 306–308, *307*;
Renaissance/Baroque compared
300–302; space as 251–254; and
transparency *see* transparency; and
type 259–260
formal gardens 93–95, *94*; distortion of
perspective in 94–95; terminology
of 93
Forsythe, William 89
Forty, Adrian 275

Foster, Norman 38–39, *39*
fountains 61, 62
Fouquet, Nicolas 93, 94
Four Elements of Architecture, The
   (Semper) 185–186
Fournier, Colin 38–39, *38*
Fowler, Charles 155
Frampton, Kenneth 131–132, 185–187,
   188, 189
France: formal gardens in 93–95, *94*;
   hôtels particulier in *see hôtels
   particulier*; *lavoirs* in 65, *65*, *see
   also* Paris; *and see specific French
   buildings/architects*
Francisci, Erasmus 67
Frankfurt Kitchen, Germany (Schütte-
   Lihotzky, 1926) 241–242, *242*
Frankfurt School 142
Frascari, Marco 214
FreelandBuck 364, *366*
Freelon Group 362–363, *363*
Freire, Paulo 141
French Communist Party Headquarters,
   Paris (Niemeyer) 316, *318*
French Revolution 278
Freud, Sigmund 61, 142, 232–235; office
   of 233–235, *236*
"Friday Mosque", Isfahan (Iran) 42, *44*
Friedrich, Caspar David 110, *111*
Friedrichstrasse Skyscraper Project (Mies
   van der Rohe) 143–144, *144*
Friehauf, Gavin *4*, *16*, *38*, *77*
frontalism 297
Fry, Edward 136
Fuente de Los Amantes, Mexico City
   (Barragan) *133*
Fujimori, Terunobu 232
Fujimoto, Sou 149
Fuller, R. Buckminster 171, *171*, 172, 180
functional integration 285
functionalism 33, 37–38, 109, 316
Furness, Frank 287
Fuss, Diana 233–234

Gahry, Frank 7
Galicia (Spain) 67, 316
Galli-Bibiena, Ferdinando 113, *115*
Galton, Francis 228
Gamble House, Pasadena, California
   (Greene/Greene, 1908–1909) 229
Gandy, Joseph 116, *116*
Garabit Viaduct (France) 202
gardens 51; astronomical 58–59, *59*;

Chinese landscape 92–93, *92*, 98;
   English *see* English picturesque
   gardens; formal *see* formal gardens;
   and picturesque 91–93, 102, 105–110;
   tectonic 182
Gaudí, Antoni 57, *58*, 193–194
Gaussian vaults 196–197
Gehry, Frank 141, 317, *319*, 376; Loyola
   Law School campus, Los Angeles
   119; Santa Monica house, California
   85–86, *87*
Geltaftan Earth-and-Fire system 193,
   197
gemeinschaft/gesellschaft 131
General Motors Building, Detroit (Kahn)
   259
Gen(h)ome Project, MAK Center, Los
   Angeles 175, *176*
Genius Loci (Norberg-Schulz) 74–75
geometry 317–329, *327*, *328*, *329*;
   and Baroque architecture 317–326;
   Golden Section/Rectangle 326, *327*,
   347; helical spiral 320, 321, 326; and
   mandalas 328–329, *330*; Platonic
   solids 328–329, *329*; *Vesica Piscus*
   327–328, *328*
German Pavilion, Barcelona (Mise van der
   Rohe) *see* Barcelona Pavilion
"Germania" (Haacke) 137, *137*
Germany 111–112, *112*, 310, *312*, 350,
   352, 356, *357*, 358–359, *359*, 361,
   362, 367, *370*
Geta (brother of Caracalla) 19–20
Giedion, Sigfried 202, 323
Gips, James 46, 47
Girardin, Marquis de 93
Giscard, Valéry 169
glass 155, 156, 158–159, 173–175, *174*,
   243, 245, 276, *see also* transparency
Glass Farm, Schijndel, Netherlands
   (MVRDV) 360, *361*
Godlewski, Joseph 143
Golden Section/Rectangle 326, *327*, 347
Gothic architecture 23, 24, 110, 277, 281,
   287, *287*, 289, 328
Goya, Francisco 112, *113*
graffiti 5, 20, 23
Graham, Bruce 374
Graham, Dan 7–8, 9, 33
grammar 13; shape 45, 46, 47
Grandville, J. J. 153, *154*
granaries (Galicia, Spain) 67
gravitas 14

Gray, Eileen 243–247, *246*, 350

Great Exhibition (1851) 185, *see also* Crystal Palace

Great Mosque of al-Mutawakkil (Samarra, Iraq) 321, *323*

Great Mosque, Cordoba (Spain) 42, 78, *79*, *325*, 326

greenhouses *see* conservatories

Groningen (Netherlands) 89–90, *90*

Gropius, Walter 229, 310, *312*

Grosz, Elizabeth 52–53

Gruen, Victor 161, *161*

Guaranty Building (now Prudential Building), Buffalo, New York (Sullivan) 288–290, *288*

Guarini, Camillo-Guarino 251–252, *252*, 323–326, *324*

Guastavino, Rafael 193–194, *198*

Guatteri, Félix 331

Guggenheim Museum, Bilbao, Spain (Gehry) 317, *319*

Guggenheim Museum, New York (Wright) 149, 174; Haacke exhibition at (1971) 136–137

Guimard, Hector 159

Gutenberg, Johannes 23, 24

Haacke, Hans 136–137, *137*, 178, 179, 180

habitus 226, 231

Hades 60

Hadid, Zaha 42–44, 141, 376

Haeckel, Ernst 153–154, *155*, 288, 290

Hagia Sophia, Istanbul, Turkey 67, 266, 367

Haiger, Ernst 137

Hamilton, Richard 33, *35*

Harcourt, Duc d' 91–92

"Haunted House", Milan, Italy (Koolhaas/ OMA) 219–220, *220*

Haussmann, Baron 278

Hays, K. Michael 143–145

hearth 185, 187, 193–197

Heatherwick, Thomas 364

Heidegger, Martin 72, 142

Hejduk, John 89, 315

Hera I, Temple of, Paestum, Greece (Labrouste's reconstruction drawing) 212, *212*

heritage sites 9

Herrmann, Wolfgang/Herrmann, Anni 275

Hersey, George 109

Herzog & de Meuron *29*, 38–39, 350, 358–360, *359*

Heydar Aliyev Center, Baku, Azerbaijan (Hadid, 2012) 44–45, *45*

hieroglyphs 16–18

High Line, New York 7, 373–377, *375*

Hill House, Pacific Palisades, California (Johnston Marklee) 83–85, *85*

Himeji Castle, Japan 190, *191*

Hinduism 58, 62, 66, 67, 328–329

Histoire de l'Architecture (Choisy) 122–123, *122*

Hitler, Adolf 137

HL23, New York (Denari) 373–377, *375*

Hoare, Henry II 105–108

Hockney, David 97–98

Hoesli, Bernhard 310, *313*

holistic approach 10, 69, 288

Holl, Steven 257, 360

Hollein, Hans 150, *151*, 172

Hollier, Denis 339

Home, Henry 110

Home Insurance Building, Chicago (Jenney) 206, *207*

"Homes for America" (Graham) 7–8

Horace 127

Horkheimer, Max 142

Hotel Casino de la Selva, Cuernavaca, Mexico (Candela) 197

Hôtel de Beauvais, Paris (Le Pautre) 238, *239*, *240*

hôtels particulier 237–241; expression of character in 239; hidden spaces in 241; privacy in 238–239, 244

hothouses 154–161; climate control/ ventilation in 156, 158–160; and colonization 154, 158; department stores as 159; public arcades as 159; shopping malls as 160–161, *161*, 182; Victorian conservatories *see* conservatories

house boats (Shanghai, China) 67

House I/II/III/VI (Eisenman) 314–315, *315*, 316

"House", London (Whiteread) 252, *253*

House on Two Towers, Pasadena, California (Escher and GuneWardena) 85, *86*

houses 7–8, *33*; Californian 80, 83–86, *83*, *85*, *86*, *87*, 229, 237, *238*, 342–343, *344*; iconography of 33, *34*, *35*; Japanese 229; Palladio's villas 46, 47, 102; and quotidian inhabitation 32–33; Roman 2, *4*, 61–62; and Semper's four elements 185–187; slum 137;

timber construction 190–192, *192*; and
weather architecture 177, *177*, *see
also* inhabitation
Hugo, Victor 23, 24, 123, 213
Hui, Wang 97–98, *100*
Hume, David 110
humidity control 175, 180–181
"Hummingbird, The" (geoglyph, Nazca
Desert, Peru) *5*
human body and architecture 40–41, 42,
66, 131, 149–150, 350; and columns
40–41, 42; and inhabitation 223–224,
226
Hunchback of Notre Dame, The (Hugo)
23, 213
Hunt, Peter Williams 2
Huxtable, Ada Louise 32
Huysmans, Joris-Karl 153
HVAC (heating/ventilating/air conditioning)
systems 159–160, 162
Hyderbad Sind (Pakistan) 67
hydrology 61–65, *63*, *64*, *65*; aqueducts
61, 73; French *lavoirs* 65, *65*; Indian
step-wells 62–63, *63*, 64; Ronan
fountains 61–62; thermal baths 63
*Hygroscope–Meteorosensitive
Morphology* (Menges) 180–181, *181*
"Hylozoic Ground" (Beesley) 290–291,
290

IAUS (Institute for Architecture and Urban
Studies) 137–138
IBA Soft House, Hamburg (Kennedy/
Violich) 177–178, *178*
icon 203
iconography 21–22, *23*, 30, 33, 320; and
Islamic architecture 42
Idenburg, Florian 360, *361*
Iglesia de Estación Atlántida, Uruguay
196–197, *200*
ikebana 230
"I'm Lost in Paris" (Roche) 177, *177*
impluvium 4, 62
Impressionism 229
Incremental Houses Complex, Iquique,
Chile (Aravena) 32, *33*
Independent Group 33
indexicality 203
India 58–59; Chandigarh 66–67, *66*;
step-wells in 62–63, *63*, 64, *see also*
Hinduism
Indian calligraphy 42, *44*
infinity 110, 111

information systems 167–169, *167*,
352–356
inhabitation 223–247; and detective's
viewpoint *see* detective fiction;
etymology of 224–225; and
habitus 226; and inside/outside
caesura 226; interior decoration
228–229; and maid's viewpoint
242–247; and privacy 223, 225,
226, 227, 238–239, 243; and
psychoanalyst's viewpoint *see*
psychoanalysis; and traces of
performance 8, 223–224, 226, 228,
243
inhumation, fear of 232, 237, 243
Institut du Monde Arabe, Paris (Nouvel)
80, *83*, *84*
Institute for Architecture and Urban
Studies (IAUS) 137–138
institutional critique 136–141
interior space *see* houses; inhabitation
International Festival of Arts and Ideas,
2012 (New Haven, US) 365
International Style 132, 146
intuition 5–6, 8–9
Ionic columns 39, *41*, 145, 204, 213
Iran 340, *342*, 350–352, *354*; Isfahan 42,
44, 194, *199*
Iraq 321, *323*
Ise Grand Shrine, Ise, Japan 73–74, *74*
Isfahan (Iran) 42, *44*, 194, *199*
Islamic architecture 42, 62, 132, 194,
see also Arabic architecture;
mosques
Istanbul (Turkey) 42, 45, 67, 266, 367
Italian city-states, fortresses of 5
Italy: and Grand Tour 102; Renaissance 7,
102, *see also* Florence; Rome
ITKE (Institute of Building Structures and
Structural Design, Stuttgart University)
356, *357*
Ivory Coast 67, *68*

Jacobs, Jane 69, 138
Jameson, Frederic 9
Jantar Mantar, Jaipur, India (King Sawai
Jai Singh II) 57–58, *58*, 67
Japan 179–180, *179*, 207–208, *208*, *293*,
294; and modernism 229; *sengu* in
73–74, *74*; tea-rooms in *see* tea-
rooms; timber construction in 190,
191, 229; woodblock printing in 229
Jarzombek, Mark 61, 142

Jeanne-Claude 360, *362*

Jeanneret, Charles-Édouard (Le Corbusier) 306, 310, *313*

Jefferson, Thomas 271–273, *271*, 279–281, *279*

Jenney, William le Baron 206, *207*

Jersey City (US) 9

Jerusalem (Israel) 42, 59

Jesuits 273, 318–319

Ji Cheng 92–93

Joachim, Mitchell *see* Terreform One

John Hancock Center, Chicago (SOM) 373–375, *376*

John and Mable Ringling Museum of Art (Sarasota, Florida) 195, *199*

Johnston Marklee 83–85, *85*

Jonas Salk Institute for Biological Studies, La Jolla, California (Kahn) 162, *164*

Jones, Inigo 102, *103–104*

Jormakka, Kari 46

Julius II 261, *262*

"Just what is it that makes today's homes so different, so appealing?" (Hamilton) *25*, 33

Kahn, Albert *259*

Kahn, Louis 162, 163, 216

Kahn, Ned 344, *345*

Kakuzō, Okakura 229–230, 231

Kames, Lord 110

Kanak building techniques 206–207, *208*

Kandinsky, Wassily 42–44

Kangxi Emperor's Southern Inspection Tour (Wang Hui) 97–98, *100*

Karnak (Egypt) *see* Amun-Re, Great Hypostyle Hall of

Kartal-Pendik Masterplan, Istanbul (Hadid) 45

Katsura Imperial Villa, Kyoto 229, *230*

Kepes, Gyorgy 309

Kepler, Johannes 319–320, 328, *329*

Khalili, Nader 193, *197*

Khan, Fazlur 374

Kipnis, Jeffrey 358, 360

Koechlin, Maurice 202

Kolbe, Georg 145

Koolhaas, Rem 7, 25, *40*, 44, 141, 161, 219–220, *220*

Korzybski, Alfred 49

Kulper, Amy 172

Kuma, Kengo 232, 367–369, *371*

Kunsthaus, Graz, Austria (Cook/Fournier) 38, *38*

La Concha Motel, Las Vegas (Williams) 197, *201*

La Rinascente department store, Rome (Albini) 164–165, *166*

Labrouste, Henri 210–213, *211*, *212*

labyrinth 1, 10

Lahdelma, Ilmari 49–50, *50*

Lahore (Pakistan) 66

Lalibela, Ethiopia 59–60, *60*, 61, 63

Lally, Sean 175–177, *176*

Lamprecht, Barbara 237

land values 69

Landscape with Aeneas at Delos (Lorrain) *108*, 109

landscape painting 91, 92, 108–109, *108*

landscapes 49; elements of 69–70; and picturesque 90, 91; and settlements 74–75

language of architecture 6, *see also* text, architecture as

Larkin Building, Buffalo, New York (Wright) 162–163, *165*

Las Arbolades, garden of, Mexico City (Barragan) 132

Las Vegas (US) 34–35

Latour, Bruno 130, 141

Laugier, Marc-Antoine 273, *274*, 275–276, 282, 285, 292

Laurentian Library, Florence (Michelangelo) 331–333, *332*, 337

Lavin, Sylvia 237

lavoirs 65, *65*

Le Brun, Charles 93

Le Carceri d'Invenzione (Piranesi) 113–114, *114*

Le Corbusier 25, 32, 169, 229, 235, 241, 247; and Chandigarh 66–67, *66*; and form 304–306, *304*, 308, 312; and Gray's E.1027 house 247; paintings of 306, 310, *313*; and parasols 66–67; and *promenade architectural* 123

Le Nôtre, André 93

Le Pautre, Antoine 238, *239*, *240*

Le Roy, Julien David 277

Le timon du capitain Ambroise Bachot (Bachot) *101*

Learning from Las Vegas (Venturi/Scott Brown) 34–35, *36*

Lebanon 320–321, *322*

Ledoux, Claude Nicolas 15, 25–26, *25*, *26*, *27*, 30n1, 272, 277–278, *280*

Lefaivre, Liane 131

Lefebvre, Henri 169

Lego 7
Leibnitz, Gottfried 321
Leoni, Giacomo 269
Lepore, Jill 227
Les Fleurs Animée (Grandville) 153, *154*
Lessing, Gordon Ephraim 127–128, 316
Letarouilly, Paul-Marie *99*
Levete, Amanda 195, *200*
Levine, Neil 213
Lewerentz, Sigurd 70–72, *70, 71*
Libeskind, Daniel 89–90, *90*, 141
libraries 19, 23
Lichdom, Nuremberg 111–112, *112*
light 66–67, *66*, 90
liminal zones/*limes* 6, 8
Lin, Maya 21, *22*
Lincoln Memorial, Washington DC 21,
    363
linguistics *see* text, architecture as
lintels 6
Lippard, Lucy 337, 345
Lisbon (Portugal) 195, *200*, 251–252, *252*
literary turn *see* text, architecture as
Liu, Jing 360, *361*
Livingston, Morna 62
Locatelli, Andrea 108
locked-room mysteries 227
London (UK) *see specific buildings*
London Zoo 316, *319*
Loos, Adolf 20, 42, *43*, 219, 235,
    306–308, *307*, 358–359
Lorrain, Claud 108–109, *108*
Los Angeles (US) 28, *29*, 30, 53, *54*,
    85–86
Lotto, Lorenzo 359
Louis XIV 93
Lovag, Antti 197, *202*
Lovell House, Los Angeles (Neutra)
    237, *238*
Lubetkin, Berthold 316, *319*
Luther, Martin 318
Lynch, Kevin 9, 69–70
Lynn, Greg 330, 331

McCullough, Malcolm 45–46
Machado, Rodolfo 195, *199*
McHarg, Ian 69
Mack, Gerhard 358, 359
MacKendrick, Paul 1, 2
McMansions 130
Maderno, Carlo 262, *265*, 266, 319
Madoff, Mark 227
magnitude 110, 111

Mahall, Mona 217, 219
Mahlamäki, Rainer 49
maids/servants 241–247
Maipua (Papua New Guinea) 67, *68*
Maison Carrée, Nimes, France 272,
    272, 273
MAK Center for Art and Architecture, Los
    Angeles 175, *176*
Malevich, Kazimir 42–44, 253–254, *254*
Mallgrave, Henry Francis 210, 219, 309
Malwiya minaret, Al-Jami Mosque
    (Samarra, Iraq) 321, *323*
mandalas 328–329, *330*
Manhattan (New York) 7, 69, 280–281,
    367–369, *372*; Fuller's dome over *171*,
    172; real estate in 136–137, 138, 204
Mannerism 297–299, 339
Manovich, Lev 354
Mansart, Jules Hardouin 279
Marly-le-Roi, France, chateau/gardens at
    (Mansart) 279
Marx, Karl 142
mashrabiyas 80, *84*
Masjed-e Jāmé, Isfahan (Iran) 42, *44*
massing 9, 119, 164
Material Immaterial (*Interni Magazine*
    event) 364
materiality 9
Materials and Applications Gallery, Los
    Angeles 181–182, *181*
Matta-Clark, Gordon 137–138, *139*, 142
May, Ernst 241
Mayer, Jürgen H. 331–334, *333*
meaning, cultural 10, 14, 24–25
mechanical systems 162–169;
    ducts/pipes 141, 162, 163, 164, 167,
    173; on exterior 166–167, *167*, 168;
    information systems 167, 168–169;
    and *Plug-In City* 168, *168*; spatial
    pockets 162, *163*
Medici family 337
Melanesian building techniques
    206–207, *208*
memory 16, 18, 127, 135, 226, 228,
    229, 282
Menges, Achim 50–51, *53*, 180–181, *181*
men's clubhouse (Maipua, Gulf of New
    Guinea) 67, *68*
Messer, Thomas 136
metallurgy 185, 187, 197–206; and height
    of buildings 204–206, *205*; and
    moment frame 204, *see also* Eiffel
    Tower

Metropol Parasol, Seville (Meyer) 331, 333–334, *333*

Mexico 132, *133*, 197, 367, *370*

Mézières, Nicolas Le Camus de 239–240

Mezquita-Catedral de Córdoba *see* Great Mosque, Cordoba

Michelangelo: and Basilica of San Lorenzo, Florence 337–338, *338*, 348; Campidoglio, Rome 97, *99*; Laurentian Library, Florence 331–333, *332*, 337; St Peter's, Rome 262, *264*, 265–266, *265*; Sforza Chapel, Rome 297–299, *298*

Middle Eastern architecture 42, 62, 80

Mies van der Rohe, Ludwig 143–147, 357; Barcelona Pavilion 145–147, *145*, *146*, 296, 297; Brick Country House 297–299, *297*; Farnsworth House 243, *244*, 276; and formal analysis 296, 297, *297*; Friedrichstrasse Skyscraper Project 143–144, *144*; Seagram Building 213–214, *214*

Milan (Italy) 50, *52*, 219–220, *220*, *293*, 294, 356, *356*

miniature silos (Ivory Coast) 67, *68*

minimalism 147, 178, 229, 230, 360

Minos, Palace of 61

"Mirage", California (Aitken, 2017) 80, *83*

Miralles, Enric 346–347, *346*

mise-en-scène 90

Mitchell, W. J. T. 13, 46, 47, 291–292

modernism 33, 71, 119, 132, 137, 159, 228, 235, 276; and form/formalism 296; and Japanese architecture 229; and organic types 285; and ornament 213–214; tabula rasa approach of 79–80, 131; and type/typology 267, 276, 285, 291

Moe, Kiel 175

Moholy-Nagy, Lázló *309*, 310

Moiré pattern *77*

Molè, Michele 356, *356*

Mollans-sur-Ouvèze (France) *65*

MOMA (Museum of Modern Art), New York 141–142

moment frame 204

Monadnock Building, Chicago (Burnham/ Root) 205, *205*

Mondrian, Piet 297

Moneo, Rafael 257–259

Monge, Gaspard 283

Monk's House, East Sussex, England 223, *224*

Monster Park, Bomarzo, Italy 350

Monticello, Charlottesville, Virginia (Jefferson) 271–272, *271*

Montreal World Fair Expo, 1967 (Canada) 171

monuments 9, 20–21

Moretti, Luigi 251–252, *252*, 348, *349*

Moses, Robert 138

mosques 42, 45; *see also specific mosques*

mostra 61

Moule, Elizabeth 120

mound 185, 187, 188

Moussavi, Farshid 185, *293*

Mud Muse (Rauschenberg) 179

multicultural context of architecture 10, 132

Murphy, G. Ronald 189

Musée du quai Branly-Jacqes Chirac, Paris (Nouvel/Blanc) 50, 290

Museo Soumaya, Mexico City (Romero) 367, *370*

Museum of Art, Architecture and Technology (Lisbon) 195, *200*

Museum of the History of Polish Jews, Warsaw, Poland (Lahdelma/ Mahlamäki) 49–50, *50*

Museum of Modern Art (MOMA), New York 141–142

Museum of Natural History, Paris 287

museums 9, 136, 167–169; critique of *see* institutional critique

Mussolini, Benito 21

MVRDV (Maas/van Rijs/de Vries) 360, *361*

Naidorf, Louis *28*

Nakaya, Fujiko *179*, 180

Nancy, Jean Luc 72

Nanjing Performing Arts Center, China (Cohen) 339, *341*

Nash, John 364–367, *368*

Natalini, Adolfo 171

National Library of France, Paris (Perrault) 30

National Museum of African American History and Culture, Washington DC, US (Adjaye/Freelon Group/Davis Brody Bond) 362–363, *363*

nature and architecture 49–51, *52*, *53*, *54*, 69, 320; biomimicry 50–51, *53*, 153–154, 156, *156*, 159; continuum between 49–50, *50*, *51*; green walls/ buildings 50, *52*, 177–178, *177*, *178*;

living structures 51, *53*, see also landscapes; picturesque
Nazca Desert geoglyphs (Peru) 2, *5*
Nazi architecture 111–112, *112*, 137
Nehru, Jawaharlal 66, 67
Nemesi & Partners 356, *356*
neoclassicism 102, 105, 111, 112, 273, 275, 276
Neolithic sites 2, *3*
Nervi, Pier Luigi 197, *201*
Netherlands 89–90, *90*, 352, *355*, 360, *361*
Neutra, Richard 235–237
Nevue, Mark 328
New Gourna, Egypt 193, *196*
New Guinea 67
New Jersey (US) 7–8, *9*
New Milan Trade Fair, Italy (Massimiliano/ Doriana) *293*, 294
New Museum of Contemporary Art, New York (SANAA) 367–369, *372*
New Urbanism 119–120
New York (US) 69, 136–138, see also Manhattan; *and see specific buildings*
Newgate Prison, London (Dance) 350
Newton, Isaac 321
Niemeyer, Oscar 316, *318*
nine-square grid 304–306, *304*, *305*, 314
Ningbo Historic Museum, Ningbo, China (Wang Shu) 134–136, *135*
Nishizawa, Ryue 173–175, *174*, 367–369, *372*
nodes/lines 9, 69–74; and Japanese *sengu* 73–74, *74*; as unifying architecture/ nature 69–72; and urban design 72–73, *73*
Nolli, Giambattista 75
Non-physical Environment (Hollein) 150, *151*
Norberg-Schulz, Christian 74–75
Norwegian Wild Reindeer Centre Pavilion (Snøhetta) 224, *226*
Notre Dame cathedral, Paris 23, 24, 326
Nouguier, Émile 202
Nouvel, Jean 50, 80, *83*, *84*, 290, 376
Noyes, Eliot *28*

O-14 commercial tower, Dubai (Reiser/ Umemoto) 370–372, *374*
observation techniques 1–2, 8
O'Herlihy, Lorcan 342
OMA (Office of Metropolitan Architecture) 39, *40*, 347

On the Art of Building (Alberti) 24–25
On Growth and Form (Thompson) *331*, 336n33
onsite fabrication 50–51
Oppenheim, Dennis 137
optical illusions 75, *77*, 91
Oratorio dei Filippini, Rome (Borromini) 319
Orchard Street house, London (Wiggelsworth/Till) 133–134, *134*
orchids 153, 154, 175–177, *176*
organic types 282–291; and biology/ comparative anatomy 283, 284–285, *286*, 287, 288–289; and Gothic style 287, *287*
ornament 185, 213–216, 219, 289, 290; and modernism 213–214, 276
Orthodox Christianity 59–60, *60*
orthographic projection 101–105, 346
Otis College of Art and Design, Los Angeles (Noyes) *28*, 30
Otto, Frei 170–171
Oudolf, Piet 375
Ouroussoff, Nicolai 175
Outsider Art/Architecture 53, *54*
Ove Arup Partnership 166–167, *167*
Overdijk, Maarten 237
Ozenfant, Amédée 310

Paestum (Greece) 212, *212*, 277
Paik, Nam June 352
Paimio Sanatorium, Finland, sink in (Aalto) 224, *225*
Pakistan 66, 67, *68*
Palais Bulles, Cannes, France (Lovag) 197, *202*
Palais idéal, Hauterives, France (Cheval) 53, *54*
Palazzetto della Sport, Rome (Nervi) 197, *201*
Palazzo Barberini, Rome (Borromini) 320
Palazzo Chiericati, Vicenza, Italy (Palladio) 102
Palazzo del Te, Mantua, Italy (Romano) 339, *340*
Palazzo Italia, Milan Expo 2015 (Nemesi & Partners) 356, *356*
Palazzo Medici-Riccardi, Florence (Bartolomeo) 206
Palazzo Zuccari, Rome (Zuccari) 350, *351*
Palladianism 102
Palladio, Andrea 25, 268–270, *268*, *269*, 292; Teatro Olimpico (Vicenza) 95, *97*;

villas of 46, 47, 102, 304–306, *304,*
305, 334n1, *see also Quattro libri*
dell'architettura
Panathenaea (festival) 121
Panathenaic frieze 122, 124, *125,* 126–127
Panathenaic Way/procession, Athens 121,
122, 123, 126
Panthéon, Paris *see* Sainte-Geneviève
Pantheon, Rome 109, 261, 268, 270, 272,
279, 367; and Pantheon at Stourhead
108, 109
Papua New Guinea 67, *68*
parallel projection 98–101
parametricism 316–317
parasols 66–67
Parc de la Villette, Paris (Tschumi) 123
Paris Exposition Universelle (1889) 197
Paris Exposition Universelle, Triumphal
Gateway (Binet) *156*
Paris (France) 167; *barrières* in 277–279,
278; see also specific buildings
Paris Métro stations (Guimard) 159, *160*
parks, public 49, 69, 375
Parthenon, Athens *105,* 121, 122, *122,*
123, 124, 145, 217, 285; and Elgin
Marbles 126–127; golden section in
326
Pascal, Blaise 147
paterae 210–212, 213
paths 70, 72
Paul V 61
Paulista, Avenida 139
pavilions 25, 26, 59, 67, 70, 94, 272–273;
and American universities 280–281,
280; and picturesque 89, 91, 105–108,
110, *see also* Elytra Filament Pavilion;
Toledo Glass Pavilion
Paxton, Joseph 155–159, *157*
Pei, I. M. 80, *82*
Peirce, Charles Sanders 203–204
pellucurality 357–358, 359
Penguin Pool, London Zoo, (Lubetkin)
316, *319*
Pepsi Cola Pavilion, Expo '70 Osaka
(Japan) 179–180, *179*
Perec, Georges 2
performance of architecture 5, 6, 10, 15,
204; *see also under* building systems;
and space 253, 254
Perniola, Mario 217
Perpendicular Gothic 281
Perrault, Claude 25
Perrault, Dominique 30

Persians (column statues) 39
perspective 7, 94–102; and axonometric
projection 98–101; in Chinese scrolls/
Canaletto paintings, compared 97–98,
100; in formal gardens 94–95; and
theatricality/set design 95–97, *96,* 109,
116; two-/multiple-point 113–114, *115;*
in urban design 95–97
Peru 2, 5, 193, *195*
Peruzzi, Baldassarre 262, 299
Pessac (France) 32
Petra (Jordan) 49–50, *51*
Petrini, Carlo 130
Pevsner, Nikolaus 260
Phaedrus (Plato) 16–18
pharmakon 18, 217
Phidias 121, 122, 217
*Phidias Showing the Frieze of the
Parthenon to His Friends* (Alma-
Tadema) *125*
*Philosophical Enquiry into the Origin
of Our Ideas of the Sublime and
Beautiful* (Burke) 110–111
Photiadis, Michael 120
photogrammetry 2–4
Piano, Renzo 166–167, *167,* 206–207, *208,*
352–354, 376
Piazza d'Oro, Tivoli, Italy 321, *322*
Piazza Grande, Livorno, Italy 281
Picasso, Pablo 323
Pictorial Alphabet (Basoli) 257, *258*
picturesque 89–93, 102; and Chinese
landscape gardens 92–93, *92;* and
emotions/moods 109–110; and English
gardens *see* English picturesque
gardens; and irregularity (*sharawadgi*)
93; and landscape painting 91, 92,
108–109, *108;* and literature/poetry
109, 127–128; negative assessments
of 127–128; and ruins 102–105; and
sublime 114–116; and urban design
116–120, *117, 118;* and views *107,* 108
pilgrimage 59
pilotis 247, 348
"Pilot's Planit House" (Malevich)
253–254, *254*
Piper, Fredrik Magnus *107,* 108
Piranesi, Giovanni Battista 113–114, *114,*
212, 277
plan libre 306, 308
plankton 153–154, *155*
planning/zoning ordinances 69, 80–85,
85, 86

Plato 16–18, 260–261
Platonic solids 328–329, *329*
Plaza San Marco Looking South and West (Canaletto) 97–98, *100*
plazas/piazzas 34, 75, 116, 167, 281, 328, 337; perspectival distortion in 97; Roman 97–98, *99*, *100*, 328
Plug-In City (Cook) 168, *168*
poché 75, 162, 237, 358
Poe, Edgar Allan 227–228, 232–233, 248n27
poesis 187, 188, 202
Poetics of Space, The (Bachelard) 224–225
poetry 13, 62–63, 92, 127–128, 162, 316
Poland 67
polychromy 217–219, *218*
Polyzoides, Stefanos 120
Pompeii 2, *4*, 61; hydro-engineering in 61–62
Pompidou Center, Paris (Rogers/Piano) 138, 166–169, 180–181, *181*, 204; at façade as information system 167–169, *167*; Beaubourg at 167–169
Ponte, Allesandra 89, 172
Pop Art 33
Portugal 195, *200*, 251–252, *252*
postmodernism 33, 267, 276, 348
Potier, Pieter 359
Poussin, Nicolas 108
power 9, 20, 42
Prague (Czech Republic) 306–308, *307*
Prato della Valle, Padua 328
prehistoric monuments 1
"primitive hut" *see cabane rustique*
printing, invention of 23–24, 25
prisons 9, 350, *352*
privacy 223, 225, 226, 227, 238–239, 243
professional personas 4–5
project 72
Project on the City II (Koolhaas) 161
promenade architectural 120–128, *122*; and cinematic montage 120, 121, 123–124, 127
proportion 9
Propylaia, Athens 121, *122*, 123, 127
Prouvé, Jean 296
Prudential Building, Buffalo, New York *see* Guaranty Building
psychoanalysis 232–241; and fear of inhumation/*poche* 232, 237, 243; and Freud's office 233–235, *236*; and *hôtel particulier see hôtel particulier*; and

interiors as analogy of unconscious 232, 233; and mirrors/windows/glass 234, 235, 237; and uncanny 232–233, 243
PTW Architects *29*
Puckey, Thom 89

Quatremère de Quincy, Antoine-Chrysostome 25, 217, *218*, 257, 273–275, 278, 282, 291
Quattro libri dell'architettura (Palladio) 47, 271, 281, 327; and centralized typology 268–271; and Inigo Jones 102, *103–104*
Queen's House, Greenwich, England 102
Quetglas, Josep 145
quotidian inhabitation 8, 14, 32–33, 223–224, 226, 231, 361; and domestic apparatuses 245

Radiolarians (Haeckel) 153–154, *155*, 290
Raguzzini, Filippo 75
Rahm, Philippe 178, *179*
Ramesses II 15, *18*
Raphael 260–266, *261*, 299
ratiocination 227–228
raumplan 306–308, *307*
Rauschenberg, Robert 179
Ray, Man 350, *353*
reading architecture: and archaeological perspective 1–4; and close observation 2, 4; holistic approach to 10, 69; and intuition 5–6, 8–9; and multiple perspectives/scales 7; poetic/prosaic methodologies 5; and professional personas 4–5; and text *see* text, architecture as; and use-patterns 8
Reichert, Steffen 180
Reichstag, Wrapped, Berlin (Christo/Jeanne-Claude) *362*
Reiser, Jesse 370–372, *374*
Renaissance architecture 7, 19, 24, 260–266, *261*, 337–339; and Baroque, compared 300–302, 317, 320; and classical revival 7, 19, 299, 339, 377n9; and computerised design 46; and geometry 326–327, 328; and Mannerism 297–299; *palazzi* 206, 309; and typological hybridity 268; *see also specific buildings*
representation 36–37
resilience 67–69, *68*, 133–134

resistance, critical 131, 132, 142, 143, 145

Revett, Nicholas 102, *105*, 277

Ricetto, Laurentian Library, Florence (Michelangelo) 331–333, *332*, 337

Richards Medical Research Laboratories, University of Pennsylvania, Philadelphia (Kahn) 162, *164*

Richardson, Henry Hobson 80

Ricola-Europe SA, Production and Storage Building, Mulhouse, Germany (Herzog & de Meuron) 361

Ripa, Cesare 21–22, *23*, 320

rituals 15, 62, 63, 210, 219, 230–232

roadside architecture 14, 30, 33, *see also* billboards

Roche, François 177

Roddier, Mireille 65

Rogers, Richard 166–167, *167*, 352–354

Roman terminology 8, 76

Romano, Giulio 297–299, 339, *340*

Romanticism 105, 112–113

Rome (Italy): and cartography 75; fountains in 61; plazas in 97, *99*, 328; Sixtus V's urban design of 72–73; *see also specific buildings*

Rome, ancient 102; and Alberti 46; Arch of Septimus Severus 19–20, *20*; *basilica* in 261, 262–266, *263*; Circus of Nero and Caligula 262, *263*; foundation myth of 20; houses 2, *4*, 61–62; and inscription 18–20, *19*, *20*; and Las Vegas 34; Trajan's Column 18–19, *19*

Romero, Fernando 367, *370*

Root, John Wellborn 205, *205*, 287

Rosetta Stone 1–2

Roskam, Cole 135

Rossi, Aldo 276, *276*, 281–282

Rousselet, Lord 62

Rowe, Colin 296, 297, 299, 305–306, 308–310, 334n1

Royal Pavilion, Brighton (Nash) 364–367, *368*

Royal Saltworks, Arc-et-Senans (France) 25–26, *25*, *26*, *27*

Rubin, Edgar *77*

Rudofsky, Bernard 67, *68*

Ruff, Thomas 358, 359

ruins, cult of 102–110, 127, 137; in English gardens 105–108; and orthographic/picturesque representations 102–105, *105*; and sublime 111, 112–113; and urban design 119

Ruins of the Palace of the Emperor Diocletian (Adam) 102, *106*

Ruskin, John 18, 216

Russ Building, San Francisco (Kelham) *259*

Saarinen, Eero 316, *317*

Sadao, Shoji 171

Sadler, Simon 168

Sagrada Família church, Barcelona (Gaudi) 57, 194

St Mark's Cathedral, Venice 266, 364

St Paul's Cathedral, London (Wren) 262, 281

St Paul's church, Covent Garden, London (Jones) 281, *281*

St Peter's Basilica, Rome 261–266, *261*, *262*, *264*, *265*, *266*; as hybrid form 268; stratigraphy of 262, *263*

St Peter's plaza, Rome (Bernini) 328

Sainte-Geneviève (later *Panthéon*), Paris (Soufflot) 262, 277, *277*, 367, *369*

Sainte-Geneviève, Library of, Paris (Labrouste) 210–212, *211*, 213

salt economy 26

salt mines (Wielicza, Poland) 67

Samarra (Iraq) 321, *323*

San Lorenzo, Basilica of, Florence 337–338, *338*, 348

San Lorenzo, Church of, Turin (Guarini) 323, *324*, 326

San Pietro (a.k.a. *Tempietto*), Montorio, Italy (Bramante) *267*, 268, 277, 300

SANAA 174, *174*, 367–369, *372*

Sanders, Joel 233–234

Sangallo, Antonio da (the Younger) 262

Santa Catarina Market, Barcelona (Miralles/Tagliabue) 346–347, *346*

Santa della Divina Provvidenza, Lisbon, Moretti's cast of 251–252, *252*

Santa Monica house, California (Gehry) 85–86, *87*

Sant'Andrea della Valle, Rome (Maderno) 319

Santiago de Compostela (Spain) 316

Sant'Ignazio, Church of, Rome (Grassi) 75, *76*

Sant'Ivo alla Sapienza, Rome (Borromini) 300–302, *300*, *301*, *302*, *303*; geometry of 320, 321–323

São Paulo Art Museum (MASP), Brazil (Bardi) 138–141, *140*

Saussure, Ferdinand de 37, *38*

scale 7, 9

Scamozzi, Vicenzo 95, *98*, 270, *270*

Scarpa, Carlo 214–216, *215*

scenography 89–128; and cult of ruins *see* ruins, cult of; and formal gardens *see* formal gardens; and *mise-en-scène* 90; and perspective *see* perspective; and picturesque *see* picturesque; and sequences of spaces *see* spatial sequences; and sublime *see* sublime; and theatricality/scenic styles 90, 95–97, *96*, 109

Scheeren, Ole *40*

Schiller Building, Chicago (Adler/Sullivan) *259*

Schindler, Rudolph 235

Schinkel, Karl Friedrich 296–297

Schliemann, Heinrich 61

Schmarsow, August 150

Schoenfeldt, Henrik 159

scholars' rocks/Taihu stones 92–93, *92*, 112

"School of Athens" (Raphael) 260–266, *261*, 299

schools 9

Schor, Naomi 228

Schumacher, Patrik 296

Schumacher, Thomas L. 348

Schütte-Lihotzky, Grete 241–242

Scolari, Massimo 101

Scott Brown, Denise 32–37, *34*; and duck/decorated shed paradigm 35–36, *36*

Scott, John Beldon 320

Scottish Enlightenment 110

scripting 45–46

Scully, Vinvent 289–290

Seagram Building, New York (Mies van der Rohe) 213–214, *214*

Seaside, Florida 119–120, *120*

Second World War 68

"Seed Cathedral" (Heatherwick) 364, *365*

Sejima, Kazuyo 173–175, *174*, 367–369, *372*

semantics 40, 42, 45, 251

semiotics 13, 37, *38*

Semper, Gottfried 25, 185–187, *186*, 193, 206, 208, 209–210, 275; on cosmetics 217, 219

"Semper Pavilion" (Cache/Beaucé) 207, *209*

sengu 73–74, *74*

Septimus Severus, Arch of, Rome 19–20, *20*

Serbest, Asli 217, 219

Serlio, Sebastiano 25, 95–97, *96*, 109, 116, 328, *328*

served/servant spaces 162

Sety I 15

Sforza Chapel, Rome (Michelangelo) 297–299, *298*

Shah Mosque, Isfahan, Iran 194, *199*

Shaker architecture 8

shan shui 92

Shanghai 2010 World Expo (China) 364, *365*

shape grammars 45, 46, 47

"Shapolsky et al. Manhattan Real Estate Holdings, A Real Time Social System" (Haacke, 1971) 136–137

sharawadgi 93

Sheerbart, Paul 158

Shelling, Friedrich 232

Shibam (Yemen) 193, *194*

"Shinden of Sanboin", Daigoji, Japan 229

Shinju-an temple, Yamashiro, Japan 229

"shinmei-zukuri" style 74

Shinto 73–74

SHoP Architects 364, *367*

shopping malls 160–161, *161*, 182

signage 9, 14, 15, 20, 33; columns as 39–40; façades as 35; and representation 36–37

signs 15, 36–37, *38*

Signs of Life: Symbols in the American City (exhibition) 33, *34*

Silent Spring (Carson) 69

sills 6

Silvetti, Jorge 195, *199*

Simpsons, The (TV series) 7

Sinding-Larsen, Staale 323

siting/situatedness of architecture 9, 10, 53, 67–68, 139; elements in 69–70; and planning ordinances 80–85, *85*, *86, see also* context; fields; nodes/lines

Sitte, Camillo 116–117, *117*

Sixtus V 61, 72–73

skeuomorph 209–213

skins 80, 149, 158, 220, 344, 356–363; and early shelters 357; and human identity 362–363, *363*; images printed onto 358–360; and pellucurality 357–358, *359*; and technological innovation 356; and wrapped buildings 360–362, *361*, *362*

Skogskapellet, Woodland Cemetery, Stockholm (Asplund) 70, *72*
Skogskyrkogården/Woodland Cemetery, Stockholm (Asplund/Lewerentz) 70–72, *70*, *71*, *72*
skyscrapers 42, *43*, 206, 209, 289; and anthropocene era 50; and nature 49, 50, *52*
Sleep of Reason Produces Monsters, The (Goya) 112, *113*
slopes 69
Sloterdijk, Peter 159, 169
slow architecture 130–131, 147
Slow Food movement 130
Slutsky, Robert 309–310
Smithson, Alison/Smithson, Peter 79–80, *81*
Smithson, Robert 149, 174
SO-IL 360, *361*
Soane, John 114–115
social Darwinism 275
social media 7, 352
socio-political context 9, 53, 131, 132, 136, 138, 142, 359
solar energy 66, 133, 178
solar orientation 49, 57, 63, 67, 69, 80, 243–244, 347
Solomon, Daniel 120
Solomon, Temple of, Jerusalem 320
SOM (Skidmore, Owings and Merrill) 373–375, *376*
Soufflot, Jacques-Germain 277, *277*, *369*
Southdale Center, Edina, Minnesota (Gruen) *161*
space 75, 125–126, 150; as form 251–254; negative/voids 60, 75, 280, 281, 363
Spain 67, 316, 317, *319*, 331, 333–334, *333, see also* Barcelona; Great Mosque, Cordoba
Spanish Steps, Rome (de Sanctis/ Specchi) *332*, 334
spatial pockets 162, *163*
spatial sequences 116–128, *117*, *118*, *119*; and promenade architectural *see* promenade architectural
Specchi, Alessandro *332*, *333*
Speer, Albert 111–112
Speeth, Peter 350, *352*
Splitting: Four Corners (Matta-Clark) 138, 142
SPSW (Steel Plate Shear Wall) system 374

Spuybroek, Lars 352, *355*
stained glass windows 23, 24
Stairs Office Building, Addis Ababa, Ethiopia (Zeleke Belay Architects) 339–340, *341*
Statue of Liberty 204
Steadman, Philip 284, 285
Steingruber, Johann David 257
step-wells 62–63, *63*, 64
stereometrics 185
Stiny, George 46, 47
Stockholm (Sweden) 70–72, *70*, *71*, *72*
Stoffweschel 210
Stonehenge 111
Stourhead, garden at 105–108, *107*, 109
Stowe, garden of 108
stratigraphy 61, 62, 124–125, 135, 262, *263*
Stuart, James 102, *105*, 277
Studio Gang 370–371, 373, *373*
stupas 67
Stuttgart (Germany) 356, *357*
sublime 110–116; and monstrous 112–113, *113*; and Nazi architecture 111–112, *112*; and picturesque 114–116, *114*; properties of 110–111; and ruins 111, 112–113; and two-/multiple-point perspective 113–114, *115*
Subotincic, Natalija 235, *236*
subterranean sites 2
suburban architecture 7–8, 9
succession 110
Suleiman the Magnificent *321*
Suleymaniye Mosque, Istanbul (Turkey) 42
Sullivan, Louis 287, 288–290, *288*
Summary of Lectures on Architecture (Durand) 282, 283, *284*, 292
Summerson, John 7
Sung, Doris 181–182, *181*
Supersurface (Superstudio collage project) 171–172, *172*
Swainson, William 153, 154
Sweden 70–72, *70*, *71*, *72*, 324, *343*
Swenson, Kirsten 8
Swiss EXPO 2002, Yverdon-les-Bains 180, *180*
Swiss Re Tower, London (Foster) 38–39, *39*
Swiss Science Center, Winterthur, Switzerland (Kahn) 344, *345*
symbols/symbolism 15, 33, 36, 37–39, 203

symmetry 9, 24
syntax 13, 42, 45, 46, 251
Syon House, Great Conservatory at, London (Fowler) 155, *157*

Tagliabue, Benedetta 346–347, *346*
Taihu stones/scholars' rocks 92–93, *92*, 112
Tail o' the Pup hotdog stand, Los Angeles (Black) *29*
Tange, Kenzo 170
Taoism 229
Taos Pueblo, New Mexico 193, *195*
tatami mats 229, 231, 232
Tate Modern Museum, London 175
Taut, Bruno 229
Taylorism 242
tea-rooms 229–232, *231*; experimental versions of 232, *233*, *234*; four components of 230; and *habitus* 231; history of 231–232; *shoji* screens in 230, 231, 237; *tatami* mats in 229, 231, 232
Teatro all'antica, Sabbioneta, Italy (Scamozzi) 95, *98*
Teatro del Mondo, Venice (Rossi) 276, *276*, 282
Teatro Olimpico, Vicenza, Italy (Palladio) 95, *97*
technological innovation 9
tectonics 185–220; and cosmetics *see* cosmetics; and detail 213–216, *215*; and hearth *see* ceramics; and height of buildings 204–206, *205*, *207*, 209; and metallurgy *see* metallurgy; and mound 185, 187, 188; and non-structural enclosure 206–209; origin/etymology of 187–188; and roof/supports *see* timber construction; and Semper's four elements/five techniques 185–187; and *skeuomorph* 209–213; and textiles 185, 206–209, *208*
Tegethoff, Wolf 146
telecommuications infrastructure 78, 169
Tempietto (Bramante) *see* San Pietro
templesEgyptian 15–16, *16*, *17*, *18*, 35, 273; Greek 210, 212–213, *212*, 217–219, 276, 277, 289, 297; and picturesque 102, 108, 109; Vesta 267
temporal factor 53, 72, 246, 310
Termeh Office Commercial Building, Hamedan, Iran (Farshad Mehdizadeh Architects) 340, *342*

Terragni, Giuseppe 21, 312–313, 347–348
terroir, architectural 57–87; and astronomy 57–58, *58*; and banality 64–65; and context *see* context; and excavation 59–61, *60*, 63; and fields *see* fields; and Gaudi 57, *58*; and hydrology *see* hydrology; and light 66–67, *66*; and resilience 67–69, *68*
text, architecture as 13–14, 14, 15–30, 32–47, 213; and *Architecture parlante* 25–30, *25*, *26*; and buildings as books 16, 18–19, 23–24, 30; and calligraphy 42–45, *44*, *45*; and cathedrals 23–24, 123; and communication–function imperative 36–38; and computer design 45–47; and duck/decorated shed paradigm 35–36, *36*; and graffiti 20, 23; and *grave/engraving* 21; and Great Hypostyle Hall of Amun-Re 15–16, *17*, *18*; and iconography 21–22, *23*, 30; and invention of printing 23–24; and Las Vegas architecture 34–35; and meaning 14; and memory/forgetting 16, 18, 20; and monuments/memorials 20–21; and Pop Art 33, *35*; and post-modernism 33; and power 20; and quotidian inhabitation 32–33; and Roman architecture 18–20, *19*, *20*; and signs/symbols *see* semtiotics; signs; symbols/symbolism; and symbolic alphabet 15, 25; and systemization of architecture 24–25, *see also* engraving
textiles 185, 206–209, *208*
Teyssot, Georges 228, 257, 285
Theatines 318–319, 323
theatricality 90, 95, *96*
Thermal Vals, Vals, Switzerland (Zumthor) 63, *64*
Theuth/Thoth 18
This is Tomorrow (exhibition, 1956) 33, *35*
Thompson, D'Arcy Wentworth 288, 331, *331*, 336n33
thresholds 4, 6, 10; and bans 65; between sacred and profane 15
Tile Arch System 193–194
Till, Jeremy 133
timber construction 189–192, *190*, *191*, *192*; American 190–192; braced/ balloon/platform frames 190–191; Japanese 190, *191*, 229; kit houses